The Table of Contents

Doctor Steadman Vincent Sanford	2
Before Sanford Stadium	9
Funding and Construction of Sanford Stadium	18
Fifty Most "Unforgettable" Games	37
Georgia Head Coaches of Sanford Stadium Era	176
Heisman Trophy Winners and Mythical National Champions	186
Greatest Opposing Coaches	206
Singularly Greatest Performances	220
Twenty-Five Significant Opposing Players	236
Notable Georgia Players of Sanford Stadium Era	263
The 1996 Centennial Olympiad Games	335
Thirteen Who Made the Supreme Sacrifice	340
Sanford Stadium Bulldog Coronation	349
The Stadium, Today and Tomorrow	356
Evolution of the Hedges	371
Attendance at Georgia Football Games in Sanford Stadium	376
Conclusion	385
Index	387

Doctor Steadman Vincent Sanford

On October 12, 1929, standing at the center of the glorious arena known as Sanford Stadium, just before the Georgia versus Yale game commenced, was a group of men in civilian attire. Among those men was one whose appearance was ecstatic with cheerfulness. Over 30,000 spectators applauded. The man was Doctor Steadman Vincent Sanford, Dean of the University of Georgia, who had been encouraged by an idea and transformed it into veracity.

Doctor Sanford stood, listening to the praise of the speaker who, on behalf of grateful fans and alumni, was bestowing upon him a silver cup and $1,500.00 in gold. It was a small wonder his eyes drifted to the magnificent scene that was his Sanford Stadium come true. Perhaps Doctor Sanford's reflections drifted, too. He obviously remembered the pessimism his plan received when he initially announced his bold intentions. And pondered, assuredly, how his large-scale proposal had been considered an impossible endeavor, even by the men who most passionately wanted to see this plan consummated.

But there were not mere doubters who had to be won to this plan by Doctor Sanford. Among the trustees, faculty, alumni, and friends, were men who believed the task was unachievable. They not only looked on Doctor Sanford as a desperate dreamer, but actually set out to discourage him; for they believed, if he failed, it would be the collapse of a man who would have shattered himself and lost his health, while attempting the impossible.

Undeterred, optimistic, and cheerful, Doctor Sanford set out, alone, towards his fundamental objective, a stadium large enough to accommodate any opponent in the nation. Not yard by yard, but inch by inch he initiated a single-handed effort to create his concept. His energy was indomitable and his enthusiasm unfailing in the face of doubts that he could not understand, and rebuffs that made him only the more determined. Little by little, the fine, unselfish spirit of the man, who would not be discouraged by the apathy of others, or the physical weariness which assailed him, won the cooperation of every man and woman interested in the University.

The silver cup, filled with gold and enhanced with words of

respect, was from appreciative alumni and friends. However, his heart was already filled with happiness, as he tried to chock back tears. He reached the pinnacle of his career by seizing a vision that would culminate with a stunning contribution to the institution to which, for years, he gave his spirited commitment and endless affection.

This man, at the forefront of the University of Georgia's pilgrimage to build its stadium, Steadman Vincent Sanford, came from very humble beginnings. He was born on August 24, 1871, in Covington, Georgia, After high school, he went to Mercer University in Macon, Georgia, where he received his undergraduate degree in 1890. Later, he pursued his graduate studies at the University of Chicago, the University of Berlin in Germany, and Oxford University in England. Afterwards, he received honorary degrees from Georgia (Litt.D., 1914) and Mercer (LL.D., 1932).

From 1890 through 1892, he taught high school at Marietta. He was principal of Marietta Male School from 1892 until 1897, then from 1897 through 1903, he became the superintendent of the Marietta schools. At the end of 1903, he took a position teaching English at Georgia.

While he was principle of Marietta, in 1895, he married Grace McClatchy, with whom he had four children, Shelton Palmer, Grace Devereaux, Charles Steadman, and Homer Reynolds.

He would guide Georgia through the numerous changes of athletic competition occurring in many sections of the nation, under many difficult, as well as pleasant conditions. He never disappointed when loyalty and honor were essential; he was never deficient when intelligence and wisdom were essential, and he was never reckless when camaraderie and kindness were greatly needed.

In 1911, he moved the university's athletic teams from Herty Field to an improved location in the valley between the North and South campuses. The new venue, called Sanford Field, would be used for both baseball and football. It had been named in honor of Will Sanford, who pitched the University of Georgia to victory over the University of Pennsylvania, in Atlanta, in the first intercollegiate baseball game played in the South.

Doctor Stanford took an active interest in every phase of the University System for which he promoted and worked for the vast building programs on the University of Georgia campus. A great academic statesman, he had been prominent in political circles and had he consented to a nomination for governor, most probably would have headed the affairs for the state of Georgia for several terms.

In 1918, on the advice of Doctor Sanford, the Georgia football team disbanded because of World War I. All members of the team, from the head coach—Alex Cunningham, to the substitutes—every man on the team joined the military by enlisting in the service to help his country defeat Germany and its allies.

In 1921, he would become the founding president of the Southern Conference. Additionally, as the faculty chairman of athletics, he emerged as the mainstay of the university's athletic association. In this role he worked to improve programs and facilities, along with freeing collegiate sports of the unsavory aspects, so common in the early portion of the twentieth century.

Sanford's path from English professor to leadership of the state's system of higher education was marked by his astonishingly extensive interests and extraordinary personal charisma. Among the academic and administrative highlights of his thirty-two-year career at Georgia were his founding and leadership of the Henry Grady School of Journalism from 1921 through 1927, his deanship from 1927 through 1932, and presidency of the university from 1932 through 1935. His role in journalism education would lead to the eventual establishment of the George Foster Peabody Award for excellence in broadcasting, one of the university's most widely recognized distinctions.

The 1920s were the age of stadium building in America. The stadiums of the era symbolized the spirit of the age, just as the Gothic temple characterized the spirit of another epoch. The whole nation had been caught-up in the excitement of stadium building, and the genesis to all of it was college football games were intended for college campuses. Originally, it was the city that attracted the football crowds; however, as the popularity of college football swept the country, the football game was what fascinated the crowds. College football games were as representative of that era as the Olympic Games were of the age of Pindar.

The lack of adequate stadiums on campuses across the nation made it necessary to play in large cities where facilities were ample. However, Doctor Sanford believed every colligate game was meant to be played on college campuses. These athletic contests primarily belonged to the students. It was never intended for college football to become hippodrome contests to attract crowds to fairs or to draw crowds to this city or that, but simply to be a normal part of college life.

During the early part of the 1920s Sanford, along with important boosters in the Atlanta area, initiated plans for the building of a large, modern football stadium. He comprehended the magnitude of a proper setting for attracting a substantial playing schedule against teams who would bring in the largest crowds and widest possible press coverage. He felt a byproduct would be the advancement of public and legislative support of higher education.

By 1924, he had discovered the epitome location for the new stadium. He felt the Tanyard basin was the perfect place for a stadium because of its natural amphitheater. The curvature of the natural hollow created a bowl shape, thus, practically no grading was necessary on either side. The area was filled with trees, and a little stream, called Tanyard branch, that ran through the middle of it.

A strong proponent for having college games played on school campuses, the Tanyard basin, located in the heart of Georgia's campus, was precisely the location where Doctor Sanford wanted the cathedral he had long envisaged. He foresaw the Tanyard Creek basin providing fans the optimum college atmosphere.

The entire nation's sentiment was very similar, and as a result, universities throughout the nation were prompted to embark on their own building of stadiums. When institutions finished constructing their own stadia—and that building frenzy hit an all-time high in the late 1920s—the majority of colligate football games were played on campuses.

Doctor Sanford, an educator by trade, hoped another primary derivative of the University of Georgia's new stadium would be to return its alumni to the campus so they might renew acquaintances with members of the faculty, have an opportunity to interact with the student body, develop an awareness of the exact needs of the University, and simply draw them more closely to Alma Mater.

Furthermore, he wanted the new stadium to bring the taxpaying citizens onto the campus so they could learn to admire, support, and protect the University of Georgia. He felt it was imperative the taxpayers respect the University because of the vital part the school had played, and continued to play, in the history, life, and development of the state of Georgia.

During this period, most colleges, including Georgia, preferred not to schedule games with institutions unable to handle large crowds, or didn't provide modern facilities for its players. The leadership at universities across America felt its athletes were entitled to facilities equal to those found at other institutions of similar rank and standing.

Doctor Sanford realized it was essential for Georgia to have a modernized and efficient stadium. In fact, though college football was still in its infancy stages, an abundance of people had ceased attending games where the facilities were not modern or weren't adequate enough to accommodate large crowds—or provide for their safety.

Doctor Steadman Vincent Sanford

While serving as dean of the Franklin College, he orchestrated the funding of a new stadium. He helped found the Southern Athletic Conference—now the Southeastern Conference, and served as president of the National Collegiate Athletic Association. He would later spear-head a campaign that would do much towards purifying college athletics in the South.

He labored long for clean athletics, fine sportsmanship and the University of Georgia. In fact, Doctor Sanford was a strong sponsor of the three year playing rule when the "tramp" athlete was prevalent throughout southern college circles.

Through it all, the stadium would become his inherent legacy. Yet, his everlasting perseverance and attentiveness to guaranteeing every aspect of the financial support and construction of the stadium was faultless, would ultimately wreak havoc on his health. In May of 1928, Dean Sanford would be confined to his home for over three weeks after an attack of influenza. Because of his general rundown condition, caused by overwork, the illness had left him in a much weakened state. He rested up for several months before resuming his duties at the University. To save his life, his family placed him in a sanatorium, located in Atlanta, and forced him to obtain a much needed rest.

It was thought he had contracted his illness on a trip to Macon with Charles Martin, managing editor of the *Banner-Herald*. In February 1928, while they were enroute to attend a meeting of the Georgia Press Institute, the car they were driving had skidded into a ditch and bogged down. The two were forced to walk for several miles, in the rain, to obtain aid in removing the vehicle. After several hours, they got the car back on the road. The two would arrive in Macon, six hours late, drenched to the skin.

In spite of Chancellor Sanford's near death experience, his $280,000 dream—a vision that grew into one of the finest football stadiums in the South, was unmatched in all of his many contributions to the University of Georgia. Over eight decades later, his dream still stands as tangible evidence of his untiring devotion and a lasting memorial to the man whose name it bears.

The minister of athletics at the University, he took his place amongst the great athletes of Georgia, like Frank Sinkwich, Charlie Trippi and Herschel Walker, who paved their way into the school's Hall-of-Fame. He was a man of dreams, with the necessary resources and fortitude to make those dreams a reality.

The great mass of concrete and steel, which forms the massive bowl between Main Campus and Ag Hill—the home of a team respected in the upper strata of collegiate gridiron society across the nation—was Doctor Sanford's vision.

Rightfully, this most magnificent of stadiums was named for Doctor Steadman Vincent Sanford; however, he was quick to acknowledge two other men who were highly instrumental in getting the stadium built. Those two men were Athletic Director Herman James Stegeman, whose ties with the Yale Athletic Director helped get the game against the Eli scheduled, and Martin, who in addition to being managing editor of the *Banner-Herald*, was also Georgia's Business Manager of Athletics.

During his thirty-two years at the University, Doctor Sanford proved to be a true renaissance man. He held multiple administrative positions—including Franklin College dean and Faculty Chairman of Athletics. While serving as the Chairman of Athletics for 23 years, he earned the title of the "Best Friend of Athletics."

Additionally, he helped establish the Grady College of Journalism, *The Red & Black* student newspaper, and the University System of Georgia—for which he later served as its chancellor.

Although he was never enrolled as a student in the University, Chancellor Sanford would be forever remembered as one of the foremost alumni of the institution.

Construction of Sanford Stadium, circa 1928

Before Sanford Stadium

Anecdotal proof exists that an assemblage of University of Georgia students engaged in a game of "football," on Herty Field, with Mercer College on January 30, 1892. The game was played ninety-one years after Georgia held its first classes on the banks of the Oconee River in northeast Georgia. Though founded in 1785, as the United States' first state-chartered university, its first classes were not held until 1801. Georgia graduated its first class on May 31, 1804; eighty-eight years before the first recorded colligate football game in the South.

As the 1890s were starting, two graduates of Johns Hopkins, Doctor Charles Herty, and Doctor George Petrie, introduced the game of football to Georgia. The sport of football, which had become popular throughout the United States, finally was introduced to Georgia. In 1891, no school as far south as Georgia had taken-up the game; however, Doctors Herty and Petrie brought the game of football to the University of Georgia.

In 1892, Georgia got its campus-area home for football. The whereabouts of this varsity athletic field was a barren, short plot of land, adjacent to the University of Georgia's quadrangle, behind the New College. The Georgia gridiron team, with the tacit permission of the newly formed athletics council, would squat on this piece of land, known as Herty Field, for eighteen years.

On January 30, 1892, the first intercollegiate football contest in the South was played in Athens, on Herty Field. Georgia was coached by Doctor Herty when they defeated Mercer 52-0. The field was a rather uneven area of land, lined with chalk. It would host thirty-seven hard fought games before being replaced in 1911. In fact, Georgia would go 22-13-2 from 1892-1910 on Herty Field.

Over the next two decades, as the sport of football steadily grew in popularity, the University became less capable of managing the expanding crowds. Realizing it was shameful for its fans to have to stand four and five deep during games, the school raised funds to enable the athletics council to expand Herty Field to a seating capacity of 3,000. Construction workers, along with students, built wooden bleachers.

The students, faculty and townspeople took pride in its football team. From 1892 through 1910, the school went through thirteen different coaches, including Coach Glenn "Pop" Warner. It wouldn't be until 1910, when Coach W. A. Cunningham arrived, that the football program received some stability and continuity within its coaching ranks. Coach Cunningham played a crucial role in launching Georgia's football program.

During Coach Cunningham's tenure, Doctor Sanford, the consummate visionary, had developed a plan of constructing bleachers and turning the swampy gorge of the Tanyard basin into a field, where both football and baseball could be played. It was an ideal location in a hollow between two hills forming a natural amphitheater. Its location was directly in the center of campus, approximately half way between the academic building and the new agricultural hall.

In 1910, in order to keep up with its most hated rival, Georgia Tech, the Georgia Athletic Association announced its intention on building a new athletic field. With an unbridled optimism, the faculty foresaw games with no more shoving and contending for elbow room. Doctor Sanford's long-range plans coincided perfectly with the changing climate within the University. It would take his leadership to develop the correct plan. The methodology employed guaranteed the funds necessary to build the stadium, coupled with the architectural design and engineering, would be an almost flawless process.

To raise the capital, it was necessary for the alumni to come to the aide of Georgia's Athletic Association. Doctor Sanford and Mr. High Gordon canvassed the state, on an endeavor to pay a visit to as many alumni as possible, in the direct interest of getting compulsory finances to build the new stadium. Of course, it was virtually impossible for them to visit everyone. Therefore, alumni were organized in cities and towns across the state, and each person was asked to send something to Chancellor Barrow for this cause, if only $5.00. Afterwards, the remainder of the money was soon being subscribed, and the University of Georgia soon had one of the finest fields in the South.

The Atlanta alumni responded graciously by pledging over $700. Chancellor Barrow was acting as a trustee for the fund, so the alumni were able to rest assure their money had been judiciously spent. By the end of June 1911, roughly $3,500 worth of work had been completed on the field.

After the main grading was completed, the sub-drainage, encompassing the entire field, ensured a dry turf during almost any kind of weather, had been achieved. The work included top-soiling, turtle-backing the diamond, along with the field, and the assembly of the grandstand and bleachers. A three thousand dollar contract, for the construction and painting of a 10-foot fence around the field, was the final project of this endeavor. It was completed on July 1, 1911.

The capacity of Sanford Field, with extra bleachers, was approximately 9,500. Unfortunately, within a few years, this newly built stadium would prove to be too small as the popularity of college football grew exponentially, attracting even larger crowds.

Sanford Field's weed-choked turf, laid out north-south, between titled wooden goalposts, would be the scene of numerous battles. Its design was rudimentary, with wooden bleachers, surrounded by a 10-foot high wooden fence, along with a hand-operated scoreboard, giving the fans the score of the game. Normally, a pistol shot signaled the game's end.

Locals would freelance within the confines of the stadium, selling baskets full of apples for five cents apiece. On several occasions, visiting teams and their fans would be pelted by apple cores while being chased by an angry mob to the train station.

Yell leaders, along with their megaphones, were the sole system of public address. These organized yells added significance to the overall spectacle. Students sat on the east side of the field, and coeds got instructions for ladylike behavior from Miss Mary D. Lyndon, dean of women. Typical halftime shows included a performance by an all-male Georgia band, or the congregation of former lettermen, or performances from local acts.

The new stadium had a rudimentary press box that blocked the view of people in surrounding buildings. Many people attending games simply paid admission, or scampered over the large wooden fence surrounding the stadium with an understanding all seats were occupied. It was not uncommon to see lots of people standing throughout games. Seeking the best possible view, fans assembled in passageways, or within a few feet of the actual field. Photographs, taken from that era, show people observing the game from trees, fences, telephone poles and the roofs of nearby houses.

During this period, football alone did not attract people to Sanford Field. In 1915, baseball still remained the big money maker, and it vied for space inside the stadium. As a result, this new multipurpose stadium surged with students competing in numerous intramural and intercollegiate sports.

On November 18, 1916, after a ten year hiatus, the Yellow Jackets of Georgia Tech returned to the Classic City. Anticipating an enormous crowd for the clash, logistical measures were taken by Doctor Sanford and school officials. In order to handle the colossal masses making this rare pilgrimage to Athens, the Seaboard Air Line ran a special train from Atlanta, and put on a special round-trip rate. The tickets cost $1.50 for a round trip, going and returning on the same day, and $2 for the return on Sunday.

Yet, the city of Athens, and the University, successfully handled the large crowds. However, it was a prelude of events to come. This game attracted more than 21,000 fans, more than twice the amount of seats available at Sanford Field.

The '16 Georgia Tech game exposed the stadium's inadequacy to support larger crowds. Understandably, Sanford Field didn't rival the more imposing stadiums of Harvard, Yale or Princeton; however, it was no worse than stadiums found on campuses of other southern state universities during this time. In addition to the popularity of college football, some speculated the increased size of crowds had been directly correlated to the improved roads and transportation throughout the state of Georgia.

Then, from 1917 through 1918, during America's involvement in World War I, and at the urging of Doctor Sanford, Georgia didn't field a team. In 1919, because of a baseball feud with Georgia Tech, athletic relations were broken off and would not be resumed until 1925.

During the 1919 season, the attendance average was approximately 12,500, including an estimated 18,500 for the Virginia game on November 7, 1919. On November 3, 1920, during the first game at Sanford Field since the moniker Bulldogs had been officially selected on that fateful trip up to Charlottesville, over 14,000 people jammed into the stadium. The heavy interest was because it marked only the second time in school history the University of Florida had traveled to Athens for a football game. An estimated 5,000 people didn't have an actual seat as they saw Georgia defeat Florida 56-0.

By 1920, nine years after its construction, attendance at Georgia football games had steadily increased to biblical proportions. Unfortunately, the amplified revenue being generated by these bigger crowds, coupled with Sanford Field's lack of adequate space, made it necessary for the rivalry game with Georgia Tech to be played at larger venues, such as Piedmont or Brisbane Park, in Atlanta. In fact, between 1900 through 1928, all games in the rivalry, except for 1906 and 1916, were played in Atlanta.

The overwhelming success of the Varsity brought in even larger crowds that would engulf the seating capacity of the stadium. Georgia's 1920 team, with stars like Fred Tanner, would bring Sanford Field to its capacity as it won the Southern Intercollegiate Athletic Association Championship, and finished with a record of 8-0-1, scoring 250 points while allowing only 17 points.

The following season, on November 11, 1921, a crowd of over 19,000 witnessed Jim Tom Reynolds and "Puss" Whelchel star in brilliant fashion against Virginia. It was one of the biggest crowds to ever witness a football game in Athens. The Bulldogs' machine sent the Virginia eleven down to defeat by a score of 21-0.

As Georgia's football popularity exploded, complaints increased. Many people who had bought tickets were unable to find seats during the games. Those who were lucky enough to gain admittance would quickly discover the seating arrangements unbecoming of a major institution, especially the state's flagship university. In essence, even in its prime, Sanford Field was basically an ad hoc, temporary structure.

Decked out in red and black bunting for big games, Sanford Field had a certain charm, as the years lent an air of tradition. After eighteen seasons as the Varsity's home, it had become a special place, the site of many exciting, hard-fought games, but it was inadequate to handle the increasingly larger crowds.

By the mid-1920s, some people entered the stadium with trepidation, petrified the bleachers could collapse. Its location, near the epicenter of the campus, and its physical building material, made of lumber and nails; guaranteed Sanford Field would not always be the home of the University of Georgia athletics.

It was understandable the Bulldogs would eventually need an honest-to-goodness stadium. The idea had been tossed about for years. Doctor Sanford, the most vigorous of them all, would spearhead the campaign of bringing it to fruition.

During much of his time on the Georgia campus he was the dominant figure, a man who made decisions, sometimes unilaterally, but with the school's best interest at heart. Though not a natural athlete, most of his sports thrills were of a surrogate nature, and nothing meant more to Doctor Sanford than watching Georgia play football. He was a very generous man who and loved Georgia.

According to Sanford biographer Charles Stephen Gurr, one of his goals since the early 1920s had always been the construction of a newfangled, grander stadium. In fact, he proposed building a football stadium at Georgia as early as 1924. A letter to Sanford, from Atlanta lawyer, and Georgia booster, Harold Hirsch, talked about the possibility of a stadium seating 12,000 at a cost of between $60,000 and $70,000. Doctor Sanford, a do-it-now type, didn't realize it would take four more years to see his long-deferred dream come true. The plan eventually settled on in 1927 called for a much more expensive and somewhat larger stadium.

In early January of 1928, according to Doctor Sanford, a stadium, seating 30,000 people, and costing between $200,000 and $300,000, would be built immediately. By the time it was officially announced, architects had already been vetted to submit plans and drawings because enough money had been secured to ensure officials the arena would be built.

In late January of 1928, Doctor Sanford, Captain J. W. Barnett, city engineer, and Mayor A.G. Dudley, departed for the University of North Carolina, where they inspected the new stadium dedicated at Chapel Hill the previous year. The terrain of North Carolina's stadium was very similar to the topography at the Tanyard basin. Therefore, Georgia's stadium would be built along the same general lines as the University of North Carolina's Kenan Memorial Stadium, at Chapel Hill.

The committee who received and passed on the bids were composed of Chancellor Charles M. Snelling, Doctor S. V. Sanford, Mayor Dudley, H.J. Rowe, George C. Woodruff, Columbus, and Hirsch.

The new structure would be in the shape of an oval, chopped off at each end; thus, every seat would be on the sidelines. The eastern end would be partially closed by a field house, known as field house number three, that would stand until 1972. The western end would remain open, leading directly into Sanford Stadium.

It was the express interest of Doctor Sanford the new stadium would be utilized for football games only. Therefore, Georgia's Athletic Association retained the old Sanford Field in order for it to be used by the track and baseball teams. In addition, the football team used it as a practice field.

The new site was located in the ravine below Memorial Hall, between the Central of Georgia fill and Sanford Field. It was a valley that separated Georgia's south campus, where the school of agriculture was located, and the older north campus, the site of the college of liberal arts. The brook, coursing down this ravine, would be diverted to run into a concrete culvert. The playing field would be built over the brook. The hills on both sides of this valley extended-upward at equal angles, forming a natural amphitheatre, similar to Sanford Field. The natural slopes greatly diminished the cost of the stadium, as very little excavating, or filling, was necessary. Of course, the agriculture dean opposed the plan, but Doctor Sanford prevailed, and the stadium would eventually bridge the north and south campuses.

The forests on both hills would be left undisturbed, and the stadium terraces, and plantings, harmonized and blended with the natural beauty of the spot. Upon the stadium's completion, it was anticipated Yale would be invited to make its first southern invasion by playing Georgia in Athens. Additionally, Alabama, Georgia's natural rival would be played on this new field on alternating years. Georgia Tech would be billed to play at the new stadium every other year, too.

The stadium was constructed in such a way that if there was a demand for a larger structure, its seating capacity could be raised to 50,000 without destroying the beauty and symmetry of the oval. Of course, there was skepticism from those who did not believe Athens was capable of accommodating the larger crowds which would soon descend upon the Classic City.

Dean Sanford pointed out the fact Athens would not make any attempt to accommodate larger than normal crowds. Trains and buses would be run to move the masses into Athens for the game and out again the same night. He referred to conditions at New Haven where, in a comparatively small town, there were sometimes crowds of over 90,000; and to Chapel Hill, a town smaller than Athens, where 30,000 fans were routinely moved in and out with ease.

By the early spring of 1928, inmates from Clarke County's prison began preliminary work on the site of the stadium, just east of Sanford Field. Initially, the course of the small steam had been successfully altered, and a culvert was built over it. A minimum amount of trees were removed, and a steam shovel had been employed to do the grading work. One specific feature of the contract, as mandated by officials, was the completion of the stadium by the opening of the 1929 football season.

It was the depression era as the University of Georgia commenced to building its new stadium. Doctor Sanford felt his institution should have an opportunity to compete with the best, and he was determined to make it happen. The primary motivational factor was Georgia played Tech every year in Atlanta, and when Tech wanted to raise the rent, Georgia partisans felt it was unfair, thus creating an incensed rallying of Bulldogs across the state.

Per legend, the new stadium had been built to finally eliminate the home field advantage Georgia Tech had appreciated during most seasons between 1899 through 1928. In fact, the 1927 loss to Tech loomed large for Georgia. At the time, the '27 'Dogs were considered the best team in the history of the South, and a triumph by the undefeated and number one ranked Georgia Bulldogs guaranteed a Rose Bowl invitation awaited the 'Dogs; however, the Yellow Jackets upset the "Dream and Wonder" team by a score of 12-0, on a rain soaked field. Most Georgia fans surmised Tech watered down the field to make it even soggier to slow down the nation's top rushing attack, Georgia's small, speedy running backs.

Less than twenty-four hours after the devastating loss, Dr. Sanford reiterated his personal mandate. His message was thunderous, yet levelheaded. Georgia would have a stadium, second to none! The overwhelming loss to the Gnats in '27, coupled with the annual home field advantage Georgia Tech enjoyed, prompted Doctor Sanford to expedite the process of building a stadium in Athens. The essential requirement was it had to be large enough to attract quality opponents, thus guaranteeing the largest of crowds. Incredibly, embarking on such a large construction project, during the early stages of the Great Depression, didn't concern anybody.

From 1911 through 1928, Georgia had endured four head coaches: W. A. Cunningham, H. J. Stegeman, George Woodruff, and Harry Mehre. Yet, despite the lack of stability, the Varsity actually improved dramatically as Georgia had an overall record of 91 wins, 43 losses, and 12 ties, including the aforementioned 1920 team that went 8-0-1, and won the conference. The Red and Black had evolved into one of the best football programs in the country. Sanford Field wouldn't be totally forgotten as it was still used by Georgia's baseball team and intramural squads until the 1930s.

Sanford Field, circa 1912

Funding and Construction of Sanford Stadium

During the 1920s, as college football's popularity spread across the nation, the South was regarded as an underling, something for eastern and western teams to practice upon. Georgia, a founding member of the Southern Intercollegiate Athletic Association (SIAA), one of the first collegiate athletic conferences formed in the United States, wanted to remove that stigma from southern teams. The Bulldogs had participated in the SIAA from its creation in 1895 until 1921. During its tenure in the SIAA, Georgia had only been conference co-champion twice, 1896 and 1920.

In 1921, to help dispel this myth that southern football was inferior to football in other parts of the country, Doctor Sanford organized the Southern Conference, and vigorously scheduled games with teams from other sections of the nation. The Bulldogs, along with 12 other teams, left the SIAA, and formed the Southern Conference. During its time in the Southern Conference, Georgia never won a conference championship; however, in time, football programs in other segments of the country would cultivate a newfound respect for southern football.

In 1923, for the first time ever, Yale had agreed to play Georgia, in New Haven, Connecticut. The 'Dogs, coached by George Cecil "Kid" Woodruff would lose to undefeated Yale by a score of 20-6; however, in 1924, Coach Woodruff's Georgia Bulldogs would return to New Haven. Though the 'Dogs lost by one point, much admiration would be heaped upon Georgia's eleven.

For many years the inadequacy of Sanford Field, as home for Georgia athletics, had been painfully evident. Georgia had grown weary of having to deal with overflow crowds and being forced to play its most hated rival, Georgia Tech, in Atlanta every season. Doctor Sanford now hoped their fortunes would soon change so Georgia would be able to host major football games.

On December 3, 1927, the aforementioned coup de grace occurred when the 'Dogs lost to Tech. Doctor Sanford was forced to act after Georgia, ranked number one in the nation for most of the season, lost 12-0, ending its dream season on Tech's home field.

Doctor Sanford, along with influential colleagues, initiated his long awaited plan. The proposal called for the construction of a superior stadium to Grant Field, not only to sustain these larger crowds, but to usher in an era of a home-and-home series with its rivals, specifically Tech and Alabama. With the advent of the new stadium, Doctor Sanford had hoped to simultaneously schedule better quality opponents.

Unfortunately, by law, the Georgia Legislature could only fund buildings for educational purposes, which meant the money for a new stadium had to be raised through other innovative methods. Students, alumni, and friends would be called upon to finance and build a greater Varsity.

Unbeknownst to many, the possibility of a bigger stadium had been deliberated since as early as 1924, but the board of directors of the athletic association delayed any serious talks because of the extraordinary amount of details to be decided, especially the one pressing question of where the money would come from.

Though many plans were offered by other institutions, none seemed to accurately fit with Georgia's unique set of circumstances. To build the type of ground-breaking stadium needed for Georgia's specific needs, it was necessary to find a way to get the money. On February 12, 1928, the last note of Woodruff Hall had been paid—therefore, the athletic association's treasury was empty.

To give credence to the University's intentions, an all-star development committee, composed of Chancellor Charles M. Snelling, Doctor S. V. Sanford, John D. Bolton, Mayor A. G. Dudley, H. J. Rowe, George C. Woodruff, of Columbus, and Harold Hirsch, of Atlanta, was formed. History would show some members did little more than attend meetings, while others took a more active role, and a few did yeoman duty on a project destined to become a watershed event in University of Georgia history—the funding and construction of Sanford Stadium. While Doctor Sanford, along with the other members, championed the campaign, the experts and engineers worked out the details of material, and cost.

On January 1, 1928, the population of Athens was approximately 21,000 people. It was estimated the university pumped a staggering $2,500,000 into the local economy. A larger football stadium would mean even more people descending upon the city, filling hotel rooms and spending money. Because a big construction project would be an economic boost to the city of Athens, Doctor Sanford, Mr. Bolton and Chancellor Snelling, all three prominent members of the development committee, continuously stressed these points during discussions with the Athens government, business and civic leaders.

Despite all that had been done, the organizing, rallies, and the sense a great and historic time had come for Georgia, most people remained unaware of the amount of work it would take to finance and erect the new stadium. Compounding the problem was most people had heard the urban legends of how northern institutions had easily raised money for their pristine stadiums.

As an example, during the mid 1920s, a fundraising drive at the University of Minnesota allegedly produced $650,000 in less than six days. And, even more amazing, Illinois was said to have raised $330,000, Purdue $460,000 and Indiana $500,000, each in a single day. It was understood most of these institutions had larger, more affluent student bodies than Georgia, and in each case, a handful of alumni made sizable pledges. It would not be the same way at the University of Georgia.

Georgia's development committee had recognized early on its plan would have to be exceptional and original. Unlike the University of Texas, where numerous fund raisers from its student body, and local townspeople, had been held, Doctor Sanford, and his associates, came up with an innovative idea. They requested loyal alumni, and friends, to lend their moral support and financial credit.

After much debate, the development committee came-up with a plan deemed acceptable, and all those who stepped forward endorsed the note of the athletic association. Georgia's ingenious plan preferred having many guarantors, rather than a few, and for that reason, they would ask for them to endorse in amounts of five hundred or a thousand dollars.

After much painstaking research, the development committee had estimated the stadium's cost would be roughly $300,000. Doctor Sanford would set-out on a mission to wheel and deal with influential alumni, the University administration and a number of banks until the necessary $300,000 could be secured for the construction project to commence.

Knowing the new stadium could not be built with pocket change, Doctor Sanford had to come up with real American currency. The University of Georgia was standing at the crossroads.

Down the right split was the stadium, epitomizing good fortune, achievement, and riches. Down the other junction lied miserable disappointment.

A few skeptical people, looking past all the hoopla, doubted fund raisers would make more than a small dent in the amount of money necessary to build this new stadium. In fact, less than $10,000 would be pledged on campus. As the committee developed its plan to raise the money, guarantying this project's success, they never lost sight of the reason why they had begun this crusade: to build the University of Georgia the best stadium in America.

When Doctor Sanford began solicitation, he faced the eternal fundraising dilemma: How pushy should he be? Obviously, a passive, apologetic approach would not get it done, but neither did he want to be so aggressive as to turn off prospective givers. He understood if people offered small pledges to build this Mecca of the South, the project would be lost before it had commenced.

Georgia's final financial scheme for the stadium was to secure a commitment of $1,000 notes from 300 stadium guarantors. The University would call for the $1,000, only if it couldn't pay off the indebtedness from gate receipts. All of the prospective donors had been informed of the stadium seating options, good for an entire lifetime. While tickets had to be paid for, a $50 donation reserved two seats, a $100 donation got four seats, and every succeeding $100 merited another seat, up to a limit of 10. Those who would give the most would sit nearest the 50-yard line.

Take a look at some of the names involved with making the $1,000 pledges: Boland, Spalding, Sanford, McWhorter, Fortson, Hodges, Myers, Barrow, Woodruff, Foley, and Tate. We still recognize them because of the streets, schools, companies, dormitories, and buildings bearing their names. In total, 264 volunteers, who were urged to make their own pledges before asking another person to give, stepped forward.

Unfortunately, for many supporters of the University, the notes were endorsed so quickly that an opportunity could not be given to numerous others who no doubt would have been pleased to be numbered among the guarantors. When the pledges were tallied, the athletic association realized it would only have to borrow a fraction of what it initially thought it would need. In the end, the

Board of Directors of the University of Georgia Athletic Association needed only $180,000 from the Trust Company Bank of Atlanta.

The University would be forever grateful to the spirit manifested by those guarantors. The school's appreciation for their cooperation, and faith they had in the men who suggested the plan to finance the building of the stadium, can't be forgotten.

On February 12, 1928, it was officially announced construction of a new stadium, with a seating capacity of 33,000, large enough to accommodate any of Georgia's football games, had broke ground. In what was considered a "wilderness," the Tanyard basin, the site of the new stadium, would be slowly worked into shape. It had been hoped between eight and twelve thousand seats would be available by the Mercer game on October 6, 1928, provided there were no delays.

The completion of the stadium would mark another step forward for Athens and the University of Georgia. The large number of people the new stadium would bring into the city for games would add much to the prosperity of the Classic City. The revenue generated from the crowds was the primary reason business leaders of the city developed a feeling of admiration for this project.

And, something more important than money motivated the University of Georgia. It had been longing for the day it would finally get its most hated rival, Georgia Tech, on its home soil. This feat could never have been accomplished without a stadium with the capacity to hold over 30,000 fans. The anticipated completion of this cathedral would be agonizing.

Doctor Sanford, along with university leaders, wanted the stadium to be completed in its entirety before the actual dedication game. They wanted plenty of time to build the perfect arena. Talks had been aboard in regard to what team would furnish the opposition in the game which would mark the dedication of the new structure.

In the early spring of 1928, a camp had been set-up for the workers, while a steam shovel, grader, tractor and several teams of mules were brought-in. Clarke County convicts worked to clear the site, and started the initial grading process. They cleared trees away and used a steam shovel to excavate dirt from the eastern slope. The convicts cleared the two hillsides above Tanyard Creek, and used mule scoops to move the dirt. It was perceived, once the workers and convicts completed this preliminary work, the remainder of the job would proceed very rapidly.

The grading force, which had been at work for awhile, was increased in early May. The reason for the rapid push was to speed up the preliminary work in order for construction work to commence, which would begin immediately after the contract was signed. The site, almost a natural amphitheatre, was expected to decrease the total construction costs.

Then, after initially agreeing to supply a portion of the labor, Clarke County suddenly backed out about halfway through the project. They received pressure from citizens who complained roads were being neglected in favor of the stadium construction.

On May 1, 1928, bids for the construction of Georgia's new stadium were opened by the committee to receive and pass on the bids, and the contract would be signed as soon thereafter as possible. The bids rolled-in soon afterwards. The lowest bid was $119,000, made by George M. Thomason Company, located in Macon.

On May 4, 1928, the committee closed the bidding and conducted its review. In all, eleven total bids were received, including one supplementary bid. These bids ranged from $119,000 to $206,778. One company, the Thomason Company, made a bid of approximately $3.95 per seat, for a total of 30,000 seats.

Finally, on May 11, 1928, Chancellor Charles M. Snelling announced a contract for the construction of Georgia's new stadium had been awarded to the Seaboard and Southern Construction Company of Jacksonville, Florida. Actual construction work was to begin as soon as the grading work was completed and a concrete culvert had been built, changing the course of the small stream, which flowed through the site of the bowl.

The figures of the Seaboard and Southern's bid was $145,000, approximately $4.85 per seat. It was slightly over the lowest bid made. The company had stated one thousand seats per day could be poured when the work reached the final stages.

Captain J. W. Barnett, city engineer, was selected as the non-resident engineer and University representative. The construction company's guarantee would be a profit of at least $8,500. The University and Seaboard and Southern Company agreed to share all savings, 75% going to the University and 25% to the company.

A clause of the contract called for the completion of the playing field, and a certain number of seats, by October, with the stadium to be finished entirely in November of 1928. The time table would allow a part, or all home games, to be played on the new field.

As mentioned, this event had given many alumni an opportunity to make a stadium pledge. Many of them showed signs of awakening from a long period of indifference to the school's progress. The reason was the nature of this project. Constructing a new dormitory or classroom building would get few people's attention; however, a big, modern football stadium for the Bulldogs? That was another matter. The alumni had taken note of this project from its inception and watched, with interest, as Doctor Sanford, Bolton and Snelling made the rounds.

Athletic Director Herman J. Stegeman leaned back in his swivel chair inside his office, and beamed a smile of content. Oddly, he felt the alumni and friends might have been inspired by the tremendous showing of Georgia's athletics during the 1928 season. The success of Georgia's athletic teams coincided perfectly with the motivational levels put forth by those people who were contacted during fundraising efforts.

The season of '28 would make history for Georgia athletics. First, Yale was expected to accept an invitation to travel to Athens to dedicate its glorious new stadium, defying all athletic traditions of old Eli. And too, Georgia Tech, bitter, but honorable rival of Georgia, agreed to play football in Athens on a rotating basis.

Coach Stegeman's '28 basketball team went 15-5 and developed into one of the South's strongest aggregations in the conference, losing during the semi-finals of the conference tournament. Additionally, Coach W. P. White's baseball team went 13-4, but lost to Georgia Tech in the Southern Conference championship game. And, Georgia's golf team won the Southern Conference championship in a tourney in Nashville, Tennessee.

In the spring of 1928, Coach C. W. Jones' swimming team returned all of its tank-men, and won the Southern Conference swim meet held at Savannah's Y. M. C. A. The 'Dogs Cross Country team, led by Bob Young, was a perennial championship contender as the harriers scintillated throughout the fall.

Captain Ira C. Nicholas's Lacrosse team won the Southern Conference championship. And, the tennis team returned all of its members, including Malon Courts, who won the Southern Conference collegiate championship in the singles matches in 1928. The time had coincided perfectly for getting the pledges needed to secure the construction of the stadium.

The 1928 football season would be Coach Mehre's first season as Georgia's head coach, as he succeeded Coach Kid Woodruff. He slipped into his football togs and sounded a call from Sanford Field. In the summer of '28, plans were in the works for Georgia's initial game of the 1928 season.

The 'Dogs were scheduled to open against the Bears of Mercer, and the game, from a provisional perspective, was scheduled to be played inside the newly built stadium, adjacent to Sanford Field, according to information from stadium officials. It would not be the "dedication game," per se, but instead a prelude to the actual "dedication game."

Once the funds had been quickly secured, Doctor Sanford turned his attention to finding an opponent for the game. There were two teams mentioned as possible candidates for the dedication game. The first choice was Yale, and the alternative choice was Georgia Tech. Either team, matched with a Bulldog squad, would prove to be a good card to draw the largest crowd, for a college football game, in the history of the South.

He felt Yale was a natural selection because many of Georgia's original school leaders were Yale graduates. The first permanent building on campus, Old College, was designed after Yale's Connecticut Hall, and Yale architect, T.C. Atwood, designed Sanford Stadium. A superior salesman, Doctor Sanford would miraculously talk the powerhouse Yale Bulldogs into making its first trip south, to dedicate the stadium.

When the Athletic Board of Control at Yale decided the Blue eleven would play Georgia in Athens in 1929, a dream was realized—the dream of a man who had for many years been the outstanding figure in advancement of Southern athletics, the father of the Southern Conference and its original president when the great association was formed. The reference, of course, was to Doctor Steadman Vincent Sanford, dean of the University of Georgia and faculty director of athletics.

In the spring of 1928, unusual progress was being shown on the stadium. What might have been called a grid across the site for the stadium had been worked into shape and the pouring of concrete, into the form of seats, had commenced. It was believed it would be only a matter of time before the structure would assume the form of the long anticipated new stadium.

As early as May, construction workers were being watched by sightseers coming to examine the changes to the Tanyard basin. As many as 75 people at a time, some of whom had traveled a great distance, would stand and view the workers, mules, equipment and mountains of material needed to complete the stadium.

Reports showed the field had already been worked into shape in July of 1928, and the stream, Tanyard Creek, which ran through the field, would run beneath the battle field. The stream itself coursed from Baxter Street, across campus, and underneath Lumpkin Street, to emerge on the south side of Stegeman parking lot below Clark Howell dormitory. It then proceeded under the cover of lush foliage, into the tunnel and below the stadium and East Campus Road, to empty into the Oconee River. After Tanyard Creek had a culvert placed over it, the field was meticulously worked down to a level form for the soil to be applied.

In August 1928, wagons were hauling top soul for the gridiron, while about three-fourths of the field had been treated with a layer of sand. The texture of the field was six inches of sand, ten inches of top-soil, and four inches of grass turf, with drain pipes every thirty feet across. The center of the field was twenty-four inches higher than the sides, giving it a true back drainage, while along the sides the drains caught the surface water. Concrete had been poured on 2,220 seats and pouring began on the end curved section on the north side. Fifty additional laborers and inmates had been put to work to expedite the project. Then, sods of grass, from Pendergrass, Georgia, were brought in and spread.

The construction project required approximately 26,000 sacks of cement mixed with 3,000 cubic yards of sand and 5,000 cubic yards of gravel. The builders used a concrete mixture of one part sand, two and half parts gravel, and three and a half parts cement. Some 350 tons of structural steel and 550,000 feet of lumber were used in building what would become the most beautiful stadium in the South.

A team of inspectors were positioned to check all material coming into the construction site. In a small office, set-up near the Westside of the site, inspectors steadfastly reviewed every aspect of the stadium's progress.

That summer several students stayed in Athens and labored amongst the 120 men and inmates. They handled picks, shovels, wheelbarrows, sledgehammers, and poured concrete into wooden forms. In all, there were approximately thirty carpenters, seventy-five laborers and inmates, eight steel workers, three painters and five foremen. Some lived in the camp set-up during the pre-construction phase, others stayed in nearby boarding houses and the inmates returned to prison. The payroll came to over $2,300 per week.

Because of the unusually fast progress being made on the construction of the new stadium, the Mercer game, on October 6, 1928, had been expected to be the first game played inside the new stadium. In fact, at least 8,000 seats had been completed. However, according to plans, if the work on the stadium was not hindered in anyway, about twelve thousand seats still could have been completed by the Mercer game.

By the end of August, in 1928, approximately 9,000 seats had been completed. Unfortunately, heavy rains began flooding the area, and the construction project suddenly sustained an inordinate amount of delays. Concrete could not be poured, and the rising waters of the Tanyard Creek basin saturated the location. A complete stoppage of work all but guaranteed the Mercer game would be played at Sanford Field, and not inside the new stadium.

However, there was still hope this new stadium could be completed in time for the October 27, 1928 game against Tulane. Then, heavy rains continued, thus delaying the blasting on the south side of the field, next to the Agricultural campus. That section was the final part scheduled to be competed on the stadium.

With the stadium construction coming to a complete standstill, Georgia's Athletic Association still considered the possibility of playing the Green Wave of Tulane University inside the new gigantic stadium for Homecoming. However, because the saturated soil further hindered the completion of the work, the Tulane game would be played at Sanford Field, too.

Out of desperation, there had been talk of playing Florida for the first game inside the new stadium on November 10, 1928, instead of Jacksonville. Alumni from the port city of Savannah had complained about the game being played on the banks of the Saint Johns' river, and the difficulty of travel. In addition to Florida, the Classic City had hoped to get Georgia Tech, Louisiana State University, and Furman. Had this spectacular act been pulled-off, Athens would have been indulged with one of the greatest football schedules of the 1920s.

In late October 1928, as work slowly proceeded on the stadium, it was officially announced no games would be scheduled inside of the new stadium until the 1929. Of the nine games scheduled for the 1928 football season, four were played in Athens, at Sanford Field. Georgia battled Mercer on October 6, Furman on October 20 (later changed to Friday, October 19 to allow Kiwanis convention members to attend the game), Tulane on October 27, and Louisiana State University on November 17, 1928. The remainder of the schedule took place on foreign soul, while the Florida game was played in Savannah to pacify alumni of the port city.

Not to be dissuaded with having to play on Sanford Field, Georgia gallantly kicked off its homecoming game against Tulane at 3:15PM in the afternoon, charging $2.50 for admission. The game was a slugfest with Georgia emerging victorious 20-14. Surprisingly, the previous week, some members of Georgia's team had attended a colligate football game between Georgia Tech and Notre Dame, as guest of its hated rival.

The 1928 season proved a big disappointment for Georgia, as the 'Dogs went 4-5, closing out the season with four straight losses. To add insult to injury, Georgia Tech defeated the 'Dogs 20-6, enroute to an undefeated national title season. But, Coach Mehre expected better things in 1929.

Opening the 1929 season, the magnificent new stadium still wasn't ready. The football team, with rather mediocre prospects, lost its opening game to Oglethorpe 13-6; however, it came back to win six of its remaining nine games. Coach Harry Mehre's men would score in every game, but lost to Florida, Tulane, New York University and Oglethorpe by close scores.

The high point of the season was the dedication game in Athens on October 12, when Yale University's squad journeyed down South to take part in a superb weekend. Little did Yale suspect, in all the hospitality and feting to which they were submitted, there was a sinister objective before the rather meekly impressing Southerners. Neither did anyone in the South expect more than a close score.

October 12, 1929, was Abraham Baldwin Day, a legal holiday, so dedicated by the members of the General Assembly of Georgia. The action, on the part of the members of the legislature, was to show honor to the founder of the University of Georgia, Abraham Baldwin, and to officially recognize the dedication of the new stadium.

The coming of the Yale football team, for the dedication game, was recognition of the close relations existing between those institutions since the establishment of the University of Georgia, by Yale graduates. The occasion was more than the ordinary importance of a football game. It brought together representatives of Yale and Georgia; cementing ties of friendship.

Months before the game, a special train had been organized in the Mid-West to transport Yale alumni from those far reaching areas of the nation to Athens. Additionally, one thousand tickets had been sent to Doctor A. H. Armstrong for Georgia Tech alumni, while Clemson alumni were given 250 tickets. Princeton and Dartmouth alumni clubs of Atlanta bought tickets in blocks of fifty.

During the week of October 29th, the Yale contingent would begin arriving by a 10-Pullman Yale Special from the East, 39 other trains, 54 planes, and thousands of automobiles. And, out of respect for the University of Georgia, Yale unselfishly donated its half of the game receipts to Georgia, to help pay off the construction loans, which would subsequently be completely repaid in only five years.

Dean Sanford had issued a number of invitations for the occasion. President H. W. Chase of the University of North Carolina was one of the first college presidents to indicate intentions to be in Athens on October 12th. President Chase was not a stranger to the University of Georgia campus. He had delivered the George Washington Day address there the previous February, in connection with the Georgia Press Institute—the message was well received by critics because of the liberalism which characterized his viewpoint.

President J. J. Tigert, of the University of Florida, was another southern college executive who was there for the game. And, of course, officials of Yale University were there for the dedication. Additionally, the Governor and Mrs. J.H. Trumbull, of Connecticut, were at the game.

Adding to the glamour of the Georgia versus Yale dedicatory game of Sanford Stadium was the presence, in the Classic City, and at the game, a large number of other prominent persons from throughout the country. Numerous college presidents, governors, state executives, and an inordinate amount of industrial leaders attended the game, which was one of the most brilliant and stupendous gatherings in the history of Athens.

Among these visitors for the dedication exercise and game, were those people who were interested in the educational institutions of the United States, the University of Georgia being one of the leaders, and the first state university to be established in the nation. It was only natural for those people to feel a great interest in the occasion which would go down in history as the biggest game to be held in the South.

This first game inside of Sanford Stadium might have been its greatest. Not only would the two great football teams of Georgia and Yale play, but both bands of those institutions would play, too. Those two music producers made it unnecessary for the people in Athens to seek musical entertainment over the radio, as there would be worlds of music in the city.

Both of those schools were boasting their best bands in years. Georgia's fifty-piece band would be dressed in red and black uniforms and play "Glory" on the day of the game. Additionally, with the fifty-piece Georgia band, would be a twelve piece drum and bugle corps, dressed in red sweaters and white pants.

Yale's Big Blue Band was famous throughout the eastern states. And, with the famous Big Blue Band, came Yale's dance orchestra. That organization would play several times during their stay in Athens. They played at the social activities held on Friday and Saturday, in honor of the thousands of visitors. In addition, George Hall and his orchestra, the favorite of New York City, were in Athens for two days.

The "Four Horsemen," as famous in the South, as the Yale dance orchestra was in the East, played, too. Branham "Blue" Watson, trap drummer and manager of the four-year old orchestra, stated they would play at several socials over the weekend; however, The Four Horsemen would not sponsor a dance.

On the day of the game, the Georgia band paraded to the stadium, wearing their new uniforms, which had been adopted the previous year, with a color scheme of red and black. Later, during the halftime festivities, the Georgia band paraded on the field and made a giant human "Y," playing at the same time Yale's alma mater. As the band came out of the formation they made a "G" and played Georgia's alma mater.

As far as the game, Georgia went into the game an inspired and enraged team. They stopped Albie Booth and the rest of the Yale stars. The 'Dogs' Catfish Smith scored two touchdowns and a safety, and the weekend was perfect with a score of 15-0.

Sanford Stadium was baptized in a manner eminently satisfying to the sons of Dixie. Saturday, October 12, 1929, was an historic day; Georgia had laughed at the jinx that supposedly plagues the team dedicating its stadium. Mother Yale, the honored invited guest, had been treated as reasonably as the mothers that once featured the old fob folksongs. The Eli left systematically trampled.

The efforts of Clarke County, and its excellent Board of Commissioners, were fully recognized for making it possible to complete the stadium with minimal setbacks. The support and interest in the enterprise stamped them as men of vision and progress. Without their untiring efforts, the construction of the stadium could have been delayed for years.

The Georgia athletic program generated enough income to cover its debts. With mortgage payments scheduled at about $32,000 a year, the athletic association made a double payment of $64,000 in the mortgage's second year.

Ironically, the first game played inside the new stadium would be on October 12, 1929, then, less than two weeks later, on October 29, 1929, the stock market crashed on a day known as "Black Tuesday." Despite the worst financial crisis in American history, none of the 264 notes were ever called.

When Abraham Baldwin, Yale, 1768, fared forth with his blue-ribboned degree from New Haven to found a college in the red clay hills of northern Georgia, he little dreamed he was rearing a Frankenstein of the gridiron, which would someday tear his alma mater's team to shreds and send it home to the Elm City thoroughly beaten and disorganized.

It was all made possible through the untiring efforts and resourcefulness of Doctor Sanford, Dean of the University of Georgia and Chairman of the faculty committee of athletics. In fact, over his stern objections, the new stadium was named in his honor as a mark of respect.

Sanford Stadium, circa 1929

264 Guarantors Who Made the Stadium Possible With Their $1000.00 Notes

Atlanta	Atlanta	Athens	Athens	Columbus	Gainesville
W. Anderson	Sanders McDaniel	A.G. Dudley	J. White, Jr.	C.D. Caraniss	O.R. Horton
P.S. Arkwright	F. M. McGonigal	A.C. Erwin	R.P. White	B.H. Chappell	H.C. Hosch
L. Arnold	M.P. McWhorter	Howell C. Erwin	W.P. White	M.B. Clason	H. H. Hosch
D. C. Helser	A. MacDougald	W.L. Erwin	**Macon**	R.E. Dismukes	J.H. Hosch
C.H. Black, Jr.	D. MacDougald	Blanton Fortson	W.D. Anderson	Jack T. Ellis	F.W. Jackson
C.H. Black	Robert F. Maddox	H.H. Gordon, Jr.	W.D. Anderson, Jr.	W. R. Flournoy	R.L. Moore
E.R. Black, Jr.	G. Middlebrooks	T. F. Green	C.J. Bloch	C.B. Foley	Sidney Smith
H.G. Block	Frank R. Mitchell	Clay Hanna	Pope F. Brock	Carl Greentree	**Crawfordville**
F. K. Boland	James B. Nevin	Robert Hodges	Pinkus Happ	B. H. Hardaway	R.G. Gunn
J.E. Boston	H. A. Newman	W.D. Hooper	C.C. Harold	H. B. Harper	**Tate**
S.F. Boykin	Lowry Nicholson	J.B. Joel	A.J. Lyndon	J.M. Hatcher	Steve C. Tate
N.A. Broyles	Charles D. Orme	P.S. Johnson	E. McKenzie	S. B. Hatcher	**LaGrange**
F.P. Calhoun	R.S. Parker	E.E. Lamkin	A.O.B. Sparks	L.D. Hill	E.T. Moon
Arthur Clarke	E.E. Pomeroy	Ernest A. Lowe	W.C. Turpin	T.W. Hill	**Marietta**
R.G. Clay	J.H. Porter	B.C. Lumpkin	Watson Walker	Tom Houston	C.M. Brown
W.B. Cody	D.W. Reynolds	C. McDorman	**Savannah**	Ike Illges	
R.W. Courts,	C.S. Sanford	R. L. McWhorter	B. Pratt Adams	Jeff Kelly	
T. H. Daniel	John A. Sibley	M.L. Manne	D. S. Atkinson	J.B. Key	
M. Dargan, Jr.	W. Hart Sibley	C.E. Martin	Craig Barrow	J.L. Mahaney	
J. T. Dennis	Victor Smith	W.K. Meadow	R.L. Denmark	W. Paul Miller	
J. P. Dick	Marion Smith	H.J. Mehre	Davis Freeman	Cecil Neill	
S.C. Dobbs	Hughes Spalding	Thomas S. Mell	A.A. Lawrence	J.E. Page	
Roy Dorsey	J.P. Stewart	D.B. Michael	A.R. Lawton	W.R. Palmer	
J. H. Draper	A.E. Thornton, Jr.	Max Michael	A.R. Lawton, Jr.	W.A. Richards	
L.C. Dulaney	W.R. Tichenor	Lee Morris	Henry McAlpin	M.D. Rothschild	
S.N. Evins	H. B. Tompkins	J. White Morton	J.D. McCartney	C.G. Scarborough	
F.L. Fleming	C.C. Torrance	J.S. Myers	P.W. Meldrim	Lester C. Slade	
J.S. Floyd	H.B. Troutman	L.W. Nelson	L. A. Miles	C.D. Smith	
Y. H. Fraser	R.B. Troutman	S.H. Nickparson	J.Rourke, Jr.	C.J. Swift	
T.K. Glenn	Oscar Venable	Abit Nix	**Albany**	George P. Swift	
J.W. Goldstein	W.C. Wardla	W.R. M. Palmer	L. Farkas	H.H. Swift	
J.J. Goodrum	G.P. Whitman	G. Palmisano	K.B. Hodges	W.C. Whittaker	
J.W. Grant	W.W. Whittington	J.K. Patrick	I.J. Hofmayer	C.F. Williams	
J. W. Grant, Jr.	Max Wright	W.O. Payne	Hollis Lanier	G.C. Woodruff	
J.R. Gray, Jr.	**Athens**	T.M. Philot, Jr.	Mercer Sherman	J.W. Woodruff	
H.J. Haas	R.O. Arnold	Frank Postero	J.A. Redfearn	**Louisville**	
T.W. Hardwick	Harry Atwell	H.I. Reynolds	M.W. Tift	Phillip Abbot	
W.P. Heath	S.G. Backman	H.J. Rowe	Richard Tift	R.N. Hardeman	
R. Hickey	J.W. Barnett	Albert D. Sams	C.Westbrook	R.N. Hareman, Jr.	
H. Hirsch	Sidney Boley	W.A. Sams	**Newton**	Roy V. Harris	
M.L. Hirsch	G.A. Booth	S.V. Sanford	Benton Odom	**Valdosta**	
M.R. Hirsch	D. W.Bridges	A.W. Scott	**Rome**	R.G. Dickerson	
W.R. Holmes,	W.M. Bryant	H.L. Seagraves	W.F. Cothran	W.M. Oliver, Jr.	
I.S. Hopkins	W.H. Cabaniss	N.G. Slaughter	Paul H. Doyal	**Elberton**	
C. Howell, Jr.	A.T. Colley	C.M. Snelling	Sidney Jones	John T. Dennis	
S.L. Hurt	Anthony Costa	H.J. Stegeman	G.E. Maddox	H.B. Payne	
E.H. Inman	R.A. Creekmore	M.T. Summerlin	George B. Smith	T.O. Tabor, Jr.	
Hugh Inman	U.H. Davenport	J.E. Tallmadge, Jr.	Barry Wright	**Toccoa**	
H. Jones	John K. Davis	F.W. Thomas	**Columbus**	Claude Bond	
R. P. Jones	Louis S. Davis	W.G. Tiller	T.Arenowitch	**Gainesville**	
G.W. Lanier	B.S. Dobbs	C.A. Trussell	W.C. Bradley	Sandy Beaver	
A.L. Lippitt	O.R. Dobbs	M.N. Tutwiler	J. R.Browne	W.T. Carlisle	
H. H. McCall	E.H. Dorsey, Jr.	S.J. Ware	E.P. Burrus	Edgar B. Dunlap	

A RESOLUTION
With the added excitement of Yale accepting the invitation, Doctor Sanford even set out to get the game day declared a state holiday. The Georgia legislature obliged by declaring it Abraham Baldwin Day, in honor of the "father of the University.

Declaring October 12, 1929, a legal holiday as a special courtesy to Yale University, the day to be known as "Abraham Baldwin Day" in honor of the Founder of the first American State Universities

WHEREAS, In this so-called materialistic age, this age of machinery, there are those who are still moved by a deep sense of appreciation and sentiment, and find occasion to pay tribute to those who have made the state great by contributing to its commercial, educational, and spiritual development; and

WHEREAS, the immigrants of Europe, the migration of citizens from other states of our own country, have made their notable contributions to the welfare and progress of Georgia, perhaps no single institution has done so much to advance Georgia to the forefront on things of permanent value as Yale University. The graduates of Yale University early fell in love with Georgia, and many came from year to year, not to find land upon which to settle, but to found schools, colleges, churches, and to become leaders in the secular professions and pursuits—to be governors, lawyers, teachers, statesmen; and

WHEREAS, Among the early graduates of Yale to settle in Georgia was that brilliant, staunch, Puritan, Lyman Hall, who from the day of his arrival was prominent in the public life of the state. His intensely patriotic services to Georgia during the Revolutionary period are well known. He was a delegate to the Second Continental Congress, signed the Declaration of Independence, and was elected governor of Georgia. He was a loyal and typical Yale man greatly interested in religion and education; and

WHEREAS, As governor he urged the legislature to make provision for the endowment of seminaries of learning in the state, and in his first message to the legislature, July 8, 1783, said:

"Every encouragement ought to be given to introduce religion and learned elegy to perform divine worship in honor of

God and to cultivate religion and virtue among our citizens. For this purpose it will be your wisdom to lay an early foundation for endowing seminaries of learning; nor can you, I conceive, lay better than by a grant of land that may, as in other governments, hereafter, by lease or otherwise, raise a sufficient revenue to support such valuable institutions;" and

WHEREAS, The next legislature acted by granting in the law laying out Washington and Franklin counties, 40,000 acres of land, to endow a college or seminary of learning. A board of trustees of seven men, was named and among these was ex-Governor Nathan Brownson, another eminent graduate of Yale University, and still another remarkable graduate of Yale University, Abraham Baldwin, whose life and service to Georgia have been rescued from oblivion by the late Doctor H.C. White, for more than fifty years professor of chemistry in the State University; and

WHEREAS, Abraham Baldwin came to Georgia from Yale University at the invitation of General Nathaniel Greene and Governor Lyman Hall; settled in Wilkes county and later represented that county in the legislature. Afterwards he was elected to Congress and to the Senate. He was an active and an important contributor to the building of Georgia, one of the group of wise men who laid securely the foundations upon which was built the present Great Republic; and

WHEREAS, That illustrious Georgian, Richard Malcolm Johnston, said of him: "He was the greatest man that ever lived in Georgia. In some respects he was superior to Jefferson. Justice has never been done to his great merits." He wrote the charter of the University of Georgia, a document that contains sentiments as lofty and as sublime and as inspiring as any found in the Declaration of Independence; as for example, "It should be among the first objects of those looking towards the national prosperity to support and encourage the principles of morality and religion, and thus early to place youth under the forming hand of society, that by instruction they may be molded to love of virtue and good order;" and

WHEREAS, Abraham Baldwin has the great honor of being the founder of the First of American State Universities and the first President of a State University; and

WHEREAS, Still another brilliant son of Yale came to Georgia to be the first active President of the University of Georgia,

Josiah Meigs. He was given authority to select his own faculty and of course selected Yale graduates; and

WHEREAS, Time will not permit to recite the contributions made by Yale graduates in other lines of activity nor their full contributions to the educational system of Georgia; and

WHEREAS, Yale University has done the University of Georgia the distinguished honor of accepting its invitation to send their football team to engage in a game which will dedicate the new stadium on October 12. It is such an unusual event for the Yale team to play at any field outside of New Haven, except Harvard or Princeton, which the University of Georgia has felt peculiarly complemented by their acceptance of its invitation, and is extremely anxious to make the occasion memorable in every way. Yale was promoted to accept the invitation because of its intimate kinship with Georgia; and

WHEREAS, Dr. George H. Nettleton, chairman of the athletic board of control, Yale University, states: "With the founding and development of this university, Yale has most intimate connections. In recognition of such close academic kinship and of the special interest of Yale graduates in the South, exceptional consideration was paid to exceptional circumstances. The determining factor is not accidental rivalry for intersectional athletic supremacy but settled community of academic interests and friendly regard;" and

WHEREAS, In recognition of the great services rendered the State of Georgia by its many illustrious graduates of Yale University: Lyman Hall, Nathan Brownson, Abraham Baldwin, Josiah Meigs, and others, and in appreciation of the coming of Yale University to dedicate the new stadium of one of her children—the State University;

THEREFORE BE IT RESOLVED, by the General Assembly of Georgia, that Saturday, October 12, be and the same is hereby designated a legal holiday for the year 1929, as a courtesy of Yale and in honor of the Founder of the First of American State Universities, to be known as "Abraham Baldwin Day."

Fifty Most "Unforgettable" Games

While some Georgia fans could squawk about not missing a game since the Depression, World War II, or some other significant event, nobody could have seen them all. Since its construction in 1929, more than 440 University of Georgia varsity football games have taken place at Sanford Stadium. In many of those games, the Bulldogs, or their opponents—sometimes both—featured dominant teams and battled to adrenaline-charged finishes. Regrettably, there have been games involving mismatches, or of two meager teams, playing ho-hum games before marginally small crowds.

During its first five decades of existence, most games inside Sanford Stadium were not sold out for various reasons. In fact, many independent variables have dictated the size of its crowds. In addition to quality of opponents, or the presence of a superstar, the weather has often played a significant part with attendance. The north Georgia weather has provided for games played under picturesque blue skies, freezing temperatures, extreme heat, pouring rain and many other climatological circumstances.

Webster's dictionary defines "unforgettable" as "something impossible to forget; indelibly impressed on the memory." Here, the terminology of "unforgettable" is a superlative that has been applied to specific games played inside of Sanford Stadium. It is a subjective term used by fans, and alumni, to describe the most extraordinary games during an exact period. The fifty games listed are considered "unforgettable," or historical, because of exceptional circumstances.

The phrase "unforgettable" has been placed in quotation marks to indicate the paradox, or call attention to the incorrectness of the term as it applies to Georgia football games. What caused this word to be subjective was because we typically list games we attended, or listened to while Ed Thilenius, Larry Munson or Scott Howard so tastefully illustrated the play-by-play over the radio, or had been told about by friends, neighbors, parents, uncles or grandparents.

Unfortunately, some of the games listed are not Georgia victories—since Georgia has suffered some close and, at times, devastating defeats in Athens. In truth, some games did not even involve Georgia, but concerned another team calling Sanford

Stadium its home, the Georgia Pre-Flight Skycrackers. The Skycrackers, a World War II service team, played a regular college football schedule from 1942 through 1944; four of these historical games were played on its home field of Sanford Stadium.

Any endeavor to go into the chronicles of Sanford Stadium and rank its top games, no matter how impartial, encourages debate and arguments. There have been so many great games played there that some were invariably excluded in this book. In fact, between 1929 through 2014, there are plenty of games that would make every Georgia fan's list; however, the following fifty games were selected as the most "unforgettable" games of all-time.

Without any further ado, here are, in chronological order, the Top-50 "unforgettable" games played inside of Sanford Stadium.

Georgia 15 – Yale 0, October 12, 1929

Per the book, "Between the Hedges," written by Jesse Outlar, he described how Coach Harry Mehre opened up his daily column on October 13, 1929, with the *Atlanta Journal Constitution,* "Christopher Columbus discovered America on October 12, 1492, and 437 years later, on October 12, 1929, the Bulldogs of Yale University came to Athens, Georgia to discover Sanford Stadium."

By the middle October, in 1929, the yellow leaves of autumn were just beginning to fall, as a brawny Yale football eleven rolled into Athens to help dedicate Sanford Stadium. It was a big game for Georgia and Coach Mehre, an old Notre Dame star. It was the first time the Eli saw fit to leave the hallowed grounds of New Haven, and head south to do battle on the gridiron of foreign soul.

Many had wondered where all those football enthusiasts would stay in the little city of Athens, but Doctor Sanford had already solved the problem. Railroad companies left Pullman and dining cars on side tracks to accommodate the droves of people journeying to the Classic City. Traffic control was under the direct supervision of Major A.T. Cofley and other officers of the U.S. Army, who worked with Athens Police Chief Beussee.

The railroads had been kept busy by the Connecticut gentlemen, too, for Yale sent a 12-car special train carrying the school's 120-piece band, plus the golf team. As anticipated, Yale came into Georgia in an array of grandeur.

Over 33,000 fans found their way into the stadium, not counting those perched on nearby buildings, or hanging out of trees. The game was played in bright sunshine, with Charles Martin's hedges encircling the field. Governors of five states, members of the House of Representative, tycoons of finance, and captains of industry, were a dime a dozen in this capacity crowd of spectators who viewed Georgia's "Game of the Century."

The voodoo curse of home teams losing "dedication games" was expected to continue in the vastness of Sanford Stadium. Most experts expected the game to end in humiliation for a 'Dogs' team loaded with sophomores. In fact, the season had started out rough for Georgia. During its season opener, the Bulldogs tasted defeat at the hands of little Oglethorpe by a final score of 13-7. On the same day, Yale defeated the University of Maine 90-0.

The 'Dogs were a heavy underdog against Yale and there appeared very little chance for a Georgia victory as the visitors, led by their backfield ace Albie Booth, took the field. And, the Eli team would meet the opening whistle on this historic day ready to send up the Bulldogs as a burnt offering on their own altar of dedication.

As the crowd breathlessly awaited the kick-off, an unusual object made its appearance in the skies overlooking Sanford Stadium. A blimp, decorated in the colors of both schools, descended over the field to drop the football to be used in the game between Yale and Georgia

The 'Dogs played inspired football against Yale in the first game in Sanford Stadium, but as in all football victories, a star emerged. That day it was the hitherto unknown Vernon "Catfish" Smith, who grabbed the headlines with his brilliant offensive and defensive play. Smith scored every one of Georgia's 15 points. Two touchdowns via the air lanes, a point-after and, to top the afternoon off, cornered Yale's All-American and Little Boy Blue, Booth, in the endzone for a safety.

Those who had expected Georgia to wilt when Yale's blue-jersey, white-helmeted giants deployed on the field, had got a stunning surprise. Yale was unprepared for the heat and humidity. The Bulldogs of Yale wore thick, wool, long-sleeved jerseys and wool stockings. During pregame warm-ups they tumbled head over heels from endzone to endzone, as they always did. By the time they were done, they were dripping wet.

The Bulldogs of Georgia elected to wear jerseys made of a very lightweight material for the first time. Its benefits were immediately felt. The stubborn sons of the Red and Black would dig their determined cleats into the fresh sod and etch a name for themselves on the immortal scroll of Georgia greats. The stars for Georgia would be Smith, Al Brown, Red Leathers, Joe Bennett, Spud Chandler, and Benny Rothstein.

Employing Rockne's tricky hop shift, Georgia packed her plays inside tackle. A superficial critic might have thought the middle of the Blue line was the last place to strike, but Georgia scouts had spotted softness there. They used the savage running plays of Rothstein to exploit this weakness.

Jack Roberts, John Davidson and Marion Dickens exploited that weak spot, too. Rothstein was a worthy successor to Bull McCrary from the 1927 team. He ran down to the turf, his nose scraping the sod. Yale's middle was split as though by a razor-edged knife. Rothstein wriggled like a snake threading a cornfield as he eluded Yale's secondary.

Line pressure would ultimately win this game, as it had decided many others. Outweighed six or seven pounds, the blocky, stocky Southerners — swarmed all over the taller, bigger Yale team. The Georgia center trio — Captain Boland, flanked by two redheads, Leathers and Ralph Maddox — chewed huge holes in Yale's midriff.

Three out of every four Georgia plays were directed over the Yale guards. They sprang out of Rockne's cleverly masked cut-in maneuver and caught Yale shifting the wrong way. Once in a while Georgia varied this close order inside assault with a wide sweep that caught Yale by surprise. On one flanking run, Dickens almost got free for a touchdown. He would have crossed the goal untouched if his interferers had mopped up properly. Line pressure forced the breaks, but it was Smith, Georgia's rugged sophomore end, who exploited them. Every football game must have its hero and Smith, dubbed "Catfish" by his classmates, surely stole Dixie's intersectional show.

Smith scored both Georgia touchdowns and kept a rod in pickle for Eli all afternoon. Oddly enough, Smith began the game as though he were destined to be the goat instead of the hero. His vertical punts, the ball traveling almost straight upwards, had

Georgia in hot water throughout the first period. Dixie supporters were mumbling unkind things about Catfish, but that was before he did his Dr. Jekyll-Mr. Hyde transformation and won the game for old Georgia.

Records show in the second quarter, Georgia's Roberts and Maddox blocked a punt behind Yale's goal line. Catfish came out of a pile in the endzone with the football, scoring a touchdown for Georgia. Smith successfully kicked the extra-point.

Later, in the third quarter, Yale All-American Booth attempted to run a retrieved ball out the endzone, after a snapped punt sailed over his head. Most historical accounts indicate Smith tackled Booth for a safety in the endzone. On the contrary, Smith forced Booth out of bounds before he got out of the endzone. Nevertheless, Smith was credited for scoring a safety for the 'Dogs.

Georgia completed only three passes the entire game, but its last completion, occurring in the contest's final minutes, was no doubt memorable. The Bulldogs had the ball on Yale's 22-yard line, facing third down. Chandler drifted a high, arching pass to Smith, who caught it over his right shoulder at the 2-yard line and fell into the endzone for his second touchdown.

Yale left on Southern beholders an indelible impression of slowness. Aside from Booth, the Blue backs were heavy footed players who tripped over their own blockers. But the chief blame for the Blue debacle rested on a line that folded up like an accordion under the berserk charges of Georgia's hell-bent forwards.

Dang-dong, dang-dong — far into Saturday night the bell atop Georgia's chapel continued to broadcast the tidings of the Southland's smashing triumph over the descendants of those hardy Yanks who founded this school at Athens.

Coach Mehre had drilled his eleven all week to stop Yale spin plays from the old Warner box formation, and his strategy, combined with sheer determination, had worked. Raw courage in the red line had baptized a fine $300,000 stadium, and initiated a new and more prosperous era in the story of Georgia football.

The victorious Georgia team climbed up the steep hill that led from its sunken stadium — a concrete gem in a sylvan setting — to the hummock top campus. A hazy, half-light, that grayish-yellow tone so distinguishing of a Southern sunset, mitigated the contours of weather-beaten college buildings aromatic of age. Dang-dong-dang-dong — the metronomic pounding of the bell came from the old chapel, a brown brick building designed on the square lines of a New England meeting house. Doric pillars, their masses bulging large in the dusk, supported the pretense. The stadium had been dedicated!

Georgia 12 - Georgia Tech 6, December 7, 1929

Less than 60 days after the Great Depression's specter engulfed America on October 29, 1929, Georgia and Georgia Tech wrestled doggedly over a brown patch of gridiron in a driving rainstorm. Over twenty-thousand spectators watched this epic struggle inside of the newly built cathedral of Sanford Stadium.

Two years earlier, in 1927, the famous "Dream and Wonder" team of Georgia had won its first nine games of the season, including Georgia's first victory over Yale. The 'Dogs had been ranked number one in the nation, and an invitation to the Rose Bowl in Pasadena would be offered after the 'Dogs beat its hated rival, Georgia Tech, in Atlanta. Unfortunately, Tech upset Georgia on an extra muddy field, 12-0, and crushed any hopes of the mythical national title. Most believe the loss incited Georgia to build a new stadium in order to play Georgia Tech in Athens every other season.

On the day of the game, in the early morning hours, there was calm before the gray dawn broke. Then, far down in the street, a voice wafted up to those asleep in the hotels, there could be heard the cry of some wanderer. "Wreck Tech!" he shouted hoarsely. As if his shout were the clarion bugle of some moral Gabriel, Athens awoke, tossed off the blankets and began to run around in circles. The great day, the day when Georgia met Tech, had arrived.

There were ginger ale bottles in the corridors of the hotels as the guests quitted their rooms and prepared to join the maelstrom in the lobbies. Quite a few, who arrived the night before, had gone into serious training for the day. The streets were a live by 8 o'clock and the colors were mostly red and black, with here and there, the old gold and white of Georgia Tech was worn proudly on a lapel.

Lunch boxes appeared on the streets corners and a myriad of taxies made their appearance. Athens was all set to put the thing over in a big way. They handled 40,000 people for the Yale game and were now taking the Tech game nonchalantly, but efficiently.

The old reliable two thick slices of bread, with whatever one chose to have spread between them, was going at 10 to 15 cents. The coffee was a nickel or a dime, depending on where it was purchased, and hotel rooms were priced as they had been all year. The Georgian hotel, which was headquarters, was jammed early and stayed that way until game time. Old Clarence, the faithful bellboy, was shouting his pages and acting as taxi-starter in front.

The Bulldogs would win the day when Vernon "Fats" Bryant, the giant native of Sargeant, Georgia, supplied his broad chest to block a Tech punt, the long arms to scoop up the bounding leather and the piano legs to run a matter of 45-yards for a touchdown. When Bryant led a raiding party of Bulldogs through the Yellow Jackets' line to block the kick, the score was knotted at 6-6. And, when he pulled-up, panting across the goal line, the 'Dogs kept their young tradition of victory on new Sanford Stadium intact.

People had gathered in a colorful array before the kickoff. None heeded the threat of rain. The 'Dogs took the opening kickoff and hurried 65-yards for a touchdown. Spurgeon Chandler flipped a 20-yard pass to Herbert Maffett, the great end, for the score. The extra-point-attempt went wide right. Then, the deluge burst on the field, and in the downpour, neither team could drive the ball over the goal line by its own plays.

The next score would not come until the second half. Picking-up speed on defense, as the game wore on, the Engineer line, led by Tom Jones, blocked one of Chandler's punts in the third quarter. It rolled over the goal line and Jim Brooke fell on it for a touchdown. The extra-point-attempt was missed and the score was tied at 6-6.

"Fats" Bryant cut the knot in the fourth period. The big sophomore delivered just the sort of versatile offensive game, and dashing defensive play, that Georgia's fond supporters expected. It remained for the Engineers, already defeated in five games in '29, to furnish the unexpected.

The Yellow Jackets, with no capable reserves, played brilliant football for at least three-fourths of the game and developed a mauling attack of surprising power. The Jackets played their starting eleven right on until one by one, they were worn out or injured and relieved. It was a last ditch fight for a depleted squad and the players in gold left the field with honor.

"Stumpy" Thomason, the little giant of the Flats, played his farewell game as a Tech halfback and he had a royal exit. His foot had been badly injured in the final play of the closing scrimmage in Atlanta, three days before the game, and he went into action against the 'Dogs limping slightly. Although the Georgia defense was designed to stop him, he tore yards from the 'Dogs in short gains on sheer fight. He took enough physical buffeting to have wrecked a player of ordinary mold.

The Bulldogs quite properly hit him by squads, by platoons and by companies. Finally, his injury became so aggravated that Coach Alexander took him out of the game. The little giant limped slowly off the field, his head hanging low, utterly fagged and in pain. And, as he made his exit from the southern football world, a mighty cheer arose, shared by Georgia and Tech fans alike.

Warner Mizell, Stumpy's understudy for three years of campaigning, played the whole game and was at his best. He had the drive and the smooth running style that landed him on the All-American team in 1928. Mizell started and finished lashing the Georgia wings and punting a wet, heavy football in masterful style.

Georgia's Bryant, Bennie Rothstein, and the other players who "graduated," passed summa cum laude. It was a game of a thousand sidelights. "Coot" Watkins played the game of his career at tackle. Maffett was a superb end and the exacting nemesis of Stumpy. Congressman Frisbee went the route at tackle and there passed a colorful figure from the Bulldog ranks. Joe Westbrook was another veteran who started and finished fighting. Joe Boland was a man of iron in the face of Tech's sledging attack. Jones was the Jones' of 1928. Unfortunately, some of the seniors sat on the bench, and never had a chance to strike a blow at the old enemy.

The battle was a complete orchestration of the gridiron score. Everything happened—more than once. Georgia swept away to a 65-yard touchdown drive with the second string starting backfield clicking as if they meant to score twelve touchdowns. Then the Yellow Jackets, with Thomason and Mizell on the loose, rushed back late in the period like a turbulent yellow torrent, but a fumble on the 10-yard line broke that up.

Then, the aforesaid rainstorms came. That was when the lid was off and the players were out to die and let die for their colors.

Tech put on a powerful advance in the second period and the 'Dogs came right back with a counter attack that carried them to Tech's 1-yard line, where penalties were called on every play and the rain-soaked spectators became agitated and went into an uproar.

As the play grew more violent, the penalties popped like firecrackers. The officials took drastic steps to keep the players within bounds. The crowd was wild. So were the players. A Tech coach spoke with truculence to officials and it seemed fatal because there was an immediate penalty afterwards, and it put Georgia right on top of the 1-yard line.

In the excitement, Rothstein bucked center and actually scored, but the referee ruled Georgia had executed an illegal shift and back went the leather 15-yards. Chandler shot a pass to Smith that got back the penalized territory, but it was ruled the pass was made less than five yards back of the line of scrimmage. For awhile the officials were gaining more ground than either Tech or Georgia.

Both teams switched to a kicking duel as the half ended. Under the extreme weather conditions, the punting exhibition staged by Mizell, of Tech, and Chandler of Georgia, was phenomenal. They punted 16 and 14 times, respectively, and the average was 39 yards for each man. Advantage varied throughout the game, contingent on the wind. Chandler and Mizell each had a kick blocked through no fault in their punting techniques.

The game dragged on with few spectacular incidents until the final quarter. In the midst of this period, Georgia's great break came. Ralph "Red" Maddox blocked a Tech punt. The ball fell in the arms of Bryant, who, with an empty field before him, and perfect inference behind, scored the final touchdown.

Georgia held an edge of less than 50 yards in rushing and had seven first downs to Tech's five, which illustrated more clearly than the score the nearly even terms on which the teams fought.

Only one pass was completed. That one was Georgia's touchdown toss that was made before the rains started. After that, neither team could connect and relied on ground work alone for their gains. A close analysis showed Georgia's real superiority rested in blocking for long runs from scrimmage. In all other departments of play, the two teams were surprisingly well matched. And in the final pinch, Georgia's superior reserve strength might have turned the balance toward the Red and Black's cause.

The Yellow Jackets executed their plays on a new balanced formation with remarkable precision for having practiced it only three weeks. And Georgia, likewise, showed the effects of sound coaching by selecting just the sort of early attack calculated to catch a veteran team unprepared. So-called "breaks" figured in all three touchdowns. It was a great game, honestly fought and won on merit.

In defeating Tech in a downpour of rain, the University of Georgia Bulldogs wound-up with a successful season after getting victories over four of its main rivals, Yale, North Carolina, Alabama, and Georgia Tech. For the entire season the Georgia squad scored 137 points to their opponent's 70. Smith led the team in scoring with 31 points for the season. Chandler had 24 to his credit, and Rothstein had 23 points. During the season Georgia won six games, lost four games and had no ties. It lost to Florida, Tulane, Oglethorpe and New York University.

The Bulldog football team in 1929 was the most colorful at Georgia in over two decades. With varied success in games won and lost, the team achieved a national following for the first time, and the season could have been called nothing, if not a successful one. From a material viewpoint, the season was brilliant with a new and much-needed stadium. As an advertisement, the 1929 team was more to be desired than even many pages in the *Saturday Evening Post*.

Georgia 9 – Vanderbilt 0, October 24, 1931

The Commodores of Vanderbilt were a perennial powerhouse since the inception of college football, in the early 1890s, until the mid-1930s. In fact, in 1931, Georgia was 3-8-1 all-time against the Commodores. Now, one week before Halloween, one of Vanderbilt's superior teams arrived in Athens on what was a very hot, humid day in the Classic City; however, it would be transformed into a slightly lukewarm afternoon as clouds obscured the sun. A brisk breeze, blowing in from the west, soothed the riotous crowds as it descended-upon Athens for Homecoming Day. They came on foot to the stadium, strolling through the old campus to renew memories. There were over 20,000 on the gently rising shelves just before the kickoff.

In a special box at the top of the south stand, draped in striped awning, Governor Richard B. Russell, Jr., and Chancellor

Charles M. Snelling entertained a distinguished group of visitors. In contrast to the diversity of the crowd, high school teams came into Athens, and bought-up all the dollar tickets in the endzone.

A half hour before game time Georgia's squad came in from their forest retreat at Camp Wilkins and worked out. The 'Dogs wore their white shirts with red numbers. The team had no intentions of changing to its red jerseys, since they had won three games in the white jerseys.

Later, the 'Dogs went to their dressing room at the west end of the field to get their final word from Coach Mehre. Vanderbilt was dressing in the field house in the east endzone, from whence no visiting team had ever marched out to victory over the Bulldogs.

Vanderbilt, loaded with All-Americans, won the toss and elected to defend the west goal. Georgia chose to receive. This game would become a titanic struggle between two of the mighty atoms of the country's gridiron.

In fact, an early freak play gave the 'Dogs a safety and a 2-0 lead just before the halftime. Georgia's Jack Roberts fumbled on Vanderbilt's 2-yard line, after catching a 12-yard pass from Austin Downes, and a Vanderbilt player had recovered the ball.

After the Commodores broke their huddle, their quarterback decided, with only a few moments left before half, it would be better to purposely throw a pass out of bounds instead of risking an interception. He dropped back and Catfish Smith rushed-in and caused him to step out of bounds as he threw the ball. The referee ruled the Bulldogs had scored a safety and the scoreboard registered Georgia 2 – Vanderbilt 0. The majority of spectators were bewildered because they didn't realize what had happened.

On the previous drive, Georgia's "Jack the Ripper" Roberts had ripped Vanderbilt's line with only a few minutes before halftime. It was the first time that season the Vanderbilt defense had actually been torn open. Roberts dashed intensely to get the ball on Vanderbilt's 40-yard line and two plays later he ripped off 18-yards more to put the ball on Vanderbilt's 23-yard line.

After Vanderbilt took a time out, he ripped off 10 more yards, carrying the ball to the 13-yard line. Downes then passed to Roberts near the Vanderbilt goal line. He grabbed it, but fumbled the ball. Thomas recovered for Vanderbilt and that was where Vanderbilt's Henderson, not wanting to turn over the ball, passed out of bounds. However, he had stepped out of bounds and gave Georgia a safety. That was how the half ended.

Head Coach Harry Mehre, true to an old Notre Dame custom, started his second-string team against the Commodores of Vanderbilt, with the exception of Graham Batchelor at center and Smith at left end.

Vanderbilt won the second coin toss and defended the east goal, thus taking advantage of a slow wind. Georgia received, again.

Georgia's Red Maddox, who had been out all the week with an injured knee, replaced James Patterson at the beginning of the second half. On the kickoff, Vanderbilt's Johnson ran through Georgia's kickoff team, and carried the ball to the 'Dogs' 35-yard line, returning it 60-yards.

The Commodores quarterback, Henderson, elected to toss a pass two plays later and Marion Dickens intercepted it for Georgia. It was a few minutes later when Downes caught Henderson's punt in his own territory and raced 28-yards to get the ball to Vanderbilt's 8-yard line. Excellent blocking aided him greatly on the play, which was one of several brilliant runs by backfield men on both teams. He almost scored a touchdown, but Vanderbilt's Will Fortune forced him out of bounds.

Georgia failed to gain on three consecutive plays. On the fourth down, Chandler took the ball and sent it sailing over the goal line. For a moment it seemed it would be caught in the waiting arms of a horde of Vanderbilt players, but all of a sudden Catfish Smith appeared from among the mass, and with one leap his outstretched hands took it for a touchdown. Georgia made the extra-point, with Downes holding the ball.

Henderson's two short punts of 36 and 30 yards and his substandard play, coupled with Bulldog quarterback, Willie Sullivan, punting deep, kept the ball in Vanderbilt's territory during most of the game.

In the middle of the third quarter, Vanderbilt returned one of Sullivan's punts from mid-field, to Georgia's 25-yard line. At this juncture, Coach Mehre sent in Chandler at left half, and put Joseph White at right half to replace Lloyd Gilmore. Vanderbilt's Coach Dan McGugin sent in his first-string fullback, Fortune, to replace Von Huhrheinrich.

The Commodores' Henderson promptly smashed center for 5-yards, then Fortune hit left tackle for 5 more yards. The situation was not any good from a Bulldog standpoint and Coach Mehre sent in Jim Hamrick for William Cooper at right tackle and Milton Leathers for Joseph Bennett at right guard. Fortune fumbled on Vanderbilt's next play, and White recovered for Georgia on the 'Dogs' 12-yard line. Chandler punted out of danger two plays later.

Late in the quarter, Vanderbilt went 60 yards, to Georgia's 15-yard line before finally being stopped. It was Vanderbilt's only real threat. Vanderbilt's quarterback, now handicapped with a leg injury, returned to the game. A pass from Henderson netted 10-yards as the third quarter ended.

Beginning the fourth quarter, two more plays failed to move the ball. Then, Henderson passed 15-yards for a first down. Two plays later, Catfish Smith intercepted a pass by Henderson and ended the threat. Next, Dickens grabbed a pass on his own 42-yard line and galloped 21-yards. The Commodores were penalized 5-yards and Georgia's Norman Mott picked-up 12 more yards to make it a first down. The next play ended in an incomplete pass. Then, the next two running plays netted no yardage. Georgia punted, held firmly, and forced Vanderbilt to punt. The 'Dogs would receive the ball at midfield, and that was how the game ended.

Statistics show the Bulldogs outplayed the Commodores in every department, except in the amount of yardage gained from the forward pass. Vanderbilt tried 13 passes and completed four for a total of 43-yards. Georgia tried only five passes and made three, good for a total of 21-yards. Georgia had no passes intercepted, while Vanderbilt tossed four interceptions.

The two teams were about evenly matched in punting, Chandler, playing the last three quarters, and Sullivan, playing the first quarter, averaged 29.8-yards. Vanderbilt's Henderson averaged 38.4 yards. Henderson did all of the Commodores' punting.

Some of the highlights of the game were Henderson's return of two successive punts for 36 and 20 yards each in the first period. Roberts' 21 and 19-yard consecutive gains in the second quarter; Downes' return of a punt for 25-yards; Johnson's return of a kickoff 60-yards for Vanderbilt in the third period; Fortunes' 42-yard run from scrimmage in the third and Dickens' 46-yard run, after intercepting a pass in the fourth quarter. Georgia triumphed 9-0.

Georgia 7 – Tulane 20, November 14, 1931

Athens played host to 39,400 people from all parts of the nation on Saturday, November, 14, 1931. The crowd who saw one of the most feared teams of the 1930s, the Tulane Green Wave, play Georgia was over five thousand more than was estimated to have witnessed Georgia beat Yale in 1929.

They arrived there by train, by automobile, by plane, and some walked. The streets, filled before 9AM, remained gridlock until kickoff. Anybody traveling through Athens, without knowledge of the game, would have thought a circus was in town.

Hundreds of distinguished visitors attended, including Governor Richard B. Russell, Bobby Jones, Grantland Rice, and Lawrence Perry. Both teams were undefeated and ranked number one and two in the nation.

An hour before game time the big concrete stadium began to quickly fill. By 2:15PM a mighty cheer arouse as the red-shirted Bulldogs paraded onto the field. The team immediately began to run practice plays. Unfortunately, because of the congestion of people, the Georgia band had not been on hand to announce the arrival of its Georgia warriors on Sanford Stadium's field of battle.

After the team finished running plays, it divided into two lines, practicing punting, getting down under kicks and receiving. Spurgeon Chandler, the future New York Yankee great, boomed long, spiraling punts during warm-ups. The Georgia team, ranked number two in the nation, had appeared taciturn during warm-ups. After twenty minutes of warming-up, the Bulldogs went back into their locker room.

Afterwards, at 2:40PM, the Green Wave, 36 strong, stormed out on the field. Tulane wore apple-green jerseys and their conventional khaki pants. They deployed over the big field and immediately got busy with practicing punts, passing, etc.... This Tulane team, ranked number-one in the nation, seemed to be confident and wore smiles as they practiced in front of a large, hostile Georgia crowd.

It was the nation's number one rated game-of-the-week. Both teams were undefeated and the championship of the old Southern Conference definitely was at stake.

The Greenies, coached by the legendary Bernie Bierman, were 7-0 and had allowed only one touchdown and that was in demolishing Mississippi State 59-7. The Bulldogs, under Harry Mehre, were 6-0 and had twice gone "up East" and conquered powerful Yale by a score of 26-7 and New York University 7-6, in their own backyards. This battle would be a game of attrition.

Opportunity would knock early on Georgia's door. Catfish Smith recovered Tulane's All-American Don Zimmerman's fumble at the Tulane 27-yard line. On third down Jack "The Ripper" Roberts, Georgia's All-Southern fullback, broke off right tackle for 19-yards. He was run out of bounds on the Tulane 6 yard line. Then the mighty Tulane team stopped the 'Dogs from scoring. The Greenies line established control of the game from then on.

Engineered by the flashy Zimmerman, a triple threat halfback, Tulane's aerial attack accounted for two touchdowns tallied by the Green Wave and put Georgia in a hole from which it threatened only once to escape. In fact, each of those touchdowns in the first half, followed strategic quick-kicks by Harry Glover that would catch Georgia by surprise, forcing them back to their own goal line.

The first of those long boots was downed by Lamar Haynes, Tulane's end, on Georgia's one-foot line. Tulane followed-up its advantage by scoring on a 33-yard pass, Zimmerman to Haynes. The Greenies rubbed the medicine in by tallying the extra-point on a similar play executed by the same players.

By a comparable process, Georgia was backed into its own territory in the second quarter and Zimmerman once more opened fire, alternating between Haynes and Captain Jerry Dalrymple, as receivers for his bullet-like tosses. On one particular play, Dalrymple had one foot on the Georgia goal line as he turned to receive the last pass. He was sent spinning headlong by the rush of the Bulldogs' defense, but the pass was declared complete on the interference. On the next play, Tulane's All-American fullback, Nollie Fields, powered across for a touchdown.

For perhaps five minutes of the third period, as Georgia played its one big hand, the crowd of Bulldog sympathizers had a plethora of things to cheer about. It looked for a time as though the courageous Georgia team might overhaul their rivals by the sheer spirit of a potentially courageous come-back.

With the ball on Georgia's 40-yard line, Homer Key faded back and tossed a long pass down the middle alley. Buster Moot, hero in the triumph a week earlier against highly ranked New York University, had grabbed the ball over his shoulder as he stepped into the clear. He outraced his would-be attackers to the corner of the endzone. It was a glorious play, to which Catfish Smith added an extra-point on a perfect point-after kick.

It looked like another quintessential Georgia rally, but the Bulldogs were nowhere equal to penetrating the close-knit Tulane defense, again. The next thrust through the air was a boomerang as Francis Payne intercepted the ball deep in Georgia territory. He returned the football to the Bulldog's 20-yard line.

Shorty afterwards, the Green Wave hit the 'Dogs with a final shattering impact. Payne dashed off tackle 26-yards for the third touchdown. Zimmerman booted the extra-point, and the door was closed to Georgia's last remaining aspirations.

Throughout the final quarter Tulane's stalwart defense, led by Dalrymple, repulsed every Georgia threat; however, the field was suddenly threatened by the surging rush of thousands of spectators who fought, pushed and scrambled along the sidelines. Time was called repeatedly while the police attempted to restore order and clear fans from the playing field, as well as the endzone. Fist fights broke-out in several areas and many a head was punched in the melee while authorities sough to maintain control.

Penalties were handed out so frequently during the final quarter that the total for the day was run-up to 18 penalties. The biggest habitual violator was Tulane, which had ten penalties for 70 yards, and eight were against Georgia for 80 yards.

Tulane not only romped off with the victory, but its star end and captain, Dalrymple, emerged with an advantage over Georgia's famous "Catfish" Smith. The two All-Americans had brawled with each other for the entire game. Dalrymple played an exceptional defensive game and his work over-shadowed that of the "Catfish."

The Green Wave registered 13 first downs to Georgia's five, rolled-up 119 rushing yards to 91 yards for the Bulldogs. Tulane completed four out of seven passes for gains of 82 yards, while Georgia completed two out of seven for 72 yards.

Except for those very few incredible moments during the third quarter, when the red-shirted Georgia team flashed their one scoring threat, the battle of Athens was turned largely into a rout by the powerful, resourceful and hard-hitting aggregation from Tulane. It carried its banner in another big stride along the championship trail of 1931.

Tulane's victory not only kept the Green Wave in a commanding position in the race for Southern Conference honors, alongside Tennessee, but helped the Greenies in the race for the national title. They had a few more hurdles to clear, but by hurdling Georgia's stubborn resistance, Tulane's forces cleared the way for their dash toward the goal of playing Southern California in the 1932 Rose Bowl classic on New Year's Day, in Pasadena, California.

Unfortunately, the battle of Athens was marred by close to a record crop of penalties, as well as disturbances along the sidelines that threatened to develop into a free-for-all fist fight in the closing period; however, the outcome was decided by a combination of Tulane's smarter play and sensational passing.

Tulane's mighty Green Wave rose to typhoon proportions and surged out over Sanford Stadium, submerging a fighting Bulldogs team by the score of 20-7. It was Georgia's first defeat inside of Sanford Stadium, and it first setback of the 1931 season. Though the 'Dogs could not withstand the crushing Wave of Green, they fought to the last minute, refusing to surrender until the final gun had ended the game. It required a great team to beat the 'Dogs.

Tulane achieved a decisive conquest before a crowd of over 39,000 spectators who had packed Sanford Stadium. The crowd overflowed onto the field and delayed the game's finish repeatedly, as the aforementioned incidents, rioting and fights were waged on the sidelines.

It would be one of the most turbulent climaxes to one of the South's most spectacular gridiron spectacles. Georgia would finish the season 8-2, losing one more game against the eventual national champions, Southern California Trojans, in Los Angeles by a score of 60-0. Tulane would win the Southern Conference title, and finish 11-1, after losing the Rose Bowl to the Trojans of Southern California by a score of 21-12.

Georgia 33 – Florida 12, October 29, 1932

As the great depression cloaked the nation, the grimness of Georgia football fans sank even deeper in the weeks leading up to the Saturday, October 29, 1932, tilt with the Gators in Athens.

Coach Harry Mehre lost everything off his '31 team that came within one game of playing for the national title. In 1932, he was off to the worst start in his five years at Georgia. He needed a win. The Bulldogs were winless as they prepared for homecoming against Florida. Georgia had lost 7-6 to V.P.I., 34-25 at Tulane, and 12-6 at Vanderbilt. On October 15, the 'Dogs had struggled mightily to a 6-6 tie with North Carolina in Athens.

Coach Charles Bachman's Florida squad owned a 2-1 record. During his fifth season as coach, Bachman had experienced his first losing season at Florida the previous year, including his first loss to the 'Dogs. The Gators had other problems, too. Right halfback A.L. Rogero, Florida's All-Conference passer and punter, suffered a knee injury earlier in the season, and would not play. Four other players, Tommy Lane, Luke Dorsett, W. Bryan, and Simon Osgood, had been demoted to the Gators' B-team and would not play, either.

Athens bulged as an enormous amount of students, alumni and fans from both teams jammed into the city. The parties intensified over the weekend. The police and local authorities were at a conundrum as they dealt with drunkard, boisterous party goers.

With a small crowd of roughly 10,000 fans looking on, both teams had little luck on their first possessions. Then, Georgia found its rhythm after a Florida punt to the Georgia 30-yard line. Georgia's legendary Leroy Young passed to Norman Mott, who was tackled at the Florida 38, after a 24-yard gain. Runs by Martin Gaston and Mott moved the ball to the 18-yard line. Unfortunately, Gaston fumbled and Gator quarterback Sam Davis recovered.

After an exchange of kicks, Gator halfback Jack Henderson, on first down from the Florida 40-yard line, threw to right halfback George Moye, who ran all the way down to the Georgia 25-yard line. The next play caught most of the Georgia players asleep as Moye shook away from Mott at the 15-yard line and knifed into the endzone. The Gators All-Conference fullback, Jimmie Hughes, missed the conversion, but Florida owned the early advantage.

The remainder of the first quarter, and the beginning of the second period, was a nightmare for the partisan Georgia crowd as the Bulldogs lost two more fumbles while threatening to score.

Midway through the second quarter, Georgia's Cy Grant eased matters for the 'Dogs' supporters with an electrifying shot through the line at the Florida 37-yard line, hitting the open field before being knocked out of bounds at the 3-yard line. On the next play, he rammed up the middle to score. Junior right end Graham Batchelor kicked the point after and Georgia led 7-6 at intermission.

After a halftime show of mules being rode around the field at Sanford Stadium, and the Georgia band's performance of the school's fight songs, both teams failed to move the ball opening the second half. The momentum seemed to have swung to the Gators, after Florida scored another touchdown. However, the touchdown appeared to act as an elixir for the wheezing Bulldogs of Georgia's offense. The 'Dogs took the kickoff and moved out to its own 45-yard line on four plays. Joseph Grant then ran wide to the left side of the Gators' line, racing for a 45-yard gain before being shoved out of bounds at the Florida 10-yard line. On the very next play, Grant scored on a 9-yard run, giving Georgia the lead, again.

Entering the fourth quarter, Florida was still within striking distance. But, Gator fullback Charles Stolz fumbled and the Bulldogs' Dick Maxwell fell on the ball at the Florida 44-yard line.

Next, Georgia's Gaston got three yards before Homer Key tore free on a 27-yard scamper to the 14-yard line. On first down, Grant piled through the line for a touchdown. Grant added the extra-point on a drop kick. Georgia had iced its win with a 27-12 spread.

Mehre sent in a wave of substitutes after the kickoff, but the demoralized giant water lizards sank deeper when the Bulldogs recovered a Florida fumble at the Gators' 40-yard line. Georgia drove to the 9-yard line before Mott coughed it up and Florida's George McCampbell recovered.

A defensive brawl ensured until there was less than five minutes to play and the 'Dogs took possession on their 45-yard line. Substitute halfback Buck Chapman made a 13-yard gallop to the Florida 11-yard line, before Davis muscled to the 1-yard line on the next play. Mott scored to give Georgia a commanding lead over one of its hated rivals. Never before in the series had the lead seesawed between these increasingly bitter enemies. Grant's off-tackle slashes and three scores proved the difference.

In the Georgia tradition, students rang the school's ancient chapel bell into the night, as part of the victory celebration. A bonfire flamed in the distance, like a funeral pyre, on old Herty Field as red-capped Georgia freshmen paraded around the fire in a rite of passage. Georgia would finish the season with a 2-5-2 record, as the Gators went 3-6.

A final death knell was delivered to the old Southern Conference on December 1, 1932, when 13 of the 23 schools in the Conference formed the Southeastern Conference (SEC). The charter members of the SEC were: Florida, Georgia, Louisiana State University, Mississippi, Mississippi State, Tennessee, Vanderbilt, Alabama, Auburn, Kentucky, Georgia Tech, Tulane, and Sewanee.

Georgia 0- Tennessee 46, October 31, 1936

Facing the Volunteers of Tennessee for the first time since 1925, Georgia's steadily improving Bulldogs played Major Bob Neyland's 1936 University of Tennessee edition inside Sanford Stadium at an inappropriate moment in time. During a ten year span, Tennessee had the best record in the South with only nine losses. Alabama, with two Rose Bowl wins, ranked second in amount of victories during this ten year period.

Georgia, crippled with numerous injuries, was a seven point underdog, as J.C. Hall and Bill Hartman missed the game because of leg injuries. Quinton Lumpkin and Bob Law were the two most valuable players for Georgia in what would go down as the worst loss the Bulldogs ever suffered in the history of Sanford Stadium.

The Vols' Marion Perkins remained the unique story of the '36 football season. It was in one of those causal conversations the night before Tennessee humiliated Georgia, where Major Bob Neyland remarked his fullback, Perkins, who was a substitute, had saved several games for Tennessee. And, ironically, Perkins was a diabetic. In fact, he had been dropped from the squad, but through hard work, he made the team, despite a handicap, which ordinarily would have confined him to a Spartan-like, circumspect life.

The drumming feet of Tennessee's great football team was a prelude of things to come as it beat out a threnody of doom for

Georgia. It was a game where the Volunteers ran, kicked and passed to a shocking 46-0 victory inside of Sanford Stadium.

Merciless as an Indian attack at dawn was this attack by the Tennessee Volunteers. It struck with an intensive power that was inexorable and unyielding in its force. The score could have gone further than the 50-point mark; however, in the fourth quarter, Coach Neyland put in his third-string substitutes to finish the game.

Only once was Georgia past the Tennessee 35-yard line. That was in the closing minutes of the first half when a pass to Spec Towns and another pass, on which Tennessee interfered, gave Georgia the ball at the Tennessee 12-yard line. Coach Neyland brought his gargantuan first-stringers back into the game and stopped the threat to end the first half.

It was Tennessee's Phil Dickens, called Phil the Phantom, who led the early attack. He was a football phantom. He seemed to be observable only to the spectators. Time after time he weaved and bobbed through the Georgia team for generous gains.

The Tennessee blocking was the dominant factor. There was blocking such as Dixie had not seen since Major Bob Neyland showed it with his 1930 team, featuring players like Bobby Dodd, Norman Hackman and John McEver. It struck unkindly.

The Georgia defense collapsed at the waist as the flying bodies of Tennesseans clobbered them. It was as effective as a broom in the hands of the blind sisters of fate, sweeping a clean path.

It was beautiful, as a beautiful woman is beautiful, in that it was sharp, chiseled and clean in its perfection. It was an art. Maybe at some time in history there had been blocking as good. But if so, it hadn't been seen before, or since. It was beautiful as a great picture is beautiful in that it was art at its best.

The Vols' Red Harp delivered another verse of that song, "Little David, Play on Your Harp," in the third period. He had run 74-yards the previous week against the mighty Blue Devils of Duke. Against Georgia, he returned a punt for a 65-yard touchdown.

He had only to run. He did have to veer slightly to his right as he sprinted. But ahead of him the broom was at work, a golden broom with straws weighing 195 pound on the average. And ahead of it the broom swept the red jerseys of Georgia as red autumn leaves go before the broom of the homeowner sweeping his lawn.

It was an attack that stunned in its intensity. A Georgia Homecoming crowd of some 12,000 looked on with staring eyes as the Tennessee team, using two full teams during the first two and a half quarters, tossed in an abundance of substitutes to finish out the game and prevented Georgia from scoring.

Before the Tennessee debacle, Georgia had scored in every single game during the season of '36. And coaches, players and supporters had hoped to see the team continue on with its play that was so exceptional during the Auburn game.

But in the face of the power of this Big Orange Rifle Brigade, the spirit of this Georgia team was broke and routed. They played with first-rate courage, but it could not match the power, the play, the energy or the proficiency of the Tennessee team.

Illustrative of just how near perfect the Tennessee offense was, one simply needs to look at its passing attack. The Vols completed five of six passes, during an era when teams didn't pass very often. Tennessee gained 70-yards on those five completed passes. The Volunteers had none intercepted. One was incomplete.

Georgia tried 18 passes and completed four. Three were intercepted. But Georgia, of course, was throwing many passes that were of the hopeless genus. And these passes were rushed; however, Georgia was not rushing the Tennessee quarterback. No quarterback who was rushed completed five of six attempts during the 1930s.

The story of the passes was almost the story of the game. Georgia fought all the way. That was the usual compliment tossed as a prop to the losing team in the 1930s. The crowd got quiet very early, and most had departed well before the last half was done. Both teams played violently until the whistle had sounded to end the slaughter. There were seven touchdown and four extra-points.

Those seven touchdowns came from old fashion American football. In the first quarter there was one. It traveled 75-yards in nine plays. The second one went 61-yards in five plays. It came in the second quarter on the first play of the period. The third one went 44-yards in eight plays. The fourth one was a 31-yard march in five plays. The fifth one required five plays to go 76-yards for pay-dirt.

Then, Red Harp, "Little David, Play on Your Harp," went 65-yards, returning a Georgia punt, in order to score the sixth one. The seventh touchdown was 11-yards in one play and a penalty.

That's six touchdowns in 33 plays for a total of 298 yards. An average of one touchdown for every five and a half plays. To that must be added Red Harp's dash, though it wasn't a play from formation. That made a total of seven touchdowns and 365 yards.

They sparred a bit at the first. Even after Tennessee had driven to the Georgia 28 yard line, the 'Dogs might have held them. But then the phantom appeared.

It was written in one of Maurer's William Shakespeare's plays when Lord Banquo's ghost appeared at the banquet table there was not much of a banquet left. Georgia was struggling there at the 28 yard line. Dickens got three. Georgia stopped McCarran. But then the ghost ran out of bounds at the Georgia one-yard line. And his run was a determined run.

Legend states that Major Bob Neyland stood out there on the field and yelled over and over one word. And the word was "Drive, Drive, Drive!" And the player who didn't drive came off the field.

They drove on Halloween Day, 1936. Yet, that one run was the most powerful of the game. That shattered Georgia. From then on, the Tennessee backs were will o' the whips of woe. Dickens really looked like a ghost on his way to the next touchdown. Georgia stopped McCarran. Then, Dickens came off right tackle for 15-yards. It saw him move, like something transparent, through the Georgia team. They reached for him and their hands seemed to go through his body. Until Quinton Lumpkin's solid canter halted him, proving him flesh and blood.

Here was the best halfback in the South. Not merely on the basis of one game. But, on the foundation of past games, plus the one game in question. After he had made the ghost-like run of 15-yards, he tossed two passes to further demoralize the Georgia defense. Everything worked. And the touchdown followed on the first play in the second quarter. There were other great backs. But Dickens had to be the number one back in the South.

Georgia's one offensive flash came in the dying minutes of the second quarter. The play that did it was a pass. The situation was this: Tennessee had just scored its third touchdown. It had been too easy, a pass on which the passer, Bib Sneed, was not rushed at all. He took plenty of time. He saw Jim Porter running free. Tennessee seemed to get pass receivers loose with unusual skill.

The kickoff came, and Georgia had the ball at its own 30 yard line. Stephens gained one yard. And then there was the big pass to Towns. It got 32-yards as Towns made a tremendous, kicking leap for the ball. It was an unusual play. It was a "fooler" because Towns was the only Georgia player to go down. He cut across from his position at left end. In a gamble, not another receiver went down field. The halfbacks and receivers faked and held in the defense. Towns got beyond the secondary and it worked.

Amazingly, Tennessee was penalized 146 yards, yet still ran-up the tremendous total of 380 yards. Georgia had a total of 143 yards. The Vols had seventeen earned first downs, to four for Georgia. And, the Volunteers completed 5 of 6 pass attempts.

Neither team would finish with spectacular records. Georgia would complete the season at 5-4-1. Coach Mehre would return for one more season before being fired. The Volunteers of Tennessee would go an uncharacteristic 6-2-2. Incredible, considering Coach Neyland's teams, from 1927 through 1932, had lost only one game, while giving-up less than 125 points during a six year period. Three years later, his '39 team finished the regular season unscored upon.

Georgia 34 – South Carolina 6, October 4, 1941

It was early October, and only sixty-four days before the attack on Pearl Harbor would change the world. Frank Sinkwich was the victim of some of the dirtiest fouling ever witnessed in a civilized football game; however, South Carolina said they would do it. And they did. But, it took longer than they originally anticipated.

The year was 1941. It was the third of Wally Butts's 22 seasons as the head coach in the Classic City. His thorough tenure would end in 1960, the year of Mark Richt's birth, when the "Little Round Man" departed Sanford Stadium's sidelines as the winningest boss in the Athenians' gridiron history. Following a losing record in his first season and a 5-4-1 campaign in his second, Coach Butts had a breakthrough year in 1941, guiding Georgia to a 9-1-1 record and its first bowl berth in school history. It would be the wake of one of the greatest eras in Georgia football.

Georgia's first home game of 1941 was against the South Carolina Gamecocks 'tween the hedges. It would be just the second night game ever played in Athens. And, the Carolina game was only the second game of the season; the Bulldogs had mauled Mercer 81-0 in its opener two weeks earlier.

The Garnet and Black of South Carolina were coached by Rex Enright, who had been backfield coach at Georgia when Coach Mehre was fired at the conclusion of the 1937 season. Enright's right-hand man and line coach, Ted Thomey, was a former Georgia assistant coach under Mehre and an ex-Notre Dame All-American.

The South Carolinians upset the North Carolina Tarheels, in Chapel Hill, to start the season. Though the Palmetto State Poultry were expected to pose a challenge to Georgia, the Classic City Canines built-up a comfortable 27-6 lead early to cruise to victory.

When the South Carolina Gamecocks took the field against Georgia, they boasted they would have All-American Sinkwich out of the game before halftime. But they reckoned without Mr. Sinkwich. It took four quarters, and a dirty play to do it.

The Red and Black newspaper related the exhibition was one of the most unsportsmanlike games ever witnessed. Sinkwich's picture hung on the wall at the Columbia Poultry Company, a.k.a. the University of South Carolina, where everyone could see it. Their watchword was not, "Stop Sinkwich," but "Get Sinkwich!"

It would be one of the most memorable Georgia versus South Carolina games played in Sanford Stadium. It was a filthy played game; typical of South Carolina football of the era. In fact, on the third play of the game, the Gamecocks were handed a 15-yard penalty for unnecessary roughness. Apparently, the Gamecocks decided to get things started off in a hurry.

Early in the second quarter, Georgia received a punt and took over on its 25-yard line. On the next play, Sinkwich raced 50-yards, to the Gamecock 25-yard line. Then, Carolina, trying to live up to its threat of having him out before the half, piled on and drew another 15-yard penalty.

Later, Sinkwich was on the receiving end of another punt, and he returned it 15-yards. On the very next play, Carolina was penalized half the distance to the goal line for "slugging."

Again, in the third quarter, Carolina drew another 15-yard set-back for unnecessary roughness. On the next play, "The Fireball" raced to the Gamecock's 10-yard line, being tackled from behind and knocked groggy when Stan Stasica piled on.

Okay, at last he was out, but it did no good. Sinkwich's teammates fought back with the ferocity of beasts and the determination of a dying man holding on to the last thread of life. The South Carolina Gamecocks were simply outshined.

Though Georgia was the superior team, Sinkwich was still in the game late in the fourth quarter. On one play, Sinkwich faked possession of the ball, ran to the right and was blindsided with a forearm to the jaw. The perpetrator was the Gamecocks' defensive left end Steve Nowak. The blow floored Sinkwich; however, he stayed in the game. On the very next play he ran his favorite play over 30-yards up the middle before being chased out of bounds on the South Carolina four-yard line.

Nowak, who delivered the forearm to Sinkwich's jaw on the previous play, piled onto Sinkwich, striking his jaw in the same spot with his knee. Sinkwich's jaw was broken. His teeth had to be wired together, preventing him from eating solid foods for weeks.

South Carolina was penalized for unnecessary roughness, and the 'Dogs got the ball at the one yard line. Georgia immediately scored on the next play to make the final margin 34-6. The win was Georgia's tenth straight over South Carolina.

Sinkwich defended the Gamecocks from accusations of dirty play and related Coach Enright subsequently sent him a written apology for Nowak's late hit out of bounds. Still, Georgia would discontinue their series with the Garnet and Black as a result of the controversy. These two rivals would not meet again on the gridiron until 1958, 17 years after the incident.

The game, like most games with South Carolina, had been a grudge match. Sinkwich missed a lot of playing time, but managed to play the remainder of the season with a mask, to protect his broken jaw. Despite his injury, he finished the season as the nation's leading rusher. He would set an Orange Bowl record against Texas Christian University, in Miami, producing 382 yards of total offense.

Georgia 14 – Ole Miss 14, October 10, 1941

In 1940, these two teams met in the Classic City. It was the first game of the series, with the cohorts of Harry Mehre, former Bulldog coach, emerging victorious. Revenge occupied the hearts and minds of every Bulldog player and coach. The fact fur would fly was an understatement. Nevertheless, Georgia fans expected to see the usual clean style of play exhibited by Ole Miss during that era of gentlemanly football.

Three former Georgia coaches returned "home," in a sense of the word, for Mehre, Weems Baskin, and "Catfish" Smith, all were coaching for Ole Miss. All three had recently been removed from Georgia's coaching ranks. Coach Mehre had compiled a 26-7 record since arriving in Oxford in 1938.

At first, it was uncertain whether Frank Sinkwich would be able to play against the Ole Miss Rebels. He would play for the first half of the game. Eventually, he was taken out for his own safety.

Sinkwich, who had his jaw broken against South Carolina the previous week, took the field against Ole Miss in one of the most courageous exhibitions ever attempted by a football player, All-American timber or not. Wearing a metal chinstrap made by an Athens machine shop, and needing the trainer to come onto the field with pliers to tighten up the wires when they came loose, Sinkwich played a very memorable game.

On the Georgia bench at Sanford Stadium, Coach Wally Butts had a snake-bit feeling. During the week, a fine tailback had left the team and a star wingback was declared ineligible. And, his All-American prospect, Sinkwich, with a broken jaw, was sustaining himself on a diet of chicken soup and oatmeal.

Ole Miss boasted they had Sinkwich's equal, and superior, in Junie Hovious. However, even with a broken jaw, Sinkwich amassed 97-yards rushing with minimal playing time. Hovious had to be content with 28-yards total.

Early in the game a Sinkwich pass was intercepted by Ole Miss and returned to the Georgia 29-yard line. Hovious then tossed 17-yards to Norman Hapes, getting down to Georgia's 12-yard line. Next, Hapes, on a no-shift play, caught the Bulldogs napping and crossed the goal-line untouched. The first half would end at 7-0. Hapes had kept the Red Clay Hounds tranquilized with three booming punts, with an astonishing average of 62-yards per punt.

In the third period, the Rebel's Raymond Terrell ran 49-yards on three quick spurts before Hovious passed to Johnny Eubanks for another score. Sinkwich covered the Ole Miss receiver on the play, but his strength gave out at the crucial moment and Eubanks out jumped him. The Rebels ran-up the score 14-0. The Bulldogs were much stronger but, understandably, their ace, Sinkwich, was not in the best of conditions.

Finally, Georgia's Lamer Davis got the ball and though the entire right side of the Mississippi defense had a shot at him, he kept tearing himself free. In effect, at one point, he was spun completely around. Finally hit hard at the 10-yard line, he was turned halfway around, again, and ended-up backing over the goal-line. Leo Costa kicked the point-after-attempt to bring the score to 7-14.

Late in the contest Hapes punted a 60-yarder out of bounds at the Georgia 13-yard line. The Canines had a good opportunity to fold; however, Heyward Allen, the 'Dogs' team captain, passing from his goal-line, hit Van Davis for a 38-yard gain, and Georgia was back in the thick of things. Ole Miss held, and Cliff Kimsey punted dead on the Rebel's 3-yard line.

Unable to move the ball, Hapes came in and punted the ball to the Mississippi 40-yard line. Sinkwich came in for one more try. His famous face-guard had not yet been manufactured, and the trainer tightened the jaw wires with a pair pliers.

Sinkwich passed to his old Youngstown buddy, George Poschner, who was hit by two men just as he caught the ball 15-yards downfield. He instantly lateraled to Lamer Davis on an impromptu version of the flea-flicker, and the Brunswick sprinter found himself in the clear. This time Davis had only to call on his speed, and the pursuing Rebels lost ground with every stride. Davis crossed the goal with a broad smile. Georgia was a point behind.

Next, Georgia's place-kicking expert, Costa, entered the game. He would hold the distinction of scoring in all of Georgia's game for three seasons. Though under pressure, Costa delivered, high and true, and the game was tied for good, 14-14.

Coach Mehre said he had never seen a greater game and Coach Butts agreed. The chapel bell pealed forth as in victory and an ole timer wrote, "No Georgia triumph of recent times has represented a finer or more stirring accomplishment."

Ole Miss would conclude the season with a 6-2-1 record, and ranked seventeenth in the final sportswriters' poll. Georgia went 9-1-1, and capped off the season with a 40-26 win over Texas Christian University in the Orange Bowl. The 'Dogs finished fifth in the final *Associated Press* poll. Georgia's greatest players returned for the 1942 season and expectations were soaring.

Georgia Pre-Flight 14 – N. C. Pre-Flight 14, Oct 2, 1942

Contrary to popular belief, the first "black-out" at Sanford Stadium didn't occur against Auburn in 2007, but instead happened on October 2, 1942. The "black-out," staged during the Georgia Pre-Flight versus North Carolina Pre-Flight game, didn't receive the complete cooperation of the attending crowd.

University of Georgia students were directly blamed. The fault did not lie entirely with the students, although many cigarettes were lighted in the student section following the darkening of the stadium. The "black-out" was part of a drill in case of an attack by either Japanese or German forces, who the United States was heavily involved in a two front war in 1942.

Coached by Raymond B. Wolf, former coach of North Carolina, who had been drafted by the United States Navy, the Georgia Pre-Flight team was considered one of the best teams in the nation in 1942. Other assistant coaches on the team were: Mike Brumbelow, from Texas Christian University, Harman Clark, former head coach of North side High School, in Fort Worth, Texas; Paul Bryant, former line coach at Vanderbilt; and Charles Jaskwhich, a graduate assistant from Notre Dame, and assistant coach at Ole Miss.

The Pre-Flight program was developed by the Navy to create a rigorous regime for incipient pilots to prepare them for war by creating a training program for one year, versus nine months. As a result, former college and professional football players, who graduated from college, and joined the Navy, were sent into the pre-flight program.

On October 2, 1942, when the two star-studded Pre-Flight schools stopped picking on the colleges, it was a battle between the two best teams in the nation. Both teams had first rate victories already under their belts. The Georgia Skycrackers beat Pennsylvania 14-6 while the Cloudbusters of North Carolina Pre-Flight downed Harvard 13-0.

As evenly matched as two peas, the teams brought together a roster of former college and professional stars. The Skycrackers had players like Bob Foxx of Tennessee, Jack Crain of Texas, and Quinton Lumpkin of Georgia.

The Cloudbusters were coached by Lieutenant Commander Jim Crowley. Some of his players were Len Eshmont, who starred for Crowley at Fordham, Hayward Sanford of Alabama and Joe Zabilski of Boston College.

After being outclassed for three quarters, an apparently badly beaten, Georgia Pre-Flight came to life in the last fifteen minutes to score twice. The Skycrackers managed to obtain a hard fought 14-14 tie with a North Carolina Naval eleven inside Sanford Stadium.

Frankie Flichock saved the day for the Skycrackers. In truth, both Skycracker touchdowns came within a space of five minutes and on each occasion, it was Flichock, former Washington Redskin star, who tossed passes for the scores. His running, especially in the fourth quarter, was enormous and his passing was sensational.

His first touchdown toss was for fifty-yards, caught by the wingback, Foxx, of Tennessee. That came after three minutes of the fourth quarter had elapsed. Five minutes later, Flichock found "Red" Rafney standing all alone in the endzone and he let him have another perfect strike. Foxx kicked both extra-points.

Except for those five minutes, the ball game was all North Carolina, with plenty to spare. Coach Crowley, who started his career at Georgia as backfield coach under Harry Mehre, wasted no time getting his machine under way.

After kicking-off to the Skycrackers, and holding firmly, Crowley's crew began a 63-yard march that required only four plays to complete. Billy Martin got three at center and Len Eshmont circled left end for 12-yards and a first down. Next, Martin rammed the middle for five more yards. Then, Walter Zwiezynski, former Lafayette star, cut over tackle on a reverse play and traveled untouched across the goal line. To complete the story, Jim Zwiezynski kicked the extra-point.

That was the only semblance of a score until late in the third quarter when the Cloudbusters took advantage of a break to get their second marker. "Spec" Sanders, attempting to kick on fourth down, got a low snap from center and fumbled the ball. He had to run and was knocked out of bounds on the Georgia 23-yard line.

The Skycrackers could have got off without a score, except for two penalties. The first one offset a brilliant hit on a defensive play by Ernie Blandi, who rushed Eshmont on an attempted pass and threw him for a 15-yard loss. An offside penalty on the next play gave North Carolina a first down on the ten yard line.

Eshmont got a yard and Martin was stopped cold. Then, Eshmont darted through a gaping hole at center to score standing-up. Zwiezynski again kicked the extra-point. That was the last time North Carolina ever threatened, and from then on, the ball game was all Georgia. The Skycrackers would finish the season with a 7-1-1 record. The Cloudbusters went 9-1-1.

Georgia Pre-Flight 20 – Jacksonville NAS 6, October 30, 1942
Coached by Raymond Wolf and Paul "Bear" Bryant, Georgia's Navy Pre-Flight school, led by professional and former college stars, was considered, by most experts, the best assembled team in the nation in 1942. In fact, many prognosticators felt Georgia, ranked number one in the nation most of the season, might have been the second best team in the city of Athens in 1942. The Skycrackers of Georgia Pre-Flight had scrimmaged Heisman Trophy winner Frank Sinkwich's Bulldogs on a regular basis, and only Coach Butts and Coach Wolf knew who the better team really was.

These Navy cadets went through one year of arduous training, heavily emphasizing physical preparation. From 1942 through 1945, about 20,000 cadets would pass through the Georgia Pre-Flight program. This pipeline meant the Pre-Flight teams never started the same team from week-to-week, because most would graduate and be shipped off to war immediately after graduation.

The Skycrackers' stars included Washington's quarterback Frank Filchock and star receiver Alex Piasecky, a Duke graduate. Another Skycracker was Noah Langdale, a Valdosta native who had been captain of Alabama's 1941 Cotton Bowl championship team.

Jacksonville drove to the Georgia 3-yard line early in the first quarter, but the big Georgia line held them on downs; however, Jacksonville's Vic Fusia would intercept Billy Patterson's pass and return it to Georgia's 19-yard line. In the second period, Jacksonville would drive deep into Georgia's territory again. George McAfee, All-Pro in 1941 for the world champion Chicago Bears, passed to Fred Golden, ex-Tulane star, who galloped 50-yards to Georgia's 25-yard line. Next, McAfee tossed to Gene Kekhelser for a 15-yard gain. Golden drove to the 10-yard line, but had three passes fall incomplete. The Skycrackers led 7-0 at the half.

In the third quarter, the Skycrackers' Darrell Tully, former Detroit Lion star, recovered MaAfee's fumble on the Jacksonville 30-yard line. Flichock, tailback in 1941 for the Washington Redskins, threw back-to-back 12-yard passes to Jim Poole, of the New York Giants, and "Red" Ramsey, of the Philadelphia Eagles, to put the ball on Jacksonville's 6-yard line. Next, Tully hit the line for two yards, before passing to Flichock in the endzone for the touchdown. Bob Foxx, former Tennessee All-American, place-kicked the extra-point.

Later in the third period, Billy Patterson, former Baylor All-American, and ex-Chicago Bear, returned punt 35-yards to the Jacksonville 4-yard line. A pass from Patterson to Noble Doss, Texas wingback on the 1941 Texas Longhorn team, gained 15-yards to the 10-yard line. A holding penalty moved the ball to the 2-yard line, and three plays later, Flichock passed to Gordon English, ex-Tulane end, for the score. Foxx again converted to make it 14-0.

Late in the third quarter, Don Hightower, star Georgia wingback from Texas A&L, returned a McAfee punt 43-yards, to the Jacksonville 38-yard line. Charlie Timmons, former Clemson fullback, carried to the 12-yard line on six straight plays, before McAfee intercepted a Flichock pass on the 4-yard line and went 96-yards for a touchdown. Jim Poole blocked George Faust's extra-point. The score was 14-6 in favor of Georgia Pre-Flight.

Now, late in the third quarter, McAfee put Jacksonville in scoring position by returning one of Tully's punts 20-yards to the Georgia 36-yard line, but Georgia was able to hold. Then, in the fourth quarter, Filchock and Tully sparked a long Georgia touchdown drive, each getting off several nice runs. The touchdown came on a Filchock pass to Poole, who snagged the ball with one hand on the 10-yard line and continued untouched. Foxx missed the extra-point-attempt. The Skycrackers would defeat Jacksonville Naval Air Station 20-6.

The Skycrackers would finish the 1942 season 7-1-1, while the Cloudbusters would go 9-3. Their game in Athens was much closer than the score indicated. Georgia Pre-Flight would only lose two games during its existence, and went 4-0-1 on its home field of Sanford Stadium. All of its games were played on Friday nights.

Georgia 34 - Georgia Tech 0, November 28, 1942

As America entered its first full year of fighting in World War II, most college football programs around the country hadn't been fully impacted, yet. Colossal changes would come very soon.

The Gnats of Georgia Tech entered the game undefeated and ranked number two in the nation behind Boston College. Three days earlier, on Wednesday, November 25, the Tournament of Roses Association revealed the winner of the game would be invited to represent the eastern part of the country in the Rose Bowl.

Ironically, earlier in the week, it appeared Georgia was destined for the Sugar Bowl in New Orleans to face Boston College. In fact, there had been few better buildups than what Coach Denny Myers, of Boston College, stirred-up when he caused a scorching feud between Georgia and Boston College. After Boston College replaced Georgia as the number one ranked team in the nation, prognosticators expected the Eagles and Bulldogs would play in the Sugar Bowl on New Year's Day for the national title.

When only 6,000 tickets had sold, Coach Myers brazenly predicted Boston College would beat Georgia 28-0. The southern media jumped on the story, and the Sugar Bowl promptly sold out. However, the match-up never occurred because Holly Cross upset Boston College's applecart in the final game of the regular season. Tennessee and Tulsa ended-up in the Sugar Bowl. A sellout, thanks to Coach Myers.

Two days prior to the Georgia versus Georgia Tech clash, nine thousand extra wooden bleachers had been brought into Sanford Stadium. The pre-game propaganda was incredible—the largest hype since Georgia lost to Tech in 1927. To add to the hysteria, two days before kickoff, members of the '42 Bulldogs, who lived in Memorial Hall, had a very rude awakening. When they gazed out of their dorm windows, they observed the words "Georgia Tech 35, Georgia 0" burned, with lime, into their sacred practice field. This desecration to their domain simply added fuel to the fire.

On game day, Sanford Stadium was jam-packed—with over 48,000 fans, many who had arrived hours before kickoff. It was the largest crowd in the history of this rivalry. This Georgia Bulldogs team, led by Heisman Trophy winner Frank Sinkwich, along with several prominent All-Americans, was considered one of the best teams in the history of the South.

Georgia, attacking with a wide variety of plays, both through the air and along the ground, left no doubt as to the outcome as early as midway of the second period. It was obviously Georgia's day. The Bulldogs' teeth were sharp. They were on a sharpened edge and refused to allow an early break—a fumble on the opening kickoff, recovered by Tech deep in Georgia territory—to upset them.

Once Sinkwich began pitching and running, and Georgia mixed it up with reverses that clicked for gains, the Bulldogs moved into a commanding position and increased their margin gradually. Sinkwich, Charlie Trippi and receivers Van Davis and George Poschner were superior. Davis scored three times. Trippi threw two touchdowns and made the game's most brilliant touchdown run.

The first nine out of 10 passes Georgia attempted were completions. It was an amazing exhibition of throwing, and of catching. The 'Dogs hit the comeback trail with vengeance after getting knocked out of the ranks of the unbeaten and dethroned as the top team in the nation the previous week in Columbus, Georgia.

Unfortunately, the extensively promoted duel between Sinkwich and Georgia Tech's Clint Castleberry failed to materialize after Castleberry was injured on a tackle in the first half.

Georgia had won the toss and received the ball. Poschner took the kickoff at the 20-yard line and returned it to the 36-yard line, where he fumbled, and Jake Manning recovered for Tech. Georgia's stout defense held and forced the Yellow Jackets to punt. Art Helms would punt out of bounds at the Georgia 24-yard line. He was aiming for the coffin corner and the ball sliced off his foot. After the 'Dogs were unable to move the ball, because of Tech's stout defensive play, and several penalties, Georgia punted it away.

On Tech's next offensive series, Sinkwich started things rolling with an interception off of Castleberry. He returned the ball to the 36-yard line of Tech. Next, he took the snap and went 17 yards up the middle. Then, Trippi gained one yard. On the third play of the drive, Trippi tossed a touchdown pass to Davis. Lee Costa would kick the first of four extra-points. He became the first player in college football history to score in every game his team played during his four year career. Costa scored in 34 straight games and would make it 35 straight against UCLA in the Rose Bowl on January 1, 1943.

For its next touchdown, Georgia advanced 92-yards. After a Tech punt, the Bulldogs started from their own eight yard line. Sinkwich did some superb passing, with Davis and Poschner on the receiving end, and both moved the ball steadily toward pay-dirt. Georgia was on the Tech 24-yard line when the first quarter ended. On the first play of the second quarter, Poschner caught an 18-yard pass and got down to the six yard line. Then, Davis sprinted across the double stripes on an end around maneuver. Costa added the extra-point.

For its third touchdown, the Bulldogs went all the way on a spectacular 87-yard broken field excursion by Trippi. He darted through an opening on his own 13-yard line, picked-up blockers and quit running after he had gone the length of the field.

The next Georgia touchdown, coming in the third period, was an amazing event. Trippi had started into the line, bounced off one defensive back, darted back after a quick recovery and threw a touchdown pass to Davis. Then, Costa started the only riot of the day after he trotted out on the field and kicked the extra-point.

After the ball sailed between the goal posts, he trotted back to his seat on the bench. The ball landed in the lap of a solider, one of several thousand occupying seats on the east end of the field. The solider passed the ball around for other military members to admire.

Unfortunately, the soldier didn't return the ball back to the field, so play could be resumed. The soldier, who had an eye for trophies, kept the football. Game officials, football players, and student managers stood in front of the section of soldiers and requested for them to return the football.

The ball was never returned and the game had to be suspended until another football could be located. A student manager, from the University of Georgia, rushed off the field to dig another ball out of stock and have it pumped up to a usable capacity. In the process, a fight broke out between the soldiers, sailors and police. State policemen, discernible in the crowd, rushed-up as the soldiers swarmed out of the stands and commenced the brawl.

Ironically, the fans appreciated it. In fact, at that point of the game, Tech fans were resigned to Tech's defeat, and even Georgia's crowd was finding itself ready for some different type of amusement. As the fight surged, football was forgotten. The battle, and its onlookers, spread into the territory Tech had been futilely attempting to defend. The football players, with hands on hips, stood back, watching the melee. The officials were unable to stop it.

Eventually, the military police of the Army and Navy prevailed, and the soldiers and sailors were forced off the field. After the fighting was over, no reports were ever filed. It was just an incident, and good fellowship was the rule of the day. The game resumed when order was restored.

Tech's quarterback, Eddie Prokop, who replaced Castleberry, came out throwing. Hardly had the crowd recovered from Trippi's spectacular score, and the riot that ensued, before Clyde Ehrhardt, one of the top pass defenders in the nation, intercepted a pass by Prokop. He returned it 27-yards for the final touchdown.

As the game ended, Georgia players went into the dressing room and held a meeting as to the bowl of their choice. They made a decision that was not to be announced until 11PM. Everyone was confident they had chosen the Rose Bowl.

The 1942 Georgia Bulldogs had won its first Southeastern Conference championship in school history. It was a great triumph for Coach Butts, who was in his fourth year as head coach. After the game, Sinkwich, the nation's total offensive leader, received the news he had officially won the Heisman Memorial Trophy.

Statistically, Georgia had 20 first downs, and was 12 of 22 on pass attempts, for 218 yards. The Bulldogs gained 294 net yards rushing. Not to be outdone, the defense had four interceptions. The 'Dogs were penalized four times for 60 yards. Tech had eight first downs, and went 2 of 18 on attempted passes, for 28 yards. The Yellow Jackets gained 120 rushing yards. Tech made four interceptions and had four penalties for 51 yards.

Castleberry finished third in the Heisman Trophy voting in 1942, behind winner Sinkwich and runner-up Paul Governali. It was the highest a freshman had ever placed in the Heisman voting. After the '42 season was over, Castleberry enlisted in the Army-Air Force and planned to return to Georgia Tech after the war.

He was a co-pilot on a B-26 Marauder bomber known as "Dream Girl." While off the coast of Africa, during the early morning hours of November 7, 1944, Castleberry's crew took off from Roberts Field, in Liberia, with another B-26. The mission was a ferrying run up the coast, toward Dakar, Senegal. Both aircraft disappeared, and were never seen again, despite an extensive six-day search involving American and British search crews. On November 23, 1944, all crew members were officially re-classified from Missing-In-Action, to Killed, No Body. In 1944, Castleberry's number 19 would be the only jersey Georgia Tech ever retired.

Georgia Pre-Flight 19 – Daniel Field 13, October 2, 1943

Not only would this game unveil both teams to critics of southern football, but it gave the Daniel Field Fliers an opportunity to seek personal revenge from Coach Rex Enright, Georgia Pre-Flight's new coach, for the 46-0 steamrolling his University of South Carolina team handed to them the previous season.

Captain Hefey H. Stovall, coach of the Fliers of Daniel Field, took a powerhouse team into Athens for its encounter. It was laden with men who had played for major college teams. They were bulky, but quick. Its starting line averaged slightly over 190 pounds. The backfield wasn't too far behind at 175 pounds. Its line included stalwarts like left tackle Vincent Secontitae from the University of Michigan; Robert Berryman, guard who played for Stanford, and George Hobson, one-time center for the Fightin' Illini.

The Skycrackers of Georgia were outweighed by 34 pounds on the line, and over 10 pounds in the backfield. The Pre-Flight team did not play any officers during the entire season, and there was only one member of its powerful 1942 eleven on the '43 team. Most of its players were members of a battalion who had arrived in Athens only a few weeks prior to this game.

When the game kicked off that Friday night at 8:00PM, there were over 5,000 spectators in attendance. The crowd, comprised mostly of Georgia students, and locals, witnessed two of the best teams in the nation square off.

The game started off slow, until midway through the first quarter when Georgia Pre-Flight struck. John Seritchfield caught Daniel Field's Anthony DiTomo's punt on his own 30-yard line and quickly handed it off to Norwood Harmon, who sped down the right sideline for a 55-yard return. Harmon stepped out of bounds on the 15-yard line.

From there the Georgia Pre-Flight machine methodically scored in three plays. First, Jimmy Randall plunged to the 8-yard line. Next, Shawn Shepherd lost 4 yards on an end-around. Then,

Tate Shugart tossed a short pass to Harmon, who plunged in from the one-yard line; however, from that point forward, it was pretty much Daniel Field, until the final quarter.

A blocked punt and a pass interference penalty enabled Daniel Field to tie it up in the second period. The Fliers' Berryman blocked Frank Hoequist's punt on the Pre-Flight 31-yard line, and took over with excellent field position. Later, Pre-Flight was penalized for interfering with a pass on the 17-yard line; conversely, Hoequist would momentarily stop the drive by intercepting a pass. Unfortunately, the Pre-Flight team was unable to move the ball and Hoequist was forced to punt out of his own endzone. He subsequently shanked the punt, and it rolled out of bounds on the 30-yard line.

Daniel Field came out passing. DiTomo fired a pass to Eric Holmes for a first down at the 10-yard line. Next, he hit Steadman Sylvester on the 4-yard line, from where he squirmed across for the score. Roger Hall missed the extra-point-attempt. The score would be tied 6-6 at halftime.

As expected, DiTomo's came out passing in the third quarter. He threw to Holmes for a first down at Daniel Field's 38-yard line. Then, he fired to Holmes for another first down at the Pre-Flight's 39-yard line. Later during the same drive, on fourth down and five, he passed to Sylvester who got the ball down the Pre-Flight's 4-yard line. After two line plunges failed, DiTomo, with his right arm still working, pitched to Sylvester for the touchdown. The extra-point-attempt was good, and Daniel Field led 13-6.

On the brink of defeat in the fatal final period, the fourth quarter would belong to the Skycrackers of Georgia Pre-Flight. Though, at first, it appeared as though Lady Luck was looking the other way when Daniel Field repulsed two drives deep in its own territory. Finally, the break came.

DiTomo fumbled and Wallace Mossmer recovered on Daniel Field's 13-yard line. After the fumble recovery, Little Bealand Thigpin, a scooter from the Arkansas Razorbacks, would be the man of the hour. His two brilliant runs, after being seemingly trapped on two attempted pass plays, would unbelievably help win the game. Hoequist, Thigpin and finally Jacob Lewis hit the line for the score; however, Craig Davidsmeyer's attempt to run for the extra-point failed by inches. Georgia Pre-Flight was down 13-12, with three minutes to play.

The final score was a thing of beauty. Grover Walker intercepted DiTomo's pass at the Fliers' 49-yard line. On Georgia Pre-Flight's first play, Thigpin faded to pass, but couldn't find any receivers open, so he raced 20-yards to the 29-yard line. Next, Thigpin dropped back to pass, but instead elected to run, where he scooted over for the score. Davidsmeyer kicked the extra-point to give Georgia Pre-Flight a 19-13 advantage with less than one minute left in the game.

Coach Enright credited his team's superior conditioning as probably the deciding factor in their monumental victory over the formidable Daniel Field Fliers. His Skycrackers finished the season with a record of 5-1; its only loss coming to Georgia Tech's professional laden team. The team would subsequently disband after its November 13, 1943 game with Clemson.

There had been a game scheduled between Georgia and Georgia Pre-Flight on November 6, 1943, but it was cancelled. Coach Butts agreed to the justification of the cancellation after Lieutenant Charles A. Burton stated, "We have been scrimmaging Georgia teams several times a week and couldn't continue these scrimmages and play a football game."

In order to make up for the canceled game with Georgia Pre-Flight, the 'Dogs rescheduled Presbyterian, a team they'd beat in the season opener 25-7. The rematch was on November 5, with the 'Dogs winning 40-12. It was only the third time Georgia played the same team twice in one season.

Athens-Pre-Flight 7 – Morris Field 19, October 15, 1944

There were over 13,000 brilliantly bedecked fans on hand for the return of Charlie Trippi to Sanford Stadium. It would mark the second time a Sunday game had been played inside the Mecca of the South. After the Skycrackers' team disbanded in 1943, it was not called Georgia Pre-Flight. Instead, the team was known as Athens Pre-Flight. And, despite the massive amount of player turnover created because of graduation from the Navy's Pre-Flight program, its grid machine remained one of the best teams in the nation.

Now, the Skycrackers of Athens Pre-Flight faced its sternest test of the season when it hosted the undefeated and unscored on

Third Air Force powerhouse called the Morris Field Gremlins, from North Carolina. The game, free to the public, kicked off at 3:00PM.

Coached by Raymond W. Pond, the Athens Pre-Flight Skycrackers drilled all week on blocking and pass defense. His Navy eleven was mindful it would need to be functioning like clockwork to withstand the illustrious Trippi's all-out assault.

By kickoff the temperature hovered around ninety degrees on a very hot, humid Sunday afternoon. The mighty Skycrackers took an early lead, but were unable to hold it. Trippi, the ex-University of Georgia romper, who had never been stopped inside of Sanford Stadium, kept his record intact as he ran, passed and kicked a powerful, well-balanced Third Air Force (Morris Field) eleven to a decisive 19-7 win over the Skycrackers.

Trippi's last performance inside Sanford Stadium had been in 1942, where he was brilliant against Georgia Tech. Based on his physical stature and tremendous performance, his two years in the U.S. Army Air Forces hadn't affected him adversely.

The Pittston, Pennsylvania native threw two touchdowns to John Kelleher, former All-American receiver from Columbia, and set-up the other with a pass to the very shadows of the goal posts.

Coach Butts, who was sitting in the press box, took a "bus man's holiday," and seemed predominantly impressed with the fine performance of Trippi, both on offense and defense. "He's a great ball-player," said the Georgia coach, "and he'll get a special 'invite' back to this school when this war is won."

It looked bad for Morris Field when Pre-Flight scored early on a 42-yard drive in the first eight minutes of the game. Trippi's first punt had been blocked, and Ted Scruggs, ex-Rice receiver, recovered for Pre-Flight. On the first play from scrimmage, Frank Stanczak gained eight yards around the left end. On second down, Stanczak completed a pass to Scruggs for a first down at the Gremlin's 11-yard line. Next, Stanczak plunged down to the 5-yard line. Leo Long, ex-Duke standout and Pre-Flight's acting captain, plunged to the 3-yard line on the following play. Finally, Stanczak gave the Pre-Flight a first down at the 18-inch line.

Next, big Long smashed across for the first score of the afternoon—and the first time the Third Air Force squad had been scored on. Buck Jones, formerly of Wake Forest, rang the bell with his extra-point-attempt and Pre-Flight led 7-0.

Morris Field was unable to move the ball on the ground during its next series, so Trippi took to the airways. First, he passed to Ted Cook, ex-Alabama receiver, for a first down at the Skycracker 40-yard line. After being thrown for a four yard loss, he completed a pass to Norman O'Hara for a first down at Pre-Flight's 25-yard line.

The Morris Field Gremlins tallied in the second period, topping off a 51-yard drive as Trippi, determined to open-up the passing game, completed a 25-yard pass to Kelleher. John Seltenreich, a former Battle Creek, Michigan high school player, missed the extra-point-attempt. Pre-Flight nursed a 7-6 lead.

Starting off the second half, Trippi became an indomitable player. It was a trait characteristic of him at Georgia, during his freshman and sophomore seasons. First, he took a punt, deep in his own territory, and came roaring down the side-line to the Pre-Flight 36-yard line. On the first play from scrimmage, he completed a long bomb to Kelleher, who almost scored. On the next play, Bob Kennedy, former Washington State All-American, plunged over for the touchdown. Seltenreich missed the extra-point-attempt, and Morris Field led 12-7.

The deciding score for Morris Field came in the third quarter at the termination of a 79-yard drive by the Gremlins. John Boneli, who once starred for Pittsburgh University, and who saw action in several big campaigns during the war, triggered the sustained drive with speedy bursts of power. Trippi climaxed the series of plays with a toss to Kelleher for 25-yards and the last score of the game. Seltenreich didn't miss the extra-point, and the final score was 19-7.

In the fourth quarter, Pre-Flight drove down on the Gremlin's 20-yard line. On a first and ten from the 20-yard line, Pre-Flight's Bill Evans, a former Louisiana State All-Conference player, was open in the endzone, but dropped a pass from Stanczak. The real "goal line stand" angle of the performance was when Athens-Pre-Flight got down to the 30-inch line and couldn't plunge it over in four downs. Right then and there, Morris Field's line proved its worth to the ranking of the best offensive line in the nation.

Having beaten Chatham Field 45-0, Charleston Coast Guard 31-0, and Fort Benning 22-0, Morris Field racked-up 117 points against only seven points from some high-quality competition. In the game against Athens-Pre-Flight, the first downs were even at 11 each, while the Gremlins, in remaining undefeated, rushed for 129 yards to 46 yards for Athens-Pre-Flight. Morris Field attempted 22 passes, connecting on 10 for 136 yards. The Skycrackers completed 10 of 25 passes for 168 yards.

Trippi had the stands in Sanford Stadium in hysterics as he sparked the Morris Field Gremlins to a 19-7 victory over luckless Athens Pre-Flight. The fans could only see the windmill of his legs slicing up everything between Trippi and pay-dirt. He put on an unbelievable show for the fans as he single-handedly defeated the powerful Athens Pre-Flight team. He returned to Georgia the following season and led the 'Dogs to the national title in 1946.

Georgia 0 – Georgia Tech 44, December 2, 1944

After America entered into World War II, Georgia Tech responded to the U.S. military's technical and manpower needs by adopting a three-term, year-round accelerated schedule for V-12 military athletes. Its campus became a virtual fort, with most students participating in either the Army or Navy V-12 program. Then, in 1944, while most colleges across the nation were forced to cancel its football programs because rosters had been decimated by the war effort, Georgia Tech actually beefed-up its football team with preeminent V-12 military athletes.

The Gnats of Tech emerged as one of the most powerful military teams in the nation as it loaded-up with semi-professional athletes from the armed forces. Meanwhile, less than two weeks before the start of the college football season, Georgia's Coach Butts almost had to cancel the '44 season. He only had 17 year old kids, or players who could not meet military physical standards, a.k.a. 4-Fs, and he wasn't sure there were enough players to field an entire team. At the last minute, he decided to play the season with what the media would refer to as a "civilian team."

The Georgia versus Georgia Tech game has always been magnetic. Its followers have continuously managed to get there, despite world wars, worldwide economical depressions, rationing of fuel, rubber, etc.... It was no different on a cold, wintery afternoon in 1944 when Sanford Stadium had comfortably filled-up several hours before kickoff.

Tech wore its yellow jerseys, while Georgia donned white jerseys, instead of its typical red. It marked the thirty-ninth meeting between these two hated rivals, and both had 7-2 records. The game would equate to Georgia's bowl toggery because the Bulldogs didn't receive a bowl invitation. Georgia Tech had already accepted an invite to play Tulsa in the Orange Bowl in Miami.

Early arrivals in frigid Sanford Stadium were trying to make something of baby tornadoes that had been whirling around the campus and funneling leaves in the hat brims' of the game's patrons. It was, some claimed, prophetic of things to come when Tech's Tornado swirled out against the Georgia Bulldogs.

People had scrimped and saved their gas rations all year to make the trek. War rations were in full effect, and gas and rubber were at a premium. Still, all the way to Athens, from Atlanta, there were old-time scenes. Cars were parked all along the route, and there were picnic groups on practically every clearing in the woodlands. It was hard to find a place to eat on a football Saturday in Athens. So, the followers of Tech and Georgia, who came from out of town, simply brought their lunch and liquid refreshment.

There had been bright sunshine for the game, but the rays of the sun couldn't dispel the chill in the air. No, especially, on the south side, where the spectators were seated in the shade of the trees, some donated by the French, high on "AG" hill, and huddled underneath blankets. Most took furtive sips of prevailing beverages.

Unfortunately for the 'Dogs, Georgia Tech's passing game was as sharp as a freshly honed straight razor, and for the second straight year, the Golden Hurricane flattened their game adversaries from the University of Georgia by a one-sided margin. Tech, largely because of its military aerial sharpshooting, defeated the Bulldogs, 44-0, before 26,000 spectators on a bright, but chilly December afternoon.

The Sanford jinx had finally been shattered, as if by the sharp blow of a double-edged sword. The Yellow Jackets had won its first game at Sanford Stadium, and the V-12 laden team did a most thorough and workmanlike job of it.

All afternoon, the passing of Frank Broyles and the pass receiving of George Mathews and Charles Murdock were eerie. The

Jackets seldom missed. When Broyles let fly, Mathews or Murdock caught the ball as if their fingers were tipped with glue. They went flying-up and down the greensward of Sanford Stadium like ghosts in the dusk of late afternoon.

Coach Bobby Dodd acted as Tech's head coach for the second straight week because Coach Alexander's wife was gravely ill. As would prove to be the case for many years to come, Dodd had the Jackets ready to play hard nose football. The figures showed it was a very one-sided game, and yet, if Georgia receivers had been able to hold on to the ball, the game might have been closer.

In all, Broyles threw three touchdown passes and ran for two more. Mathews and Murdock each scored twice. And, Charlie Nixon scored the final touchdown on an interception.

When Tech moved up the field for its first touchdown, the Jackets really moved. They covered 60-yards in three plays. Tech's Dinky Bowen hauled one of Al Perl's kicks back to the 40-yard line. On the first play from scrimmage Broyles threw a pass to Mathews, who made an impressive run to the Georgia 39-yard line. Next, Broyles faked a pass and ran down to the 10-yard line. Tech scored on the next play when Georgia's James Rutland fell down, and Mathews made a pass over Rutland's prostrate body and hit Murdock in the back of the endzone for the game's first touchdown. Bowen kicked the extra-point.

A few minutes after their first touchdown, Tech scored again. Georgia's quarterback, Billy Hodges, tried a long, wobbly pass that was intercepted by Tech's Bowen, who returned it to the Georgia 45-yard line. After several running plays, Broyles passed to Mathews, who was all alone in the endzone.

In the second quarter, Georgia's Perl had a poor punt of nine-yards. His punt went out of bounds at the Georgia 44-yard line. It would set-up Tech's third touchdown. Broyles promptly passed to Jack Tinsley who got the ball within striking distance of the goal line. Then, Bowen churned his feet and ran down to the 12-yard line; however, Bowen injured his leg and was put out of the game. Next, Tex Ritter passed to Murdock who made it to the two yard line. Broyles punched the left side of Georgia's line for the third touchdown. Tinsley replaced Bowen and kicked the extra-point.

On the kickoff, Georgia's Danny Edwards returned it to the 38-yard line. On the first play from scrimmage, Tech's Ritter intercepted Georgia quarterback Kenneth McCall's long pass, which was intended for Perl. Ritter was tackled at the Tech 44-yard line. After several running plays, Broyles tossed a lateral that went awry, but Logan caught-up to the ball and got back to the line of scrimmage before Georgia's George Bradberry made the tackle. An official named Hackney, football's most active headlines-man, called a 15-yard penalty against Tech, forcing the Jackets to punt.

After the punt, McCall hit Reid Mosley with a pass to the 47-yard line. But, Hackney called his fifth penalty of the game. It was 15-yards against Georgia for clipping. A box score of Hackney's activities throughout the season revealed a startling discovery. He picked-up more ground than any team in the country.

Perl ran for a first down after the penalty. It was Georgia's initial first down. But, eventually, the 'Dogs were forced to punt, and Tech took over at its own 44-yard line. The Yellow Jackets wasted no time as Mathews made a remarkable catch from Broyles, taking the ball away from a Georgia defender and almost running for a touchdown. Mathews was finally tackled at the eight yard line. With a minute left before halftime, Broyles rushed for a one yard gain. Next, he threw an incomplete pass, before tossing a touchdown to Mathews. Tinsley's extra-point-attempt was wide right. The score at halftime was 26-0.

Later, in the third quarter Ritter and Murdock collaborated when Ritter threw a long pass to Murdock, covering 31-yards. It was followed-up with a screen pass from Broyles to McIntosh, who got to the 15-yard line. After Georgia was penalized for unnecessary roughness, Broyles plunged through the line for another touchdown. Tinsley's kick was no good. Georgia Tech took a 32 – 0 lead.

In the fourth quarter, Georgia finally moved the ball before McCall's intended pass to Mosley, at the 47-yard line, was intercepted by Ritter. He returned it back to the Tech 49-yard line, a runback of 16 yards. On the first play from scrimmage, there was a handkerchief on the play as Broyles hit Murdock with a touchdown pass. The penalty was against Georgia. Tinsley's try for the extra-point was no good. Georgia Tech led 38-0.

Mosley returned the kickoff to the 32-yard line. Georgia promptly fumbled and Tech recovered. After the Yellow Jackets lost 15-yards for unnecessary roughness, William Mitchell caught a pass from Frank Carpenter. On the next play, John Carver lost five yards trying to run. Next, Norm Basler caught a screen pass, but Tech had nine yards to go on fourth down. Carpenter caught another pass, but Georgia got the ball on downs, as time was about to expire.

On the very next play the Yellow Jackets' Nixon made an interception and returned it 35-yards for the game's final touchdown. It was the closing feature of a miserable game. The pass, intended for Mosley, was batted by Nixon, who took it along the boundary.

The game was marred by over 200 yards in penalties and injuries to players on both sides. Bowen, Tech's primary kicker, was injured and his replacement, Tinsley, missed five out of six extra-point-attempts. From a statistical perspective, Tech completed 28 of 39 passes in a game where 72 passes were tried by both teams. Tech's average of completions was phenomenal. The Jackets V-12 military athletes were simply too sharp and alert. In a role of pinch-hitter for ailing Coach Bill Alexander, Coach Dodd came through with flying colors. And those who saw something prophetic in those swirling miniature tornadoes were on the right track. The Golden Tornado blew with a vengeance.

Georgia 14 - Alabama 0, November 2, 1946

Sanford Stadium was jammed to capacity on this early November afternoon, for a clash between two teams piloted by two of the nation's all-time great coaches, Alabama's Frank Thomas, and Georgia's Wallace Butts. Over 50,000 rain-soaked fans could have readily affirmed the Red Elephants were just as hypersensitive to dogs, specifically Bulldogs, as they were to the perennial mouse.

The rains had returned to Sanford Stadium and would wash Thomas's Alabama Crimson Tide down the drain. Georgia, led by its captain, Charlie Trippi, played its best game of the season, and prevailed 14-0. Georgia turned-in a complete performance as they sparkled on defense, blocked like demons on offense, and broke-up the Tide so bad that 'Bama never penetrated beyond the Georgia 25-yard line.

History shows the 'Dogs had correctly anticipated Alabama would be its toughest opponent for the season. The Tide returned most of its team that had won the Southeastern Conference title the previous season, going undefeated and whipping Georgia 28-14 in Birmingham, in 1945.

"Hurling Harry" Gilmer, Alabama's 1945 All-American, was completely eclipsed by Trippi in all departments. Gilmer, whose trusty right arm was depended on to sharp-shoot the Alabamians back into the battle for the Southeastern Conference title, failed to complete a single pass in eight attempts. In all, 'Bama tried nine passes, the other, thrown by Johnny August, was without success. The Georgia defense was too tough to crack, and was alert enough to make two interceptions, one of which led to the first Bulldog score.

Midway in the first period, Dick McPhee, who had an injured leg, intercepted Harry Gilmer's first attempted pass on the Georgia 43-yard line. He quickly lateraled to Johnny Donaldson, who was unhampered in speed, and blocked an onrushing Alabama player. Donaldson ran the ball to the Alabama 12-yard line before he was run out of bounds.

After Trippi got the ball to the ten yard line, Donaldson gained one yard on the next play. Then, the Pittston, Pennsylvania powerhouse faded back and tossed a pass to Dan Edwards in the endzone. Alabama halfback, Hal Self, leaped high and slapped the ball with his fingers, causing the ball to spiral into the air, just beyond his reach. Edwards, doing a remarkable imitation of a man on a treadmill, dived after the pigskin and snared it inches off the ground for a touchdown. It was one of the most sensational catches ever witnessed in Sanford Stadium.

Next, George Jernigan trotted out to convert the first of two for his contribution to the Georgia victory. He ran his 1946 record to 28 of 29 extra-point-attempts.

The Bulldogs' second touchdown came late in the first half. After Gilmer had thrown three incomplete passes in a row, he punted down to the Georgia 21-yard line, where Trippi caught it. After an off-side penalty set Georgia back to the 16-yard line, Trippi passed down the middle to Johnny Rauch, who made it to the Alabama 46-yard line, the play covered 34-yards. Joe Tereshinski recorded an assist on the play by seizing a hold of Rauch, and the ball, for protection.

After back-to-back pass attempts to Donaldson and Jonathan Smith were broken-up, Trippi called his own number, a running play. He ran 46-yards though the entire Alabama defense, travelling on a wide end sweep that was assisted by some skilled blocking. Seemingly hemmed-in, and stopped at least twice, Trippi side-stepped, twisted and danced his way through the Tide offense as he skidded across the goal line. Jernigan made the extra-point and Georgia led 14-0.

That completed the scoring for the day. The steady drizzle that had soaked the gridiron all morning resumed, and the tempo of game was slowed down considerably. The ball was wet and slippery, and several fumbles were made by both teams. The rushing attack became the order of the day, with neither team completing a pass out of two attempts by each team. The highlights of the punt exchanges were two kicks by Trippi that stopped dead within the Alabama 10-yard line and set the Crimson Tide back on its heels and kept them there until the final whistle.

The Battle of the Halfbacks—second edition—was an absolute coup for Trippi. The statistics showed how completely he had dominated the game. He completed five out of 11 passes for 109 yards. Rauch, who played about 58 of the 60 minutes, peering through his iron mask that protected his broken cheekbone, completed two out of three passes in the flat for a total gain of one yard.

Trippi had 16 rushes for 98 yards. He punted from behind his own goal line three times, booting the ball 49, 50 and 54 yards. One of his punts was blocked by Charlie Compton, an Alabama tackle, and as the two raced after the pigskin, Trippi outsmarted Compton and recovered the ball on the Georgia 4-yard line. On the next play, a fourth down and long, he punted out to the 45-yard line.

The Great Gilmer was limited to attempting only eight passes and he was zero for eight—not a single completion for the first and only time in his outstanding career—two of his passes were intercepted. He rushed the ball twelve times for 55 yards.

Outstanding performances on the line were turned-in by Bulldog Williams, Jack Bush, Herb Saint John, Jerry Deleski, and Clayton Devers. Rauch contributed a well-generated game from the quarterback slot, and the balance of the backfield showed-up well.

There were standouts on both teams, including Vaughn Mancha, All-American center for Alabama and two Crimson Tide running backs, Lowell Tew and Self. It was Self who let Dan

Edwards get by him for the remarkable circus catch that went down in Georgia football annals to rival some catches made by George Poschner, star for the Big Red Legions in their game against Alabama in 1942.

The entire Georgia team rose to the occasion and played an almost flawless game. Trippi played the full 60 minutes and was at his very best in pacing a 14-0 Bulldog victory en route to an undefeated season and Sugar Bowl conquest of North Carolina.

Harry Mehre, former Georgia head coach, who was covering the game in the press box stated, "... I saw Charlie doing everything except selling programs and ushering between halves." Unfortunately, Trippi, the greatest player in the nation, was denied the Heisman Trophy because of the northeast bias towards the South.

Georgia 35 - Georgia Tech 7, November 30, 1946

Georgia had a record of 9-0-0, and was ranked number three in the country, only behind Army and Notre Dame. The 'Dogs were averaging 37 points per game behind the outstanding play of Charlie Trippi. Similarly, Coach Bobby Dodds' Yellow Jackets had been rolling along with an 8-1 record, with its lone loss coming in the season opener against Tennessee by a score of 13-9. Tech rolled into Athens as the seventh highest ranked team in the nation.

As tranquil and unyielding as a silent black boulder overlooking a raging river, the magical Trippi, and his crimson-liveried teammates, threw the book at the Yellow Jackets. Georgia's Seven Mules came through—and plastered Tech. They would watch as Trippi staged an unforgettable gridiron classic.

The stout-hearted Sicilian, who knew he could turn the trick, manufactured three touchdowns, including a 66-yard burst that completely broke Tech's back. After that mammoth run, the superiority of Georgia's team, a dominance that had often been controversially contested by northern sports' writers, and fans from coast-to-coast, was never questioned again.

On a cold afternoon, a brilliant Georgia football team would ride on the twinkling heels of All-American Trippi to its first undefeated, untied football season since 1896. The 'Dogs had a January 1, 1947, date with North Carolina and Charlie 'Choo-Choo" Justice, in the Sugar Bowl after demolishing Georgia Tech 35-7 before 55,000 boisterous fans inside of Sanford Stadium.

The great Trippi gave a heart-stirring exhibition in his final appearance before an Athens crowd. In addition to his three touchdowns—he completed six of 10 passes for 151 yards. Even those thousands who were unable to get into the stadium, and had to watch from the roof of near-by Memorial Hall, were able to tell. Trippi was a Herculean of a man amongst boys.

He did everything possible for one to do, and at times the Yellow Jackets probably thought he had doppelganger. The Jackets' couldn't get him out of their hair all day, and when he limped from the field, late in the game, he was given a standing ovation by the entire stadium.

Trippi was not alone, as usual. John Rauch and Rabbit Smith, who played just about the entire game in the place of the injured John Donaldson, were other stars of the backfield. Each scored a touchdown.

It was a hard fought game throughout the first half with the Bulldogs managing to push over two touchdowns for a 14-0 advantage at halftime. However, they put the clincher on after a couple of minutes of the third quarter had been played, ran-up another seven points as the fourth started and capped the day's work with Trippi's run after James Bowen had gone across for the losers.

Georgia's first touchdown came after a march of 80-yards, which moved as steadily down field as the chant of the Georgia students. Trippi, Smith and Rauch ran for consistent gains for two first downs before Trippi completed the first pass of the drive—a nine-yarder to Joe Tereskinski, who carried to the Tech 40-yard line.

The Bulldogs went back to the ground and Trippi, Dick McPhee and Rauch quickly added another first down on the Tech twenty-nine. Trippi then passed to Smith, but the play lost a yard. Trippi faded back on the next play and appeared trapped before he ran around in the backfield, after dropping back some 15-yards. With uncanny coolness, he hit Tereshinski right in the stomach with a bullet pass. It got Georgia down to the Tech nine-yard line.

After a roughness penalty put the Bulldogs back to the 20-yard line, Rauch passed to Edwards who made a leaping catch on the Jackets nine-yard line. Smith ran for three and Trippi added two more yards. On fourth down, Trippi started to his right, saw daylight over Tech's left tackle, and cut for home. The Jackets found out there was no stopping him short of those double stripes.

That score came after three minutes and twenty-five seconds of the second quarter had been played. Georgia was to add another before halftime. This one was a result of a 41-yard drive which followed a fumble by Tech halfback, George Mathews, and was recovered by Bulldog Williams of Georgia.

On the first play, Trippi was apparently trapped, trying to pass. However, he gave ground, twisted and turned away from would-be tacklers and spotted Smith down the field. He passed to Smith, who tried to lateral to McPhee; however, it wasn't a lateral, and the Bulldogs were penalized five-yards for an illegal forward pass. As it turned out, an apparent loss of 15-yards was turned into a play for no gain by Trippi.

Trippi then passed to Reid Mosely for seven yards and Rauch shot one in the flat to McPhee, who bulled his way down the sideline to the Tech 17-yard line. Rauch then tossed to Trippi for three yards before Smith tore through the line, getting to the Tech 9-yard line.

Next, Trippi threw a jump pass over the line which, except for the amazing speed of the ball, would have been intercepted by Frank Broyles. Trippi then passed to Rauch in the coffin corner, who was quickly tackled by two Yellow Jackets at the 4-yard line; at least, they tried and thought they had tackled him. Rauch somehow pulled loose from the defenders and dove over for the touchdown.

That was all of the scoring in the first half, although Tech had an opportunity just before the whistle. McHugh recovered a fumble by Gene Chandler, who had taken a lateral from Rauch, on the Georgia 36-yard line. On the next play, Rauch made a leaping interception and ended the half.

Tech came out fired-up in the second half; however, Trippi made an interception off of a weak pass by Bowen. He sailed down the sidelines for 17-yards, to the Tech 29-yard line. Six plays later, Rauch calmly passed to Trippi in the middle, on the four-yard line, and the All-American pivoted across for the touchdown.

Following two punt exchanges, Georgia drove 82-yards, in fourteen plays, for its fourth touchdown. The march started late in the third period and ended after three plays in the final quarter. Taking Broyles' kick on their own 18-yard line, the Bulldogs were aided by a 15-yard penalty for roughness against Tech. But, the longest gain of the drive was a pass from Rauch to Edwards which carried in the air for 38-yards, to the Tech 14-yard line.

Trippi bucked for six yards and Rauch gained four more yards, to the Tech four-yard line. Smith carried it to the three, but Trippi lost seven after taking a lateral from Rauch and fumbling out of bounds on the 10-yard line. Finally, Smith caught a Rauch pass on the nine-yard line and rumbled in for the touchdown. The score was 28-0.

Now, even though down by an insurmountable four touchdowns, Tech did not give-up. The Yellow Jackets came roaring down the field to score in eleven plays, covering 74-yards. On the final play, Broyles passed a scoring strike to Bowen.

Trippi caught the ensuing kickoff on the 35-yard line and pounded Georgia Tech one last time. He cut off his own right tackle and cavorted 66-yards for the last touchdown. It was a chef-d'oeuvre of broken running as he followed his blockers flawlessly—a fitting finale for a superior halfback during his last regular season game; culminating one of the greatest college careers of all-time.

Afterwards, the Georgia players had voted unanimously to accept a Sugar Bowl invitation. Coach Butts, pale and sick from nervous excitement, walked into the dressing room and told the team no bowl bid was yet official; however, he asked them to indicate whether they would prefer the New Orleans' Sugar Bowl or the Dallas Cotton Bowl, if each bowl made a bid.

"Sugar Bow, Sugar Bowl," shouted the delirious team, then one player, stark naked, leaped off a bench and yelled: "Let's give 15 cheers to Coach Butts!"

Trippi, Georgia's captain, whose brilliant offensive and defensive play won the game, lay on a training table moaning with pain from cramps, which knotted his leg muscles from the hips down. He was placed in a special tub with hot water. Coach Butts later related Trippi was not seriously hurt.

Georgia outgained Georgia Tech 431 yards to 284 yards. The 'Dogs went 11-0, won the Southeastern Conference and beat North Carolina in the Sugar Bowl, a game featuring a duel between two of the country's most spectacular tailbacks—Georgia's triple-threat Trippi, and North Carolina's 160-pound freshman, Justice. Georgia Tech would defeat Saint Mary's in the Oil Bowl.

Georgia 27 – Maryland 7, September 23, 1950

One of the most powerful football teams ever to file through the gates of historic Sanford Stadium would battle Georgia in a grudge match which had been brewing for two years. The bitterness originated on New Year's Day 1948, in the Gator Bowl, in Jacksonville, Florida, when the Terrapins and the Bulldogs fought to a 20-20 tie. And, to add insult to injury, Coach Jim "Split-T" Tatum and his gridiron warriors had walked off the Gator Bowl field with the game ball, which always goes to the winner.

When asked to flip a coin to determine the rightful ownership, Tatum said flatly, "We deserve the ball and we intend to keep it!" And, his Terrapins headed home with the game ball. For two years the Bulldogs had waited for a crack at Tatum and Company, to see who really should have taken home the ball.

Now, two years later, as leaves were falling and the humidity was beginning to become tolerable, they'd met again. Fall had arrived, and so had football. This gargantuan Maryland team, ranked tenth in the nation, would be led by Ed "Mighty Moe" Modzelewski, a 210 pound right halfback, who would viciously slam head on into the 'Dogs the entire afternoon.

The Terrapins entered the game with three All-Americans: tackle Ray Krouse, Bobby Ward at guard and Modzelewski. An improved Georgia team wasn't nearly as talented; however, Coach Butts had never been beaten until the last whistle had sounded, and this team would be taxed to the limit, and beyond, against Maryland's potent assault.

During the summer of 1950, there had been 6,000 new concrete seats installed to replace the old wooden ones inside of Sanford Stadium. The stadium now held 18,000 on each side of the field, with an additional 14,000 to be erected, if necessary. Now, including the endzone stands, it comfortably held 50,000 fans. Additionally, another upgrade included paving the ole dirt road that led to the press box, which was welcomed by visiting newsmen.

Late in the first quarter, Fred Billyeu, Georgia's top sophomore, brought a near capacity crowd of 49,000 to its feet by tossing a pass to John Duke, after being trapped behind the line. Georgia kept the ball on the ground, and scored from a yard out, putting 'Dogs ahead 14-7.

Patrick Field's super-human punting kept Maryland driven deep into their own territory the remainder of the period. Field's best efforts of 53 and 56 yards helped the Irishman compile an astounding 42.9 yard average from scrimmage, despite one punt that went into the endzone.

The defensive star was Art DeCarlo, who was singled out by Coach Butts as playing one of the best defensive stints for Georgia. Late in the quarter, DeCarlo recovered a fumble at the Terp's 33-yard line, and from there it was smooth sailing to the goal for the Bulldogs. With Billy Mixon, Lewis Brunson, Dick Raber, and Lauren Hargrove sharing the load to the one-yard line, Mixon hurled the line to score. Jeff Keith blocked Robert Walston's extra-point-attempt, to leave the score at 20-7.

DeCarlo got another Terp fumble at Maryland's 29-yard line to initiate the final touchdown drive. On the first play, Zippy Morocco uncorked an astounding 15-yard run to Maryland's two-yard line. On the very next play, Richard Raber piled over for the touchdown. Walston's first extra-point-attempt went wide, but a penalty against Maryland, for being offside, gave him a second opportunity. Walston's second attempt was true.

It was taps for the Terps when Maryland's vaunted Split-T giants made its last costly fumble. It was recovered by Dick Steele at the Terp's 29-yard line. Georgia was unable to move the ball, and was forced to punt; however, Maryland was equally ineffective in its last minute barrage of passes, with Scarbath heaving the final toss as the siren sounded.

Georgia's offensive line was stellar, and refused to buy into the hype that Maryland boasted the best defensive line in the country. In fact, after the game, Coach Tatum stated, "We weren't ready for Georgia in a game as early as September 23. We weren't in shape, and this ninety-two degree heat and humidity killed us."

The loss, however, did not impact Maryland's poll ranking as the situation surrounding the game was generally understood. Maryland finished the season 7-2-1; however, over the course of the next three seasons, Maryland would emerge as the top team in the nation, while enroute to winning two national titles. Georgia had entered the game a six point underdog, but the 'Dogs out-played and out-conditioned its visitors and won by a score of 27-7. The 'Dogs finished the season at 6-3-3, and unranked.

Georgia 14 - Auburn 13, November 14, 1959

The University of Georgia football team, the weather man, and some fine musicians and entertainers, combined their talents to treat 54,000 fans to a day in the Classic City they still talk about decades later. People from all over, but especially from Alabama and Georgia, began filling hotels and motels around the city on Thursday night.

The Auburn Tigers' team arrived at lunchtime on Friday. Afterwards, they worked out lightly inside Sanford Stadium during the afternoon, and looked the town over on Friday night. Their hulking size would impress those who saw these gargantuan athletes.

Scalpers, souvenir salesmen, and just plain beggars, recognizing this rare opportunity, arrived earlier and in larger numbers than usual, to take advantage of the influx of persons with some inflated wallets. The gigantic pep-rally on Thursday night had raised spirits to a high pitch for the 2PM clash. Hopes were high for a repeat of the only other Auburn-Georgia game ever played in Sanford Stadium, a game in which the Bulldogs triumphed 24-0 in 1929, the year of the arena's inception.

Just like the true champions they were, Georgia's tenacious Bulldogs struck for a touchdown in the final thirty-seconds of play to whip Auburn 14-13, and win the 1959 Southeastern Conference championship.

Quarterback Francis Tarkenton threw a fourth-down strike to his receiver, Bill Herron, for a 13-yard touchdown with the clock showing thirty seconds left in the game. Then, Durward Pennington, a sophomore place-kicker, gave the Bulldogs their improbable victory and the conference championship.

The overflow crowd of 54,000 fans cheered wildly and uncontrollably as the resilient 'Dogs simply refused to give-up, even after Auburn scored on a blocked punt to take a 13-7 lead with only 7:30 left in the game. Georgia stomped back and on the strength of Tarkenton's passing and Pennington's conversion, clinched the elusive 1959 Southeastern Conference title. The win gave Georgia a 6-0 conference record, good enough for the crown, regardless of the result of the 'Dogs' November 28, 1959 final game against Georgia

Tech. This was during an era before the Yellow Jackets defected from the Southeastern Conference in its attempt to emulate the Pope's pupils of Notre Dame and the prosperity the Irish enjoyed as an independent school.

The conference title was the fourth for the 'Dogs. Other crowns came during the 1942, '46, and '48 seasons. The game against Auburn was fitting for a worthy Georgia team, which started the season picked to finish ninth among conference teams. The 'Dogs' spirit was high, the line play was extraordinary against the mammoth Plainsmen, and the thrills plentiful—the ingredients that marked the 'Dogs all season.

The Georgia line, outweighed some 14 pounds per man by the Tigers, deserved much of the credit for the triumph. The ferocious Bulldogs allowed Auburn, the Southeastern Conference's second ranked offensive power, a total offensive production of only 38-yards during the second half.

Then there was Charlie Britt's sparkling 39-yard punt return for Georgia's first touchdown. The return was a thing of beauty for the partisan Georgia fans, and Britt's outstanding run was made possible by a half-dozen key blocks by fired-up teammates.

In the first quarter, Auburn would score first. After winning the toss and electing to receive, the Tigers moved from their own 40-yard line, down to Georgia's 23-yard line. They used a series of running plays to move the pigskin. The Plainsmen drew a five-yard penalty for delay of the game, then end, Gordon Kelley, spilled quarterback Bobby Hunt for a nine-yard loss. Joe Dolan kicked out of bounds at the Bulldogs 11-yard line, but the play was nullified when Georgia was penalized 15-yards for a personal foul. That gave Auburn the ball, fourth down at the Georgia 26-yard line.

Fullback Ed Davis kicked a 43-yard field-goal to give Coach Shug Jordan's team a 3-0 lead with 8:10 left in the first quarter. Auburn would be handed another scoring opportunity late in the first quarter after Britt fumbled a Dolan punt and Bobby Walden recovered for the Tigers. The ball was on Georgia's 34-yard line.

On the last play of the first period, Davis ripped off 20-yards, down to the 'Dogs 14-yard line. Three plays later, including a 15-yard penalty against Auburn, Davis booted another three-pointer.

The field-goal was from 40-yards away. The Plainsmen held a 6-0 lead with only one minute gone in the second quarter.

Georgia threatened before intermission when a Tarkenton pass, to Fred Brown, covered 39-yards for a first down at the Auburn 18-yard line. Next, Brown gained five, but Tarkenton would lose one yard before a fourth down pass to Herron was broken-up at the goal line. Later, Georgia would bully the Plainsmen back deep into their own territory throughout the third quarter. Walden, doing some of the best punting of his career, punted to the Auburn 19, 10, 10 and finally out of bounds at the Tiger two yard line, all during the third quarter. That fine exhibition of kicking set the stage for Britt's inexplicable touchdown return.

Georgia punted the ball out-of-bounds at the two yard line, but the Tigers weren't able to gain any yardage in three plays. Davis punted to Britt, who caught the ball on a dead run at the Auburn 39-yard line. He broke away from two Auburn defenders, headed towards south sidelines, and scored. Several crucial blocks were thrown by Pat Dye, Larry Lancaster, and Jimmy Vickers, as Britt reached the endzone with an escort of Bulldogs. Pennington kicked the extra-point to give Georgia a 7-6 lead with ten seconds left in the third quarter.

The Bulldogs got the ball right back and had another chance when Don Leebern and Vickers caused Lamar Rawson to fumble the kickoff. Larry Lancaster recovered for Georgia at the Tiger 28-yard line. Brown picked-up six yards in two carries before Tarkenton was hit for a one-yard loss. Pennington tried a field-goal from the 30-yard line, but the kick was wide right of the goal posts.

On the next series, when Georgia got the ball back, on third down, a Walden punt was blocked. Auburn recovered at the Georgia one-yard line. On the first play, Auburn's quarterback, Bryant Harvard, sneaked over. Davis booted the extra-point to give Auburn a 13-7 lead with 7:30 remaining to play.

Georgia took the kickoff and drove to the Auburn 39-yard line before turning the ball over on downs. On a second down play, Harvard went back to pass, was hit from his blindside and fumbled. Luckily, Dye pounced on the ball at the Tiger's 35-yard line.

Next, Walden tried a halfback pass to Bobby Towns that was incomplete. On fourth down, Tarkenton called the game-winning play, connecting to Herron in the left corner of the endzone.

Pennington kicked the extra-point and Georgia had a 14-13 lead with just 30 seconds left in this classic battle royal.

The Georgia defense was superb, particularly in the second half. Hunt, the Southeastern Conference's leader on total offense before the game, carried nine times and broke even, gaining 2-yards and losing 26. He completed one of three passes for seven-yards. Davis was Auburn's big ground-gainer with 56 yards on 11 carries.

Brown paced Georgia's rushers with 41-yards on eight carries. Soberdash, playing fullback, and doing a fine job, picked-up 29-yards in eight carries. Tarkenton completed seven of 15 passes for 97 yards and that all-important touchdown. Walden punted six times for a 45.2 yard average.

Statistics tell the tale, too. Georgia had a total offense of 229 yards, as compared to Auburn's 148 yards. It was the first Georgia victory over Auburn since 1952. The win couldn't have made Georgia fans happier. The Bulldogs finished with a 10-1 record for the season, and beat Missouri in the Orange Bowl. The one loss 'Dogs team finished ranked ninth in the nation.

Georgia 14 – Florida State 17, October 17, 1964
Moral victories don't count in standings, or statistics. But Florida State, and the sports writers, wouldn't soon forget the thunderbolt that stuck in Sanford Stadium on that Saturday afternoon. Still, a thousand times bravo went to the 'Dogs for one of the finest, most determined efforts Georgia fans had witnessed in many seasons.

The fans were devastated when Preston Ridlehuber's glorious 81-yard touchdown was voided by a penalty. These same fans cheered as their Bulldogs shoved Florida State's vaunted defense around throughout the afternoon, chalking-up two touchdowns and came within a hair of two more touchdowns.

Georgia's defensive team, which allowed the Seminoles only three first downs rushing, received a standing ovation almost every time it left the field. One of the loudest applauses followed a spirited defensive stand that forced Florida State to settle for a first-quarter field-goal, rather than a touchdown.

The Bulldogs' offensive team drew cheers throughout the game, too. The loudest occurred after the 'Dogs quarterback,

Ridlehuber, cut around left end, waded through the "Seven Magnificent," and refused to be brought down until he entered the endzone 80-yards away. The play was called back because of a holding penalty.

Coach Bill Peterson, of Florida State, called Georgia "the best prepared football team we have faced. Those backs were the hardest runners we've encountered this year or any other year."

Spirit in the student section was never higher. Ovation, after thunderous ovation, and cheer after rousing cheer, was evidence of the unbroken support of every person in a student seat.

Florida State, sparked by its great passing combo of Steve Tensi to Fred Biletnikoff, bounced off the deck for a last period touchdown to gun down an upset-bent Georgia squad 17-14 inside of Sanford Stadium.

A crowd of over 31,000, including President Johnson's younger daughter, Luci Baines, saw heavy-underdog Georgia play the unbeaten Seminoles off their collective feet for three and a half quarters, only to succumb to a gamble that paid off.

With time running out, the Seminoles, trailing 10-14, marched 27-yards to Georgia's 45-yard line, where they faced a fourth down and five. Florida State went for it. Tensi tossed a 13-yard pass to Biletnikoff for a first down. Two plays later, they teamed-up again for 20 yards, and a touchdown.

For the majority of the game it had been almost sacrilegious the way Georgia treated Florida State's touted defense, allegedly the tenth best in the nation. The 'Dogs gained 240 yards and lost approximately 100 yards because of penalties.

The most costly penalty wiped out an 80-yard scoring jaunt by Ridlehuber in the third quarter, and killed a desperation Bulldog attempt after Florida State scored late in the final quarter.

A fumble erased Georgia's bid for a first quarter touchdown as the normally glue-fingered Pat Hodgson coughed-up the ball after a 21-yard pass got down to Florida State's 3-yard line. From there the Seminoles marched down to the Bulldogs' 4-yard line in three plays. The Seminoles eventually registered the first score of the game, a 23-yard field-goal by Les Murdock.

An error cost Florida State a second quarter touchdown. Ed Pritchett's punt was touched by Georgia's Doug McFalls, 16-yards from the 'Dogs' goal line. Those 16-yards were duck soup for the Seminoles.

Georgia did its scoring in the second and fourth quarters, driving 79-yards in 13 plays for the first touchdown, then going 23-yards in seven plays, after a fumble recovery, for the second score. Ridlehuber went in from the 4-yard line in the second quarter and Fred Barber scored from the 7-yard line in the fourth quarter.

Georgia started out like it intended to run the tenth-ranked Seminoles back to Tallahassee on a rail. During the opening series Georgia drove from their own 33-yard line, to the Florida State 3-yard line, before losing the ball via a fumble.

On Florida State's first play from scrimmage halfback Phil Spooner broke away for 40-yards, prior to being brought down from behind by Joe Burson. Two plays later, Tensi fired a strike to end Don Floyd, who covered 52-yards, to the 'Dogs four-yard line, where Burson rolled him out of bounds.

The Bulldogs put-up their stiffest defensive stand of the first half, stopping Florida State on three downs. On fourth down, Murdock hammered through a 23-yard field-goal. With 6:52 remaining in the first quarter, Florida State was on the scoreboard.

Early in the second quarter, Florida State got another break from the Bulldogs. Stymied at the Georgia 47-yard line, the Seminoles punted. McFalls accidently touched the ball at his own 16-yard line, and McDowell pounced on the football for Florida State.

Spooner slashed for three yards on two successive plays before Tensi and Lee Narramore clicked on a nine-yard pass play to the one-foot line. On the next play, Narramore muscled over right guard for the score. Murdock made it 10-0 with 4:42 in the half.

Georgia came back and did what no team had done all year: scored a touchdown on Florida State. From their own 21-yard line, the 'Dogs did it in 13 plays, beginning with four straight carries by Phil Hughes to put Georgia on the 49-yard line. Barber got six, and Ridlehuber got to the 17-yard line. Three plays later, Hughes hit Porterfield for 21-yards, to the eight-yard line. Runs by Barber and Taylor nettled two yards each, and Ridlehuber kept off left tackle for the final four yards. Etter booted the point that made it a three point deficit, 10-7, at the half.

In the third quarter, the 'Dogs fashioned a 29-yard move, to the Seminole 36-yard line, before an official caught a Georgia lineman holding. That 15-yard assessment began a 60-yard taxation against Georgia during the period. Late in the quarter, Florida State reciprocated with a holding infraction that smothered a drive. Tensi had passed to Biletnikoff for 34-yards, then five yards, on successive plays. A personal foul against Georgia put the ball on the 'Dogs' 21-yard line, from where Tensi hooked-up with Floyd on a five-yard pop. Then a penalty was called and the Seminoles were stopped.

Murdock tried a 48-yard field-goal, but toppled the ball into the endzone. From their own 20-yard line, the 'Dogs began serious business. On the second snap, Ridlehuber bolted into the open and raced 68-yards to score; however, another holding penalty nullified the run, and the longest play of the day. Next, Mack Faircloth punted 58-yards, to the Florida State 20-yard line.

Georgia's line mobbed Spooner on Florida State's first effort. He fumbled and McFalls claimed the ball for Georgia at the 23-yard line. With Ridlehuber at the controls, Georgia scored in six plays. First, Ridlehuber gained five. Then, Hughes returned to pick-up two yards. Next, Barber got five, then three yards, before Ridlehuber got to the seven-yard line. Barber got the call again and bulldozed his way for those last seven-yards, sending Georgia into the lead 14-10, with 12:13 left in the game. It was the first time all season Florida State had trailed.

The Seminoles showed championship class on the following offensive do-or-die drive. During a 16 play drive, the Seminoles methodically moved the ball into Georgia territory. On the 45-yard line, Tensi was faced with a fourth down and five play, where he called on his favorite receiver, Biletnikoff. The sticky-fingered flanker reeled in a 13-yarder for a first down at the 32-yard line.

Next, Spooner broke loose for 12-yards. Then, Tensi speared Biletnikoff inside the five, and the Seminoles' great refused to go down until he had scored the touchdown. Murdock made it 17-14.

Georgia's ball control tactics proved a disadvantage as small bites of yardage moved the ball, but ate-up too much valuable time. Eight plays covered 30-yards and required nearly four minutes. Faced with a fourth down at midfield, Georgia needed one yard for a first down. Barber apparently got it on a plunge into the line, but an over-zealous lineman jumped the gun and cost the 'Dogs five-yards.

Again, on fourth down, with six yards needed, Hughes flipped to Hodgeson, who dropped the ball.

The 'Dogs did regain possession with 1:15 remaining, but were backed-up to their own one-yard line. Three passes fell incomplete, including one to Porterfield, who was wide open on the right sidelines. Georgia punted away its last dim hope of victory.

The 'Dogs ground out yardage as no previous Florida State foe had done all season, netting 167 yards to the Seminoles 92 yards. The statistical difference was in the air where Florida State gained 193 yards to 73 for the 'Dogs.

Tenis-to-Biletnikoff was indeed an All-American combination. They clicked on eight occasions for 114 yards and the winning touchdown.

Dooley's first team at Georgia would finish the season at 7-3-1, and defeat Texas Tech 7-0 in the Sun Bowl. Coach Bill Peterson's Florida State Seminoles would go 9-1-1, and beat the Oklahoma Sooners 36-19 in the Gator Bowl.

Georgia 18 - Alabama 17, September 18, 1965

The Georgia-Alabama series started in 1895, when Coach Glen "Pop" Warner's Georgia team won 30-6. By 1965, the 58-game series was decidedly in Alabama's favor. However, the season opener in '65 would be one of the most exciting games ever witnessed inside of Sanford Stadium.

In this 1965 season opener, Georgia pulled off one of the most surprising upsets of the intercollegiate football season when, during Vince Dooley's second year at Georgia, the 'Dogs upset defending national champion Alabama. Surprisingly, a year earlier, Georgia had been humiliated by Alabama, in Tuscaloosa, by a final score of 31-3. In the '65 game, a questionable play occurred that would break Alabama's back, and has been psycho-analyzed by experts, and novice fans, decades later.

In the first quarter, Bobby Etter kicked a 37-yard field-goal to draw first blood for the 'Dogs of Georgia. Then, six plays later, Georgia's defensive tackle, Jiggy Smaha, hit Alabama quarterback, Steve Sloan, from the blindside, as he attempted to pass. The ball fell short, and Georgia's All-American tackle George Patton, from Tuscumbia, Alabama, intercepted it and ran fifty-five yards, untouched, for the touchdown. Etter made it 10-0 and pandemonium reigned inside Sanford Stadium. Ironically, Patton's older brother, Jim, played on Alabama's 1961 national championship team.

Late in the half, Alabama finally scored, after recovering a fumble at the Georgia 11-yard line. The Bulldog defense held and the Crimson Tide's David Ray booted a 26-yard field-goal to make the score 10-3, in favor of Georgia. However, another Georgia fumble, recovered at the Georgia 29-yard line, resulted in Alabama tying the score at 10-10. Later, the Tide roared back with a 90-yard drive to go ahead, 17-10. Then, the play in question happened.

Three plays after Alabama scored, deep in the fourth quarter, came possibly the most sensational play in Sanford Stadium annals. It was a 73-yard touchdown pass thrown by Kirby Moore, who was playing his first game at quarterback for the varsity. He passed the ball to Pat Hodgson, who made a lightning-quick lateral-pass to halfback Bob Taylor, who sped down the sidelines to glory.

The play was recognized as the "flea-flicker," and Oklahoma's coach Bud Wilkinson, on NBC, stated it was the "most electrifying" play he had ever seen.

But when that great play was over, Georgia still trailed 16-17, and had a long way to go for a victory. The Bulldogs faced the great Alabama defense from the three yard line. Georgia could have settled for an almost certain tie with an Etter extra-point, but Coach Dooley never gave it a thought. He waved quarterback Moore back into the game for a two-point attempt that would win or lose the game once and for all.

In the turmoil of the moment a time-out had to be called. For Georgia and Alabama fans alike, it was a never-ending period of misery, and television fans had to suffer through three commercials and a station break. Finally, the whistle blew as the tension in the stadium rose to a climax. But, when the ball was snapped, complete silence engulfed the stadium.

Moore rolled to his right, looking for an open receiver, when he suddenly saw Hodgson running parallel to the back of the endzone. Moore delivered the ball and it was over. He had calmly hit Hodgson in the endzone for the two-point conversion. This time an explosion of noise engulfed the stadium.

Georgia's 18-17 upset broke a five-game winning streak by Alabama over Georgia. Hodgson, from Atlanta, had a grandfather,

Morton Hodgson Sr., who lived on Prince Avenue, where the Georgia Power Co. building is now. Hodgson Sr., was Georgia's first four-year letterman and All-Southern first baseman in 1908.

In 1965, the "flea-flicker" play Georgia perpetrated against national champion Alabama, on national television, would be the talk of the football world. Those who witnessed it, would never forget the sight of Taylor galloping all alone down the north sideline, in the direction of the railroad tracks. All alone, except for the Georgia cheerleader who matched him step-for-step, shoulder-to-shoulder, just outside the boundary line.

It would be the only defeat inflicted on Alabama that season, as the Pachyderms went 9-1-1. Its lone tie came against Tennessee. The Crimson Tide defeated Nebraska 39-28, in the Orange Bowl, to win the national title. Dooley's 'Dogs would go 6-4, but did not receive a bowl invitation.

Georgia 9 – Ole Miss 3, October 8, 1966

For the first time during the 1966 season, Georgia had the role of the underdog, though only slightly, when Ole Miss invaded Sanford Stadium. The Bulldogs would eventually put the Rebels down by a final score of 9-3, and leave Coach Johnny Vaught's Ole Miss Rebels defending a hopeless cause.

The Rebels scored on a 39-yard field-goal early in the first quarter. Ole Miss had recovered a Kirby Moore fumble, but could not move the ball the required 10-yards for a first down, and were forced to go for three points. Mississippi quickly led 3-0.

During the first series, when Ole Miss had the ball, the Georgia defense was the talk of the day. Terry Sellers, Mark Holmes, Lynn Hughes, Jimmy Cooley, Steve Neuhaus, Bill Stanfill, and, of course, George Patton, all turned-in the performances that left even the most confident Bulldog fans in doubtful amazement.

Patton and Stanfill spent much of the afternoon in the Rebel's backfield, while Sellers, Hughes, Holmes, and Neuhaus were busy downfield intercepting Ole Miss pass attempts. Sellers intercepted two, and the others got one apiece.

The hard-running of fullback Ronnie Jenkins figured greatly in the Georgia win. He gained 90-yards, more than any other team had against the Rebels' defense. Forty-six of those yards came on six carries during the Bulldogs' 78-yard touchdown jaunt.

Ole Miss purportedly had the best defense in the entire nation. Jenkins shredded this highly touted Ole Miss defensive unit, as he ran behind some of the most first-rate blocking Bulldog fans had observed in many years.

Georgia had begun to take command of the game early in the second period with its touchdown drive. Jenkins ran for 12, seven, and four yards. Then, the 'Dogs pulled some razzle dazzle. It was that three-man play which had become known as the "Alabama play." This time it was Moore-to-Billy Payne-to-Randy Heeler, and it was good for 29-yards to the Rebels' 20-yard line. At that point, Georgia was assessed 15-yards for ineligible receiver downfield and had to start at the 35-yard line. From there, it was Moore and Jenkins, behind the kind of blocking a ball carrier dreams about.

Moore rolled to the left for 15-yards. Then, Jenkins carried for seven. An Ole Miss personal foul gave the 'Dogs a first down on the Rebels' 13-yard line. Moore lost three, but Jenkins gained 15-yards on the very next play. Two plays later, the big fullback was in the endzone, and Bulldog fans were in "Dawg ecstasy!"

For the first time during the 1966 season, Georgia's defense scored. After a Moore punt was slapped out of bounds at the Rebel four-yard line, big Patton slipped through the beefy Ole Miss line and nailed Bruce Newell in the end-zone for a safety.

The Georgia Bulldogs led 9-3.

Though all the scoring came in the first half, the second half was not any less exciting. As everybody had predicted, the Rebels were a 'never-say-die team.' They fought back late in the game, and were moving toward the Georgia goal, on their most spirited drive of the afternoon, when Sellers made his second interception of the game. Georgia took over at their own 44-yard line.

Offensively, Georgia was so effective on the ground that Moore and Rick Arrington didn't pass at all in the second half. Instead, the Bulldogs ran the ball directly down the Rebels' throats.

During the course of the game, Georgia rolled up 150-yards against a Rebel line that allowed top ranked Alabama only 81-yards. Additionally, the 'Dogs had 48 passing yards, which got them close to the 200-yard mark in total offense.

The win kept Georgia's record blemish-free at 4-0. Ole Miss went to 2-2 overall and 0-2 in Southeastern Conference play. The Bulldogs, who were squarely in the Southeastern Conference title picture, smelled something akin to orange blossoms. In truth, the 'Dogs would finish the season at 10-1 and won the Southeastern Conference title after throttling Steve Spurrier and Florida 27-10 in the World's Largest Outdoor Cocktail Party in Jacksonville. Its only loss came against Miami by a score of 7-6. Georgia went on to beat Southern Methodist 24-9 in the Cotton Bowl. Ole Miss finished 8-3, and lost to Texas in the Bluebonnet Bowl by a score of 19-0.

Georgia 23 – Georgia Tech 14, November 27, 1966

As Georgia prepared to meet Georgia Tech in its annual rivalry, most Americans still hadn't heard of a small Southeast Asian country called Vietnam, or the conflict that was just beginning to explode. On a cold afternoon, in late November of 1966, Georgia's unrivaled Bulldogs, greedily smacking their jaws for Texas Methodists, drilled Georgia Tech's Gold and White into Sanford Stadium's brown turf.

Georgia left little doubt in the minds of 48,272 spectators the collegiate football champion of the state of Georgia resided in Athens, not Atlanta. Coach Dooley's Cotton Bowl-bound Bulldogs tuned-up for its New Year's Eve clash with Southern Methodist by soundly whipping its bitter rival 23-14, in a game that wasn't nearly as close as the final score indicated.

Prior to their clash in Sanford Stadium, Tech was one of two undefeated college teams in the nation and was the fifth ranked squad in the country. Tech was 9-0. Georgia was 8-1. Coach Dooley admitted he was somewhat apprehensive the week of the game, but said by Thursday morning's practice he knew the Bulldogs were ready to play. And he added, "When your opponent is fifth ranked nationally, and your state rival—if you're not ready to play them, you're not ready to play anybody.

Knowing his team was motivated for the game helped soothe his psyche. Dooley said he didn't feel as much strain during the game. And the 'Dogs' 17-7 lead at halftime was energizing.

Coach Bobby Dodd's fifth-ranked Yellow Jackets had one impressive touchdown march of 96-yards, but other than that, it left most of the fireworks to Georgia all afternoon. The Bulldogs had several other chances to score, and they did twice more, but penalties and mistakes stopped or nullified those touchdowns.

Kent Lawrence, a 9.5 trackman from Central, South Carolina, had two touchdowns called back because of penalties. One came on a 25-yard run in the first quarter and the other came in the fourth quarter, on a 13-yard pass from Kirby Moore.

Dooley's 'Dogs were the 1966 Southeastern Conference champions. Georgia completed its best season since 1959, when Wally Butts troops went 10-1 and won in the Orange Bowl. Whereas, Tech's Gnats had won nine straight in '66, before being whipped by Georgia and still had a date with Florida in the Orange Bowl, on January 2, 1967. Astonishingly, Georgia had defeated both the Engineers and Gators, the two Miami opponents.

On the auspicious day of the game, 48,000 fans had come to see the national "game of the week," but, as far as most were concerned, it was the "Game of the Century!" And, for just plain good football, they were not disappointed.

Tech won the coin toss, yet elected not to receive. The Yellow Jackets' Tommy Carmichael kicked-off to start the game. The Bulldogs kept the ball for seven plays and two first downs, but couldn't make the required yardage on its third attempt for a first down. Georgia's Stan Crawford punted deep into Tech territory.

The Jackets ran three plays, but found themselves confronted with a fourth and eleven, and elected to punt. The Yellow Jackets' Charlie Mason punted directly into the waiting arms of Lawrence. Georgia's punt return team had an unbelievable lane set-up for his return, and the fleet footed sophomore used it to its full advantage for a 71-yard run into the endzone. The play set-off a fury amongst Georgia partisans, and created a celebration that would last all afternoon and deep into the night.

Unfortunately, Bob Etter, a senior from Chattanooga, who closed his regular season career by scoring in his thirty-first straight game since arriving at Georgia, missed the extra-point, leaving the Bulldogs with a shaky 6-0 lead. Etter later admitted he had been disturbed by an untimely explosion of cannon fire, and missed the point-after-attempt. It had been his first and only missed conversion attempt of the season.

On the next series of Tech plays, Kim King experienced the same feelings as Steve Spurrier, the great Florida quarterback and '66 Heisman Trophy winner. The Tech quarterback quickly lost 28 yards and the ball. It was big All-American George Patton who forced the fumble, and who then recovered it.

Georgia was in business again. On the fourth play of the series, Lawrence scooted through the middle, and around the end for another touchdown; however, it was nullified by a penalty. Georgia couldn't get back the lost yardage and was forced to punt.

It was there that Tech finally got something going. They marched 96-yards for a touchdown, and the go ahead point-after-attempt. Tech's first score came with 9:09 to play in the first half. The Yellow Jackets, paced by brilliant tailback Lenny Snow, who accounted for 54 of the yards, took 18 plays to go 96-yards for the touchdown. King scored from six yards out on a sweep. Afterwards, Bunky Henry connected on one of two extra-points for the day. Tech led 7-6.

The Yellow Jackets lead was short-lived, however. Georgia came right back a few minutes later, marching 54-yards in six plays. Terry Sellers downed a punt at the Georgia 31-yard line. From there Moore passed twice to Ronnie Jenkins, the first one covered 10-yards and a second pass went for 22-yards. Next, Lawrence carried for no gain. On the following play, Moore skirted around the end for 16 yards. Faced with a first and goal to go at the seven yard line, Jenkins and Brad Johnson teamed-up for the last yards, with Johnson going over for the score. Georgia led 12-7.

Coach Dooley called time out, and talked it over. Georgia elected to go for the two-point conversion. Moore tossed to Hardy King and the 'Dogs had a 14-7 lead with three minutes left in the first half.

Tech took the ensuing kickoff, but had the football for only three plays. King had tossed a pass that was deflected by Patton and fell right to Larry Kohn, who returned it 12-yards to the Tech 13-yard line. The 'Dogs couldn't move the ball across the goal and called on Etter to attempt a three-pointer. The kick was good and the 'Dogs took a 17-7 lead into halftime.

During the halftime show, the Dixie Redcoat Band used its allotted time to make its presentation through demonstrations. First, facing the Georgia fans, they blasted forth with "Take the 'A Train," deceptively saluting the 'Dogs locomotive railroading of Tech.

Then, the music makers "saluted" Tech with "I can't Get Started," a suitable selection for the visiting team. And, finally, the band turned back to the Georgia partisans for a boisterous version of "Woodchoppers' Ball," denoting the "ball" the Bulldogs were having "chopping down" Tech and "building up" a lead.

After the two teams returned to the field, they spent the third quarter exchanging punts; however, neither team was able to muster much of a drive. When the next score was recorded, it was again for the Bulldogs. Lynn Hughes, repeating his performance from the 1965 Tech game, intercepted King's pass and returned it back 39-yards to the Tech eight-yard line. The interception was so perfect it looked as if Hughes knew they play.

Disappointingly, Georgia was plagued by penalties and was forced to go for another Etter field-goal. The attempt was good. With 9:03 remaining in the game, the Bulldogs led 20-7.

On the next series of downs, the Jackets were unable to make the necessary ten yards for a first down. Instead of punting, Coach Dodd elected to take a gamble and go for the first down on a fourth and one. Tech failed, and Georgia took over on Tech's 25-yard line.

Again, the 'Dogs weren't able to make a first down, and were forced to have Etter attempt yet another field-goal. His 34-yard kick was good and the 'Dogs led 23-7.

Tech's next possession was short-lived. As King dropped back to pass, All-American Bill Stanfill covered him. King got the pass off—directly to Patton.

Having a 16-point lead, and the ball deep in Tech territory, Coach Dooley took out his first-string, and they would not return to the game. With a big thorn out of their sides, Georgia would let the Jackets score with just five seconds remaining in the game. And, not a single member of the 'Dogs first-string was on the field. When the final horn sounded, the scoreboard read: Georgia 23 – Tech 14.

Georgia's Cotton Bowl-bound Bulldogs took a lot of the luster out of the Orange Bowl by beating Georgia Tech 23-14. The win was the third straight for Coach Dooley over Georgia Tech. And, it ran his all-time record to 22-8-1. Coach Dodd, who was in his twenty-second year as head of the Jackets, went to 12-10 all-time against Georgia and 5-6 inside of Sanford Stadium.

From an historical perspective, it marked the fourth time these two hated rivals had met with a single loss between them. The first time was in 1927, when Georgia invaded Grant Field with a 9-0 record. Tech was 7-1-1 and pulled a 12-0 upset. Next, in 1942, the Yellow Jackets had a record of 9-0 when they came to Athens. Georgia was 9-1 and destroyed the Yellow Jackets 34-0. In 1946, Georgia was 9-0, and Tech was 8-1 and the 'Dogs won that game 35-7. And, in 1966, Georgia proved Tech's undoing again.

The 'Dogs would go on to beat the Southwest Conference champions, the Southern Methodist Mustangs, 24-9, in the annual Cotton Bowl in Dallas, Texas, on December 31, 1966. Tech lost to Spurrier and Florida in Miami's Orange Bowl.

Georgia 21 – Ole Miss 31, October 10, 1970

The impossible dream lasted 46 minutes and 43 seconds on this ill-fated day, then died in the warmth of an October Sanford Stadium afternoon. Georgia the "underdog," was a team that wasn't supposed to beat the undefeated and nationally ranked Ole Miss Rebels. However, the 'Dogs matched the Rebels point-for-point, for two and a half quarters, then mental errors and interceptions mounted up for a 31-21 Mississippi victory.

The afternoon saw the return of the Georgia offense, led by the extraordinary running of Ricky Lake and engineered by Mike Cavan, the senior who had yielded his quarterbacking slot to sophomore James Ray before the year even started.

Lake, making his first varsity appearance, after sitting out three games with a knee injury, rushed for 85-yards in 15 carries, 60 of them in the first half. Cavan, who entered the game after Ray injured his left knee, hit nine of 18 passes for 160 yards and one touchdown, a six yarder to Julian Smiley.

The killing goof came with a minute gone in the fourth quarter. Ole Miss's quarterback, Archie Manning, a.k.a. Archie the Magnificent, caught Georgia sleeping on a 52-yard touchdown bomb to Floyd Franks.

The ensuing kickoff, a short lob, sailed over the heads of Paul Gilbert and Smiley, and rolled around until the Rebel's Ronnie Moses jumped on it at the Georgia seven-yard line. That was when the bottom fell out. Though Ole Miss eventually had to settle for a field-goal, it put the Rebels ahead for good.

Afterwards, a dejected and defeated Georgia football team filed slowly thought the gate, located on the east end of Sanford Stadium. A scattered combination of girlfriends and wives walked with them, offering what little encouragement and consolation that remained. Occasionally, a bright red helmet would tilt upward to the mammoth scoreboard that stood lighted guard over the Bulldogs' dressing room. With its single bulbs blending into figures, it rubbed salt into the afternoon's wounds. Under "Georgia" it read 21 and under "Visitors" it read 31.

But the 10-point difference, and the pregame smart money, that had given Georgia and seven and one-half, couldn't begin to tell the true story. Neither could Dooley, as he picked ice from his Coke in the dressing room and reviewed, as best he could, what had gone into the final outcome.

"The only way to beat Ole Miss," he surmised, "is to go ahead late in the game so they won't have time to come back." The memory lingered, however, that for three quarters the Rebels had been beaten. They had been outscored 21-14, by an inspired Georgia offense that drew life from a Bulldog defense that played with the militancy of a Colombia University student rally.

For three quarters they stopped the unstoppable Manning and Ole Miss. But Georgia's lead didn't last. It was only one of several designs in the game that fizzled. Something was amiss when the halftime show had been held almost two hours before kickoff. The senior parade was next. The Mickey Moose production was its usual fiasco, but in consolation, it was over.

Then, there was Georgia's dismal fourth quarter production, which included two fumbles and 17 Rebel points. The killer, and at the same time the clincher for Ole Miss, came on a Rebel kickoff which Smiley and Gilbert watched bounce into the Rebels' hands at the Georgia seven-yard line.

The turnover culminated in an Ole Miss field-goal that gave the Rebels a lead of 24-21, an ultimately, the momentum to win the game. Afterwards, Manning evaded his waiting army with the help of two armed uniformed guards. He had passed for three scores and added a fourth himself, but the All-American was vulnerable to penetration. He threw three interceptions and had one fumble.

Coach Vaught had been extremely pleased in the way the Rebels came from behind to steal a win. "This was a real tough game, probably tougher than any game we've had all season. It is hard for any team to come back and win, especially in a place like this," he added, pointing towards Sanford Stadium.

Georgia 20 – Auburn 35, November 13, 1971
The game that was supposed to have everything had it; except for a miracle finish.

The game, supposed to pit two of the premier teams in the Southeastern Conference, did just that.

The Auburn passing attack of Pat Sullivan to Terry Beasley, with liberal doses of Dick Schmalz sprinkled in, that was supposed to be devastating, was just that.

The Georgia ground attack that was to eat-up yards. and time, did, most of the time. Anybody who paid $100 for a ticket got his money's worth. The game was everything it promised to be.

Except Auburn won 35-20.

In the end, it was super-athlete Sullivan who proved too much for Georgia. He threw long, he threw short, he ran the ball sometimes, and it seemed that whatever play he called was correct.

When the day's work was done, he had 14 completions, including four touchdowns, for 248 yards. He established himself as the leading Heisman Trophy candidate, especially after Cornell and Ed Marinaro suffered a 24-14 upset loss to Dartmouth.

Georgia's sophomore quarterback, Andy Johnson, did his best to upstage the Plainsman, rushing for 163 yards, the most yardage gained in a single game by a Georgia back in many years. In the end, however, it was his, and Georgia's style of play that lost the game. The Bulldogs were not a come-from-behind type team, and they spent most of the game in that position.

Auburn took over right away, starting from its own 38-yard line. Only twice during the game did the Tigers have poor field position. Sullivan made the first big play of the game, appropriately enough, moving the ball from his own 41-yard line, to the Georgia 44-yard line on the second play of the game.

Fullback Tommy Lowry gained five yards on two carries, then gathered in a Sullivan screen pass to the right and followed blockers for a 12-yard gain, to the Georgia 27-yard line. Next, Auburn got caught for a delay, but Lowry would gain three of the five penalty yards back. Sullivan dropped back and found Schmalz wide open across the middle. The wingback shook one tackle and was finally pushed out of bounds at the two by Phil Sullivan.

Auburn's tailback, Terry Henley, gained one and then Lowry dived over for the score. Gardner Jett added the extra-point and Georgia was in a very unfamiliar spot, behind.

Auburn kicked-off and Georgia started from its 19-yard line. Johnson replaced James Ray, hero of the past two games. The Bulldogs went nine yards and punted. Auburn then proceeded to go 63-yards and kicked—an extra-point that is. The drive started on a bad play. Henley was stopped for no gain. Then, Lowry went 10 yards on another screen pass. Sullivan would later convert a third down play by passing to Schmalz for an 18-yard gainer to the Georgia 34-yard line.

Beasley turned it into athlete against athlete, and he won. He beat Jerome Jackson to the endzone after grabbing a perfectly thrown pass from Sullivan for a 34-yard touchdown. Jett added the extra-point to give Auburn the 14-0 lead.

However, Johnson wasn't through, and he brought the partisan crowd of 62, 841 to its feet on the next series. Starting from the 20-yard line, Jimmy Poulos could gain nothing. Then, Johnson gained eleven yards on the quarterback draw, down to the Georgia 31-yard line. The next play was the biggest play of the first half.

Johnson faked to Robert Honeycutt, followed him around left end, cut back to the right and sprinted 57-yards to the Auburn two where he was caught from behind by fleeter defenders. Two plays later, and Jimmy Poulos scored. Kim Braswell kicked the extra-point to cut Auburn's lead to 14-7.

In the second quarter, with Ray back at quarterback, Poulos, on second down, slithered right and sped by defenders for a 26-yard gain, to the Georgia 49-yard line. Next, Honeycutt blasted through the middle for four yards. Ricky Lake came on for his one and only run of the day, picking up 10-yards over left tackle. It was an expensive 10-yards. He limped off the field and never returned.

Georgia got the ball down to the Auburn 13-yard line, with a first and 10. First, Ray rolled right for four yards. On the next play, Ray went right, and was almost engulfed, but pitched to a wide open

Donnie Allen, who went into the endzone, untouched. Braswell added the extra-point, to tie the game at 14-14. The extra-point was the costliest extra-point of the year as All-American Royce Smith went down with an injured knee, and never returned.

Auburn didn't let the game stay tied for very long. Sullivan went to work and eventually hit Schmalz for a 15-yard touchdown. Jett made the score 21-14. There would be no more scoring until the fourth quarter when Georgia caught its biggest break of the game on a fumble recovery at the Auburn 26-yard line. Johnson would eventually dive over from the two-yard line to score the touchdown; however, the extra-point would be blocked when Roger Mitchell burst through to block Braswell's kick.

If that wasn't demoralizing, the next play from scrimmage certainly had to be. From his own 30-yard line, Sullivan passed to a very well covered Beasley. Two Georgia tacklers bounced off the fleet receiver and he turned and ran and ran and ran before scoring a 70-yard touchdown. It was the longest scoring play of the year against Georgia. The score was 28-20.

The game was over for Georgia. The Bulldogs never were able to reach the midfield marker again, much less get into Auburn territory. Auburn stopped one drive with an interception of a Ray pass. Sullivan passed to Beasley for 12-yards, down to the five yard line before making the play only a superstar could make. Faced with a ferocious rush and protection breaking down, Sullivan rolled left, saw Schmalz open in the endzone and threw for a touchdown as he was falling down. Jett closed the scoring for the day at 35-20 with his fifth extra-point.

The rest of the game was just an agonizing wait for the inevitable—the Bulldogs were going to lose. Lose the game, the Southeastern Conference Championship, a big bowl bid, a high ranking and a perfect season. But they lost to a great player, a very great player, a Heisman Trophy winning player.

Georgia 21 – Alabama 0, October 2, 1976

Gillis Bridge, on the west end of Sanford Stadium, smelt like whiskey and stale beer. Thousands milled around, attempting to buy and sell tickets in a Saturday afternoon version of the American Stock Exchange. Ticket scalpers were asking $80-$100 each.

Football carried the day as Athens almost entirely turned over in what was undoubtedly one of the most anxiously-awaited games in its history. Sanford Stadium was the epic center of the Southeastern Conference's attention as Paul "Bear" Bryant's five-time defending Southeastern Conference champion Crimson Tide of Alabama took on Coach Dooley's Georgia Bulldogs.

Though the Tide had won the conference title five straight seasons, Georgia had been given a chance, by the prognosticators, to finally dethrone the Pachyderms. Moreover, the previous week, Coach Bryant's team had been upset by Ole Miss. Now, the Bulldogs had an opportunity to effectively knock Alabama out of the race, while asserting their own candidacy.

An estimated 60,200 fans swarmed the stadium while another 12,000 viewed the game from the bridge on Sanford Drive, or surrounding rooftops, and the railroad tracks, where crowds started camping out early Friday morning.

The near-hysteria was evident on Friday night, as traffic on Milledge Avenue approached levels reminiscent of the spring of '74, when streakers dashed from fraternity house to sorority house, forcing Athens police to actually close sections of the city to cars.

Horns blew all night, and frequently shouts of "Go Dogs" and choruses of "Glory, Glory to old Georgia," echoed through Athens. There were carloads of Bulldog fans driving-up and down the city's streets, some hanging out of windows, others stuffed into trunks, but all wearing red and black, with pom-poms in one hand and, sometimes, a bottle of beer, or a liquor bottle, in the other. Everybody, with all of their energy, was shouting their support for the 'Dogs.

People parked wherever they could on game day. Hundreds of vehicles were abandoned on sidewalks, while others were parked on the lawn in front of the law school. Somebody drove his Fleetwood along the walk in front of the library, stopping behind Old College on north campus.

Several groups were seen on Baldwin Street, near the Journalism Psychology Complex, where they set-up chairs and a table lined with plenty to eat, and large quantities of alcohol, while listening to Larry Munson over a transistor radio.

Coach Dooley said it would take three touchdowns to beat Alabama. Georgia did score three touchdowns; however, it only needed one for the victory. Georgia won 21-0. Questions immediately arose about how good this '76 Georgia football team was? The throng of more than seventy-four thousand who witnessed the game, in and around Sanford Stadium, on a sunbathed fall afternoon, no doubt would have insisted the 'Dogs were as good as any team Coach Vince Dooley had ever put together.

However, many, including Coach Dooley, and some players, were not convinced they had conquered a team of the caliber of Michigan, Pittsburgh, Oklahoma or the like. Their statements left unanswered the enigma of Georgia's strength, despite its hefty number six national ranking, which improved after its solid win over the Pachyderms.

It was the Junkyard Runts, formerly trading as the Junkyard 'Dogs, who held the game together until the Georgia offensive team overcame its suicidal tendencies. Then, with a flourish of steady, level-headed direction, Matt Robinson and group conducted themselves with applaudable decorum 67-yards into the endzone, just eight seconds before halftime.

With the game still scoreless, Georgia began its long drive towards the endzone. Kevin McLee picked-up 13-yards on back-to-back carries, taking the ball to the Alabama 44-yard line. Then, the next three plays only netted eight-yards, and Georgia faced a fourth and two at the 36-yard line. Rayfield Williams got three-yards and the drive stayed alive. But the clock was running out. With less than 20 seconds to go, Robinson passed to Steve Davis, on the Alabama three-yard line. With no more time-outs, Robinson hurled an incomplete pass to Gene Washington, who was open in the rear of the endzone, stopping the clock at ten seconds. The crowd was in a fury. The situation undoubtedly called for a short pass over the goal line because a running play would use up all the remaining time.

Instead, Robinson would follow Moonpie Wilson's block on a slant over the goal line, requiring only two seconds, covering three yards. Coach Dooley aged several years on the bench, and Larry Munson was gasping into the microphone high in his radio booth. Robinson had spotted an opening, broke a tackle, with great effort, and dove precisely on the goal line. Leavitt added an extra-point and Georgia took a 7-0 lead into halftime. Then, bedlam erupted in the raucous crowd.

The next score would not come until late in the third quarter, when Williams scored on a two-yard touchdown run, giving Georgia had a 14-0 lead. In the final quarter, Robinson would toss a six yard touchdown to Ulysses Norris—culminating in Robinson's seventh scoring pass in only four games.

At the end of the game, not only had Georgia snapped a 69-game Alabama scoring streak, but dominated the Red Elephants from start to finish. The Tide had entered the game with the Southeastern Conference's best rushing offense and rushing defense. As a matter of fact, Alabama was the best rushing team in the nation, averaging 297 yards per game. Georgia would grudgingly give them 49 yards on the ground and embarrassed the Tide with minus 15-yards in the second half. In contrast, Georgia gained 190 rushing yards on 56 carries. McLee picked-up 98-yards on 22 carries.

During the fourth quarter, Georgia dominated the game. The Bulldogs sacked Alabama's quarterback, Jeff Rutledge, on four consecutive plays. Still, by everyone's admission, it was Robinson's touchdown that was the death knell for the Pachyderms, and eliminated the Crimson Tide from the conference race.

A dejected Coach Bryant, whose Alabama teams had won 55 of its past 58 regular-season games, rarely witnessed his team get so thoroughly whipped. "We lost to a superior team," Bryant said in the gloomy dressing room. "… and when I say superior, that is an understatement. I still thought we could win when we were down 7-0 at halftime, but they got better and we got worse as it went along. Dooley and his staff did a great job of preparing for us. They have a fine team…but I can't judge how good they are."

Though Georgia dominated the first half, the Bear had reason for optimism. The Georgia offense had sputtered and wasted an early chance to score. The second time the Bulldogs handled the ball, Dooley reached into his bag of tricks. He inserted freshman quarterback Jeff Pyburn in a halfback slot. Pyburn took a pitchout from Ray Goff and threw to Washington. Alabama was penalized for pass interference, and Georgia had its first scoring shot from the ten yard line.

The next trick play would backfire. On a fake field-goal, Robinson missed the mark, and the Bulldogs came away empty handed after going 72-yards against Alabama's top rated defense.

There was no indication the game would be a mismatch. Initially, the Bulldogs squandered an opportunity to take an early lead when they committed four infractions on one drive. But, late in the second quarter, Robinson generated that infamous 67-yard touchdown drive, and thereafter it was all "Glory to Old Georgia."

McLee ripped for 13-yards, in two carries, to ignite the scoring excursion. On fourth and two, at the Alabama 36 yard line, Williams gained a vital three-yards. Four plays later, Robinson nailed Davis at the three. He then hurled a quick pass to stop the clock ten seconds before halftime. On the next play, Robinson kept the ball and went around the right side for three yards and six points. Allen Leavitt made the extra-point, and Georgia went ahead for keeps.

Alabama boosters still had hope until the Bulldogs called on the infantry for a 61-yard touchdown production on ten rushes in the third period. Goff let McLee, Al Pollard, and Williams do the running through huge holes created by its offensive line. McLee had the longest gain of 12-yards, to the 17-yard line, and Williams scored from the two-yard line with 3:18 left in the third quarter.

Erk Russell's Runts kept dropping Tide tailbacks for losses, and Georgia cashed-in a surplus touchdown after Brad Cescutti recovered a Cal Culliver fumble at the 'Bama 20-yard line. Then, two plays later, Robinson rifled to Norris for a six-yard touchdown.

When it was all over, Bryant had no more success eluding the Bulldogs than his tailbacks had during the game. They encircled the winningest coach alive to shake his hand. Finally, the Bear gripped paws with Coach Dooley and congratulated him.

It would be a memorable day in Sanford Stadium when Dooley was floating on air after the Bear and his Tide sank to the bottom of the Southeastern Conference standings. It didn't take Dooley too long to get his feet back on the ground. He was cautioning one and all that Ole Miss would be on the rebound after its loss to Auburn. Georgia played the Rebels the next weekend and had their undefeated season derailed in Oxford, Mississippi.

Georgia 13 – Georgia Tech 10, November 27, 1976

On Saturday, November 27, 1976, inside of Sanford Stadium, Georgia Tech was not convinced the Bulldogs, 10-1, were any better than the Jackets, 4-6-1. Grimly, dejectedly, Georgia Tech's gallant underdogs trudged off the field of battle. A steady rain dripped from Yellow Jacket uniforms. A loss to Georgia dripped from their eyes.

Georgia Tech had traveled into Sanford Stadium to play one of the strongest Georgia teams of all-time. The Southeastern Conference champion 'Dogs were 9-1-0, and ranked number four in the nation. Five weeks later, Georgia had a date to play number one ranked Pittsburgh, and Heisman winner Tony Dorsett, for the mythical national title in the Sugar Bowl. In the intervening time, the 'Dogs had to play a 4-5-1 Georgia Tech squad that hadn't been ranked in years, and had its worst defense in team history.

It was what Coach Dooley called, "championship football." Some called it luck. Others called it "Devine Providence," that saw the University of Georgia through, again, in Dooley's words, "real stress," in the 13-10 victory over its most hated rival, Georgia Tech. A crowd of over 60,500, along with another 10,000 looking on from outside of Sanford Stadium, were left stunned and in disbelief.

Cornerback Bill Krug, who recovered a fumble, which led to a field-goal, which won the game, with five seconds remaining, chose the latter explanation. With just over three minutes remaining, Georgia quarterback Ray Goff fumbled the ball and Don Bessillieu, a Georgia Tech defensive back, recovered on Jackets' 29-yard line.

On the first play, Gnats' halfback Adrian Rucker slashed for four yards, to the 34-yard line, where he was simultaneously dealt a crushing blow from Dickey Clark, Jeff Sanders and linebacker Ben Zambiasi. Rucker coughed-up the ball and Krug recovered.

The show wasn't over. After three plays, Georgia was a fraction of an inch shy of a first down, on Tech's 24-yard line. Coach Dooley decided not to send kicker Allan Leavitt in to attempt a 41-yard field-goal, though it was within his range.

There wasn't any need for imagination on the fourth-down play. Everybody in the stadium knew Goff would run a quarterback sneak to the right of center Joe Tereshinski and over All-American guard Joel Parrish. Goff got the first down, and after one more running play, plus a timeout to kill the clock with nine seconds left, Leavitt was sent in to save the season.

It was apparent from the opening kickoff that both teams had similar game plans—keep the ball on the ground and don't make mistakes. A low scoring game was in the making.

It was a waste of time to pump air into the ball for this one. Even though Tech's pass defense had been extremely vulnerable, Goff only attempted five passes, completing four for 63 yards. He had one interception. Tech's freshman quarterback, Gary Lanier, was a strong runner, who almost broke clear on a 45-yard run, was intercepted on both his passes. Drew Hill accounted for Tech's nine air yards when he hit John Steele on a triple reverse.

Junior running back Kevin McLee rushed 30 times into a Tech defense and gained 105-yards. His total for the season was 1,058 yards. He accomplished something no other Georgia running back before him—including Frank Sinkwich, Charlie Trippi, and Glynn Harrison—had been able to do. He gained over 1,000 yards in a single season. Al Pollard had 112 yards on 24 carries. Pollard and McLee accounted for most of Georgia's 246 rushing yards.

Tech's Lanier had 73-rushing yards, Dave Sims had 70-yards, and Eddie Lee Ivery 63-yards, as the Wishbone rolled for 275 yards against the Junkyard Dogs. But the 'Dogs rose to the occasion when it counted, halting Tech at the ten-yard line, via a fumble, in the second quarter and at the one yard line, when Coach Pepper Rogers went for a field-goal on fourth down, in the final quarter.

Down 10-0, as a result of Goff's three-yard touchdown run in the second quarter, and a 22-yard field-goal by Leavitt in the third period, Tech had moved to the Georgia one-yard line, after Lucius Sanford recovered a Goff pitchout on the Bulldogs 19-yard line.

With 12:07 remaining in the game, and down 10-0, Coach Rogers decided to go for a field-goal on fourth down, with the ball at the one yard line. Dan Smith kicked an 18-yard field-goal and cut the deficit to 10-3.

The Yellow Jackets struck again on an 80-yard drive, with Ivery circling around the left side on a 26-yard touchdown. Smith made the extra-point to set the stage for the cardiac finish with 6:53 remaining. Gene Washington returned the ensuing kickoff 33-yards. Then, Goff, McLee, and Pollard hammered it to the Tech 29-yard line. That was when Goff fumbled and Bessillieu recovered for Tech. With 3:09 remaining, Tech would fumble the ball on its first play from scrimmage. Rucker was struck by the aforementioned Georgia players and Krug recovered on the 34-yard line of Tech.

Once Goff found his helmet, he had tossed after his previous fumble, he exhibited amazing poise. He worked on the ground against the Yellow Jackets and the clock. His quarterback keeper, for a first down at the 23-yard line, enabled Georgia to win. Three snaps later, with nine seconds left, the Bulldogs used their last time out. Leavitt then broke the tie and Georgia Tech's heart with his winning field-goal.

It had been a rainy day in Athens, and the game started out sloppy with Tech punting the ball on its first drive. Georgia took over at its own 40-yard line and Goff quickly moved the ball down to the Tech 33-yard line before the drive stalled. Leavitt proceeded to miss on a long field-goal attempt.

After exchanging several punts, Tech started at its own 33-yard line, late in the quarter, and started building confidence against Georgia's defense. Inside the 10-yard line, Ivery fumbled and Georgia's Lawrence Craft recovered the ball.

With less than three minutes before halftime, Goff started to his right, and cut sharp into a path cleared by Georgia's All-American tandem of Mike Wilson and Parrish. He lunged into the endzone—minus his jersey—left behind in the hands of Tech linebacker Reggie Wilkes. Georgia led at halftime 7-0.

Georgia opened the second half by marching down to Tech's five-yard line, before a fumble knocked the ball back to the 13-yard line, where Georgia recovered. Leavitt kicked a field-goal from there and made the score 10-0.

Afterwards, the rains came pouring down, and Georgia's problems started.

Tech used its wishbone to move down to Georgia's eight-yard line. That was where the Junkyard Dawgs' defense stopped Tech. The Yellow Jackets got down to the one-yard line. There, Tech called a time-out. Instead of going for the touchdown, Coach Rogers decided to go for the field-goal. Smith kicked it perfectly through the uprights.

Georgia's entire season would come down to the final few seconds of the game, not simply Sugar Bowl pride and national ratings, but Georgia against Tech. Then, just before the last gush of fog rolled-in, with nine seconds left in the game, Leavitt kicked the 33-yard field-goal to beat Tech 13-10, and keep the 'Dogs national title hopes alive. "It was like a graveyard on the sidelines," Leavitt later admitted of the tension-filled moments leading up to the winning kick. "Not a soul would say a word to me." Georgia finished the season 10-2 after getting stomped in the Sugar Bowl 27-3. Tech stayed home for the holidays.

Georgia 0 – Kentucky 33, October 2, 1977

Prince Charles captivated a cheering Sanford Stadium crowd of over 60,000 as he took a stroll between the hedges. Escorted by University President Fred C. Davidson, Charles proceeded to walk from the west end of the stadium to the east end, stopping just in front of the goal post. The Prince was greeted there by Georgia Coach Vince Dooley, Kentucky Coach Fran Curri, Jeff Lewis of Georgia, Art Still of Kentucky and several game officials.

The Prince smiled as he talked with the coaches and players, and Lewis presented him with an autographed football from the team. People in the stands stood on tiptoes and strained to get a better view of the Prince. "He's too short," one woman commented as the Prince walked beside the taller Davison. Unfortunately, after the small in stature Prince returned to the President's box to watch the game, the carnage commenced.

In 1977, the Wildcats of Kentucky had the best football team money could buy. It seemed Kentucky proved why many believed the Wildcats would be the team to claim the Southeastern Conference title when they soundly defeated the Bulldogs 33-0.

Kentucky did what few teams had been able to do against a team coached by Vince Dooley. First, the Cats handed Dooley his largest margin of defeat, in a regular season game, and his third of four shutouts ever.

"We were whipped soundly by a great football team," a tactful Dooley said afterwards. "Anybody who saw the game observed us hang in there for one quarter, but after the first quarter, Kentucky dominated the football game during the second, third and fourth quarters."

Dooley supported the idea Kentucky had a team capable of capturing the Southeastern Conference title. However, recruiting violations eliminated the Wildcats from participating in any bowl games, specifically the Sugar Bowl. "Kentucky was not a one-game affair," he said. "They've soundly won five football games, defeating some very fine teams. This has been Kentucky's year since they got beat early in the season by Baylor. Three of the five games they've played, and won, were in their opponent's backyard."

Wildcat's Coach Curci had no inkling the game would unfurl as it did.

"Never in my wildest dreams did I think we would dominate Georgia like we did," he said. "I know we have a good team, but today we got a blocked punt, an interception and a fumble recovery. Whenever we get that, and play well, we're going to whip anybody."

The game began slowly, and appeared to be a defensive battle, but the Wildcats suddenly sprang to life and posted 10 points on the board in the second quarter. Joe Bryant's one yard field-goal, following a missed attempt from earlier, put the Wildcats ahead to stay at 8:14 of the first quarter. Kentucky quarterback Derrick Ramsey tossed the first of three touchdown strikes to Freddie Williams, and put the Cats on top by 10 at halftime.

There was an elongated intermission featuring the Prince of Wales and the King of Soul, James Brown. Brown did his rendition of "Dooley's Junkyard Dogs," and other "Georgia" songs. Still, Kentucky picked-up where it left off in the third quarter. Moving 79-yards in just over two minutes, 47 of them on a Williams burst around end. The Cats tallied again when Ramsey sought out wide receiver Dave Trosper on a 17-yard touchdown pass, to put the Cats up 17-0.

Shorty before the end of the third quarter, Bryant struck gold from 51 yards and Kentucky surged on, avenging its 1976 loss of 31-7 to the 'Dogs, in Lexington. Ramsey, who accounted for 187 yards passing and rushing, again led his offensive unit on a sustained scoring drive, moving 60-yards in 12 plays before hitting wide receiver Felix Wilson in the left corner of the endzone. Bryant added his ninth point of the afternoon and, as the crowd began to file out of Sanford Stadium, the scoreboard showed Kentucky up by 27.

Sophomore reserve quarterback Mike Deaton, whom many Wildcat followers felt should have been playing in place of Ramsey, came in to throw a touchdown pass, for good measure, with 3:34 remaining to play. Deaton's pass to tight end Greg Nord covered 10-yards and, for the first time all day, Bryant failed on an extra-point-attempt to close the scoring.

Georgia 16 – Baylor 14, September 16, 1978

Two college football teams recuperating from the malady of identical 5-6 seasons, met on the road to recovery in Sanford Stadium, and only one came away with its health—and that one was the long shot. The Georgia Bulldogs had been looked upon by the specialists, who operate in the sporting grooms, as a bad risk—by a 3-point margin—but rising-up from their bed of thorns, they scratched and clawed out a 16-14 win over the Baylor University Bears of the Southwest Conference before a moderate crowd.

There would no joy on the banks of the Brazos River back in Texas, for the one great scorer had come to write against the team that Grant Teaff had called the best since he came to Baylor's campus to coach six years earlier. It made it all the sweeter for Coach Dooley, who had viewed his own Georgia group as the mystery team of the year.

Dooley's middle name is Joseph, but after what happened against Baylor inside of Sanford Stadium, between the hours of 1:30PM - 4:28PM, a large quantity of Georgia followers requested that Dooley change Joseph to Wolf.

The 43,000 fans, approximately 42,950 of them Georgia rooters, saw the much maligned Bulldogs, criticized by the coach himself, open the season by putting the bite on Baylor's heavily favored Bears. It was what one would call a victory balance. When Georgia needed defense, it came up with defense. When Georgia needed offense, it came up with offense. When it needed Noble Rexford Robinson, the player with the golden foot came through with such admirable results that he would go into the record book as one of the few who had kicked four field-goals in an NCAA game, all clean and acceptable, but gets credit for only three. Georgia threw one back in the first half, for bigger fish, when Baylor jumped offside and the "Dogs chose the first down.

Prior to the game, and ever since Georgia Tech beat Georgia during the last game of 1977, Dooley had been crying 'wolf' to anybody who would listen. It was a very familiar shtick: Georgia is too young; there are only one or two proven winners on the defense; 10 players are starting their first college game; Baylor has its best team ever, etc....

If that was Coach Teaff's best outfit ever, folks should have been worried for him. If Georgia's players were too young, they forgot their diapers. When they played Baylor, they came of age. If the defense was lacking, nobody told Ricky McBride, or Jimmy Payne. Georgia proved Coach Dooley wrong.

The Bulldogs, playing before a regional ABC-TV audience, uncovered several stars, two already known in the South, and a third name, which would become quite familiar throughout the state during the weeks that followed.

Rex Robinson and Willie McClendon, the old hands, were quite a one-two punch by themselves. The new comer, freshman Jimmy Payne, out of Cedar Shoals, proved to be the Johnny-on-the-spot several times, coming up with a key fumble recovery late in the game to help preserve the win.

Robinson's right foot accounted for ten of Georgia's points. The Marietta sophomore toed field-goals of 43, 38, and 36 yards, including one extra-point. McClendon, looking every bit the part of at least an All-Southeastern Conference player, rushed for 106 tough yards on 26 carries.

Payne, giving the appearance of a senior, rather than a first-year man, made a fumble recovery in the fourth period that led to Georgia's lone touchdown of the afternoon.

Baylor, though perhaps not as good as advertised by Dooley, did have a few stars of its own to brag about. Running back Greg Hawthorne carried the ball 24 times for 127 yards, and linebacker Mike Singletary wouldn't be forgotten around the South for many decades. He was in on an unbelievable number of 24 tackles, six solos, and 18 assists.

The game itself boiled down to a 15-minute contest between the Bears and the Bulldogs, with the Bulldogs proving superior in the fourth period by a 10-7 count.

Late in the third period, with Georgia trailing 7-6, the Bulldogs started a march that would result in three points.

With 4:48 to play in the period, the 'Dogs took the ball on their own 20-yard line, following a missed field-goal attempt by Baylor's Robert Bledsoe. Fourteen plays later, Georgia had driven 60-yards for the go ahead field-goal when Robinson split the uprights from 36-yards away.

Ronnie Stewart, an impressive performer in the late going, came-up with big runs to keep key drives alive.

Hawthorne, who was pretty optimistic about the way the Bear offense performed on the afternoon, hauled in three Steve Smith passes for a total of 26-yards, his longest an 11-yarder.

"We played good offensively as a whole, but we made too many mistakes. We busted assignments, missed play calls, and fumbled the ball when it counted," Hawthorne commented.

Oddly enough, it was Hawthorne, the Bear's offensive star of the game with 153 total yards, who coughed-up the football to kill a Baylor drive late in the game.

With 2:54 left to play, the Baylor quarterback handed off to Hawthorne, who ran into a wall of Georgia defenders and fumbled. Georgia's Pat Collins recovered and the 'Dogs ran out the clock.

"The turnover was the key play," said Jeff Pyburn, "In the huddle we said, 'Fellows, it's ours for the taking.' We were jacked-up because we knew if we ran out the clock, we had the game."

Collins tried to be a bit modest about the fumble recovery, not wishing to sound like a braggart, but he beamed when he said, "It helped. It inspired the offense. They knew if they could hold on, they had the game."

Dooley called the win as "satisfying" as any opening-day victory. "Of course, I think back to beating Alabama, but that was so long ago that my memory is fading."

"We whipped a good football team today, but I'm glad we played Baylor for the first game in September instead of late in November, in Waco, Texas." Such was Vince Dooley's assessment of his Georgia Bulldogs win over the Baylor Bears in Sanford Stadium before a less than overflow crowd.

Georgia 29 - Georgia Tech 28, December 2, 1978

The day began with a heavy fog hanging over Athens most of morning. The crowd was shoving its way into position early, out of the motels, to the parking lots, and gathering around the trunks of their cars, which looked like large-mounted animals with their lids up. On the trestle, at the east end of Sanford Stadium, the eaves-peeping mob had assembled early, and great was the conviviality and the booziness among them. Their numbers indicated the tempo of the day and their mood.

In the final synopsis, it had come down to Georgia leading 29-28. There were two minutes and fifteen seconds blinking on the big scoreboard clock. Tech's Mike Kelley, the freshman, throwing to George Moore, the big sophomore end from Columbia High School in Decatur, so slightly recruited he hadn't even made Tech's press guide. It was Kelley to Moore for 20-yards. Kelly again to Moore, and the ball was at midfield. Kelley to Moore again to the 37-yard line of Georgia, with Moore making catches with a complete and blatant disregard for his body.

Only one more throw, and one more catch was needed to get the ball within chunky Johnny Smith's field-goal range, with time to spare. "Kelley drops back," as they say on the radio, 'he's looking, he's looking, he throws and...." David Archer, a freshman from Atlanta, on the field for the first time—he didn't even have his name above his number "14"—threw himself in front of the sinking ball, sparing nothing of himself, and pressed the ball to his chest. Georgia Tech was dead.

In 1978, they called them Bulldogs, Underdogs and Wonderdogs, but most of all they were called Winning Dogs. In fact, during his first fifteen seasons as Georgia's head coach, Vince Dooley had never had a team like this 1978 team that continuously flirted with defeat before figuring out some way to win.

Georgia boosters were so stunned and silent that you could hear a fumble drop as Georgia Tech zipped into a 17-0 lead in the first quarter, and boosted the lead to 20-0 before the Bulldogs did anything to promote a cheer. The 59,700 who saw the nationally televised game live inside of Sanford Stadium never dreamed they would see, before the afternoon was over, perhaps the most exciting game since they kicked the first football at Herty Field in 1892.

When they apparently had run out of miracles, the Wonderdogs put it all together and finally downed Georgia Tech 29-28, as Anthony Arnold crossed into the endzone on a two-point run with 2:24 left on the clock. Minutes earlier he had caught a 42-yard touchdown pass from quarterback Buck Belue.

The state-championship shootout was even more exciting than the score indicated. The back-to-back scoring plays, covering 173-yards, in the explosive 22-point third quarter, was an accurate idea of what kind of contest it was. Old timers vowed there hadn't been one like it since Doctor Sanford built his stadium.

Cornerback Scott Woerner, voted the game's outstanding defensive player, scored on a 72-yard punt return to put Georgia ahead for the first time at 21-20. But on the ensuing kickoff, Drew Hill raced 101-yards, to put Tech ahead again 26-21. Then Kelley passed to Moore for two points to give Tech a 28-21 lead.

There were many heroes wearing red and black, and white and gold. Even the most ardent Georgia zealot wouldn't have argued the outstanding individual was Tech's tailback Eddie Lee Ivery. In less than three quarters, he gained 160-yards on 25 carries, and scored one touchdown. Ivery went down as Tech's all-time career and single season rushing leader.

When he was assisted off the field with 1:09 remaining in the third quarter, suffering a severely sprained right ankle, an eerie hush fell over the Tech fans. He ended the season with 1,502 rushing yards. Most Tech fans felt if Ivery, possibly the best player in the nation, had not been injured, the Gnats would have likely been able to hold a lead that vanished at the 11th hour.

Georgia tailback Willie McClendon, the Southeastern Conference Player of the Year, lost his yardage duel with Ivery, but he was the 'Dogs leading rusher with 73-yards on 23 carries, and scored two touchdowns. He boosted his record Georgia rushing total to 1,312 yards on the season.

The co-stars of the winning Georgia 84-yard march in the fourth quarter were freshman quarterback Buck Belue, and sophomore flanker Arnold, a former quarterback at Cedar Shoals in Athens. Belue had come in to replace Jeff Pyburn when Georgia was down 20-0, late in the second quarter. But, it was Arnold who passed, caught and ran to spark the winning drive.

The drive started when freshman tailback Matt Simon threw an incomplete pass. Belue then hit Lindsay Scott, who had seven receptions for 50-yards during the game. Later, on fourth and two, Belue rolled to his right for six yards and a first down. Then, Arnold came in and passed 20-yards to Simon. Faced with a fourth down and three yards, on the Tech 42-yard line, it was Belue, exhibiting amazing poise for a freshman, who rolled to his right and started to run for the first down. He quickly spotted Arnold, who had slipped past the cornerback, and hit him with a 42-yard scoring strike with 2:24 left in the game.

The Wonderdogs, who a week earlier lost an opportunity for a trip to the Sugar Bowl and the Southeastern Conference title, after not going for two against Auburn, refused to consider a tie this time. The 'Dogs promptly lined-up for a two-point attempt. Belue picked Mark Hodge as his target in the end-zone, but a Tech linebacker, Henry Johnson, belted Hodge down and was called for pass interference. Now, Georgia needed one yard for two points.

Once again, Belue and Arnold bamboozled the Jackets. On what started as a fake to McClendon up the middle, Belue kept the ball and pitched out to Arnold, who ran, untouched, into the endzone with the winning two-pointer under his arm.

Ironically, one of the most important plays of the game might have occurred in the second quarter when Tech had a first down on the Georgia six-yard line, and settled for a 20-yard field-goal by Johnny Smith. On third down at the one-yard line, Kelley missed a handoff to Ivery, then slipped and fell for a two yard loss.

At the outset, there was no indication the Jackets would be worrying about a two-yard loss. In fact, on the first offensive series, McClendon had fumbled on the Georgia 31-yard line, and Al Richardson recovered for Tech. Kelley flipped to Hill for 14-yards on the long gainer, then, Ivery scored the touchdown from four. Smith converted and Tech led 7-0.

Next, the Jackets startled the Bulldogs with an onside kick, so neatly executed by Don Bessillieu that many fans thought he'd crudely missed the ball. Jeff Shank recovered for the Jackets on the Georgia 42-yard line. The elusive Ivery accounted for 28 of the yards before Rodney Lee scored from the one.

When Scott fumbled the ensuing kickoff, Sheldon Fox recovered at the Bulldogs' 17-yard line. Georgia's defense held, and forced a field-goal. Smith hit a 28-yarder. The underdog Gnats held an astonishing 17-0 lead with 4:09 remaining in the first quarter.

Nothing was working for Georgia. After Woerner returned a punt 45-yards, to the Jackets 23-yard line, the 'Dogs forked it over again when Ronnie Stewart fumbled at the Tech 18-yard line. That was when Kelley slipped down at the one yard line for the big two yard loss. Smith boosted the bulge to 20-0 with a 20-yard field-goal.

After several exchanges of the football, Woerner took a wallop when a Tech defender prematurely hit him as he attempted to catch a punt. With excellent field position after the penalty, Belue came in to replace Pyburn. Georgia then proceeded to score its first touchdown just before halftime.

Woerner, who had a tremendous day for Georgia, intercepted Kelley on the first series in the third quarter, and Georgia moved 39-yards in nine plays. On the ninth play, McClendon scored from the two-yard line. When Robinson converted, Georgia trailed 20-14. In the fourth quarter, Woerner finally put the Bulldogs ahead after he shed at least four would-be tacklers, enroute to a captivating 72-yard punt return. On the following kickoff, with the fevered fans roaring, Robinson kicked the ball one-yard deep into the endzone, where Hill took it. He shot forwards, split the alley, enroute to a 101-yard touchdown.

With less than three minutes to play, on a fourth-and-four, Belue passed to Arnold for a 43-yard touchdown. On a two-point attempt, Belue pitched back to Arnold, who went untouched into the endzone. Georgia was up 29-28 with 2:35 seconds left in the game. On the ensuing drive, Tech made it to the Georgia 37-yard line before Archer came in and made an interception to end the game.

However, there was no brighter star wearing Georgia colors than senior linebacker Ricky McBride, who made 15 solo tackles and had four assists. Woerner, and rover back Chris Welton, each had a total of ten assists and tackles.

Georgia went on to play Stanford in the Bluebonnet Bowl in Houston, Texas, where the 'Dogs lost 25-22, after leading at halftime 22-0. The Bulldogs finished the season at 9-2-1. Tech would go on to lose the Peach Bowl against Purdue.

Georgia 42 – Texas A&M 0, September 13, 1980

"Go you Silver Britches!" These signs and posters, proclaiming the return of Georgia's silver pants, littered the campus. From World War II until the beginning of the Vietnam era, circa '64, that was the cry heard many a Saturday afternoon in Sanford Stadium as Georgia did battle 'tween the hedges.

Georgia's all-time greats ran on the field to the exhortations of the Bulldog fans who loved their team wearing those silver britches. Among those legends were Georgia's only Heisman Trophy winner Frank Sinkwich, as well as Charlie Trippi, and Zippy Morocco.

In 1964, after suffering through three straight losing seasons, Georgia hired a new coach, Vince Dooley, and he brought in a new scheme of things. One move to revamp the situation at Georgia was to change the image of the team, which was partially achieved by changing the uniforms. Out went the silver britches and silver helmets, and in came what most of the younger fans remember, the red and black jerseys, with white pants and red helmets.

The Texas A&M game would be Herschel Walker's first game inside of Sanford Stadium. After a 16 year absence, the Dogs roared into Sanford Stadium wearing their silver britches, to the approval of over 60,000 fans.

The previous week against Tennessee, in Knoxville, Georgia fans saw a small piece of history because the 95,288 fans had been the largest crowd to ever see a football game in the South; however, the most historical part of what occurred was the debut of Walker.

Those who saw Walker were comparing him with Earl Campbell, Tony Dorsett, Red Grange, Jim Thorpe, O.J. Simpson, and anybody you cared to mention. In the Sanford Stadium debut of the "Wrightsville Wrecker," he had twenty-one carries for 145-yards and three touchdowns. The most gained by a Georgia back since Willie McClendon ran for 149-yards against Virginia Military Institute in '78, to break Frank Sinkwich's single-season Georgia rushing record. Walker's domination was so incredible that he would spend the last 19 minutes of the game sitting on the bench as a spectator. He was given the afternoon off after he broke loose on a 76-yard touchdown run in the second half. Walker was only half of Georgia's wide-open offense against A&M, though, while a deadly Bulldog aerial attack accounted for three other touchdowns in the 42-0 burial of A&M.

But quarterback Buck Belue saw the freshman speedster as a factor, even in the passing category. "Herschel just opens a lot of things up in the passing game," Belue said.

In truth, Walker single-handedly rejuvenated a Bulldog offense which was disadvantaged by a lack of speed in '79, and he spurred the Dogs to a 2-0 start in '80.

Excellent playing on both the offensive and defensive lines, and good overall play by special teams, kept A&M in trouble. Jim Broadway's punting kept the 'Dogs out of strife. Rex Robinson drilled six extra-points to extend his consecutive point-after-attempts record to 73.

Coach Dooley was so satisfied with the play of his squad, he admitted it would take him a second look to find anything wrong with its performance on Saturday.

Georgia's offense rolled-up 417 total yards with a balanced attack, gaining 207 on the ground and 210 yard through the air. Belue riddled the Aggie secondary, completing six of 13 passes for 147-yards and two touchdowns, both to flanker Anthony Arnold.

Georgia first got on the scoreboard when Belue found Arnold in the endzone with a three-yard strike in the first quarter. The quarterback from Valdosta would hit Arnold with a 19-yard throw late in the first half for the 'Dogs' third touchdown of the game.

Arnold, who caught another pass for 27-yards, to later set-up his own scoring reception, said after the game he was pleased with the more wide-open passing game the Dogs adopted against A&M.

Georgia's other touchdown pass came in the second quarter when second-string quarterback, Jeff Paulk, hit Chuck Jones in the endzone with only seven seconds remaining before half time.

Four other Georgia receivers had catches of 23-yards or more against the Aggies, most notably Norris Brown's 53-yard grab that made it to the A&M two yard line. The catch would set-up Walker's first touchdown early in the second quarter.

Walker's power running was incredibly dominant. After a 58-yard punt return by Scott Woerner, Walker powered his way into the endzone from the one yard line. Coach Dooley was fascinated with the goal-line play on his tailback. "That is the value of Herschel—he is big and strong and can get that extra foot or yard that is the difference in scoring."

But Walker was most impressive in the third quarter when he broke loose on a 76-yard touchdown scamper for Georgia. On the strength of a couple of good blocks from his linemen, most notably Hugh Nall, Walker went practically untouched through the A&M defense. He ran with no one in front of him for most of the 76-yards. Walker had 21 carries for a 6.9 yards average.

Walker's performance followed a stunning entrance against Tennessee in which he ran over, instead of around, the Vols defense, for most of the night. If truth be told, on his first touchdown run against Tennessee, a 16-yard burst up the middle, he ran straight into sophomore defensive back Bill Bates, then through two other would-be tacklers, to score. And, except for his second scoring run, a nine-yarder, most of this other runs were straight into, not around, Tennessee defenders. His two touchdown runs, plus a Georgia safety after a fumbled Tennessee punt, brought the Dogs back from a 15-0 first half deficit.

In 1980, after playing in six quarters of two games, Walker had scored five touchdowns and rushed for 229-yards in helping Georgia to its best start in two seasons. What was Walker's explanation for his running style? "They say the shortest distance between two points is straight ahead—at least I've found that was true."

Georgia 20 – Clemson 16, September 20, 1980

A legend was gone. William Tate, dean of men emeritus, and an institution at the University for over two generations, died during the week of the Georgia versus Clemson game. Whether watching hawk-like over late registration at the Coliseum, helping to quell a student demonstration, or taking new students on a tour of the campus, he represented all that was good at the University of Georgia.

Woerner's 67-yard punt return versus Clemson, 1980

Against Clemson, on a hot fall afternoon, Georgia's offense showed-up for only the second half; however, the 'Dogs' defense compensated with some big plays to guide Georgia to a 20-16 win.

The offense entered the game in the second half and accounted for six points of its own with two Rex Robinson field-goals, but it was the Scott Woerner-led defense which was responsible for 14 first half points, enabling the Dogs to win a Clemson-dominated battle.

Buck Belue and his cohorts were only on the field for five minutes during the first half, garnering no first downs and only 33 total yards. Clemson's offense ran over the Dog defense for 16 first downs and 239-yards, while holding the ball twenty-five minutes.

But Woerner, who did not start on defense for the first time in his collegiate career, assumed an offensive role. He returned the Tigers' first punt for a 67-yard touchdown early in the game. Later, during the first quarter, the cornerback from Jonesboro intercepted a Tiger pass in the Georgia endzone and returned it 98-yards to the Clemson two-yard line. The interception return gave Georgia an easy touchdown.

Coach Dooley had nothing but compliments for Woerner. "What a great day he had," Dooley said, "returning the punt, then the interception. He gave us our only points of the half."

Dooley didn't complain about the rest of Georgia's performance, either, even though the Tigers whipped the 'Dogs everywhere but on the scoreboard. Georgia had only 10 first downs to Clemson's 26 and 157 total yards to Clemson's 351 yards.

"Despite the things that happened to us, and things went against us during the game, we came back and we held on in some really adverse conditions," Dooley related.

Most of that holding-on was done by the 'Dogs' defense, who was stingy around their own goal line when it counted. When the Tigers threatened at the 'Dogs' 10-yard line late in the game, senior safety Jeff Hipp picked-off a Mike Gasque pass to finally kill a Clemson offense which had annoyed the Georgia defense all day.

The only Clemson touchdown came on a fluke play midway through the second quarter, after an interference penalty put the Tigers on the Georgia one-yard line. The 'Dogs defense forced a fumble on a Clemson run-up the middle, but Gasque scooped-up the ball and ran into the endzone to score.

Clemson's only other score of the half came in the last minute of the period when Obed Ariri, who had missed his first field-goal earlier during the game, breaking his streak of 14 straight, kicked a field-goal from 22-yards away to narrow the Tiger's deficit to 14-10.

Finally, the defense got a little help in the second half when the 'Dogs scored on their first drive of the half, with a Robinson field-goal from 42-yards away. Georgia was powered mostly by the running of freshman tailback Herschel Walker. The 'Dogs went from their own 23-yard line to the Clemson 25-yard line, before being stopped by a strong Clemson defense. Georgia settled for a field-goal.

The defense returned the favor on the next drive when Robert Miles picked-off a Gasque pass meant for wide receiver Jerry Gaillard. Miles' interception culminated in another Robinson field-goal that gave Georgia a 20-10 lead. Robinson's two field-goals and two extra-points were the difference in the game.

After the Dogs looked like they might take control, Clemson drove down the field again. Aided by a roughing the passer penalty, which kept their drive alive, the Tigers narrowed the deficit with a 45-yard field-goal by Ariri.

After the two teams exchanged the ball several more times, Clemson finally scored again, late in the fourth quarter. It was another field-goal, by Ariri, from 25-yards away.

Georgia looked like it was in control after getting the ball back. The 'Dogs' drove to the Clemson 42-yard line, and had a first down with less than six minutes remaining. On the next two plays, the 'Dogs were thrown for two losses. Jim Broadway had to come in to punt. Broadway fumbled the punt from center, and the Tigers took over on the Georgia 41-yard line.

The Tigers picked-up two yards on the first play, then Woerner was called for pass interference, which put the ball on the Georgia two-yard line. It set the stage for Hipp's heroics. After Hipp's interception, Walker took the Bulldogs out of trouble by running 20-yards to the Georgia 27-yard line. Georgia held-on to win the game 20-16.

Georgia 13 – South Carolina 10, November 1, 1980

On November 1, 1980, the South Carolina Gamecocks were 6-1, and ranked fourteenth in the nation. Georgia was 7-0 and ranked fourth in the polls.

The 62,200 fans who packed Sanford Stadium witnessed a classic. There had been a lot of discussion about the matchup between Herschel Walker and George Rogers. In fact, it all came down to a Walker 76-yard jaunt, a Rogers fumble late in the fourth quarter and a Herschel dominated drive that reached the Gamecock one yard-line.

Georgia missed at least two scoring opportunities in the first half. Rex Robinson, the old reliable, missed a field-goal, and the Gamecocks stopped one Bulldog drive at their one yard line. Midway in the second period, the Bulldogs started a long drive from their own 20-yard line, seemingly in command and headed for the endzone. On the Carolina one-yard line, with a fourth down situation, Dooley said, "go for it." The Gamecocks defense was unyielding at their goal line. George Haffner called a pass play and the Carolina rush was effective. Buck Belue's pass fell incomplete.

In the third quarter, with Georgia on its own 24-yard line, Haffner sent word to Charlie Whittemore, who was on the sideline, to signal play "22" to Belue. This was a play which had not been all that good to the Georgia offense. Still, the coaches had spent time before the game analyzing what they were doing wrong. They decided, perhaps, they were delaying too much in giving the ball to the tailback, or maybe the defense was recognizing the play and having time to recover. The coaches made a decision to force the play to develop sooner. It required the offensive line to execute quicker. The tailback was instructed to start sooner, in order not to give the defense that extra split second to read and react.

When Haffner sent in the play everything clicked. The right guard blocked his man to the inside and fullback Jimmy Womack shot through and knocked down the middle linebacker. Lindsay Scott got on the left cornerback quickly. Walker blasted through the line in a flash, hit the sidelines, and outran the secondary 76-yards and gave Georgia an early 10-0 lead.

The South Carolina safety appeared to have the angle on Walker, but Herschel's afterburners could leave a lot of good athletes behind. Later Robinson added another field-goal, before South Carolina kicked one of their own to make the score 13-3.

Late in the third period, Carl West rushed for a Gamecock touchdown, leaving Georgia out front by the slim margin of 13-10. With seven minutes and 20 seconds remaining, Carolina had gained possession at Georgia's 47-yard line. Rogers commenced to pounding for yardage. It didn't look good for the home team, but like Erk Russell preached to his defense, bend but don't break. Even so, the Gamecocks had the advantage.

Rogers went for nine-yards. Next, he picked-up three-yards. Then, he gained eight-yards. Finally, he went for seven-yards, down to the Georgia 20-yard line. The 'Dogs needed a break.

Scott Woerner versus South Carolina, 1980

Rogers went out of the game for a play on which West gained three-yards. On second down, from the Georgia 17-yard line, an obviously tired Rogers, back in the game, got the handoff and headed to his right. He faked Scott Woerner, who missed with a straight ahead tackle. Instead, Woerner's headgear landed on Rogers' right arm, under which he was carrying the football. The ball had been loosened from Rogers' hold by the Woerner miss-hit. In the next second, defensive end Dale Carver rendered a jolting blow to Rogers. The ball was free. It was loose. A mass scramble ensued. There to recover it at the Georgia 16-yard line was defensive guard Tim Parks.

Carver and Parks never made any all-star teams. They claimed no awards. They were not household names, but they will forever be enshrined in the hearts of all Bulldogs who witnessed the 1980 regionally televised South Carolina game.

Georgia 38 - Georgia Tech 20, November 29, 1980

Saturday November 29th, 1980 would mark the last home game inside of Sanford before its east endzone would be enclosed. About 6,000 fans took to "The Tracks" for one last view of a football game from the perch many had come to know and love. It was the end of an era.

While Notre Dame would decide, in the Sugar Bowl, on New Year's Day, whether Georgia remained the number one ranked team in the nation, freshman tailback Herschel Walker had already proven he was the number one tailback and the greatest first-year back ever.

It would be the first time since 1927 that Georgia Tech played Georgia when the 'Dogs were ranked number in the nation. Unlike '27, when the Yellow Jackets cost Georgia a Rose Bowl trip and national title, the Maggots found themselves down 17-0 at halftime, in what experts figured to be a preliminary match into a heavyweight event. But, the great Walker guaranteed the Bulldogs remained unbeaten as the 'Dogs cruised to a 38-20 win.

After the 220-pound Walker scored three touchdowns and rushed for 205-yards on 25 carries, the partisan crowd of 62,800 wanted to reopen the Heisman Trophy polls which closed the previous Friday. His superb performance enabled him to break the freshman rushing record of 1,586 yards held by Tony Dorsett of Pittsburgh. Walker finished the regular season with 274 carries for 1,616 yards, with an average of 5.89 yards per carry.

Georgia Coach Vince Dooley, exhilarated about his first perfect season, he served as a spokesman for the Georgia delegates. "I wish they'd wait until after the last game to vote on the Heisman Trophy," Dooley related in the interview room after the game. "I don't think there's a player in the country more deserving. He has broken one of the great, great NCAA records and is on a team with a perfect record. What else can you say?"

Walker gained over 200-yards four times during the season and would rush for 151-yards against Notre Dame. Against Tech, he scored his first touchdown on a one-yard plunge in the first quarter. Then, he darted 23-yards for his second touchdown in the third quarter. Later, he broke Dorsett's record with a 65-yard touchdown run in the fourth quarter.

He was the difference between the nation's number one team and the state's number two team. In fact, Tech won only one game during a 1-9-1 campaign, which included a 3-3 tie with then top-ranked Notre Dame that elevated Georgia to the top spot. Georgia needed a huge game from Walker, because the Jackets had scored 20 points in the second half to trim the deficit to 31-20. The death knell for Tech was when Herschel broke loose on the 65-yard touchdown.

Walker wasn't the only player revising records on that momentous day. Tech junior quarterback, Mike Kelley, idle most of the season with a shoulder injury, riddled the Georgia defense for 335-yards. Completing a Tech record of 27 passes in 46 attempts to nine receivers, Kelley became the Jackets' all-time passing and total-yardage leader. He had a total of 4,407 yards, eclipsing the career mark of 4,262 set by Eddie McAshan from 1970-72.

As usual, quarterback Buck Belue had a big hand in the Georgia victory. The Bulldogs would go 26-3 in games where he had started. Against Tech, Belue hit on eight of 16 passes for 98 total yards, despite a season's high three interceptions. He got the Bulldogs moving on their first possession, completing a 31-yard pass to Walker. When the Jackets held, Rex Robinson kicked a 57-yard field-goal, with the 18-mile-per-hour wind behind him, breaking his own Southeastern Conference mark of 55-yards.

The next time Georgia got the ball, Belue negotiated a 43-yard touchdown drive in nine plays. He passed 15-yards to Norris Brown, then, connected with Lindsay Scott for 18-yards. On fourth and one, Walker got a first down, before picking-up the final yard for his first touchdown of the game and thirteenth of the season. Robinson kicked the first of his five extra-point attempts, which boosted his consecutive streak to 101 at the end of the game.

Leading 10-0, after one quarter, Georgia struck again with 4:16 remaining in the half, going fifty yards in seven plays. Walker got 36-yards in three snaps to launch the drive, and Belue passed five yards to Ronnie Stewart for the touchdown. With the score 17-0 at halftime, Georgia boosters were anticipating a rout, but those Gnats never gave-up. Despite all the adversity against them, the Jackets gave it 100 percent, providing Georgia an exhilarating finish.

The Jackets got on the board early in the third quarter on a quick 55-yard thrust. Tailback David Allen, having a career day, got 45 of his 98-yards on a run to the Georgia 5-yard line. After Kelley was dropped for a 10-yard loss, he rifled 15-yards to Leon Chadwick for a touchdown. Johnny Smith kicked his seventy-fourth extra-point, breaking the Tech record previously held by Bunky Henry.

During the Maggots' victory dance in the endzone, the Jackets' hit Georgia safety Scott Woerner in the celebration. It cost the Jackets a 15-yard penalty. The annoyed Woerner returned the ensuing kickoff 71-yards, to the Tech 24-yard line. As Curry said, every time Tech did something good, Walker did something better. This time he would skirt the right side for a 23-yard touchdown.

Herschel Walker breaking freshman rushing record, 1980

Once again, the rivals did the see-saw act. Tech went 55-yards in nine plays, with Allen scoring from the four yard line. But, the 24-14 score didn't stand for too long, because the 'Dogs went 58-yards in eight plays, with Belue scoring from the one, after Walker made a 20-yard run up the middle.

Next, the Jackets used thirteen plays for an 86-yard scoring drive. Kelley passed to Steve Henderson for the five-yard touchdown. With 11:11 remaining, it appeared Tech was in contention at 31-20, but Walker busted 65-yards, and it was all over with the final score of 38-20 on the boards. Georgia would defeat Notre Dame 17-10 on New Year's Day to claim its national title.

Georgia 13 - Clemson 7, September 6, 1982
Georgia and Clemson decided to move their annual rivalry to Labor Day night, in order for the game to be broadcast nationally, in prime time, by ABC. The game marked the first ever opening-week showdown between the two previous national champions, Georgia in '80 and Clemson in '81. It was a prelude to the "Kick-off Classics." This game would feature the largest nationally televised audience to ever view an opening-day college football game in colligate football history. Unfortunately, sixteen days before the game, the greatest player in the country, Herschel Walker, broke his thumb during practice and was not expected to play.

During the off season, Georgia's Athletic Department spent over $800,000.00 on a new lighting system so football games could once again be played at night inside of Sanford Stadium. It had been thirty-one years since the last night game had been played in Athens, in a game against Louisiana State University. A dozen poles, outfitted with 420 metal-halide bulbs, positioned 150 feet above the field, were mounted. The previous lights, from 1940, were unprepossessing and were taken away when Joel Eaves became Georgia's Athletic Director in 1963.

It would be difficult to exaggerate the implications of this game. Georgia was ranked as the seventh best team in the nation, while Clemson was ranked number nine. Coach Dooley, who turned fifty-years old a couple of days before this fifty-first game between Georgia and Clemson, was going for his 141st career win. The victory would move him past Coach Butts as the all-time winningest coach in Georgia football history.

The suspicion that Georgia had an ordinary offensive unit without Walker was quickly confirmed shortly after the ABC-TV cameras focused on the biggest night football game ever staged inside of storied Sanford Stadium. Over 82,000 fans watched as Clemson middle guard William 'Refrigerator" Perry recovered a fumbled exchange between Georgia center Wayne Radloff and first-time starting quarterback John Lastinger. Clemson quickly capitalized off the turnover and scored to take a 7-0 lead early in the first quarter.

The 'Dogs would have an opportunity to answer late in the first quarter. Georgia downed a punt at Clemson's one yard line and from there the Tigers were powerless to move the ball against Georgia's tightfisted defense and had to punt on a fourth and one from its ten-yard line. Georgia's Dale Carver blocked the punt as it left the foot of punter Dale Hatcher. The 'Dogs scored off the blocked punt and placekicker Kevin Butler efficiently converted the extra-point to tie the game 7-7.

In the second quarter, a 40-yard touchdown by Tron Jackson would be called back because of a holding penalty. It was a trick play that worked flawlessly after Walker had been sent in as a decoy, and Jackson got the ball on a reverse. Later, Butler attempted a 59-yard field-goal try, but missed. On Clemson's next possession, Tony Flack, the first true freshman to start a season opener for Coach Dooley, made a critical interception on Georgia's 40-yard line.

Georgia took the ball down into Clemson territory; however, faced with a fourth and one situation, Dooley elected to attempt the field-goal instead of going for the first down. Butler kicked a 39-yard field-goal to give Georgia a 10-7 lead at halftime.

During the second half Walker, whose thumb was wrapped in a large cast, was utilized more and gave Georgia the spark essential to drive down and score a touchdown. He plunged over from three yards out; however, the touchdown was called back on an offensive penalty. Butler came on and kicked a 23-yard field-goal to give Georgia a 13-7 lead.

As the game was nearing an end, Clemson rallied to get into Georgia territory. After the 'Dogs held, Clemson was forced into a fourth down situation. Coach Danny Ford called a time-out, and on the ensuring play, Nate "The Termite" Taylor intercepted Homer Jordan's pass. It was Jordon's fourth interception of the game.

Coincidentally, the previous season, Georgia's Buck Belue had thrown eight interceptions against Clemson at Death Valley.

In winning, the Bulldogs did unto Clemson what the Tigers did to them a year earlier. They ended Clemson's 13-game winning streak, the longest in the nation, and defeated the defending national champions. Clemson won the Atlantic Coast Conference after finishing the season with a 9-1-1 record. The Tigers would finish as the eight ranked team in the nation.

Georgia would finish the '82 season with its unprecedented third straight Southeastern Conference title, and an undefeated and untied season. The 'Dogs would play Penn State for the mythical national title. Unfortunately, Georgia finished fourth in the nation after losing the Sugar Bowl, while Penn State won its first ever national title. Walker, who played sparingly against Clemson, because of a broken thumb, would win the 1982 Heisman Trophy.

Georgia 17 – Brigham Young University 14, September 11, 1982

The Georgia Bulldogs opened the 1982 season with an almost impossible job of facing two teams with the nation's longest winning streaks. One team, Clemson, was the defending national champions. The other, the Cougars of Brigham Young, led by quarterback Steve Young, would become the greatest passing team to ever come into Sanford Stadium.

Unfortunately, Herschel Walker's broken thumb didn't seem to be all that was afflicting Georgia's offense. In the Georgia's 17-14 win over Brigham Young, the offense often looked as miserable and gloomy as the overcast weather.

A week earlier, Clemson provided a sprint-out type passer in Homer Jordon; whereas, pass-happy Brigham Young boasted a pure, drop back passer in the pro-set of Young. In fact, Young showed he meant business when he started the game off with eight straight passes. The Cougars drove to Georgia 24-yard line before being forced to attempt a field-goal. Though Young, passing the majority of the game, amassed 285-yards in the air, he tossed six interceptions. Georgia's defense held in crucial situations, and miraculously held the high-powered Cougars to 14 points.

Brigham Young's potent passing attack stretched Georgia's defense like salt water taffy, but those six interceptions kept the Cougars from pulling away. Georgia spread the pickoffs among five players: cornerback Ronnie Harris, who had two, safety Jeff Sanchez, cornerback Tony Flack, defensive end Tim Bobo and roverback Terry Hoage. Five interceptions came in the first half.

The teams traded touchdowns in the first quarter. Georgia scored first on a Barry Young 12-yard burst. Brigham Young was stopped on its first series after the score, then, Georgia tried to crank-up its passing game. A John Lastinger pass to Clarence Kay went astray and Tom Holmoe made an interception he would return, untouched, 63-yards for a touchdown. The Cougars scored their only offensive points against Georgia's defense in the third quarter when Young hit Scott Collie on a 21-yard touchdown play.

With less than six minutes to play, Georgia found itself down 14-7. Then, an unusual play occurred. Call it the "BYU Play." Call it the "Mike Weaver First Down Play." Or, call it the "Hot Football Play." Regardless of the name, Georgia offensive guard Mike Weaver won't forget it. Georgia started the drive on the Brigham Young 36-yard line. With a fourth-and-one on Brigham Young's 17-yard line, Georgia's Lastinger fumbled the snap from center Wayne Radloff. The fun commenced.

"I fell on the ball and pushed it as far as I could," Lastinger said of the fumble. "Herschel and I were lying face to face in the pile and he told me to give it to him, so I pushed it forward a little bit. I guess he passed it on up to Mike."

The fans rose and waited breathlessly. Lastinger stood-up and held his hand in the air. He didn't have the ball. "I heard the Brigham Young players saying, "The quarterback's got it, so I stood up and said, 'No, I don't have it.'"

The fans waited a little longer. Weaver rose and held the ball high in the air. Georgia picked-up the first down. The crowd went berserk. "John handed me the ball, and Mike was up a little ahead of me so I pushed it up to him," Walker said. "We were having fun."

Walker, who gained 127-yards in the game, had put Georgia back in the game during the fourth quarter. He would score over the middle, in the typical over-the-top manner from the one-yard line. With 5:36 left, Butler's extra-point tied the game at fourteen a piece.

The magnitude of two Brigham Young missed field-goals in the first half loomed large as the game clock wore down in the final minutes. Kurt Gunter missed a 41-yard attempt in the first quarter, then a 38-yard effort on the last play of the first half. Either would have forced Georgia to go for a touchdown to win late in the fourth quarter; however, with the score 14-14, Lastinger only needed to maneuver the 'Dogs into Butler's considerable long range.

The game winning field-goal was set-up by a 40-yard drive that started on the Georgia 33-yard line. Lastinger threw two incomplete passes, before hitting Kevin Harris for an 11-yard gain. Herschel then broke a 23-yarder to put Georgia on the Brigham Young 44-yard line. The final two plays put Georgia at the 28-yard line, when Tron Jackson swept right for a 1-yard gain. From there, Butler kicked the winner.

"I asked Tron to run right," Butler said. "My good kicks come from the right. Tron gave it his best shot at getting over there, and it helped a great deal."

Butler calmly made the 44-yard winning field-goal with 1:11 remaining. A few plays later and Harris would end Brigham Young's last drive with the sixth Georgia interception of the day, sealing Georgia's second win of the week.

Coach Dooley said something after the Brigham Young game that even the biggest Georgia fan would have had to agree with. "We were lucky," said Dooley, following his fifth-ranked 'Dogs' win over nineteenth ranked Brigham Young. "No question about that. We were fortunate to win this ball game. You have to have a little luck sometimes. We had our share. Brigham Young deserved to win. Give our team credit for finding a way to win. Coach LaVell Edwards knows his team played good enough to win."

While Georgia's front four only sacked Young three times, those six interceptions cost Brigham Young. Georgia amassed 275 yards of total offense, but its passing game was almost non-existent. Lastinger completed four of 15 pass attempts, including one interception, for thirty-six yards. With only four and a half days to prepare, the Georgia rushing attack gained yards in spurts. Of the five fumbles it incurred, the 'Dogs lost two.

Still, in the span of four and a half days, Georgia beat teams that were ranked number one and ten at the end of the previous season. In addition, Georgia ended the nation's two longest winning streaks in back-to-back games; all during the same week.

In the season opener against Clemson, the Tigers were ranked ninth by the *Associated Press*, and in its second game, against Brigham Young, the Cougars were ranked nineteenth in the nation by the *United Press International*. Georgia, ranked seventh in its season opener, beat both opponents, but would drop to eighth in the polls' of America's expert sports writers. Two years later Brigham Young would win the mythical national title.

Georgia 7 – Auburn 13, November 13, 1983

All good things must come to an end. On so many Saturday afternoons, in the locker room beneath the endzone seats of Sanford Stadium, eyes had sparkled and smiles had covered grimy faces. On twenty-four Saturdays, spanning four years, to be exact, the voices were cheerful, talking about what had to be done to win. The slaps on the back had been strong and sturdy in victory.

Before 82,122 fans, Georgia, proud possessor of a couple of the country's longest college football winning streaks, saw them abruptly end when a strong Auburn team whipped the Dogs 13-7. It should have been Herschel Walker's last home; however, he departed the previous season, after signing a sixteen million dollar contract with the New Jersey Generals of the now defunct United States Football League. The streaks snapped by Auburn included the Bulldogs' twenty-four game consecutive home winning streak, and twenty-three straight conference victories. Auburn had been the last conference team to beat Georgia on November 17, 1979.

Coach Dooley's Georgia Bulldogs were ranked fourth in the nation with an 8-0-1 record. Coach Pat Dye's Tigers of Auburn were ranked third in the nation with a record of 8-1. Auburn simply had too much defense and too much Bo Jackson and Lionel James for the Bulldogs to handle on that November afternoon.

For the third week in a row, Auburn faced a top-ten team with "The Belt" on the line. Against Georgia, Auburn running back James rushed for 84-yards on 13 carries, and scored the Tigers' only touchdown. Al Del Greco, Auburn's kicker, booted two field-goals, and the Tigers' offense held the ball for a total of 38:59.

Auburn got the first break of the game when Tigers' defensive tackle Doug Smith stripped John Lastinger of the ball on an option play. The ball was recovered by defensive end Quincy Williams at the Georgia 23-yard line. Auburn drove the 23-yards in five plays. James scored the touchdown when he went four yards around the right end, with 4:34 remaining in the first quarter.

The highlight of the drive was a punishing 10-yard run by Tigers' All-American running back Jackson. He got down to the Georgia 4-yard line, as he broke the tackles of four Bulldog defenders, before being brought down. Del Greco's field-goals came in the second quarter when he hit from 21 and 41 yards giving, Auburn a 13-0 halftime advantage.

Jackson nearly gave the Tigers another score when he broke a 28-yard run around left end from the Auburn 3-yard line. He stepped out of bounds at the Auburn 31-yard line, but would have gone the distance for the score without the misstep. Both defenses dominated the second half as neither team was able to mount a scoring challenge in the third quarter. Del Greco could have put the game out of reach with two 30-yard field-goal attempts but both kicks from the center of the field sailed wide to the left.

The Bulldogs only touchdown came with 2:11 left in the game after an 87-yard drive. Lastinger, who completed 7 of 8 pass attempts on the drive, threw a 13-yard touchdown pass to receiver Herman Archie. The highlight of the drive was a 23-yard pass completion from Lastinger to receiver Fred Lane.

Georgia recovered the on-side kick at their own 45-yard line, but they were still unable to move against the suffocating Auburn defense. Tigers' cornerback Jimmie Warren broke-up the final pass.

Lastinger threw for 110 yards, and one touchdown, while the Bulldogs were held to just 51 yards rushing and 117-yards passing in the loss. Campbell threw for 95-yards, completing 12 of 15 pass attempts. Jackson added 115-yards rushing for the Tigers.

Auburn finished the season 11-1, won the Southeastern Conference title, and finished the season ranked third in the nation. The 'Dogs finished 10-1-1 and ranked fourth nationally.

Georgia 26 – Clemson 23, September 22, 1984

In 1984, twentieth ranked Georgia hosted the number two ranked Clemson Tigers, during an era when games between the two institutions were as big as any in all of college football. With only two regular starters returning off the 1983 team, Waycross native Todd Williams would quarterback an inexperienced offense.

Unfortunately, Williams came out during the first half and threw four interceptions. He tossed a fifth interception in the second half. In fact, on the day he only completed three of eleven passes.

In the second quarter, after the 'Dogs made it to Clemson's 42-yard line, Coach Dooley sent Butler to try a 59-yarder. Butler's kick fell two yards short of the crossbar. The previous season, at Clemson, Butler had kicked the game-tying field-goal, after the 'Dogs came from behind. After Butler had tied the game, the Tigers attempted a long field-goal, too. After reaching the 49-yard line, Clemson's kicker, Donald Igwebuike, tried a 68-yarder and came-up well short. Georgia took over with time to run one more play, in an effort to break the deadlock and get the win. Butler came on to attempt a 66-yard field-goal into the wind. He didn't make it, but he would have his chance to hit a game-winner in 1984.

On this crucial September day in '84, after the Tigers built-up a 20-6 halftime lead, it looked like the Bulldogs were going to be embarrassed on their home field. However, during the second half, Williams inexplicably rejuvenated his offense.

Georgia slowly worked its way back, and tied the game at 20-20. Under Williams' leadership, Georgia eventually took a 23-20 lead late in the third quarter after Butler kicked a 43-yard field-goal. However, Clemson wasted no time by driving 48-yards, in twelve plays, to tie the game with a 48-yard field-goal.

It looked like the two rivals were playing for their second straight series draw with just over two minutes left in the game. Then, the Bulldogs took possession at their own 20-yard line. Tron Jackson took a draw play and picked-up 24-yards. His run helped Georgia get into Clemson's territory. Next, Butler ran onto the field to attempt a 60-yard field-goal. Larry Munson stated, "So we'll try to kick one 100,000 miles. We're holding it on our own 49 and a half, gonna try to kick it 60 yards plus a foot and a half."

When Butler put his foot into it, Munson's voice got higher as the ball did. "Butler kicked a long one," he began to yell, "a long one. Oh, my God! Oh, my God! The stadium is worse than bonkers. . . . I can't believe what he did!"

Lewis Grizzard wrote an open letter addressed to the son he hoped one day to have, Lewis wrote:

"I hugged perfect strangers and kissed a fat lady on the mouth. Grown men wept. Lightning flashed. Thunder rolled. Stars fell, and joy swept through, fetched by a hurricane of unleashed emotions. When Georgia beat Alabama 18-17 in 1965, it was a staggering victory. When we came back against Georgia Tech and won 29-28 in 1978, the Chapel bell rang all night. When we beat Florida 26-21 in the last seconds in 1980, we called it a miracle. And when we beat Notre Dame 17-10 in the Sugar Bowl that same year for the national championship, a woman pulled-up her skirt and showed the world the Bulldog she had sewn on her under britches. But Saturday may have been even better than any of those.

Saturday in Athens was a religious experience. I give this to you, son. Read it and re-read it, and keep it next to your heart.

And when people want to know how you wound up with the name "Kevin" let them read it, and then they will know.

Son, that football hung in the air for six seconds, which is an eternity when you're waiting to find out whether you've won. Kevin Butler knew immediately. As the pigskin flew westward, the placekicker ran eastward, sank to his knees, where he was mobbed by his teammates after officials signaled the kick was good."

The official need not have bothered. It tied the longest field-goal in the history of the Southeastern Conference, but it cleared the crossbar by at least five yards. Butler could have split the uprights from 70 yards. Butler was still trembling in the locker room afterwards, when he related: "It was the best feeling I've ever had."

The legendary Coach Danny Ford, the Clemson coach whose team lost its shot at the national championship because of what Butler did, told the press, "That ball must be flat now. He kicked the fool out of it." Coach Dooley realized immediately how important that field-goal would prove to be in the course of Georgia football history. Coach Dooley stated:

> I think it will be in the Butts-Mehre Heritage Hall, where people can walk-in, and pick-up that phone and push the button and see Kevin Butler kick the record-breaking field-goal to win the ballgame. That was an exciting play, just as Buck's pass to Lindsay, and . . . this has got to be one of the greatest in Georgia history.

During his four year career at Georgia, Butler was responsible for 34 points against Clemson. In games against the Country Gentlemen, he kicked one field-goal as a freshman, two field-goals as a sophomore, three as a junior, and four as a senior.

He was not perfect against Clemson, though. In fact, he missed a combined four long field-goals against the Tigers in his sophomore and junior seasons. In 1982, when Georgia played the first night game in Sanford Stadium in more than 30 years, during a nationally-televised Labor Day showdown with defending national champion Clemson, Coach Dooley asked Kevin before the game how long he could kick one. Kevin confidently stated he could make a field-goal from 57-yards. He would kick two field-goals to help Georgia defeat Clemson 13-7.

Georgia 18 – Southern Mississippi 17, September 15, 1990
On a very hot and humid day in the Classic City, an unheralded quarterback named Bret Favre, who had not completely recovered from a very serious automobile accident during the summer, led Southern Mississippi into Sanford Stadium. He almost led the Eagles to another upset of a Southeastern Conference (SEC) team, in as many weeks.

It was not very pretty, but Georgia's much-criticized defense came through when it needed to in the Bulldogs 18-17 victory. Georgia's defense was far from perfect, allowing 267 total yards and 17 points, but the 'Dogs stepped-up and thwarted Southern Mississippi's attempt to capitalize on opportunities afforded to them.

Georgia took a 3-0 lead in the second quarter; however, Georgia quarterback Greg Talley would cough-up the football on Georgia's 26-yard line. But, the 'Dogs' defense stiffened, and knocked the Eagles back five yards. The Eagles' Jim Taylor salvaged the drive by booting a 49-yard field-goal to tie it 3-3.

On its first possession of the second half, Southern Mississippi drove to the Georgia 11-yard line before a hard hit popped the ball loose from running back Eddie Ray Jackson. Georgia recovered the fumble to end the threat.

With the exception of a third quarter breakdown in the defensive backfield, where Southern Mississippi quarterback Favre found receiver Michael Jackson all alone for a 63-yard touchdown pass, Georgia's defense stifled the Golden eagles attack. The play woke-up the Dogs. Georgia forced Southern Mississippi to punt four times and miss one field-goal in their last five possessions.

After Georgia took the 18-17 lead in the fourth quarter, the Bulldog's defense held Southern Mississippi to 29 yards in the final period. The 'Dogs hunkered down one more time on Southern Mississippi's last possession of the game, when the Golden Eagles got the ball on the Georgia 24-yard line, after a long punt return. Yet, the Eagles penetrated no further into Georgia territory. The Bulldog's defense knocked the Eagles back on three straight plays. It proved to be crucial for the Dogs as Taylor missed the potential game-winning 42-yard field-goal by inches.

The win was much needed for Georgia, after losing 18-13 the previous week to the Bayou Bengals of Louisiana State. The home crowd gave the 'Dogs a lift too, when Southern Mississippi found itself backed-up against its goal line, on the closed end of Sanford Stadium. The deafening roar of the crowd hindered the Golden Eagle offense and contributed to forcing a punt from the endzone. It gave the 'Dogs excellent field position at the Southern Mississippi 46-yard line, which led to Georgia's winning touchdown.

Favre and Southern Mississippi had upset the Crimson Tide of Alabama the previous week, and had been seeking a sweep of SEC teams. Favre would go 11 of 20 for 136 yards, along with two touchdowns, and no interceptions.

Georgia 17 – Alabama 16, September 22, 1990

As the Crimson Tide rolled away from Sanford Stadium, after Georgia's miraculous 17-16 victory, the Bulldogs discovered more than just a satisfying win. The Bulldogs had a renewed life in the Southeastern Conference title race.

Garrison Hearst, a freshman, rushed for 106-yards, on 16 carries, and solidified himself as the Bulldogs' top tailback not only with his totals, but with his clutch runs in the fourth quarter.

"We made the plays and we came up with the plays when we had to," Coach Ray Goff stated. "Especially Garrison!"

On Georgia's fourth-quarter touchdown drive, the Bulldogs had a third and two at the Alabama 24-yard line, Hearst gained four yards, for a first down on the Tide's 20-yard line. On the next play,

Hearst picked-up sixteen yards. Quarterback Preston Jones smelled a Georgia upset at that point, even with Georgia still trailing 16-6.

"When Garrison got the ball down to the four, I knew we were going to win," Jones stated.

Then on the winning field-goal drive, with the ball resting on the Alabama 47-yard line, Hearst got the ball on third and 12 yards to go, and gained 16-yards for a first down, keeping the drive alive. According to Hearst, the play was originally planned to be a draw.

"The play was a draw. It was clogged up the middle, but it was open to the right," Hearst stated. "I was just trying to get the first down, and everything just opened-up."

Although it was only Hearst' third colligate game, and he wasn't a starter, he quickly became the focal point in the Bulldog offensive arsenal. In the previous two games Hearst carried the ball 29 times for 178-yards. Meanwhile, Georgia, as a team, rushed for 318-yards on 98 attempts, making him accountable for over half the Bulldogs' rushing yards on less than a third its carries.

"This is my third game now and I'm starting to feel a little more confident about what is going on," Hearst said. "Earlier in the Alabama game I was kind of nervous, but by the time the fourth quarter came around I was really confident."

Nervous would be a good word to use as Georgia lined-up at the Alabama three-yard line, for a crucial two-point conversion in the fourth quarter. The Crimson Tide had blitzed the Bulldogs from the corners all day, keying on shutting down the Bulldogs sweep. However, offensive coordinator George Haffner had a trick.

Jones pitched left to tailback Larry Ware. Typical Georgia power sweep right? Wrong! Ware pulled-up around the seven and lofted a duck into the endzone where tight end Chris Broom snagged the pass, snatching the hearts out of the phenomenal Pachyderms.

"That play was on the backburner," Haffner said. It's something we thought would work against Alabama. They bite so hard on the sweep. The players executed it perfectly."

Ware added, "I had to calm down and execute. Everybody did their job on the play and allowed me to complete the pass."

Georgia's defense made no excuses. They didn't have to. The much-beleaguered group bent to frightening extremes, but didn't break in a thrilling come-from-behind win. Coach Goff's working class men could have used any number of excuses to fold the tent, and count their losses. Instead, players stepped forward to fill vacancies left void by injury, academic casualty and suspensions.

In fact, after strong safety David Hargett broke his leg in practice the prior week, Georgia's casualty count had reached five—all of whom were slotted for starting roles.

"We didn't get down on ourselves," said linebacker Bryant Gantt, who had seven solo tackles and three assist against Alabama. "No matter what kind of adversity we face, we are going to come out and fight no matter what the score of the game."

During the game, Tide quarterback Gary Hollingsworth had been largely effective against the Bulldog defenders, mixing the run and pass very well. But, Alabama produced just 17 total yards in the last 12 minutes of the game. Georgia would finish the season a miserable 4-7, while Alabama lost to Louisville in the Fiesta Bowl and finished 7-5.

Georgia 17 – Florida 52, October 28, 1995

The best way for fans to have avoided traffic during the Georgia versus Florida game, in Athens, on that fateful day in October, would have been to stay until the end of it. Few fans remained in Sanford Stadium by the time the Gators 52-17 dismantling of the Bulldogs was over. Florida's victory, before a capacity crowd of 86,117, was thorough, and never in doubt.

The undefeated Gators, playing in Athens for the first time since 1932, used two miscues to get ahead 14-0 after only eight minutes into the game. Coach Steve Spurrier's Gators never looked back enroute to their sixth straight victory over the Bulldogs.

Even after the duel was over, Sanford Stadium would be burning for many years to come. The Gators' last seven points came when back-up quarterback Eric Kresser threw an eight-yard touchdown pass with 1:10 left to play. That late touchdown prompted a perfunctory handshake between Georgia Coach Ray Goff and Spurrier.

"A lot of our coaches' had mentioned to me that no one had scored 50 points in there before, so we wanted to do that," Spurrier said. "We had our back-ups in and they want to play hard and score just like the other guys."

In 1995, for the first time in 63 years, the third ranked Florida Gators came calling to Athens for a meeting 'tween the hedges. Disappointingly, Georgia overplayed the role of gracious host, sending the Gators back to Gainesville, Florida with an easy win.

The '95 game would be the second straight year Florida scored 52 points on Georgia. In fact, the 52 points marked the highest total the Gators had ever scored in the stored rivalry, and the most points ever scored against Georgia inside of Sanford Stadium.

After Florida built a 28-3 lead at halftime, it sent many Georgia fans toward the exits. By the start of the fourth quarter, the Gators' 15,000 fans nearly equaled those still cheering for Georgia.

Florida displayed every weapon in their offensive arsenal. The Gators rolled up 542-yards of total offense and gave up only 281 total yards. Gators' junior quarterback Danny Wuerffel completed 14 of 17 passes for 242-yards and five touchdowns.

Late in the third quarter, Florida junior quarterback Kresser came on in relief of Wuerffel. He completed 6 of 9 pass attempts, for 71-yards and two touchdowns. Sophomore wide receiver Ike Hilliard was on the receiving end of five passes, gaining 99-yards and scoring two touchdowns.

The Dogs' defense held Florida on its first possession; however, Georgia's offense would subsequently be pinned deep in its own territory. On Georgia's second play from scrimmage, fullback Selma Calloway took a toss left and fumbled the ball at the 14-yard line. Florida cornerback Anthone Lott recovered it, setting-up a short scoring opportunity for the Gators.

On the very next play Florida took a 7-0 lead, and the Bulldogs never got any closer. "We heard that Georgia was saying they were ready for us," Spurrier said. "Our guys really responded well, forcing that early turnover gave us an easy score. That gave us some early momentum."

On Georgia's next possession, the Dogs were held to nine-yards on three plays and were forced to punt. Long-snapper Matt Rabon sailed the snap to punter Dax Langley. He couldn't handle the snap. After he recovered the ball he was hit and tackled by back-up cornerback Shea Showers.

Three plays after the botched snap, Wuerffel lofted a 2-yard touchdown pass to wide receiver Chris Doering. "Our defense set the tone early with those turnovers," Wuerffel said. "We wanted to get up on them early, and because our defense, we did."

Sophomore Elijah Williams ran 15 times for 143-yards, to pace the Gators' ground attack. Bulldog sophomore quarterback Hines Ward, who played with a sprained right thumb he sustained in the third quarter, completed 20 of 33 passes for 226-yards and a touchdown in the most impressive start of his college career at the quarterback position. He had eight rushes for 65-yards.

"We're going to use this week to recuperate from our injuries, and recover mentally, "said Georgia senior offensive tackle Troy Stark. Goff stated, "We've got to get people healthy. If you go back and look, unfortunately, the same thing happened last year, except we were a little better offensively than we are this season."

In the end, the Dogs' ended-up with a total of four turnovers on a day when the Atlanta Braves won their first World Series Title against the Cleveland Indians. Georgia would go to a bowl, but Coach Goff would be terminated at the end of the season.

Georgia 21 - Tennessee 10, October 7, 2000

Georgia's fans have only rushed the field at Sanford Stadium once in its history, and that occurred on October 7, 2000. The 'Dogs had finally busted through that Big Orange roadblock as they powered past the twenty-first ranked Tennessee Volunteers. Georgia broke a 12-year stranglehold the Volunteers held on them. The last time Georgia had defeated Tennessee was twelve years earlier, when Coach Dooley was still head coach in 1988.

Once Tim Wansley picked-off a hopeless pass by Tennessee, very late in the fourth quarter, a large quantity of fans tried swarming the field, even though 1:13 remained in the game. Once officials got those overzealous fans off the field, they waited until the end of the game before storming the field for a second time.

The Vols trailed 7-3 at halftime; however, Tennessee promptly reasserted itself on the first drive of the third quarter when they took a 10-7 lead, after a touchdown by Travis Stephens. The go-ahead score was set-up by Travis Henry's 58-yard run off right tackle. It was the best play of the night for the Volunteers' star. In the first half he had been restricted to 15-yards, on six carries.

The 'Dogs recaptured the lead after Jasper Sanks' second touchdown run with 10:08 remaining in the third quarter. The touchdown had been set-up by a 33-yard completion from Quincy Carter to Terrence Edwards. Georgia led 14-10.

The devastating offensive jolt, however, came in the fourth quarter when Georgia pushed 99 yards, on 10 plays. The coup de grâce was a one-yard touchdown run by Musa Smith, who excelled throughout the second half. Georgia led 21-10.

Nursing a 21-10 lead, the game was still in doubt before the 'Dogs tackled Henry, just shy of the first down marker, on a fourth-and-one from Georgia's five-yard line. Once it became evident Henry was short, the public address announcer shouted, "First down, Georgia!" There was a deafening roar from the sold-out stadium.

With Georgia holding onto a 21-10 lead, with only 73 seconds remaining, it prompted some of Sanford Stadium's near capacity crowd of 86,520 to leap over the famous hedges, storm the field and attempt to tear down the goalposts before the game was officially over. In reality, they attempted to tear down the goal posts on both ends of the field, though there was still 1:13 left in the game. It took officials several minutes to clear the field, temporarily postponing a wild celebration.

After the fans were cleared from the field, Georgia ran the clock down to 29 seconds before the fans stormed the field again. As the final seconds ticked off the clock, the goal posts at Sanford Stadium came down for the only time in its history.

It was the one hundredth overall win in Coach Jim Donnan's career. His total record, in eleven years at Marshall and Georgia, stood at 100-37. It was his first conquest, in five attempts, against the Riflemen.

Tennessee's A. J. Suggs completed 13-of-21 passes for 96-yards and was sacked four times. He split time with Casey Clausen, who was 5-for-11 for 40-yards.

The Bulldogs profited from a violent defense that included a pair of interceptions by cornerback Wansley. Georgia's Carter was unspectacular but efficient, completing 8-of-17 passes for 134 yards, without an interception. Sanks had 15 carries for 53-yards, including a pair of one-yard touchdown runs. Early in the third quarter, Georgia scored its second touchdown to take the lead for good at 14-10. Edwards had four catches for 109 yards.

Fans destroying goalpost, Tennessee game, 2000

The Red Clay Hounds displayed heart and intensity Coach Phil Fulmer's Vols usually had beaten out of them by halftime during the entire decade of the '90s. Using a smothering defense, coupled with dominant running, the same formula the Volunteers used to win the previous nine games in the series, the 'Dogs defeated Tennessee 21-10. Georgia would finish 8-4, and beat Virginia in the Oahu Classic, while the Vols went 8-4 and lost the Cotton Bowl to Kansas State.

Georgia 31- Clemson 28, August 31, 2002
Georgia's best offense was its receivers, but instead of getting their yards from passes, Fred Gibson and Damien Gary made their biggest impact off the foot of Clemson kickers. The 'Dogs had 203 returns yards, the exact amount of yards its offense gained.

The bulk of those return yards were on a 91-yard kickoff return by Gibson, and a 40-yard punt return from Gary. Gibson's return in the second quarter put Georgia on top 14-7, and would help the eighth-ranked Bulldogs escape a major upset by rallying for a 31-28 victory over Clemson.

On Clemson's next series, after Gibson's return, Tigers' punter, Wynn Kopp, dropped the snap and shanked his punt. It went just 17-yards. Thomas Davis picked-up the wayward football and returned it 18-yards, to the Clemson 15-yard line. D. J. Shockley would score three plays later to give Georgia a 21-7 lead. Later, Clemson's Willie Simmons successfully tossed a 21-yard touchdown pass to Kevin Youngblood, with just eight seconds left in the first half, pulling Clemson to 21-14.

Shockley, playing in his first college football game, showed the world why he was the nation's top high school quarterback prospect coming out of high school. He displayed his scrambling ability—leaving Eric Meekins in the dust on his touchdown run—and his rocket arm. If there hadn't been a Bulldog quarterback controversy, there was one after the events of this clash between the 'Dogs and Tigers at Sanford Stadium.

As David Greene watched from the sidelines, Shockley came in for three plays and ran twice for 15-yards, including his first touchdown from nine-yards out. In the second half, it appeared Shockley wasn't coming back, but he did and again he excelled. With Georgia trailing 28-21, Shockley brought the 'Dogs back from the brink. On one play, as he pulled back from center, he tripped; however, he regrouped and scored two plays later.

Clemson's punter, Georgia transfer Kopp, had earlier set-up Shockley's touchdown run by dropping a snap, and shanking the punt 17-yards. In addition to his running ability, Shockley proved himself a great drop-back passer in his first appearance as a Bulldog, completing 3 of 4 passes for 50-yards and a score. Greene, the Southeastern Conference Freshman of the Year in 2001, was 12 of 21 for 67-yards—the worst performance of his career.

Shockley rifled the ball across the field to Gibson, then, he threaded the needle to Terrence Edwards on the 24-yard score. Later, with 5:19 left in the game, Billy Bennett kicked a 43-yard field-goal to give Georgia an improbable 31-28 lead. Oddly, Bennett had struggled throughout the preseason camp, but successfully held on to his starting job after fighting off Brett Kirouac just one week prior to the opener. Bennett kicked the game-winning field-goal.

To preserve the win, Musa Smith picked-up a first down on fourth and one, at the Georgia 38-yard line, with 40 seconds remaining. The Bulldogs' high-powered offense managed 203-yards, but Shockley did very well in his three series. He ran for a 9-yard touchdown in the second quarter and threw a 24-yard scoring pass to Edwards early in the fourth, tying the game at 28 each.

Greene, who tossed a critical 4-yard touchdown pass to Damien Gary, was adamant about not being concerned with giving-up playing time. "It's a win," Greene said. "We're all the same team. It's a team game. We're both thrilled for each other."

Clemson's special teams play was horrendous, and the Red Clay Hounds took full advantage of the Tiger's mistake prone antics. Gibson exposed their weaknesses after scoring on a 91-yard kickoff. And, to add insult to injury, Clemson's Aaron Hunt missed two critical field-goals, including a 46-yard attempt, with just 1:43 remaining, that would have tied the game for the Tigers. Two other special teams blunders, a shanked punt and a long punt return, set-up two more Georgia touchdowns.

Though only ninety miles apart, it would mark the first time, since 1995, that these two institutions met on the gridiron. Unfortunately, both teams made numerous errors, however, it's typically par for the course in season openers. Still, it made for an action packed spectacle late in the game. If fact, if not for all the mental errors, especially from the special teams, the Tigers most likely would have won the game. As mentioned, when Clemson got in position to put the game into overtime, after driving to Georgia's 26-yard line, its offense stalled out. Hunt entered the game for a field-goal attempt, but amazingly his kick was several feet short.

When Gibson made his game-jolting kickoff return for a 91-yard touchdown—he was hardly touched—oddly, the play shouldn't have happened. Bowden's Tigers were forced to kick-off again after it had been penalized for an illegal procedure on its initial attempt.

"I have never had that many breakdowns in all my years of coaching," Clemson coach Tommy Bowden said. "If I had a special teams coach, this would have been his last game."

The Tigers of Clemson wasted several other opportunities as well. Georgia's Decory Bryant made an interception after Simmons didn't see an open receiver in the endzone, instead, he tossed into deep coverage. However, Simmons' receivers let him down on two other throws. A long pass connected with Airese Curry, on a fly pattern, at the Georgia 15-yard line, but the ball went right through his fingertips. On another perfectly tossed pass, Derrick Hamilton was all alone in the endzone; however, he clumsily fumbled away another perfectly thrown pass by Simmons.

The Tigers appeared awkward, and without skill or grace as they fumbled six times; however, even though they managed to recover all six, they lost valuable yards. Georgia went on to have its best record since 1980, by going 13-1, and winning the Southeastern Conference title for the first time since 1982.

Georgia 51 – Georgia Tech 7, November 30, 2002

Silhouetted against an orange-gray November sky, Georgia played an almost perfect game. The 'Dogs overwhelmed another struggling Georgia Tech team that was brushed over the precipice at Sanford Stadium while a crowd of 86,520 peered down on the mystifying scenery spread across the brown field below.

Georgia, scheduled to play Arkansas in the Southeastern Conference (SEC) championship game the following weekend, had aspirations of playing for the national title. In fact, after building-up a 34-0 halftime lead against Tech, the Bulldogs learned third ranked Oklahoma had lost to Oklahoma State, thus eliminating another Tostitos Fiesta Bowl contender. Georgia just needed Miami to lose to Virginia Tech the following weekend, coupled with the 'Dogs beating the Razorbacks, to earn a spot in the national title game.

Georgia beat Arkansas, and won its first Southeastern Conference title since 1982; however, Miami defeated Virginia Tech and played Ohio State for the national title. The 'Dogs, 13-1, were locked-out of the national title game, and finished ranked third.

Against Tech, Georgia cruised to a 51-7 victory—Georgia's most lopsided win in the series, which began in 1893. Musa Smith rushed for 121-yards and became the first Georgia back, since Garrison Hearst, in 1992, to reach 1,000 yards in a season. David Greene completed 10 of 14 passes for 205-yards and a touchdown. And, fullback J. T. Wall added a couple of touchdown runs.

The Bulldogs were stimulated by the return of David Jacobs for senior day. In 2001, Jacobs had been a defensive lineman for Georgia when an almost fatal stroke suddenly ended his career. Once all the other seniors had been introduced, he put on his old number 99 uniform, and though weakened on his right side, he trotted onto the field to a thunderous standing ovation. Jacobs would watch from the sideline as Smith started the drive with a 22-yard run as Georgia marched right down the field on its first possession. Smith finished it by scoring from the one yard line.

A few minutes later, a 46-yard field-goal by Billy Bennett pushed the Bulldogs in front 10-0. Afterwards, things really got nasty for the Gnats of Georgia Tech. First, D. J. Shockley scored on an 8-yard run to make it 17-0. Then, Greene came back on the next possession to complete two straight long passes to extend the lead to 24-0. Initially, Greene completed a 31-yard pass to Terrence Edwards, who took the ball away from Jeremy Muyres as the Tech defensive back was primed to make an interception. Next, Greene came back with a 49-yard touchdown pass to Fred Gibson, who made the catch once cornerback Marvious Hester misjudged an underthrown ball.

Edwards, who wasn't suppose to return until the SEC championship game against Arkansas, because of an injured shoulder, came back one week early. He made two receptions, for 48-yards. Sean Jones returned a punt 26-yards, then Smith had a 22-yard run to set-up Bennett's second field-goal, a 30-yarder, to make the score 27-0.

The 'Dogs immediately got the ball after Tech's P. J. Daniels fumbled a kickoff. Moments later, Wall crashed into the endzone on an 18-yard run, carrying Muyres on his back the last couple of yards. In the first half, Tech tallied two fumbled kickoff returns, and A. J. Suggs tossed an interception. The Yellow Jackets' only threatened to score when Luke Manget attempted a 49-yard field-goal. It was blocked by Boss Bailey. Tech didn't get on the scoreboard until early in the fourth quarter, narrowing the gap to thirty-seven points. The 'Dogs answered two drives later to produce the final result.

With less than four minutes remaining, Tyson Browning scored on a 19-yard run to help the 'Dogs notch their most points ever against the Tech. In 1994 and 1999, Georgia scored 48 points on the Yellow Jackets; however, if the 2001 game turned the rivalry in Georgia's favor, the '02 game solidified it, leaving no doubt.

With the fifth-ranked Bulldogs in the midst of an 11-1 season, and pointed towards an SEC title, and a spot in the Sugar Bowl, Georgia rolled to 552-yards of total offense and scored the game's first 44 points. Six different Georgia players caught at least two passes, and the Bulldogs' defense forced five turnovers.

Georgia 17- South Carolina 15, September 10, 2005

Georgia fans left their homes on Saturday foaming at the mouth, like Uga VI, for the much-anticipated return of The Sith, Steve Spurrier, to Sanford Stadium. The 'Dogs wouldn't have a chance to annihilate South Carolina. The Georgia faithful, in the sold-out crowd of 92,746, went from wanting coach Mark Richt to run-up the score, to simply hoping Georgia would find a way to score more points than Spurrier's Gamecocks.

South Carolina was an 18-point underdog, but left the ninth-ranked 'Dogs hanging on for dear life in Georgia's Southeastern Conference (SEC) opener. Georgia, trailing by two points at halftime, was happy to escape with a 17-15 win against the reviled coach, who wore a white Gamecock visor.

The last time Spurrier had been inside of Sanford Stadium was 1995. His Florida team had won 52-17, after tossing a touchdown pass with 1:10 seconds left, to become the first visiting team to score over fifty points against Georgia on its home field. Returning to the Bulldogs' hallowed turf, during his first season as South Carolina's coach, Spurrier came without the dynamic offense that symbolized his Florida teams. Still, the Gamecocks gave Georgia all it could handle.

The 'Dogs kept hitting. Play after play after play. Another handoff, another glimpse of light, another burst of speed. Gradually, the 'Dogs moved down the field. Georgia's Thomas Brown and Danny Ware never seemed to tire. The two tailbacks never avoided contact, instead they pounded straight ahead, through the mass of bodies, like Georgia's hopes relied on them.

They continued to pound, grind, break tackles and spin out of trouble. And when the 'Dogs needed a touchdown, needed something to break-out of its offensive quagmire, they turned to Brown and Ware. Eight plays. All runs. Seventy-one yards. All on the ground. It was the type of drive that would make Coach Dooley proud. The results of Brown and Ware's efforts culminated in a fourth-quarter touchdown that gave the 'Dogs the winning margin.

After D. J. Shockley tossed an interception that was returned for a touchdown by South Carolina's Jonathan Joseph, Richt turned to the running game. Especially after witnessing four other passes slip through the hands of various defensive backs. It might have been the only choice.

Clinging to a 10-9 lead, Georgia wore down the Gamecocks with its running game. With Shockley, the hero in the season opener against Boise State, struggling, the tailbacks were the only real option to rescue the 'Dogs. Brown and Ware were interchangeable and had nearly identical running styles, despite the fact that Brown was 4 inches shorter and 40 pounds lighter than Ware. With the way Brown unleashed punishment, by knocking folks backwards when he hit them, it was nearly impossible to distinguish between them.

Brown muscled his way through the center of the line, through guys 130 pounds heavier than him, to rush for career high 144-yards. He slightly sprained his right shoulder late in the game, but he had done his damage. He had already scored a touchdown that made Spurrier's Gamecocks play catch-up the rest of the game.

Ware, who was a lot less patient than Brown, had 69 yards rushing; 25 of those yards came on the drive that overlapped the third and fourth quarters. He was effective on the next drive, the one that allowed Georgia to march out of the shadow of its goalpost and eventually enable the 'Dogs to pin the Gamecocks deep with a punt.

On third-and-18, South Carolina's quarterback Blake Mitchell spotted a safety blitz. He quickly connected with Syvelle Newton over the middle for 34-yards. Going down the middle again, Mitchell threw a 24-yard pass to Sidney Rice. Next, Mitchell found Rice on a 4-yard touchdown play with 6:52 remaining. An earlier missed extra-point forced the Gamecocks to go for two. Mitchell overthrew Rice, preserving Georgia's narrow lead.

The Bulldogs were able to burn more than 5½ minutes, mainly because of Shockley's 27-yard pass to Bryan McClendon on third-and-22, from Georgia's 8-yard line. South Carolina finally got the ball back with just over a minute to go, but went four-and-out, deep in Georgia's territory.

Booed every time he was shown on the scoreboard monitor, Spurrier jogged to midfield for a swift salutation with Richt and then turned for the locker room as the crowd ruthlessly heckled him.

Shockley, who had five touchdowns the previous week, tossed two interceptions in the first half against Carolina—one was returned for a Gamecock touchdown, while the other one was picked-off in the endzone. He went eight for 17 for 112-yards.

Mitchell completed 22 of 34 for 236-yards, and was intercepted twice. He regretted the two-point conversion that failed.

Georgia fans definitely wanted a blowout, a Spurrier stomping, something they could laugh about for years down the road. Instead, they saw Georgia could win without the bombs away mentality, without receiving gifts from an overmatched offense.

The fans discovered the 'Dogs possibly weren't quite as good as what they thought after dismantling Boise State. The 'Dogs found out its defense remained speedy and stout and could come through with big plays during crucial situations.

Outside the stadium, Georgia took part in the SEC relief effort for victims of Hurricane Katrina. Venders were accepting money inside, and outside of Sanford Stadium, before and during the game. Eventually, the SEC donated over $3 million to the relief efforts to help rebuild New Orleans after the destruction caused after the levies busted on August 29, 2005.

Georgia 15 – Georgia Tech 12, November 25, 2006

The 2006 season had been an unusual one for Georgia. In late November, when sixteenth ranked Georgia Tech came-calling, Georgia was a heavy underdog. The Bulldogs had lost to Vanderbilt and Kentucky, before knocking-off a highly ranked Auburn team, on the road, two weeks prior to the Tech game. Nobody knew what to expect against the Yellow Jackets of Georgia Tech.

In reality, three weeks earlier, it would have been tough to picture Georgia in the position it was in after the 2006 edition of "Clean Ole Fashion Hate," had been completed. Three weeks earlier, the 'Dogs had woke-up on a Sunday morning, fresh off a loss at Kentucky, their fourth loss in five games, and gawked wide-eyed into the high beams of two ranked teams, Auburn and Tech.

Some Georgia fans didn't believe the 'Dogs could beat Auburn or Georgia Tech. Two more losses would culminate in a 6-6 finish, and leave the Bulldogs to pick at the bowl table scraps. This team was going nowhere. It was all hardship and misery. Armageddon was right around the corner. Then, three weeks later, the 'Dogs woke-up with two upsets in their rearview mirror. The smiles that were on their faces after defeating Auburn 37-15, two weeks prior to Tech, somehow got bigger after Georgia pulled-off the comeback and beat Georgia Tech for the sixth straight time.

The hurtful sound of boos that Georgia sophomore receiver Mohamed Massaquoi had heard during his previous game inside of Sanford Stadium, became a serenade of cheers against Georgia Tech.

Massaquoi caught the game-winning 4-yard touchdown with 1:45 remaining, then, snagged the two-point conversion to help Georgia knock off the sixteenth ranked Yellow Jackets.

Appropriately, Reggie Ball's last pass attempt was intercepted by Paul Oliver. Before he made the game-clinching interception, in Georgia's 15-12 upset win, the junior cornerback had helped with shutting-down All-American Calvin Johnson. Johnson was limited to 13-yards on two receptions.

Not long after the interception, the heckling came pouring out of the Sanford Stadium stands, random at first, then the Georgia faithful took it up as a chorus.

"Reg-gie."
"Reg-gie."
"Reg-gie."

Paul Oliver interception, 2006

His lone fumble was returned for a touchdown and one of his interceptions came on a last-gasp effort in the closing minutes. "We knew he was going to give it to us," Georgia defensive tackle Ray Gant said of Ball. "He's a competitive guy. When he gets rattled, when he gets frustrated, he can't handle his emotions too well. We took advantage of that. He pretty much gave us the game!"

Georgia's Mathew Stafford played a big role in both wins. He accounted for 302-yards rushing and passing against Auburn, then, rallied from a lethargic start, to direct the biggest drive of the season when Georgia Tech reclaimed the lead, 12-7, after Tech's Tashard Choice scored on a 10-yard run with 8:50 remaining.

Stafford completed four straight passes on a 12-play, 64-yard drive. His last pass was to Massaquoi, on third-and-goal from the four-yard line. Massaquoi went outside, as though he was heading for the corner, and Stafford sold the ruse with a pump fake. Massaquoi then glided free over the middle, hauling in Georgia's only offensive score of the day. Next, Georgia converted a 2-point conversion on a Stafford-to-Massaquoi pass.

Ball, a four-year starter, endured four painful performances against Georgia. He sustained a concussion against the Bulldogs his freshman year. As a sophomore, he lost track on the downs on a late drive, allowing Georgia to hold on for a 19-13 win. In 2005, he threw an interception at the goal line with just over a minute remaining in a 14-7 loss to the Bulldogs. Then, 2006 was considered the worst performance of his career.

Georgia Tech's quarterback was an easy target for Georgia fans in the rivalry game. He completed his career against the 'Dogs with another mistake-filled performance, underscored by his individual stat line: 22 attempts, six completions, two interceptions, 42-yards, no touchdowns, four sacks and one fumble.

Most damaging was Ball's fumble that Georgia ran back for its first touchdown. The play appeared over until line-backer Tony Taylor snatched the ball from a pile of players and took off the other way for 29-yards. "I walked-up to the pile and saw the ball lying there," Taylor said. "The first thing that went through my mind was, 'I hope they don't blow it dead."

Choice rushed for 146-yards, but he was a one-man show for Tech. Johnson, a future first round National Football League draft pick, managed just two catches for thirteen yards.

Early in the second quarter, Stafford gave Tech its first points when he fumbled the snap. The ball was recovered by Philip Wheeler on the Bulldogs' 13-yard line. Thankfully, the Jackets went rearward from there; however, Travis Bell booted the first of his two field-goals, a 35-yarder.

The score was 3-0 in the third quarter when Taylor altered the entire nature of the game. As Ball attempted to jostle on third-

and-15, Marcus Howard jarred the football loose when he hit him from behind. There was a pile-up when players jumped on top of the football; however, as everybody searched for the ball, wondering who had recovered, Taylor took the ball from underneath Nate McManus' legs, and was off to the races. He rumbled all alone toward the endzone, and the touchdown stood after the replay officials took another look.

Stafford rallied in the second half, finishing 16-of-29 for 171-yards. Most importantly, he didn't throw any interceptions for the second week in a row. "When the protection was there, Matthew did a good job of hitting his targets," said Georgia coach Mark Richt, who had never lost to the Yellow Jackets. "When it wasn't, he did a great job of throwing it away or taking a sack. It's called managing the game. It's not exciting, but that's what you've got to do."

Georgia 45 - Auburn 20, November 10, 2007

On November 10, 2007, during the 111th game between Georgia and Auburn, Coach Richt sent out his tenth ranked Georgia Bulldogs in black jerseys for the first time in the modern era. Matthew Stafford tossed two touchdown passes, Knowshon Moreno rushed for 101-yards, and Georgia kept its Southeastern Conference title hopes alive with a 45-20 win over the eighteenth ranked Tigers.

"That was a lot of fun," said Richt, who suddenly has gone from a phlegmatic, by-the-book coach, to someone willing to explore all sorts of inspirational tactics. "That was maybe first or second on the fun-meter for me."

Several weeks prior to the game, Coach Richt motivated his lethargic 'Dogs by encouraging the players to have fun, in an excessive manner, once they scored their first touchdown against a despised Florida team. After Moreno scored an early touchdown, the entire Georgia sideline stormed the endzone, drawing numerous penalties. The 'Dogs went on to a 42-30 victory over the nation's defending national champions in Jacksonville, Florida.

Coach Richt actually devised his plan for a jersey switch during the summer, allowing Georgia's seniors the opportunity to wear black, instead of Georgia's traditional red jerseys. The Bulldogs wore red in pregame warm-ups, and then returned to the locker room for their normal ritual of praying behind closed doors, with the lights turned-off. However, when Georgia got into the locker room, everybody had black jerseys waiting at their lockers.

"We were so jacked-up," related senior receiver Sean Bailey, who had four receptions for 96 yards.

Georgia had an 8-2 record, and was tied with Tennessee for the top spot in the Southeastern Conference's Eastern Division, with a 5-2 mark. However, the Volunteers held the tiebreaker over Georgia, and they would not surrender it.

It was Thomas Brown's first game back after suffering a broken collarbone. Early in the fourth quarter he put the final nail in the Tiger's coffin with a 53-yard run to the Auburn 1-yard line. Brannan Southerland bruised his way into the endzone on the next play, commencing a huge celebration for the Bulldogs.

Georgia ended-up scoring the last 28 points against Auburn's defense, ranked fifth nationally in points allowed, at 14.5 per game. It marked Georgia's third straight game where the 'Dogs scored over 40 points; the first time that had occurred since 1942.

"I thought we looked chaotic out there at times," Auburn coach Tommy Tuberville said. "When you give up 45 points, you've been taken to the woodshed." Still, the Tigers recovered enough to take the lead in the third quarter; however, those four interceptions tossed by Brandon Cox were too much to overcome.

"Just one of those nights," said Cox, who threw four interceptions against Georgia the previous season, too. "Their defense really got too much pressure on us."

Auburn had defeated the 'Dogs in twelve of its last fifteen games inside Sanford Stadium. Coach Richt needed a motivational tactic and elected to have Georgia wear black jerseys. In fact, earlier during the week, he suggested the fans wear black, stating he was simply passing along the wishes of the seniors.

The team stormed-out through the main entrance wearing black jerseys, sending the 92,000 fans into an uproar, as a song from an old rock group from the 1980s, AC/DC, "Back in Black," blasted over the stadium's speakers.

When the War Eagles ran its first play from scrimmage, Kelin Johnson made his first of two interceptions. The play afforded Brandon Coutu an easy 32-yard field-goal, thus contributing to Georgia's 17-3 lead by the start of the second quarter.

Auburn's seemingly "home field advantage" inside Sanford Stadium resurfaced as the Tigers' scored 17 straight points. First, Ben Tate ran in from the seven-yard line. Next, Mario Fanning caught a 12-yard touchdown toss from Cox. Finally, Wes Bynum kicked a 33-yard field-goal to give Auburn its first lead of the game, with slightly less than seven minutes remaining in the third quarter.

But Georgia refused to lose. "We just looked in the mirror and said, 'This is our house. We don't want to get embarrassed,'" Johnson said. The Bulldogs dominated the rest of the way, reclaiming the lead with two big plays. First, Stafford went deep down the right sideline for a 45-yard pass to Bailey that was actually called by Richt, instead of offensive coordinator Mike Bobo.

Next, Moreno took off on an outstanding run, where he galloped into a mammoth size opening over his left tackle. While making a beeline for the corner, he suddenly cut to his right and left Auburn safety Zac Etheridge seizing empty air. Moreno masqueraded in the endzone, with hands on his hips.

After the game was over, the Bulldogs galloped toward the student section, pirouetting along with one more playing of "Back in Black." In what was Georgia's original "Blackout" game, the Bulldogs returned from the locker room in black jerseys, a moment that ignited what some called the best home atmosphere ever in Sanford Stadium. While this was an emotional boost, the tenth ranked Bulldogs actually won the game late, scoring 28 unanswered points in the final twenty minutes, to pull away from the Tigers.

Moreno scored on runs of twenty-four and three-yards, while Stafford fired a pair of touchdown passes, one of them to Sean Bailey, who had 96 receiving yards in the victory. Georgia would win its final four games—including a Sugar Bowl rout of Hawai'i—to finish 11-2. Georgia ended the season ranked number two.

Georgia 30 – Alabama 41, September 27, 2008

The game will forever be known as "The Blackout."

It was getting tougher for Alabama Coach Nick Saban to be grimace. He tried to keep the carnival floats padlocked after Alabama's rout of ninth ranked Clemson in the season opener. On September 27, he was back wiggling his finger of caution after a convincing victory over third ranked Georgia.

There had been talk of Alabama's springing into the top-five, and becoming part of the national championship debate, but Saban had a succinct response. "I'm not interested," he said.

Entertainment and Sports Programming Network's College GameDay broadcast their show live from Athens before the Alabama game. The trip was the show's first broadcast from the Classic City since the Tennessee game in 1998. This game was notable because it was only the third "blackout" game where Georgia wore black jerseys. However, unlike the earlier two contests, which Georgia won, the Pachyderms took control early in the game, and built an insurmountable lead.

Saban's pleas slowly became less reasonable to outsiders because his team was arriving ahead of schedule as a national powerhouse. The Crimson Tide had scored on its first five possessions against Georgia, built-up a 31-0 halftime lead, and coasted to 41-30 win. Georgia's eleven game winning streak ended.

The eighth ranked Alabama Crimson Tide started the game running behind its superb left side of the offensive line, left tackle Andre Smith, left guard Mike Johnson and center Antoine Caldwell. The linemen's play set-up play-action plays for quarterback John Parker Wilson, who threw darts into the Georgia secondary.

Wilson completed 13 of 16 passes, for 205-yards and one touchdown. Tailback Glen Coffee gained 86-yards rushing against a Georgia defense ranked third in the nation, allowing only 45 rushing yards per game.

Alabama's front seven, anchored by nose guard Terrence Cody and linebackers Rolando McClain and Dont'a Hightower, knocked Knowshon Moreno out of any Heisman Trophy deliberations by holding him to 34-yards rushing. The Pachyderm's defense was excellent in the box, the region in between the hash marks and near the line of scrimmage, and did not need to assign a defensive back to its run defense.

The Bulldogs entered the game with the dreams of taking Southern California's place as the nation's number one ranked team, after the Men of Troy's astonishing loss to Oregon State two nights earlier. Instead, it was the Bulldogs who were astonished. The Pachyderms quickly destroyed any ambitions Georgia had of reclaiming the country's top spot in the polls.

Alabama set the tone of the game early when, on its first possession the Tide drove 80-yards in eleven plays. The 2009 Heisman Trophy winner, Mark Ingram, scored on a seven-yard touchdown run. On Alabama's next possession, Leigh Tiffin kicked a 23-yard field-goal.

Astonishingly, Georgia had ten penalties for 81-yards. The 'Dogs entered the game as the most penalized team in major college football. In point of fact, the Bulldogs were ranked 119 out of 119 teams in total penalties, managing 10.75 per game.

In effect, on Alabama's first two possessions, Georgia assisted the drives by getting roughing-the-passer penalties. The Fat Lady started warming-up on the Pachyderm's third possession. Alabama got the ball on Georgia's 48-yard line, after a 19-yard punt. The Tide only needed five plays to score. Coffee went into the endzone, and Tiffin's extra-point-attempt made it 17-0 with eleven minutes and fifty-eight seconds remaining in the second quarter.

Alabama's achievement on offense was accredited to staying out of bad situations. Wilson only faced one third-and-long situation during the first half, and Georgia assisted him with one of its roughing-the-passer penalties on the first series, affording the Tide's offense a first down on Georgia's eleven yard line. Incredibly, the Crimson Tide held a 31-0 lead at intermission.

In the third quarter, the Bulldogs put an extra player in the box to make Alabama pass. Additionally, Georgia utilized some crossing blitzes to get at Wilson and unsettle his pocket presence.

The Bulldogs scored seventeen answered points, including a 92-yard punt return by Prince Miller on the first play of the fourth quarter to make it 31-17. However, Saban simply remedied any attempt at a Georgia comeback by relying on the left side of his mammoth offensive line. During a display of power, on first down, Coffee gained five yards around the left side, behind the pulling guard Johnson. On the next play, a reserve tailback, Roy Upchurch, caught a screen pass and went 22-yards behind the bulldozing block of the left tackle Smith. Eventually, Alabama would settle for a 32-yard field-goal from Tiffin to make the score 34-17.

Alabama charged back down the field on its next position. Coffee went twelve yards for another touchdown and Tiffin's kick made it 41-17, with 4:13 remaining. As Georgia fans made a mass exodus towards the exits, the Bulldogs continued fighting. Indeed, the 'Dogs scored twice, to make it a respectable final spread. Humiliated, Georgia had started the season ranked number one in the nation; now, the Bulldogs were regulated to focusing on its Southeastern Conference Eastern (SEC) Division schedule, with games against Tennessee, Vanderbilt, Florida, and Kentucky.

It was a peculiar season. Georgia opened the season with back-to-back victories, yet dropped in the rankings each week. The "blackout" game against Alabama was an opportunity to get to that top spot again; however, instead of impressing a national television audience, the Bulldogs went to the locker room with its largest deficit under Richt. It was Georgia's worst beat down since trailing Auburn 31-0 in 1999.

After the "Blackout" game, the Bulldogs joined the ranks of one-loss teams that included Southern Cal, Florida, Auburn, Ohio State and Kansas.

"We just wanted to come out and take care of business and we didn't do that," said Georgia cornerback Prince Miller. "We saw Southern Cal and Florida go down and we really shot ourselves in the foot. We had a significant opportunity to get back in the driver's seat and we really dropped the ball. Bama played great tonight."

"We don't see it as a big body blow," Geno Atkins said. "If we can somehow win out, we should still go to the SEC championship, and maybe play for the national championship."

The destruction impacted more than Georgia's win-loss record and national rankings. Matt Stafford went 24 of 42, for 274 total yards. He tossed touchdowns and an interception; however, he sustained a head injury in the third quarter. Trainers escorted him away before postgame interviews occurred. A. J. Green led all Georgia receivers with six catches for 88-yards and one touchdown.

Moreno suffered an elbow injury as he rushed for a career low of 34-yards on nine carries. It was the kind of game that made Georgia deliberate scrapping its blackout jerseys forevermore.

It was the first game in six years that pitted two top-ten teams inside of Sanford Stadium. Murphy's Law was in effect, because anything that could go wrong went wrong for Georgia, at least during the first half.

As an example, Akeem Dent was whistled for roughing the passer, negating an Alabama fumble that Georgia recovered deep in its own territory. Two plays later, Ingram scored a touchdown. Next, a Stafford pass to Green turned into a fumble when it was knocked out of Green's hands and into the hands of Hightower. That led to a four yard Upchurch touchdown run and a 24-0 lead.

The game was a definite mismatch in the first half as the 'Dogs were outgained in total yardage 231-86. And, the Pachyderms of Alabama amassed 17 first downs to Georgia's four. The Bulldogs would finish the season a very respectable 10-3, and would defeat Michigan State 24-12 in the Capital One bowl game. Alabama finished 12-2, and lost the SEC title game against Florida.

Georgia 13- Louisiana State University 20, October 3, 2009

The referees' calls were a disgrace to the Southeastern Conference (SEC). Georgia's defense held the fourth-ranked Louisiana State University Bayou Bengals out of the endzone for fifty-seven minutes. But the talk amongst the 'Dogs defenders, after Georgia's 20-13 upset loss, was of those remaining three minutes when the Tigers scored twice to win the game.

A.J. Green, the hero of the Arizona State game the previous week, after blocking a game saving field-goal, wasn't able to pull another miracle against the Bayou Bengals and an incompetent group of referees. Green's late 16-yard reception put Georgia ahead with 1:09 remaining. It was surely cause for a celebration inside Sanford Stadium; however, the officials elected to rule Green had celebrated too much. In the end, the fourth ranked Louisiana State Tigers was the team celebrating during a 20-13 victory over the eighteenth ranked 'Dogs.

"I guess you can't stay energized too long or they'll throw a rag on you," said Coach Richt, who said officials did not tell him clearly what had occurred to cause the celebration penalty.

As mentioned, the previous weekend Green blocked a fourth quarter field-goal that would have put Arizona State ahead. Against the Bayou Bengals, he was penalized after he jumped-up and grabbed the football over the outstretched arms' of cornerback Chris Hawkins. It was a fade pattern into the right side of the endzone. "I was surprised, but you can't argue with them," said Green, who had five receptions for 99-yards. As a team, Georgia was held to 274 total yards of offense.

With 1:09 remaining, little did anybody know in the delirium, after Green's apparent game-winning touchdown catch, the tide was going to turn. Georgia was penalized for unsportsmanlike conduct after the touchdown, forcing Blair Walsh, Georgia's kicker, to kick off from the Bulldogs' 15-yard line. The Tigers' Trenton Holiday returned the ensuing kick to the Georgia 43 yard-line, setting-up Charles Scott's winning touchdown run.

Somehow, despite the Tigers penetrating the 'Dogs 20-yard line three times in the opening half—the Tigers led only 6-0 at halftime. "We could have been down 28-0 at halftime," Richt said. "The first half was a defensive masterpiece."

For most of the day, it was a defensive struggle. However, as the clock prepared to expire, the two teams started trading touchdowns almost as if there were no defense on the field. In fact, the Bulldogs and Tigers combined for three touchdowns in the final three minutes. Scott scored the one that mattered most, a 33-yard run, with 46 seconds remaining, to give the Tigers the 20-13 win.

J. Green, 2009

Scott appeared stopped at the line, after being hemmed in by at least three Georgia tacklers. But he stumbled out of the pack, putting down a hand to stay-up, and didn't stop running until he got into the endzone. "I played mad, a controlled rage," said Scott, who rushed for 95-yards on 19 carries, after struggling in the first four games. Neither team reached the endzone through the first three quarters, but they made-up for it in the fourth.

In the end, Louisiana State benefited from an excessive-celebration penalty after Green came down with the concentrated catch. The good field position, culminating from the penalty, helped put Scott in position to win it with a hard-nosed run, which would have been a pass if those on the sideline had their way.

Bayou Bengal quarterback, Jordan J. Jefferson, convinced the coaches to let him hand off to Scott, instead of putting the ball in the air. They were sure glad he did.

"I would rather give it to Charles and let him pound it in there," said Jefferson, who was 18 of 27 for 212 yards. "Charles is a big power back. I didn't want to pass it. That situation required a running play. I saw the hole, and once he hit it, I knew it was a touchdown."

Georgia took control in the third quarter, after being sparked by a hard-rushing defense that sacked Jefferson six times and the hard running of Washaun Ealey, who gained 33-yards on eight carries in his first college appearance. The 'Dogs finally scored in the opening minute of the fourth quarter when Joe Cox tossed a 1-yard touchdown pass to Shaun Chapas on fourth-and-goal.

The Bayou Bengals were down 7-6 when Jefferson converted a third and 16-yard pass to Rueben Randle. Next, he tossed a pass to Scott for another 16-yards. Then, Scott got open down the sideline for a 27-yard gain that set-up Scott's first touchdown, a 2-yard run, with 2:53 remaining. The Tigers led 12-7 after failing to convert a 2-point conversion as Jefferson was sacked.

Georgia answered fast. Tavares King caught a Cox pass and went 46-yards. Next, Cox tossed-up a pass for grabs in the endzone. Green extended over Hawkins, and grabbed the football before he was shoved into the hedges.

Afterwards, Georgia received a penalty for another excessive celebration penalty. Green related, "I was simply celebrating with my team." However, Southeastern Conference officials released a statement from the officiating crew stating, "Following a brief team celebration, Green made a gesture, calling attention to himself."

Georgia missed their 2-point try, and had to kick-off from the 15-yard line. Holiday, a track and field sprint champion, returned it to the Georgia 43-yard line. A 5-yard penalty, for an illegal formation, pushed the Tigers even closer. Next, Scott won it for the Tigers. He got loose, with Jeff Owens clutching for his ankles, and linebackers Rennie Curran and Marcus Dowtin trying to tackle him.

Both teams would have uneventful seasons. Georgia ended the season at 8-5, with a third place finish in the East. Louisiana State finished 9-4, and third in the SEC West.

Georgia 44- Louisiana State University 41, September 28, 2013

The game was between Southeastern Conference (SEC) titans. Aaron Murray tossed four touchdown passes, including the game winner to Justin Scott-Wesley, with 1:47 remaining, to give the ninth ranked Bulldogs a 44-41 victory over the sixth ranked Bayou Bengals. Georgia was glad to have won.

The Bulldogs opened the season running the gauntlet of some of the nation's premiere football teams by defeating the Bayou Bengals, and subsequently getting back into the national title talk. "We've played some brutal teams," Scott-Wesley said. "It shows we're a great team. We can handle anything thrown at us."

Georgia emerged as the fourth team, since 1998, to play three Top-10 teams in its first four games of the season. The 'Dogs lost to Clemson 38-35, rebounded to defeat South Carolina 41-30, then beat Louisiana State 44-41. "We've grown-up a lot this past month," Murray said. "I think the nation knows what Georgia football is about now. We're a tough group. We're fighters!"

Georgia's team returned to the field less than ten minutes after the game in order to rejoice and celebrate with 'Dog fans. "I'm honored to be a part of something like that," Coach Richt said. The triumph placed Georgia in a position to make a run at their third straight SEC East title. Unfortunately, the Missouri Tigers would later ruin Georgia's plans.

"We're definitely happy," Murray said. "If we had to lose one of these games, obviously Clemson was the one, just because they're in the Atlantic Coast Conference. Not saying we wanted to lose. Don't get me wrong. But this is colossal."

With 4:14 to go, the Bengal Tigers went ahead 41-37, on Jeremy Hill's 8-yard touchdown run. On a day when neither defense accomplishment very much, Murray had plenty of time. He came out of the gates throwing. He completed three passes in a row to quickly move the Bulldogs into Tiger territory. J. J. Green got down to the Tigers' 18-yard line, after busting free for an 18-yard run. Next, Scott-Wesley got behind the secondary, hauled in a pass from Murray and tiptoed just inside the pylon for the winning score.

In 2010, Murray and Louisiana State quarterback Zack Mettenberger were part of the same amazing recruiting class at Georgia. They both competed for the starting job in the spring of '10. Mettenberger, out of Watkinsville, grew-up a Bulldog; however, after pleading guilty to misdemeanor charges, involving an incident at a bar, he was dismissed from the team. However, his connection to Georgia remained—most notably, his mother, who was employed in football operations for the Bulldogs. Coach Richt gave her the week off because of the attention surrounding her son.

Mettenberger tossed three touchdowns passes, and ended-up going 23-of-37 on pass completions. His 25-yard pass completion to Odell Beckham, on third-and-22 yard, miraculously kept a Tiger drive alive. Eventually, it led to Hill's go-ahead touchdown. But Murray was afforded too much time to dispense the final wallop.

Georgia did sufficient damage on the ground in the first half; however, it came with a cost. Todd Gurley suffered an injury to his left ankle when he busted loose on a 25-yard run. He watched the second half, as a spectator, in a windbreaker and walking boot.

Keith Marshall, one of the top running backs in the nation out of high school, handled the load; however, Murray and his receivers took-up the slack. Chris Conley had five catches for 112-yards and a touchdown. Michael Bennett grabbed two passes for touchdowns.

In the end, Georgia had 494 total yards, and the majority of the gains came in a back-and-forth first half. Murray ran for Georgia's other touchdown, and finished with 298-yards passing.

Kadron Boone, who was rarely utilized, scored two early touchdowns for the Tigers; however, Jarvis Landry emerged to be Mettenberger's go-to receiver. Landry had ten catches for 156-yards, including a 39-yard touchdown to tie the game late in the third quarter. Mettenberger passed for a staggering 372-yards.

Georgia 45- Clemson 21, August 30, 2014

Todd Gurley was only trying to rebound from an injury-plagued sophomore campaign. He sustained an injury to his quadriceps that regulated his carries in a season-opening loss to Clemson. Later in the year, he wrenched his ankle against Louisiana State and missed three games. He ended the season with slightly less than 1,000 yards rushing.

Now, on this historic date, Georgia eventually broke open a game that was tied 21-all at halftime. Without Tajh Boyd and Sammy Watkins, Clemson's fast-break offense wasn't as effective, and the 'Dogs' defense shut down the Tigers. In fact, in the second half, the Tigers were held to one first down and 15 total yards.

Gurley started off the scoring with a 23-yard touchdown run in the first quarter. Later, he electrified the crowd of more than 92,000 when he took a kickoff at the goal line, burst through a gap and went straight-up the middle of the field for another touchdown. He displayed an extraordinary amount of speed.

Cognizant of Gurley's injuries from the previous season, and attempting to protect him in the extremely humid conditions, Georgia's coaching staff limited the amount of times he touched the football. Still, the nation watched Gurley have a record-setting performance for Georgia, totaling 293 all-purpose yards. He turned-in his fourteenth 100-yard rushing performance by gaining 198-yards. Additionally, he became the fifth Georgia player to have a 100-yard kickoff return for a touchdown. Besides his all-purpose yards, Gurley accounted for four touchdowns.

Hutson Mason led the passing attack for Georgia, going 18-for-26 for 131-yards. He rushed for one touchdown. Michael Bennett collected 60-yards on five catches. Nick Chubb had four carries for 70 yards and a touchdown.

Initially Clemson had taken a 7-0 lead on the first drive of the game, going 70-yards in 12 plays. After going 69-yards, the Tigers had a fourth down on the one yard line before scoring a touchdown.

Georgia promptly scored on their second drive of the game. Mason started the drive with an 11-yard pass to Sony Michel, putting them on the Clemson 46-yard line. After a nine-yard pick-up by Isaiah McKenzie, Mason found Bennett down the sideline for 19-yards, setting-up a first down at the Clemson 23-yard line. Two plays later, Gurley went 23-yards for the score. Marshall Morgan converted the extra-point to tie the game at 7-7.

Next, with less than one minute to play in the first quarter,

Georgia took a 14-7 lead. After an overwhelming defensive stand, that included a sack of Clemson's Cole Stout, Gurley took the first handoff of the drive 14 yards, to the Clemson 22-yard line. His following rush set-up a 12-yard completion to Bennett. In turn, Bennett's reception set-up a two-yard touchdown dash by Mason.

Clemson immediately answered with a pair of touchdowns that gave the Tigers a 21-14 lead. The first touchdown came on a 30-yard pass from Deshaun Watson to Charone Peake, with 13:52 left in the half. Next, the Tigers took the lead on a one-yard touchdown run by C.J. Davidson.

Afterwards, Clemson kicked-off, with Gurley back deep for the Bulldogs. He proceeded to tie a school-record with a 100-yard kickoff return for a touchdown. The score was knotted at 21 each. It was Gurley's second career touchdown from a kickoff return.

To start off the second half, Mason coordinated a 10-play, 57-yard drive that culminated in a 27-yard field-goal by Morgan. Georgia led 24-21. With less than 10 minutes left in the game, the score remained 24-21.

While Gurley kept pounding away, Clemson discovered it was becoming increasingly harder to tackle him. In fact, during Georgia's first drive of the fourth quarter, he rushed for 58 of the 82-yards. He topped off the drive with an 18-yard rush, up the middle, to give Georgia a 10-point lead at 31-21.

Georgia's defense continued to frustrate the Tiger's offense, as the ensuing possession saw Clemson post negative yardage. The 'Dogs subsequently took over on their own 47-yard line. Riding the momentum, Chubb took the first play of the drive 47-yards into the endzone for his first career touchdown. Georgia went up 38-21.

After the Tigers went three-and-out, Gurley grabbed a handoff from Mason and went 51-yards for pay-dirt. It was his fourth touchdown of the game. Mason completed 18-of-26 passes for 131-yards.

Gurley turned-in one of the more dominant performances in Sanford Stadium's history. He finished the night with 198-yards on 15 carries and scored three rushing touchdowns. However, it was his fourth touchdown that thoroughly captured the attention of the talking heads at ESPN.

Georgia Head Coaches of Sanford Stadium Era

Football can be merciless to men. Coaching can make a man even more peculiar than an alcoholic drink can. The men who ply their trade on the windy, time-worn college football fields across America appear innumerable, as they lie in wait for football season to start. History has shown the intricacies of college coaching can be so vast, and grandiose, it is sometimes hard to imagine some of the details therein.

Statistics indicate, in a sample of hundreds of college football coaches, outliers will occur in both vast success, and staggering failure. Historically, when a football program is successful, its coach can stay for decades; however, as college football emerges into a multi-billion dollar enterprise, nine or ten win seasons are no longer sufficient to guarantee job security.

Throughout the history of colligate football there have been many men who have posted incredible winning percentages, and the majority of them reside in the College Football Hall-of-Fame. Unfortunately, most of the gentlemen who've held the head coaching position in Athens will most likely never reside in the College Football Hall-of-Fame, despite their allegiance to Georgia,

Here are the eight head coaches the University of Georgia has had since Sanford Stadium's inception on October 12, 1929. Some are legendary, while others aren't too well known. All are exceptionally important people because each one had the distinct opportunity of being the chief executive officer at one of the greatest college football institutions in the annals of American sports history.

Harry Mehre, 1928-37

Harry Mehre played for Knute Rockne at Notre Dame, and coached the Georgia Bulldogs for a decade prior to moving on to Ole Miss. A renowned humorist, Mehre declared he had a lifetime contract at Georgia, but the University decided he was dead.

He coached the University of Georgia football team from 1928 to 1937. His most memorable game was on October 12, 1929, during the dedication game of Sanford Stadium. His '29 Bulldogs, mostly sophomores, upset invincible Yale 15-0, with the famous Catfish Smith scoring all 15 points.

Coach Mehre had an overall record of 59-34-6; however, he never won a conference championship. He had four teams that contended strongly for the conference championship (1930, '31, '33, '34) and each would have gone to a bowl game had there been as many post-season games as there were during the 1990s. His 1931 team went 8-2, with its only two losses coming against the two teams that finished the season ranked number one and two in the nation, the University of Southern California, and the Tulane Green Waves, respectively.

In 1936, the year before his termination as head coach, there had been alumni who had been critical of Coach Mehre; however, the "whispering" campaign against him slowly quieted down. Then the murmur started back after the Tennessee game on October 31, 1936. Georgia suffered its worst loss ever inside of Sanford Stadium by a final score of 46-0.

In November 1936, Coach Mehre's Bulldogs tied the undefeated Fordham's "seven blocks of granite," and knocked the Rams out of the Rose Bowl picture. This game in New York would again quiet down his naysayers, temporarily. Nevertheless, Coach Mehre left Georgia at the end of the season to assume the head coaching duties at Ole Miss. He remained with the Rebels for eight seasons and compiled a 39-26-1 record. In 1945, he left Ole Miss and became a soft drink wholesaler and football analyst for the *Atlanta-Journal* for 22 years.

Joel "Lil' Joel" Hunt, 1938

Joel Hunt, born on October 11, 1905, was a dumbfounded replacement for the Coach Mehre. Although Hunt's 5-4-1 record as a head coach was respectable, his most important contribution to Georgia football was one of the assistant coaches, Wallace Butts, he brought with him.

During the week of January 14, 1938, after a month of conflicting reports, rumors, and guesses, the name Joel Hunt, a youthful backfield coach at Louisiana State, was announced as Georgia's new head football coach. He brought with him Elmer Lampe and Butts.

Lampe, praised by "Red" Grange as "the best end I ever tried to get around," was Hunt's end coach and took over the varsity basketball assignment, too. Whereas, Butts, the former Mercer star, and coach of Male High school, in Louisville, Kentucky, served as Georgia's new line coach.

Coach Hunt, who had five years professional baseball experience in the Saint Louis Cardinal system, was considered for the Georgia baseball coaching position, too; however he never accepted the position. Before the football season started, he added Forrest Towns to his staff, in addition to appointing him as an assistant track coach to his former mentor, Weems Baskin.

Many experts boasted the most talented back on Georgia's football squad was 32-year old Coach Hunt. He had been a great player during his collegiate hey-day at Texas A&M, under Coach Dana Bible, where he complied the most sensational record ever to reach the books in the Southwest Conference—the league a whole lot of grid critics felt was the toughest in the country. Hunt won that school's award for being its top athlete in 1927, when he scored 19 touchdowns for the Aggies.

Coach Hunt had been an athlete, and an All-American selection his senior year in 1927. In 1938, he still could have stepped on the field and received the snap from Captain Quinton Lumpkin, at center, and booted or passed the ball better than anybody on Georgia's team. It wasn't that Georgia lacked a capable punter, or bomb-tosser, but it was merely happened stance that Coach Hunt was still as nimble and as agile as a jack-rabbit.

Coach Hunt came to the University in the winter of 1937, but only stayed for one season. Hunt never captured the favor of Georgia's fan or alumni and left Athens after the '38 season. He went on to coach at the University of Wyoming and later returned to Louisiana State University.

Wallace Butts, 1939-1960

Born in the heart of the state, Milledgeville, on February 7, 1905, Butts was a direct descendant of one of Georgia's earliest settlers, Captain Samuel Butts, for whom Butts County, Georgia was named. In 1814, Captain Butts had been killed leading a charge of Georgia militia against Creek Indians in the Battle of Chalibbee.

Coach Butts was a football, basketball and baseball standout at Georgia Military College in his hometown of Milledgeville. In 1928, he graduated Mercer University, in Macon, after making All-

Conference under Coach Bernie Moore, later Southeastern Conference (SEC) Commissioner, in 1932.

Coach Butts had remarkable success in 10 years of prep school coaching, losing only 10 games. He never failed to turn out an undefeated championship team at each of the three schools he coached. He was at Madison Georgia A&M in 1928-31; Georgia Military College in Milledgeville: 1932-34, and Male High, in Louisville, Kentucky, from 1935-37.

He became head coach at the nation's oldest state chartered university in 1939, and in 22 seasons at Georgia, Coach Butts posted a 140-86-9 record. As mentioned, he originally arrived at Georgia as an assistant to Joel Hunt in 1938, but Hunt left Georgia after a 5–4–1 season in order to take over at Wyoming.

During his reign as head coach, Georgia claimed a national championship in 1942, after being selected by six polls recognized by the NCAA. In 1946, his team, led by a gauntlet of All-Americans, finished undefeated, and was selected as national champions in several of the national polls.

He coached Heisman Trophy winner Frank Sinkwich, and Maxwell Award winner Charlie Trippi. His teams won four SEC titles in '42, '46, '48 and '59 and his bowl record was 5–2–1. His teams and players held more SEC offensive records, particularly in passing, than any other conference school.

From a monetary perspective, in 1946, during Georgia's undefeated season, Coach Butts' regular salary was a modest $8,166, or the equivalent of $99,934 in 2015 currency. Additionally, he would receive nearly $1,900, or $23,251 in 2015 currency, as a Sugar Bowl bonus. He received a subsistence allowance of $1,749, or $21,403 in modern exchange, for six months.

The professional football teams of the 1940s and '50s used pass patterns similar to those Butts used while at Georgia, when Sinkwich and Trippi were dominating college football. In fact, the late Frank Leahy of Notre Dame referred to Coach Butts as, "… the greatest offensive genius of all-time." And, Fran Tarkenton, who starred for Georgia before revising the National Football League quarterbacking records, said Coach Butts knew more about offense than any coach he ever knew.

After twenty-two seasons at Georgia, Coach Butts resigned to become full-time Athletic Director. The Dean of SEC Coaches,

Coach Butts brought Georgia into national prominence as a football power and had taken his teams to every major post-season bowl. Although his flashy pass patterns were called the best in the game, hard-nosed defensive tactics were his trademark.

In 1959, he was named SEC Coach of the Year for the fourth time after his Bulldogs won the conference crown, defeated Missouri in the Orange Bowl, and finished fifth in the nation. Later, in 1962, he was embroiled in a controversy with Coach Bryant of Alabama, about fixing the 1962 Alabama versus Georgia game. They would be vindicated in a lawsuit against the *Saturday Evening Post*.

Coach Butts "Saturday Evening Post" redemption, circa 1963

Georgia sports lovers rank James Wallace Butts with two other athletic immortals born and bred in the Empire state of the South: Jackie Robinson and Bobby Jones. Coach Butts went on to a highly-successful career in the insurance business. The Butts-Mehre Heritage Hall on Georgia's campus is named in his honor.

Johnny Leonard Griffith, 1961-63

Born on May 27, 1924, in Crawfordville, Georgia, the home of Alexander H. Stephens, Coach Griffith and his family moved to Atlanta when he was a youngster. He played at old Boys' High in

Atlanta, under the famed R.L. "Shorty" Doyal. Coach Doyal shifted Griffith from guard to halfback because of his sprinter's speed. He became a standout on the great juggernauts Doyal was producing annually at Boys' High.

After serving in the U.S. Navy, 1943 through 46, during World War II, Coach Griffith entered Georgia and was a substitute back as a freshman on Georgia's great undefeated and untied Southeastern Conference and Sugar Bowl champions of 1946.

Griffith was known as an excellent recruiter in his days as a Georgia assistant from 1956-1960. Coach Griffith became Georgia's nineteenth head football coach in 1961, replacing the legendary Coach Butts. Unfortunately, because of systemic problems, he was unable to establish a winning program in those three years after Butts, going a combined 1-8 against Florida, Auburn, and Tech, along with three straight losing seasons. He compiled an overall record of 10–16–4 during his three-year career as head coach. While he had few successes during this time, he did have two big victories, a 30–21 upset win over Auburn in '62, and a 31–14 victory over highly favored Miami in '63.

He coached one of Georgia's all-time greatest passers, Larry Rakestraw, who is prominent in the Bulldog's record books. Griffith resigned his coaching duties in December, 1963, and later went on to establish a successful construction business in Atlanta. He became a tireless worker on behalf of the State of Georgia Sports Hall of Fame and was selected for induction into the Hall in 1997.

Vincent Joseph Dooley, 1964-1988

He was born in the Alabama coastal city of Mobile on September 4, 1932. His mother, the former Nellie Agnes Stouter, was a native of Mobile, of German-Italian descent. His father, William Vincent Dooley, an electrician, was a native of New Orleans, Louisiana.

He played quarterback for Auburn during the 1950s, and later joined the United States Marine Corps. He returned to Auburn to coach the freshman teams, and would eventually be hired by Georgia's new Athletic Director, Joel Eaves, to replace Coach Griffith as the twentieth head coach at Georgia. Coach Dooley would hold the head coaching position longer than any other Georgia coach, leading the Bulldogs from 1964–88.

During his tenure as head coach, Georgia won its second consensus national championship in 1980. Coach Dooley's '68 team finished first in one national poll, giving Georgia a claim to a third national championship. The '67 Cotton Bowl win over Southern Methodist University made Georgia only the third school in college football history to have won all four of the historical major bowls: Rose, Cotton, Sugar, and Orange.

Coach Dooley's teams won six Southeastern Conference titles and he had one Heisman Trophy winner, Herschel Walker, in 1982, and one Outland Trophy winner, Bill Stanfill, in 1968. He amassed a record of 201–77–10, while going to twenty bowl games. His bowl record was 8–10–2.

Coach Dooley's offenses were known primarily for power running. He converted Georgia's single-wing offense to a Split-Back Veer during the early '70s, and later ran a professional I-type offense with the arrival of Walker in 1980.

The 1977 was a disappointing season for Bulldog supporters. The team, plagued by inexperience and injuries, finished the season with a 5-6 record. It would be Coach Dooley's only losing season in 25 years at Georgia. As a result, the Georgia players and coaches found themselves sitting at home watching Alabama paste the Ohio State in the Sugar Bowl on January 2, 1978. Staying at home for the Christmas holiday's season was something Coach Dooley was not accustomed. When asked about the sub-par season, he cited inexperience and injuries as the main problems.

During his tenure, seven of his players earned the prestigious National Football Foundation post-graduate scholarship and eleven former players received equally-coveted NCAA post-graduate scholarship. Seventy-seven of his players earned Academic All-SEC recognition. He holds the unique distinction of being inducted into the Sports Hall of Fame in two different states, Georgia and Alabama. Coach Dooley was a 1994 inductee into the National College Football Hall of Fame.

Ray Goff, 1989-95

Goff, born on July 19, 1955, was a former player and All-Southeastern Conference (SEC) quarterback under Coach Dooley from 1973-1976. He was captain of the SEC champions in 1976 and was named SEC Player of the Year. After serving three years as an assistant coach at South Carolina, Coach Dooley hired him as one of his assistants at Georgia from 1981-1988. Goff was the recruiting coordinator, tight ends coach, and running backs coach. When Coach Dooley, the winningest coach in Georgia football history, retired after the 1988 season, Coach Erk Russell was expected to replace him; however, after Coach Russell declined the offer, Goff—a 33-year-old running backs coach—was the surprise choice to succeed Coach Dooley.

Coach Goff compiled an overall record of 46-34-1 during his seven years as head coach. His coaching career got off to a rough start, with only ten wins in his first two seasons. Then, his teams won nine games in 1991 and ten games in 1992. In fact, only five points separated Georgia from an undefeated season in 1992. A 34-31 upset loss to Tennessee and a 26-24 loss to Florida derailed what potentially could have been a national title season. Instead, Georgia's '92 campaign finished with the 'Dogs ranked eighth by the Coaches Poll.

Unfortunately, from 1993 through '95, Coach Goff's teams never won more than seven games. His last three teams made brief appearances in the Coaches Poll in '93, '94 and '95, reaching as high as number thirteen in the '93 preseason polls. His '95 squad was on the receiving end of Steve Spurrier's "Half a Hundred" game where Swamp Lizards put-up 52 points on the struggling Bulldogs. In truth, short passes, reverses, double passes and, finally, an eight-yard touchdown pass, with only one minute remaining, capped a 76-yard drive and a final score of 52-17 for Florida in Sanford Stadium.

Coach Goff's teams were 0–5 against Tennessee, 1-6 versus Florida, 2-4-1 in games against Auburn, and 5-2 in opposition to hated Georgia Tech. In 1995, at end of the injury-plagued season, he was fired, despite Georgia receiving an invitation to the Peach Bowl.

Jim Donnan, 1996-00

A native of Burlington, North Carolina, and graduate of North Carolina State, Coach Donnan came to Georgia following a record-setting run at Marshall. In his six years with the Thundering Herd, his teams won sixty-four games, one national championship, three national runner-up finishes, and earned five consecutive trips to the post-season playoffs. He was named National 1-AA Coach of the Year twice. Coach Donnan had previously been the architect of Oklahoma's high powered offenses from 1985-1989, where the Sooners won 49 games during those five seasons, including 27 straight Big Eight contests and the 1985 National Championship.

In 1996, Coach Donnan left Marshall to take over as head coach at Georgia. He coached from '96 through '00, where he obtained a record of 40-19, including 25-15 in the Southeastern Conference. He was the first coach in Georgia history to take the program to four consecutive bowl victories, winning the '98 Outback Bowl, '98 Peach Bowl, '00 Outback and the '00 Oahu Bowl. He gained fame on the Armed Forces Network when the television station aired the way he motivated his team before the '97 Mississippi State game. He drove a steamroller onto the practice field and told his players they "were either going to be the steamroller or the pavement." Georgia won the game 47-0.

After posting back-to-back eight-win seasons, Coach Donnan was terminated by University President Michael F. Adams, against the advice of Athletic Director Vince Dooley. Nevertheless, Georgia had lost three straight to its most hated rival, Georgia Tech

Mark Richt, 2001–present

Coach Richt was born in Nebraska. His family later moved to Florida, where he became an outstanding athlete in high school. He signed a scholarship with the University of Miami, where he backed-up one of the greatest quarterbacks of all-time, Jim Kelly.

After college he was a graduate assistance at Florida State before becoming offensive coordinator at East Carolina in 1989. In 1990, he returned to Florida State where he eventually took over as the offensive coordinator, under Coach Bobby Bowden. He became the most successful offensive coordinator in the nation after leading Florida State to nine straight Atlantic Coast Conference titles. Additionally, he coached two Heisman Trophy winners, and guided the Seminoles to two national title appearances, winning one against Virginia Tech, while dropping one against Oklahoma.

On December 26, 2000, after taking Florida State to its pinnacle, Coach Richt accepted the head coaching position at Georgia. While in Athens, he has rested calmly in the eye of the storm for well over a decade, while winning at least 10 games on seven different occasions. His Georgia teams have won two Southeastern Conference (SEC) titles in 2002 and 2005, and six SEC Eastern Division titles in '02, '03, '05, '07, '11 and '12.

At the end of the 2014 season Coach Richt's record at Georgia was an exceptional 136-48, including a bowl record of 9-5. Under his guidance, Georgia is 10-4 versus Tennessee, 5-9 in games against Florida, 9-5 in opposition to Auburn, and 13-2 versus Georgia Tech.

Coach Richt, the Dean of SEC coaches, has maintained his head-coaching job in an industry not conducive to longevity. Georgia has been a mainstay near the top of the polls and his teams have reached a bowl game every season since his arrival. His winning percentage is the best in Georgia football history.

In fact, he was selected as SEC Coach of the Year twice, in 2002 and 2005. With an endless supply of stellar recruits continuously being signed to scholarships, another SEC title, along with Georgia's first national title, since 1980, isn't too far away.

Train Crossing Trestle, circa 1977

Heisman Trophy Winners and Mythical National Champions

The Heisman Trophy, long distinguished as the most prestigious individual award in American college football, was created in 1935. It is the oldest of several awards in collegiate football, including the Maxwell Award, Walter Camp Award, and the *Associated Press* Player of the Year.

The trophy has been awarded yearly to the most exceptional college football player in the National Collegiate Athletic Association (NCAA) Division I, whose performance has best demonstrated the quest of excellence with integrity. Winners have exemplified great talent, merged with conscientiousness, determination, and hard work. Each year, in early December, it has been presented by the Heisman Trophy Trust, successors of the awards from the Downtown Athletic Club, at an annual ceremony in New York City.

The Downtown Athletic Club, a privately owned recreation facility, located on the lower west side, in New York City, initially developed the trophy to "recognize the best football player "east of the Mississippi River," however, it was eventually broadened to include players west of the Mississippi. In 1935, the trophy was first known simply as the Downtown Athletic Club Trophy, and its first winner, Jay Berwanger, played for the University of Chicago.

In 1936, the Club's president, John Heisman, died and the award was renamed in his honor. Larry Kelly, the second winner of the trophy, was the first man to win it as the "Heisman Trophy." In 1942, Frank Sinkwich would become the first person from outside the northeast to receive the award.

Eight winners of this award have played inside of Sanford Stadium. Two recipients of the award, Sinkwich and Herschel Walker, played for Georgia. The six other beneficiaries, who graced the field of Sanford Stadium, played on teams that would go a combined 8-1-1 in games played inside of Sanford Stadium.

Frank Sinkwich, Georgia, 1939-42

Frank Sinkwich was born October 10, 1920, in McKees Rock, Pennsylvania and raised on the west side of Youngstown, an

Ohio steel town, by Croatian immigrant parents from Russian Georgia.

During the Great Depression of the late 1930s, he played running back for the Chaney High School football team. In 1939, he was recruited by University of Georgia backfield coach Bill Hartman. He accepted Hartman's offer on the condition his friend, George Poschner, be granted a scholarship, too. That season, in 1939, both Sinkwich and Poschner would make headlines playing for the "Point-a-Minute Bullpups," the university's greatest freshman football squad of all-time.

On the physical side, the two-headed sensation stood a shade above five-feet-ten, and was powerfully built. Pictures of 1940 games show him violently bowling over would-be-tacklers. But his main asset was his ability to get under way in a hurry. He took off much faster than Georgia's other talented backs, although several could out-sprint him in the 100-yard dash.

In 1941, Sinkwich earned All-American honors as the team's leading halfback. After breaking his jaw against South Carolina, he played the rest of the season with his jaw wired shut. He wore a large jaw protector attached to his helmet. He had the guard when he led Georgia to a 40-26 victory over Texas Christian University in the 1942 Orange Bowl, Georgia's first postseason appearance. His performance was considered one of the best individual performances in Orange Bowl history. He completed nine of thirteen passes for 243-yards, and three touchdowns, while rushing for 139-yards. He capped off his efforts with a 43-yard touchdown run.

The following season, Sinkwich shared the backfield with a greenhorn, Charlie Trippi, by switching to the fullback position, while Trippi played halfback. The pair led Georgia to an 11-1 record, culminating with a 9-0 Rose Bowl victory over the University of California at Los Angeles. Sinkwich, known for his sturdiness, if not his bulk, played that game with two very badly sprained ankles.

For his stellar play in 1942, which included a still-unbeaten school record of twenty-seven touchdowns, he was awarded the Heisman Trophy by a unanimous vote, the largest margin of victory in the award's history and was a two time All-American. Additionally, the *Associated Press* named him the "The Number One Athlete for 1942." The second place finisher was Ted Williams, who won baseball's triple-crown that year. Sinkwich rushed for 2,271 yards, and passed for 2,331 yards during his career with Georgia. The school retired his jersey, number 21.

In 1943, the Marine Corps rejected Sinkwich for having flat feet; however, the Detroit Lions, a professional football team, drafted him in the first round. In his two seasons as a running back with the Lions, Sinkwich was named All-Pro twice and league Most Valuable Player in 1944.

The next season, he was accepted into the Army-Air Force. However, he suffered a serious knee injury playing for the 4th Air Force football team. The injury ended Sinkwich's career at the age of twenty-five. After the setback, he coached at Furman University, in Greenville, South Carolina, and the University of Tampa, before settling in Athens as a businessman. In 1954 he was inducted into the College Football Hall of Fame.

In later years Sinkwich's success as a wholesale beer distributor allowed him to be a major supporter of Georgia athletics. Along with his former coach Bill Hartman, he chaired the committee to raise funds for construction of the Butts-Mehre Heritage Hall, completed in 1987. Frank Sinkwich died of cancer on October 22, 1990. His Heisman Trophy is on display at the Butts-Mehre Hall.

Pat Sullivan, Auburn, November 15, 1969, November 13, 1971

It would be almost thirty years before another Heisman Trophy winner would grace the field of Sanford Stadium. Pat Sullivan, born in Birmingham, Alabama, began his athletic career as a three-sport star at Birmingham's John Carroll High School. Although a talented baseball and basketball player, he chose to play football for Auburn University, where he would become the starting quarterback in 1969, under the guidance of head coach Ralph Jordan.

The 6'-0", 190 pound Sullivan would break school and NCAA records for passing, while leading Auburn to a 26–7 record. In 1970, he led the NCAA in total offense with 2,856 yards and set an NCAA record for most yards per play with 8.57. During his career, he was responsible for 71 touchdowns.

In 1971, his senior season, Sullivan completed 162 passes on 281 attempts for 2,012 yards and 20 touchdowns. He eventually edged out Ed Marinaro, of Cornell University, for the 1971 Heisman

Trophy. He finished his college career with 6,284 passing yards and 57 touchdowns, along with another eighteen rushing touchdowns.

Auburn defeated Georgia 13-6 in the 1969 game, and despite his already impressive career, 1971 proved to be Sullivan's greatest year. With Sullivan and Terry Beasley as the center piece, the Auburn Tigers went 8-0, with notable wins against Kentucky, Georgia Tech, and Florida before its showdown with the Georgia.

On November 13, 1971, the two undefeated teams met inside Sanford Stadium on a crisp autumn day, with Southeastern Conference (SEC) and national championship implications on the line. It was considered the biggest game in the history of the SEC and was the first time two unbeaten SEC teams met late in the season.

Georgia, ranked seventh in the nation, was a three point favorite over fifth ranked Auburn. The Tigers of Auburn were cast as the underdog because the Bulldogs had the conference's best defense, having surrendered just four touchdowns in eight games. Coach Dooley boasted his '71 squad was the best team he coached.

It was an elimination game. Auburn would play unbeaten Alabama two weeks later and Sullivan was locked-in a tight race for the Heisman Trophy with Cornell's Marinaro. The atmosphere on this epic day was so electric it still brings chills to those who played and those who viewed.

"Things were different then," said Sullivan. "The hype of the game, and the atmosphere were astonishing. We stayed twenty or thirty miles outside of Athens. Some Georgia students, or fans, met us and started circling our buses. They were shouting stuff, throwing beer cans, all kinds of stuff. Coach Lorendo and I normally rode in the second bus, along with Spence McCracken. Us three usually played Jeopardy near the rear of the bus. Once all that crazy stuff happened, you could have heard a pin drop on that bus."

It was Coach Vince Dooley versus his old mentor, Shug Jordan—and it definitely contributed to the hype of the looming slugfest between these two unbeaten teams. Conversely, there would be no championships settled that day.

After arriving in Athens, the Tigers went straight to Sanford Stadium. There they worked out; however, the pesky students went with them. "Everybody has their own memories," Sullivan related. "I remember walking into the stadium and seeing somebody had stretched a sheet in the stands that said 'Piss on Pat.' It was gone the next day."

Auburn stayed at a local Holiday Inn, and things got increasingly rowdier. Students and fans drove around the hotel, blowing their vehicle horns until the wee hours of the night. Some entered into the hotel, banging on doors. Lorendo, a large, hulking man, threatened one party goer, only to have him getaway by scuttling through his legs.

"We didn't get any sleep," Sullivan said. "Then we got to the stadium and it was just unbelievable. They were hanging from the railroad trestle, the trees, anywhere anybody could be in sight of the field."

The hype of the game unquestionably lived-up to its billing. Most say the Heisman Trophy was clinched by Sullivan when he tossed four touchdown passes, while guiding his team to a 35-20 victory. His primary target, Beasley, was double covered the entire day, but Sullivan still found him four times for 130-yards and two touchdowns. Georgia's shadowing of Beasley allowed Sullivan to throw two more touchdowns to his secondary target, Dick Smaltz.

He ended the day completing 14 of 24 pass attempts, for 248-yards and four touchdowns. During an era when defense, along with "three yards and a cloud of dust" dominated college football, those numbers were colossal.

Coach Dooley stated, "We were beaten by the best quarterback I've ever seen. Sullivan was a super player, having a super day and if Sullivan is 'Superman,' then Beasley is 'Boy Wonder.'"

Piggybacking on Coach Dooley's statement, *Sports Illustrated* captioned its article about the game with the title, "Underneath That 7 Is an S." The magazine claimed Sullivan could, "do everything but leap tall buildings in a single bound."

Dooley's response was often reiterated by other SEC coaches, such as the legendary Alabama coach Bear Bryant, who considered Sullivan one of the finest to ever play the game. During the 1970 Iron Bowl, immediately after Sullivan picked-up Auburn from the brink of a 17-0 drubbing, and won an improbable 33-28 game against the Pachyderms of Alabama, Coach Bryant stated,

"Sullivan does more things to beat you than any quarterback I've ever seen."

Sullivan was a two time All-American, and was selected as the SEC Player-of-the-Year, twice. He finished his three year career with 6,284 passing yards and an NCAA record seventy-one total touchdowns. He led the nation in total offense in '70.

The Heisman Trophy winner was announced at halftime of the Georgia-Georgia Tech game on Thanksgiving Day. There were no invitations to New York City during that era. The winner got the news at the same time the rest of the country did.

"The announcement was made and Coach Jordan came by," Sullivan said. "Then we went to the coliseum. That was probably as emotional as any locker room or anything. The players knew, and I knew, they shared the award as much as I did. The power and the feelings were extremely special. The next day, we had to get on the bus and go play Alabama in the biggest game of the year."

Sullivan, and others who played that Saturday, were positive the outburst of sentiment over the Heisman Trophy proved costly on game day. Alabama won 31-7.

"I'm not saying we would have beaten Alabama, but our senior class had never lost to them," Sullivan said. "We didn't play very well. It was 14-7 going into the fourth quarter, but I threw an interception and they kind of took over. One thing I will always remember is being introduced. The Auburn fans cheered. The Alabama fans cheered, too. They were very gracious. I'll always remember that."

Anthony "Tony" Drew Dorsett, Pittsburgh, September 15, 1973 and September 6, 1975

The son of Wes and Myrtle, Dorsett grew up in Aliquippa, Pennsylvania, near Pittsburgh. He attended Hopewell High School, where he played football and basketball. In 1970, while a high school sophomore, Dorsett started at cornerback, because his coaches did not believe that, at 147-pounds, he was big enough to play running back, the position he played in junior high school.

In 1971, a competition for the starting running back position, between Dorsett and sophomore Michael Kimbrough was brewing. It abruptly ended when Dorsett caught a screen pass and went 75-yards for a touchdown against Ambridge during the season opener.

At the University of Pittsburgh Dorsett gained 1,586 yards as a freshman, with 101 of those yards coming against Georgia on September 15, 1973 in his first collegiate football game. Coach Dooley, the quintessential pessimist, stated, "They had speed on the outside that hurt us." That statement was directed at Pitt's high school All-American tailback Dorsett. The threat of his 9.6 speed opened up the middle of the line for fullback Bill Englert, who averaged ten yards per carry. Dorsett was quick and hurt Georgia badly when he got to the outside. Still, the game ended in a 7-7 tie.

He would become the first freshman, since Doc Blanchard of Army, in 1944, to be named All-American. He finished second in the nation in rushing with 1,586 yards in eleven games and led the Pittsburgh Panthers to its first winning season in ten years. He was Pittsburgh's first All-American selection since the 1963 season, when Paul Martha and Ernie Borghetti were named first team All-Americans. His 1,586 rushing yards was the most ever recorded by a freshman. The record would stand for seven years, until, in 1980, Herschel Walker would break it with 1,618 yards.

Nobody had ever accused Dorsett of being too small to play college football; nobody except for Penn State's Joe Paterno.

"For as long as I can remember, I wanted to play football for Penn State," Pittsburgh's All-American running back said following his team's 19-9 opening game win over Georgia on September 6, 1975 in rainy Athens. "But when it came time to decide on a college, Penn State was one of the last schools to contact me. Word was they thought I was too small."

So, at 5'-11" and 180 pounds, Dorsett opted for the Nittany Lions' arch-rival Pittsburgh. During a short two years under coach Johnny Majors, Dorsett established himself as the premiere running back in college.

And although Erk Russell's inexperienced defense did another good job on Dorsett during the Bulldogs '75 home opener, "holding" him to 104 yards, the pride of Pitt still had his sights set on the Heisman Trophy. Dorsett, who only had 17-yards rushing in the first half, took advantage of a fourth quarter Georgia letdown and finished the rainy afternoon with 104-yards on 17 carries. A fourth quarter, 36-yard burst, gave the talented junior a slight edge in his statistical battle with Georgia's All-American hopeful, Glynn Harrison, in this season opening duel.

"My goal for this season is to regain my first-team All-American status. I figured if I accomplish that, the team as a whole will profit, and who knows, I just might win the Heisman Trophy in the process."

Dorsett would finished eleventh in the Heisman balloting in 1973, and was thirteenth in 1974. Ohio State's Archie Griffin would win the Heisman Trophy in both 1974 and 1975.

Prior to his rematch with Georgia, Dorsett saw the Bulldogs' defense as one he could easily shred. However, the "Junkyard Dogs" wasted little time in changing the Pitt star's mind. "Georgia's defense really surprised me in the first half," Dorsett said, referring to his unimpressive six carried for 17-yards. "After all, they had lost eight starters and we outweighed them close to twenty pounds a man on the line. But they were beating our offensive line off the ball. And man, were those Georgia linebackers aggressive!"

In addition to the 104 rushing yards by Dorsett, Pitt had a well-balanced rushing attack. Elliot Walker had 17 carries for 74-yards, and quarterback Robert Haygood had 24 carries for 65-yards.

In 1976, as a senior, Dorsett opened the season with a total of 290-yards against Notre Dame. He darted 61-yards on his first run of the season and tacked on an additional 120-yards by the end of the 31–10 Pitt victory. Pittsburgh went on to win the mythical national title after defeating Georgia 27-3 in the Sugar Bowl. In fact, Dorsett set a Sugar Bowl record of 203-yards rushing.

In addition to winning the Heisman Trophy, Dorsett won the Maxwell Award, the Walter Camp Award for Player of the Year, and the *United Press International* Player of the Year award. He was the nation's leading rusher with 2,150-yards and finished his college career with 6,082 total rushing yards and was a four-time All-American.

George Washington Rogers, South Carolina, September 29, 1979 and November 1, 1980

Born on December 8, 1958, he was heavily recruited out of high school. The Georgia native elected to attend the University of South Carolina once Coach Jim Carlen told Rogers he could play his freshman season.

Because of his large size, he seemed fated to play fullback rather than tailback. However, the Gamecocks had two running backs who graduated at the same time, so Rogers began his college career as the starting tailback midway through his freshman season.

During his sophomore season he only played in eight games, but still rushed for 1,006 yards, despite splitting time with Johnnie Wright. However, after gaining 1,681 yards during his junior campaign, he was launched into the national spotlight as one of the top tailbacks in the nation.

On September 29, 1979, the bruising running of the 6'-2" junior blasted through the 'Dogs for 152-yards on 28 carries. He set-up the Gamecocks' winning touchdown by catching a flare pass from quarterback Garry Harper, where he rumbled 24-yards to the Georgia 1-yard line. On the next play, Harper plunged into the endzone for the winning score. Rogers was awarded Second Team All-American honors by the *Associated Press*, National Editorial Alliance, *United Press International*, American Football Coaches, and Football News.

In 1980, the stage was set when the Gamecocks returned plenty of talent, including the All-American Rogers. While South Carolina's 8-3 record was good, Rogers' final season was better. His 1,781 yards was the best in the nation and earned him the Heisman Trophy.

November 1, 1980, was a brisk day when the Gamecocks of South Carolina came into Sanford Stadium with the second best running back in the nation. The Georgia defense held Rogers to 168-yards on 35 carries, and no touchdowns. On South Carolina's final drive, Georgia's Dale Carver put a helmet on Rogers's body and jarred the ball loose. His teammate, Tim Parks, fell on it to secure the victory for Georgia. The fumble wasn't the only thing Rogers lost on that fateful day, as the battle between himself and Herschel Walker ended in Walker's favor. Walker had 219-yards on 43 carries.

In December 1980, the Downtown Athletic Club in New York City selected Rogers as the winner of the 1980 Heisman Trophy. Rogers beat out an impressive group of players, including Pittsburgh defensive lineman Hugh Green, and Walker. He would be the first University of South Carolina player to have his jersey retired while still active at the school.

Rogers left the Gamecock football program as its most successful running back. His 5,204 yards remains the highest career total by any Gamecock running back, and his 31 rushing touchdowns tied Harold Green for second. He scored 202 points and gained more than 100 yards in each of his final twenty-two colligate games.

Herschel Junior Walker, Georgia, 1980-1982

Herschel Walker was born in Wrightsville on March 3, 1962, to Christine and Willis Walker. On Easter Day, 1980, Georgia football coach Vince Dooley signed Walker to a scholarship. Walker would leave an indelible mark on the University of Georgia football history books as he emerged into the most dominate player in the history of colligate football.

Sonny Seiler, Uga IV, and Herschel Walker

Ironically, as a youth, Walker exhibited little interest in playing sports. In fact, he was an avid reader and spent most of his time writing poetry. But, something happened when he was twelve years old that prompted him to embark on an incredible exercise program. Over the next year, he racked up 100,000 push-ups, 100,000 sit-ups and sprinted hundreds of miles. Before being recruited by Georgia, Walker led his Johnson County High School to the 1979 state championship game and *Parade Magazine* recognized him as the nation's "High School Back-of-the-Year."

In three seasons at Georgia (1980-82), Walker piled up 5,259 yards and 49 touchdowns. He won the Heisman in 1982, although many felt he should have won it as a freshman, when he led the Bulldogs to the national championship. What Walker meant to his team says the most. During his Georgia career, the Bulldogs went 32-1 during the regular season, and 1-2 in bowl games. Georgia won three straight Southeastern Conference (SEC) titles during his era.

As a freshman, Walker led the team to an undefeated regular season and a Sugar Bowl victory over the University of Notre Dame, enroute to winning the national championship. He was a consensus All-American, and finished third in the Heisman Trophy balloting, setting the freshman rushing record with 1,616 total yards. He averaged 146.9 yards per game and scored fifteen touchdowns during an eleven game season. Unfortunately, bowl game data was not counted towards statistical totals during the 1980s.

Walker was a consensus All-American in each of the three seasons at Georgia, setting eleven National Collegiate Athletic Association (NCAA) records, sixteen SEC records, and forty-one Georgia records, including the most rushing yards in a game (283 against Vanderbilt University in 1980). He ran for more than 100-yards in eleven games as a sophomore. At the end of his Georgia career, Walker's total of 5,259 yards gained was the most ever by a college running back in a three-year career and made him the third leading rusher in NCAA history.

Most experts of the game consider Walker to be the top player in college football history. His three seasons for Georgia were the most successful in the school's extensive football history. In his sophomore year, he finished second in the Heisman Trophy balloting. Finally, in his junior year, Walker won the Heisman Trophy, despite having a broken thumb, and earned the 1982 Maxwell and Walter Camp Award. He was later selected as the all-time best athlete in the history of the University of Georgia.

Walker competed on Georgia's track and field team, twice drawing All-American honors. He left Georgia after his junior season to play for the New Jersey Generals of the now obsolete

United States Football League (USFL). In 1983, during his first season with the Generals, he set a professional single-season rushing record with 2,411 yards rushing, and was named the USFL's Most Valuable Player. After his first season in the USFL, Walker earned his Bachelor of Science degree in criminal justice from Georgia. He was inducted into the College Football Hall of Fame in 1999.

Vincent Edward Jackson, Auburn, November 12, 1983 and November 16, 1985

He was born on November 30, 1962, in Bessemer, Alabama and attended McAdory High School in McCalla, Jefferson County, Alabama. Early during his high school career he began drawing the attention of collegiate scouts from three sports: football, baseball, and track and field. In 1982, the New York Yankees drafted him out of high school, but Jackson rejected their contract offer and instead accepted a football scholarship from Auburn University.

During his time playing for the Auburn Tigers, he ran for 4,303 career yards, and finished his career with an average of 6.6 yards per carry. Some of those yards came against Georgia.

In fact, if there were a professional football, or baseball team in Athens, you could have bet Jackson would have tried to sign with it. When the Tigers provided the opposition for the Diamond Dogs' first night game ever, Jackson collected four hits, including three home runs and a triple. Some folks still talk about his first home run, a thunderous shot to center field which bounced off of the new light tower.

In 1982, Jackson's freshman year, he was shut down by Georgia as Auburn was defeated 19-14. In 1983, as a sophomore, Jackson rushed for 1,213 yards on 158 carries, for an average of seven yards per carry. He rushed for 115-yards on 18 carries against Georgia, as Auburn won the game 13-7. In 1984, he spent most of it injured, and his totals weren't impressive. He did, however, come back to earn Most Valuable Player honors in the Liberty Bowl.

Jackson returned to Athens in 1985 as the leading candidate for the Heisman Trophy. He unquestionably did nothing to hurt his chances to be named the best collegiate football player in the nation as the 8-2 Tigers destroyed Georgia's hopes for the Sugar Bowl with a 24-10 win. Jackson ended-up with 169-yards, 121-yards on the ground and 48 receiving yards.

In the first quarter Auburn wasted no time getting the ball to Jackson as he incorporated his well-known long touchdown sprints into the Auburn attack. Highlighting a five-play drive, where he carried four times, he took a pitch from quarterback Pat Washington and headed to the sidelines. Georgia's Greg Williams, playing in his first game as a defensive back for an injured Michael Willis, spun off a blocker and tried to tackle him at the line of scrimmage.

Jackson busted away from Williams, eluded Georgia safety Tony Flack with an acceleration of speed, then cut away from Gary Moss and John Little, who had been pursuing. Before you could say, "You can't spell Sugar without UGA," and 67 yards later, Jackson was in the endzone for his fourteenth touchdown of the year.

In the third quarter, after Georgia's Jonathan Crumley connected on a long 50-yard field-goal, the lead was cut to 17-10. Then, early in the fourth quarter, Jackson added his second touchdown of the afternoon to give Auburn a 24-10 lead.

For the season, he rushed for 1,786 yards and averaged 6.4 yards per rush. For his performance in 1985, Jackson was awarded the Heisman Trophy in what was the tightest margin of victory in the annals of the award, winning by less than fifty points over Iowa's Chuck Long. He completed his career at Auburn with 4,675 all-purpose yards and forty-five touchdowns, forty-three rushing and two receiving. He averaged approximately 6.6 yards per carry.

Daniel Wuerffel, Florida, 10-28-95

Born on May 27, 1974, in Pensacola, Florida, he was the son of a Lutheran minister, who was a chaplain in the United State Air Force. Wuerffel went to Fort Walton Beach High School where he was a standout in football and basketball. He led the Vikings of Fort Walton Beach to an undefeated season as its quarterback and his team finished ranked number two in the nation by *USA Today*.

Wuerffel, the valedictorian of his high school class, was rated the best high school football recruit in the state of Florida, and he was *USA Today's* High School Player of the Year in 1992. In 1993, he accepted an athletic scholarship, from Steve Spurrier, to attend the University of Florida.

In 1995, he led Florida to the Bowl Alliance national championship game against the Cornhuskers of Nebraska, where

Florida was manhandled 62-24. However, in 1996, he led Florida to a 12-1 record and a 52-20 Sugar Bowl victory over Florida State. Florida went on to claim the mythical national title and Wuerffel was awarded the Heisman Trophy. Later, he declined to be included on *Playboy* magazine's All-America team, as well as declining its Scholar-Athlete of the Year award, saying, "That's not the type of person I am or would like to portray myself as."

He only played once inside of Sanford Stadium, on October 31, 1995. Florida defeated Georgia 52-17 and he displayed every weapon in his offensive arsenal. The Gators rolled up 542-yards of total offense, while the defense surrendered 281-yards. The junior quarterback completed 14 of 17 passes for 242-yards and five touchdowns. The controversial 52 points were the most ever scored against Georgia on its hallowed field of Sanford Stadium.

He finished his Florida career by completing 708 of 1,170 passes for 10,875 yards and 114 touchdown passes. He had a career pass efficiency rating of 163.56. In 1996, during his Heisman-winning season, he completed 207 of 360 passes for 3,625 yards for thirty-nine touchdowns.

Mark Ingram, Jr., Alabama, September 27, 2008

The son of former National Football League wide receiver Mark Ingram, Sr., Ingram was born on December 21, 1989, in Hackensack, New Jersey. He attended Grand Blanc Community High School, in Grand Blanc, Michigan, for three years before going to Flint Southwestern Academy, in Flint, Michigan, his final season.

He started all four-years on those high school teams. He accumulated a combined 2, 546 yards, and thirty-eight touchdowns during his last two seasons. He earned Saginaw Valley Most Valuable Player awards, and was twice an All-State selection.

In 2008, he decided to sign an athletic scholarship to play for Coach Nick Saban's Alabama Crimson Tide. Later that season, on September 27, 2008, his Alabama Crimson Tide played Georgia inside of Sanford Stadium. The Pachyderms ran-up the score to 31-0 at halftime as Ingram started the scoring bonanza by running seven yards for a touchdown, after only eight minutes into the game. He was sparsely used the remainder of the game, with a total of seven rushing attempts for 17-yards. Alabama cruised to a 41-30 victory.

On December 12, 2009, during his sophomore season, Ingram would become the first player in Alabama colligate football history to be awarded the Heisman Trophy. Additionally, he would set the Crimson Tide's single-season rushing record with 1,658 yards, and scored 17 touchdowns. He was a unanimous All-American and helped lead the Tide to an undefeated 14–0 season and the Bowl Championship Series National Championship.

Ingram won the Heisman Trophy in the closet vote in the history of the award, as he beat out Stanford's Toby Gerhart by less than thirty points. Ingram was the third consecutive sophomore to win the award, and at the time, was nine days shy of his twentieth birthday, making him the youngest player to win the Heisman. On January 7, 2010 Alabama defeated Texas 37–21 to win the Bowl Championship Series. Ingram received honors as Offensive Most Valuable Player after rushing for 116-yards and two touchdowns on 22 carries.

Sanford Stadium's Mythical National Champions

In addition to Georgia's 1942 and 1980 teams, Sanford Stadium has played host to seven teams selected as national champions, by major polls, during the season those teams played inside of Sanford Stadium.

The National Collegiate Athletic Association (NCAA) Division I Football Bowl Subdivision (FBS) is a designation awarded annually by various organizations to their selection of the best college football team. Division I FBS football is the only NCAA sport for which the NCAA does not sanction a yearly championship event. As a result, it is unofficially referred to as a "mythical national championship."

While the NCAA has never officially endorsed a championship team, it has documented the choices of some selectors in its official *NCAA Football Bowl Subdivision Records* publication. In addition, various analysts have independently published their own choices for each season. These opinions can often diverge with others, as well as an individual institution's claims to national titles, which may not correlate to the selections published elsewhere.

The concept of a national championship in college football dates back to the early years of its inception in the late 19th century. In 1901, the earliest contemporaneous polls can be traced to Casper Whitney, Charles Patterson, and *The Sun*. The hypothesis of polls and national champions predated statistical ranking systems; however, it would be Frank Dickinson's mathematical scheme that would be one of the earliest to be extensively popularized.

In 1926, Dickinson's system named 10–0 Stanford its national champion, two weeks before the Indians of Stanford tied with Alabama in the Rose Bowl. Later, Knute Rockne, then coach of Notre Dame, requested for Dickinson to predate the prior two seasons, 1924 and 1925, and it produced Notre Dame as its 1924 national champion and Dartmouth at its 1925 champion.

A number of other arithmetical methods were born in the 1920s and '30s, and these methodologies quickly emerged as the only organized methods of selecting national champions. Then, in 1935, the *Associated Press* (AP) began polling sportswriters to obtain its rankings. In a prelude to the convolutedness to colligate football polls, Alan J. Gould, the creator of the AP poll, named Minnesota, Princeton and Southern Methodist University as champions. In 1936, the polled writer's opinions resulted in a singular national champion, when it selected Coach Bernard Bierman's Gophers of Minnesota.

In 1950, the *United Press International* (UPI), the AP's main competition, created its first poll of coaches. For that season, and the next three, the AP and the UPI agreed on its national champion; however, the first "split" championship occurred in 1954, when the writers selected the Buckeyes of Ohio State and the coaches picked the Bruins of UCLA. Eventually, the two polls would disagree again in 1957, 1965, 1970, 1973, 1974, 1978, 1990, 1991, 1997, and 2003.

The Coaches' Poll would stay with the United Press when they merged with International News Service to form UPI, but was acquired by *USA Today* and CNN in 1991. The poll was in the hands of Entertainment and Sports Programming Network (ESPN) from 1997 to 2005 before moving to *USA Today*.

A variety of selectors have named national champions throughout the years. They generally can be divided into four categories: those determined by a mathematical formula, human polls, historical research, and the playoff system. The selectors below are listed in the official NCAA FBS records as having been deemed to be "major selectors" for which the criteria was for the poll, or selector, to be "national in scope, either through distribution in newspaper, television, radio and or computer online."

"Consensus" selectors in the official NCAA FBS records correspond to the period from 1950 to present, which began with the introduction of the two poll system upon the appearance of the Coaches Poll in 1950. Selectors used to determine teams listed as "Consensus National Champions" in the NCAA FBS records include: the AP poll, Coaches Poll, Football Writers Association of America, and the National Football Foundation/College Football Hall of Fame.

Here are the teams, listed in chronological order, that have played inside of Sanford Stadium during the season they were crowned as national champions.

Louisiana State University (LSU), 1935

In '35, the Bayou Bengals, led by All-American Gaynell Tinsely, would become the first team to play inside of Sanford Stadium during the same season they were selected as college football's national champions. Coached by the legend Bernie Moore, the Bengals went 9-2 and were selected by the Williamson System's poll as the national champions. The only losses for Tigers came against Rice, and Sammy Baugh's Texas Christian University in the Sugar Bowl. LSU defeated Georgia 13-0 on a cold, wet day in November, as Tinsely harassed the 'Dogs offense all day.

Georgia, 1942

The 1942 Bulldogs of Georgia, led by Heisman Trophy winner Frank Sinkwich and All-American George Poschner, were selected by eight national polls, including Berryman, Billingsley Report, DeVold System, Houlgate System, Litkenhous, Poling System, Sagarin Ratings, and the Williamson System as national champions after going 11-1 and beating UCLA in the Rose Bowl.

Charlie Trippi and Frank Sinkwich, 1942

This '42 Georgia football team had Charlie Trippi, whom some would argue was Georgia's greatest running back of all-time. World War II broke-up that great team, as most players left school to join the military soon after Georgia won the Rose Bowl. Between 1942 and 1945, a total of eighty-two players from Georgia would leave school for the military

Georgia, 1946

In '46, Georgia, led by Charlie Trippi, who had recently returned from World War II, was the next national championship team to play inside of Sanford Stadium. The Bulldogs were selected as national champions by the Williamson System after going 11-0, and defeating Charlie "Choo-Choo" Justice's North Carolina team in the Sugar Bowl.

Maryland, 1951

In '51, Coach Tim Tatum's University of Maryland, led by Chet "The Jet" Hanulak, beat Georgia 43-7 on October 13. Many researchers consider the '51 Terrapins the greatest team in college football history. The Terrapins went 10-0 and were selected by the majority of national polls, including the College Football Researchers Association, Devold System, Dunkle System, Sagarin

Ratings, and National Championship Foundation, as national champions. The Terrapins outscored its opponents 381 – 74. In the Sugar Bowl, they defeated Coach Neyland's number one ranked Tennessee Volunteers by a score of 28-13.

Georgia Tech, 1952

In '52, Coach Bobby Dodd's Georgia Tech Yellow Jackets, led by George Morris, were selected as national champions by the majority of polls, including the Berryman, Billingsley Report, Poling System, Sagarin Ratings, and International News Service, after going 12-0 and defeating Georgia 23-9 on November 29. The Yellow Jackets would go on to beat an Ole Miss team led by one of its all-time great quarterbacks, Jimmy Lear, in the Sugar Bowl by a final score of 24-7.

Alabama, 1961

It would be nine years before another national champion graced the fields of Sanford Stadium. In '61, Coach Bryant's Alabama Crimson Tide, led by Mal Moore and Lee Roy Jordan, was selected as consensus national champions by the majority of national polls including: the Berryman, Billingsley Report, Devold System, Dunkle System, Litkenhous, Sagarin Ratings, Williamson System, *Associated Press*, *United Press International*, National Championship Foundation and National Football Foundation.

In late September, the Crimson Tide beat Georgia 32-6; however, the Tide dropped one spot in the polls the following week. Alabama rebounded and went on to an 11-0 season, defeating Arkansas, led by All-American Lance Alworth, in the Sugar Bowl. Ten players on that Alabama team went on to play in the National Football League.

Alabama, 1965

In '65, Ken Stabler helped lead Alabama to the national title after Alabama went 9-1-1, with its only loss coming on September 18, to Georgia, by a final score of 18-17. Coach Bryant's team was selected as national champions by the *Associated Press*, College Football Researchers Association, Football Writers Association of America, and the National Championship Foundation.

Georgia, 1980

It would be fifteen years before the next census national champion would play inside of Sanford Stadium. In 1980, Georgia, led by Buck Belue, Jim Blakewood and Herschel Walker, went 12-0, and defeated Notre Dame in the Sugar Bowl 17-10. The 'Dogs were census national champions by the majority of national polls. It would be the first time the 'Dogs finished undefeated since Charlie Trippi's team went unbeaten in 1946. The only other Georgia team to go unbeaten was Coach Glenn "Pop" Warner's 1896 team that went 4-0.

Georgia Tech, 1990

Ten years after Georgia won its undisputed national title, Bobby Ross's Georgia Tech team would become the next national champions to play inside of Sanford Stadium. The Yellow Jackets defeated Georgia 40-23 on December 1, 1990. Georgia Tech, led by Calvin Tiggle and Jim Lavin, went 11-0-1, and split with Colorado as mythical national champions. The Jackets were selected by *United Press International*, Dunkel System, Sagarin Ratings, Rothman, and the National Championship Foundation. Georgia Tech scored 379 points, while allowing only 186 points. They overpowered Nebraska 45-21 in the 1991 Florida Citrus Bowl.

Tennessee, 1998

Eight years after Tech split a national title, the Volunteers of Tennessee would be the next national champions to play inside of Sanford Stadium. On October 10, 1998, Tennessee beat Georgia 22-3. The Tennessee defense limited Georgia to only 254-yards of total offense and held the 'Dogs without a touchdown. The majority of national polls recognized the 13-0 Volunteers as the consensus national champions. The Volunteers, led by Tee Martin and Peerless Price, defeated Florida State in the Fiesta Bowl by a final score of 23-16.

Greatest Opposing Coaches

Without a doubt, whenever the subject of "greatest" coach is brought up, it is inherently controversial. There are no tried and true methodologies, or barometers, to accurately determine the greatest coaches off all-time. It is an opinionated speciality, and here we will recognize the most formidable legends who have plied their trade inside of Sanford Stadium.

Normally, coaches in collegiate sports are often looked upon as legends for their longevity with their respected schools. In fact, a football program's identity has often been shaped by its head coach. As an example, a hard-nosed rushing attack, consisting of three yards and a cloud of dust, has often been associated with Coach Vince Dooley's Bulldogs or Tom Osborne's Nebraska Cornhuskers.

Time after time it has been legendary coaches, like the aforementioned, who have been the ones to find success where no one thought it could be found. Legends have often turned plodding programs into powerhouses and been stewards in steering the way for the innovation and evolution of the game. As the colligate game continues to evolve into an even bigger money enterprise, versus a game meant to be played by students, for the students, the job of the coach will continue to develop into an even more demanding occupation; however, the ultimate goal will never waiver or change.

Since it held its first game on October 12, 1929, Sanford Stadium has hosted plenty of legendary coaches. However, what measurement, or formula, should be used to determine the greatest opposing coaches of all-time in Sanford Stadium history? Should the amount of wins, conference and national championships won, be used? Or, should the amount of time the coach spent at his school, coupled with the memories he gave back to the landscape of the sport be used? This subject is controversial and open for argument. Nonetheless, the following coaches are the fifteen greatest opposing coaches to have coached on the sidelines of Sanford Stadium.

Bernard W. "Bernie" Bierman, Tulane 1931

He was born on March 11, 1894, to European immigrants. Coach Bierman avoided the spotlight, and was known to be a man of few words. He once stated, "I don't think I'd be able to make a sentimental dressing room talk. I'm afraid I would end up laughing at myself."

He coached Tulane during its greatest era of football, 1927-31. During his last three seasons at Tulane, Bierman's Green Wave won twenty-eight of twenty-nine regular season games—a record tarnished only by a loss to Northwestern in 1930. In 1931, his Tulane Green Wave finished the season undefeated and untied, and played the Southern California Trojans for the national title. Tulane lost 21-12. Afterwards, Coach Bierman left Tulane and returned to his alma mater, the University of Minnesota where he won five mythical national titles, and seven Big-10 conference titles, including five undefeated seasons.

The only time he coached inside of Sanford Stadium was on November 14, 1931, and his second ranked Green Wave of Tulane defeated an undefeated Georgia team 20-7.

Unfortunately, one of his most famous halftime speeches consisted of three simple words. Tulane was trailing Georgia 15-14 during the 1929 game, and assistant coach Lester Lautenschlaeger chewed out the Greenies during the intermission. He concluded his remarks by throwing his hat on the floor, stomping on it and shouting, "Georgia! I can lick the whole state of Georgia by myself!" Bierman then stepped forward, driving his own heel into the crumpled hat, and added, "So can I." Tulane won that game 21-15.

Paul William "Bear" Bryant, Kentucky: 1946, '48; Texas A&M 1954; Alabama 1958, '59, '61, '63, '65, '72, '76

Coach Bryant first attracted national attention as a coach when he was Kentucky's mentor in the late '40s and early '50s. In 1950, he was coach of Kentucky's first Southeastern Conference Championship team in football. His Kentucky teams went into Sanford Stadium in 1946 and '48, and lost both games; however, his 1947 and '49 teams defeated Georgia 26-0 and 25-0, in Lexington.

In 1954, he took his Junction Boys of Texas A&M into Sanford Stadium and won the game 6-0. The Aggies won a defensive dual, and intercepted Jimmy Harper twice. It was the Aggies only win of the season; however, two seasons later, Texas A&M would go undefeated and win the national title.

In 1958, after returning to his alma mater, Alabama, the Pachyderms' football soared to new heights. Bryant's return ended an 18-year absence for the former Crimson Tide star and assistant coach. In '58, his first Alabama team came into Sanford Stadium and won 12-0. During his time at Alabama, his teams would win four games and lose three inside of Sanford Stadium.

Bryant's fame as a rebuilder of ailing football machines, which grew after his achievements as head coach at Maryland, Kentucky and Texas A&M, was enhanced more than a little by the accomplishments of his Alabama football teams. In actuality, when he returned to Alabama, the Tide had won two games, tied one and lost seven the previous season. The Tide's record for the three seasons prior to his return was a miserable 4-24-2.

During his 25-year tenure as Alabama's head coach, he amassed six national championships and thirteen conference titles. When he retired in 1982, he had more wins, 323, than any other collegiate football coach. Additionally, Coach Bryant had an overall record of 5-5 inside of Sanford Stadium while coaching Kentucky, Texas A&M and Alabama.

Robert Lee Dodd, Georgia Tech, 1946, '48, '50, '52, '54, '56, '58, '60, '62, '64 and '66

He was born on November 11, 1908, in Galax, Virginia. Dodd was named after another famous Virginian, General Robert E. Lee. He was the youngest of Edwin and Susan Dodd's four children. In the fall of 1921, the Dodd family relocated to Kingsport, Tennessee. In 1926, Dodd graduated high school and was admitted to the University of Tennessee with a football scholarship. He was a legendary quarterback for Coach Neyland's powerful Volunteer teams of the early 1930s, as they went 27-1-2.

After his college career ended, he would become an assistant coach at Georgia Tech, under Coach William Alexander. Dodd eventually succeeded Alexander in 1945, as the third head coach at the Institute. Under Dodd's watch, the Yellow Jackets, a charter member of the Southeastern Conference, withdrew from the conference after the 1963 season, but the Jackets maintained a prominent spot in the archives. The Gnats were the only major college team to have three coaches in a row who won more than 100 games each: John Heisman, Bill Alexander and Dodd.

In twenty-one seasons, Dodd's Jackets won six straight bowl games, and his 1952 team was selected as the mythical national champions. In 1966, he retired from coaching after compiling a 165–64–8 record. Coach Dodd was 5-6 inside Sanford Stadium while coaching Georgia Tech.

Reuben LaVell Edwards, Brigham Young University, 1982

He was born on October 11, 1930, and grew-up in Utah. He attended the University of Utah, and would later earn a doctorate degree from Brigham Young University (BYU), where he was head coach from 1972 through 2000. He was the Cougars most successful coach of all-time with a total of 257 career victories, 101 losses, and three ties.

Among his many notable accomplishments, Edwards guided the Cougars to the mythical national title in 1984 and coached 1990 Heisman Trophy winner Ty Detmer. Other notable players he coached in BYU's passing-dominated scheme were Steve Young, Jim McMahon, Marc Wilson and Virgil Carter.

A coaching icon, whose success, and longevity, is paralleled by few others, Coach Edwards guided BYU to heights never before reached in its program's history. In twenty of twenty-nine seasons, the Cougars claimed nineteen Western Athletic and one Mountain West Conference titles.

Edwards led BYU to twenty-two bowl game appearances, reaching the apex of his coaching success in 1984 by winning the national championship. He was named NCAA District 8 Coach of the Year eight times, Bobby Dodd National Coach of the Year in 1979 and AFCA National Coach of the Year in 1984. The stadium at BYU was renamed LaVell Edwards Stadium in his honor.

During his one appearance inside of Sanford Stadium, his Cougars turned the ball over seven times, and would lose to Georgia 17-14, after Kevin Butler booted a long, last second field-goal.

Phillip Fulmer, Tennessee, 1992, '94, '96, '98, '00, '02, '04, '06 and '08

He was born on September 1, 1950, in Winchester, Tennessee, and attended Franklin County High School. After enrolling at Tennessee, as a student in 1968, he would earn a scholarship on the football team the following season. He received All-American honors as an offensive lineman, and helped guide the Volunteers to a 30-5 record between 1969 through 1971.

In 1992, he replaced Coach Johnny Majors, who was laid-up in the hospital at the time, to become the twentieth head coach at Tennessee. He would remain head coach until 2008, compiling a record of 152-52. In 1998, he reached the pinnacle of his coaching career when Vols won the Bowl Championship Series national title. At the end of his tenure at Tennessee, Fulmer was twenty-one games behind Coach Robert Neyland as the winningest coach in Vols history. Despite a decline in the program during his later years, he was considered an icon of college football, especially one of institutional loyalty.

The Volunteers won two Southeastern Conference (SEC) titles in 1997 and 1998, along with the national title in '98. His teams posted ten or more wins from 1995 to 1998, with Peyton Manning at quarterback from 1995 through 1997. In 2005, Coach Fulmer experienced his only losing season at Tennessee. The Volunteers went 5–6, and lost to in-state SEC rival Vanderbilt for the only time during his 14-year tenure. He would go 6-3 inside of Sanford Stadium.

Louis Leo "Lou" Holtz, North Carolina State, 1973; South Carolina 1999, '01, '03

Lou Holtz was born on January 6, 1937 in Follanbee, West Virginia. He grew-up in East Liverpool, Ohio and attended East Liverpool High School, before going to Kent State University. He played linebacker at Kent State and graduated in 1959.

In 1969, he got his first head coaching job at William & Mary, where he led the Indians to the Tangerine Bowl. In 1972, he took over at North Carolina State where he went 33-12-2, and took the Wolfpack to four bowl games. In 1977, he accepted the head coaching position at Arkansas where he went 60-21-2; however, he was subsequently fired by Athletic Director Frank Broyles. In 1984, he coached at Minnesota before leaving for Notre Dame in 1986. His Fighting Irish would win the 1988 National title.

During his first visit to Sanford Stadium, on September 29, 1973, his Wolfpack was led by All-American Willie Burden, who rushed for 160 yards, and lost by a score of 31-12.

In 1999, he returned to Sanford Stadium as head coach of the University of South Carolina. His Gamecocks would lose; however, in 2001, Carolina would finally give him his lone victory inside of Sanford Stadium. In 2003, during his final game inside of the Mecca of the South, the Gamecocks lost 31-7. He would go 1-3 inside of Sanford Stadium.

In all, Coach Holtz coached at William & Mary, Minnesota, Arkansas, Notre Dame and South Carolina. He retired with 249 wins, 132 losses, and seven ties. He was selected Coach of the Year in 1988, after his Fightin' Irish of Notre Dame team won the national title. On May 1, 2008, Holtz was elected to the College Football Hall of Fame.

Ralph (Sug) Jordan, Auburn, 1959, '61, '63, '65, '67, '69, '71, '73 and '75

Born September 25, 1910, in Selma, Alabama, Sug—so called because of his taste for sugar cane—was a three sport standout at Auburn, 1929-32. He earned freshman letters in four major sports at Auburn, but dropped track when he became a sophomore. He was a star center at Auburn, under Coach Chet Wynne, an outstanding forward in basketball, leading the old Southern Conference scorers in 1929, and he was an outstanding left-handed pitcher, doubling at first base.

His coaching career began at Auburn in the fall of 1932, following graduation with a civil engineer's degree. He coached the Auburn frosh, 1933-36; then he was varsity assistant coach under Jack Meagher 1937-41.

In July 1942, he joined the Army, and remained on active duty until October 1945, earning seven battle stars as a major with the First Army Engineers' Brigade. He received the Purple Heart when shell fragment stuck him on D-Day, at Omaha Beach.

In 1946, he coached Auburn basketball, and was an assistant to Meagher with the Miami pro Seahawks. He joined the Georgia staff in October 1946, as assistant coach in football and basketball.

In 1951, Coach Jordan returned to Auburn to become its head football coach. He inherited an Auburn football team that lost all 10 of its games in 1950. Additionally, from 1947 through 1950, Auburn only had five wins in four seasons.

Jordan brought Auburn into a new era of football. The Tigers would eventually run-up a 24-game winning streak and finish the 1957 season as the nation's only major unbeaten, untied team, while winning the *Associated Press* National Football Championship. From 1951 to 1975, Coach Jordan compiled a record of 176–83–6. He went 5-4 inside Sanford Stadium.

Johnny Majors, Pittsburgh 1973, 75 and Tennessee 1981, 88, 89, and 92

He was born on May 21, 1935 in Lynchburg, Tennessee. He played high school football for the Huntland Hornets in Franklin County, Tennessee. He attended Tennessee, where he was an All-American halfback in 1956, and was selected as the Southeastern Conference Most Valuable Player in 1955 and 1956. He was a triple-threat running back whose Volunteers used the single-wing formation versus a modified T-formation. During his senior season he would finish second in the Heisman Trophy balloting to Paul Hornung, who played on a Notre Dame team that went 2-8.

In 1968, he became the head football coach at Iowa State. Then, in 1973, he inherited a Pittsburgh team which had won just one game the previous season and hadn't had a winning record in eleven years. He coached his first game as Pitt's head coach inside of Sanford Stadium. The game ended in a tie 7-7. He guided his '73 team to a 6-5-1 record, and took Pitt to its first bowl game in seventeen years. He was voted National Coach of the Year by both the Football Writers Association and the Walter Camp Foundation.

In 1975, he returned to Sanford Stadium, along with Heisman Trophy candidate Tony Dorsett. Pitt won the game 19-9, finished the season 8-4 record, and defeated Kansas in the Sun Bowl.

In 1976, Majors led the Panthers to the national championship after destroying Georgia 27-3 in the Sugar Bowl and was voted Coach of the Year by the American Football Coaches Association. He had an overall record of 185-137-10, while going 9-7 in bowl games. He was 1-0-1 inside of Sanford Stadium, while coaching Pittsburgh, and he went 2-3 while at Tennessee.

Robert Reese Neyland, Tennessee, 1936

Born on February 17, 1892, he served three stints as the head football coach at the University of Tennessee from 1926 to '34, then from '36 to '40, and finally from '46 to '52. He was one of two college football coaches to have won national titles in two non-consecutive tenures at the same school. Frank Leahy, of Notre Dame, was the other coach. Neyland won 173 games of the 216 games he coached and had six undefeated seasons, nine undefeated regular seasons, won seven conference championships, and four national championships.

Coach Neyland was considered the best defensive football coach ever. His teams had 112 shutouts and his '38 and '39 teams set a colligate record when they shut out 17 straight opponents for 71 consecutive shutout quarters. In fact, his '39 team was the last college football team in history to hold every regular season opponent scoreless.

Neyland was credited with being the first coach to utilize sideline telephones, and game film to study opponents. His teams were some of the first to wear lightweight pads and tearaway jerseys. Such measures exemplified Coach Neyland's "speed over strength" philosophy.

In 1936, on Halloween night, Coach Neyland's team mauled Georgia 46-0. His Volunteers administered the worst loss Georgia ever experienced in Sanford Stadium. Coach Neyland was 1-0 inside of Sanford Stadium.

Nicholas Lou "Nick" Saban, Jr., LUS 2004, Alabama 2008

He was born on Halloween, October 31, 1951, in Fairmont, West Virginia. He played high school football at Monongah, in West Virginia. Later, Saban attended Kent State, where he played defensive back.

In 1989, he became head coach at Toledo, where the Rockets had some of its greatest success in the program's history. In 1995, he became head coach at Michigan State; however, after five seasons with the Spartans, he resigned and took over head coaching duties at Louisiana State. After leading the Bayou Bengals to the national title in 2003, he accepted a job in the National Football League with the Miami Dolphins. After two seasons, he departed to take the head coaching position at Alabama.

He achieved resounding success as a head coach and earned a reputation as an outstanding tactician, leader, organizer, and motivator. Those qualities, coupled with a slight touch of narcissism, sparked impressive turnarounds at every stop of his career. His teams repeatedly exhibited grit, determination and resilience, often prevailing over adversity to achieve a victory.

During his five-seasons at Louisiana State, he produced a 48-16 record, one national championship, and two Southeastern Conference titles. In 2004, he brought his only LSU team into Sanford Stadium and lost 54-28.

In 2007, Coach Saban was named the twenty-seventh head coach at Alabama. In 2008, his Pachyderms came into Sanford Stadium and, after building-up a 31-0 halftime lead, cruised to a 41-30 victory. As of 2014, his Alabama teams have won three national championships, and five Southeastern Conference titles. He has an overall record of 1-1 inside of Sanford Stadium.

Stephen Orr "Steve" Spurrier, Florida 1995, South Carolina 2005, 2007, 2009, 2011, 2013

He was born on April 20, 1945, in Miami Beach, Florida and later attended Science Hill High School, in Johnson City, Tennessee. Spurrier was a three-sport athlete who starred in football, basketball and baseball for the Hilltoppers. As a starting pitcher, he never lost a game for Science High, and his teams won back-to-back state baseball championships. Additionally, Spurrier was an All-State selection in football, basketball and baseball, and a high school All-American at the quarterback position.

In 1963, Spurrier signed a scholarship with the University of Florida, coached by Ray Graves. He became an All-American quarterback while completing 392 of 692 attempts, for 4,848 passing yards and 37 touchdowns during his three year career. In 1966, he won the Heisman Trophy, the Walter Camp Memorial Trophy, was selected as first-team All-Southeastern Conference, and All-American by the Football Writers Association of America. Still, his Florida teams never won a conference title during his playing days.

In 1987, after a lackluster career in the National Football League, he retired and got his first head coaching job at Duke. In 1989, he led the Blue Devils to their first conference title since 1962.

He was selected as Coach of the Year for the Atlantic Coast Conference in 1988 and '89. On December 31, 1989, he became head coach at the University of Florida.

In 1990, he guided the troubled program away from the scandals it had been involved. Florida had the best record in the conference; however, the Gators weren't eligible for the title because of NCAA probations. In 1991, Florida won its first officially recognized Southeastern Conference (SEC) title.

In 1995, he crowed about wanting to set the record for most points ever scored against Georgia inside of Sanford Stadium by hitting the "half a hundred" mark. His Gators destroyed Georgia 52-17; however, the game became controversial after he continued to call deep pass patterns, late in the game, in order to set the record.

Spurrier would win seven SEC titles, and reach his apex in 1996, when the Gators finished 12-1, and won the mythical national championship. In twelve seasons with Florida, he went 122-27-1.

In 2005, he took over as head coach of South Carolina. As of 2014, his overall record with the Gamecocks is 84-45, including a 2-3 record inside of Sanford Stadium.

Yet, an internal feud subsists within Spurrier because of the loss to Georgia during his Heisman Trophy season of 1966, the year Florida was supposed to "win it all." In fact, the Gators started the season with seven straight victories, and were primed to finally win its first ever SEC title.

On November 5, 1966, unranked Georgia spoiled the seventh-ranked Gators' unbeaten season and the SEC title hopes by defeating Florida 27-10. The Gators were just another Florida team that couldn't get it done against Georgia when it mattered most.

"They write books about this game," Spurrier once said. If truth be told, he learned there was no substitute for championships. "When we have our reunions of the guys who played in the '60s, we don't have any championships to talk about. We don't have any rings to flash to each other," Spurrier said. "We don't talk a heckuva lot about the ballgames we had because we don't have any memories of winning a championship."

Bill Stanfill, Georgia's All-America defensive lineman from 1966-68, who, as a sophomore, dominated in the Bulldogs' victory over Spurrier's Gators, stated, 'Florida fans may not think it's still a big game, but I can assure you it's still the biggest game on our schedule. A lot of Georgia fans dislike him because of his attitude. Do I hate him? I don't really want to use the word hate. Let's put it this way, if I were still playing, I guarantee I'm going to burn an extra quart of oil trying to get to him."

In 1966, just days before the Georgia game, Spurrier had a reporter from *Sports Illustrated* over to his house for dinner. A week earlier, Spurrier kicked a 40-yard field-goal to win the game against Auburn; a kick most people believe earned him the '66 Heisman Trophy. He learned that individual focus and attention always take away from the team's goal.

"That wasn't real dang intelligent," Spurrier related. "But we didn't know any better back then. We let all the media attention get to us, like about every other Florida team has. It didn't help, not that it costs us, but it didn't help."

It would take Spurrier twenty-four years to redress that loss as coach of the Gators. As of 2014, Coach Spurrier, the 1966 Heisman winner, was 3-3 inside of Sanford Stadium.

It was a big blow, but I think we can come back.
--Florida quarterback Steve Spurrier,
November 6, 1966

James Moore Tatum, Maryland, 1950, 1951 and 1952

He was born in McColl, South Carolina on July 22, 1913, where he went to high school before moving on to the University of North Carolina. With the Tarheels, he played football and baseball and was named All-Southern Conference tackle in 1935.

In 1936, after graduation, he played semi-pro baseball before joining the football coaching staff of Carl Snavely, his Tarheel coach. In 1942, after coaching at Cornell, as assistant to Coach Snavely, he returned to his alma mater to take over the head football reigns after Coach Raymond Wolf had been drafted into the Navy.

Upon completion of the season, he entered the United States Navy, too, and was assigned as assistant football coach under Don Faurot with the Iowa Sea Hawks. It was there he learned the split-line T, a system he later became a supreme authority on. He taught numerous clinics and lectured on its phases during the season. Coach Tatum was considered a wizard of defensive tactics, too.

After his duty at Iowa, he was appointed head coach at Jacksonville Navy Pre-Flight. While coaching the Pre-Flight teams, he used variations of the Split-T option offense, the 'Wishbone,' the 'Veer,' the 'I,' and the 'Spread.' Coach Tatum and Coach Bud Wilkinson would use variations of these formations to win national championships at Maryland and Oklahoma, respectfully. After his discharge from the military, he coached the University of Oklahoma for one season, before moving on to take over at Maryland.

Coach Tatum brought three highly ranked and powerful teams into Sanford Stadium and went 2-1 in those games. After losing the 1950 game, his '51 squad trounced Georgia 43-7, enroute to the national title, with a 10-0 record. In 1952, he brought another nationally ranked team into Sanford Stadium and beat Georgia 37-0.

Frank W. Thomas, Alabama, 1935, 1946

He was born on November 15, 1898, in Muncie, Indiana, where he became a star athlete in high school. In 1922, he attended Notre Dame, where he played quarterback for Knute Rockne. Per Rockne, "Thomas was the smartest player I ever coached." Thomas's roommate in college was George "The Gipper" Gipp.

After graduating from Notre Dame, Thomas became an assistant coach at Georgia for two years before earning his first head coaching job, in 1925, at the University of Chattanooga. His teams' record was 26–9–2 in four seasons. In 1931, Thomas took over as Alabama's head coach and stayed until 1946, compiling an astounding record of 141-33-9.

During his tenure, Alabama won four Southeastern Conference titles and its 1934 team went undefeated, and was selected as national champions. His total wins, and winning percentage at Alabama rank second all-time among Crimson Tide football coaches. He's only behind Coach Bryant, who he coached during the mid-1930s. He never had a losing season, and his teams twice had undefeated, 10-win campaigns. He was 1-1 inside of Sanford Stadium, winning 17-7 in 1935, and losing 14-0 in 1946.

Johnnie Howard Vaught, Ole Miss, 1966, 1968, 1970, and 1973

Born on May 6, 1909, he graduated valedictorian from Polytechnic High School in Fort Worth, Texas. He later attended

Texas Christian University, where he was an honor student and was selected as an All-American in 1932.

During World War II, he served as an assistant coach with North Carolina Pre-Flight School. In 1946, a year after World War II ended, he took a job as an assistant coach at Ole Miss. In 1947, he was named the Rebels' head coach, and Ole Miss proceeded to win the university's first conference title. Mississippi enjoyed unprecedented success under Vaught, as he led them to Southeastern Conference (SEC) titles in 1947, '54, '55, '60, '62 and '63.

As of 2015, he was the only football coach in the history of Ole Miss to win an SEC championship. His 1960 team received the Grantland Rice Award, from the Football Writers Association of America, as the best team in the nation. Vaught took Ole Miss to 18 bowl games, winning ten, including five victories in the Sugar Bowl. The only coaches who held a winning record against him were Coach Bryant, with a record of seven wins, six losses, and one tie, and Tennessee's Coach Neyland, with three wins, and two losses.

Coach Vaught wasn't a complex man, and was easily recognizable in his suit, tie and hat. He preferred the quiet life on his farm with his family. During his tenure at Ole Miss, the Rebels experienced heights never before seen in the history of the program. His overall record at Ole Miss was 190 wins 61 losses and 12 ties.

He was considered one of the easiest people to conduct an interview with and was a true gentleman in the mold of Georgia Tech's Coach Dodd, Coach Jordan of Auburn, or Coach Dooley of Georgia, who fell into the same category. He was a coach who might have been the least talkative man in the South and could name his starting line-up with a "yes" or "no."

His Ole Miss teams went 1-3 inside of Sanford Stadium. And, the 1970 Rebels, led by Archie Manning, was his only team to beat Georgia inside Sanford Stadium, by a score of 31-21.

Bill Yeoman, Houston 1968 and 1974

Bill Yeoman was born on December 26, 1927, in Elnora, Indiana. He attended high school in Glendale, Arizona. In 1945, he signed a scholarship with Texas A&M; however, in 1946, Yeoman received an appointment to West Point. At 6'-2" and 200 pounds, he played center for Army from 1946 through 1948. The Cadets went

22-2-4 during Yeoman's era under legendary head coach Earl Blaik. In fact, the 1946 team was 9–0–1, with a backfield of two Heisman Trophy winners: Glenn Davis and Doc Blanchard. In 1948, Yeoman became the only underclassman to become captain an Army football team. He was selected as an All-American in '48.

In 1962, he started coaching for the University of Houston and would coach there until he retired in 1986. In 1964, he revolutionized offensive football across the nation by developing the Veer option offense. Contrary to popular belief, this Veer offense, which dominated college football in the 1960s, got its initial start in 1962, at the University of Houston.

Coach Yeoman stumbled onto the Veer while trying to block for the power sweep. Each time the Cougar offense ran the power sweep, problems developed with the defensive tackle, who kept busting the play. In disgust, Coach Yeoman told his quarterback, Billy Roland, to hand the ball off on the dive play, to settle his defensive tackle down to where the power sweep would work.

In 1964, Yeoman played a leading role in the racial integration of collegiate athletics in the South. He was the first coach at a mostly white school, in the state of Texas, to sign a black player. On July 11, 1964, he awarded a scholarship to high school All-American Warren McVea, from San Antonio.

From 1966 through 1974, Houston went 64-20-3 running the Veer. In fact, the Cougars led the nation in total offense for three straight years and set several NCAA records during the 1968 campaign of 562.0 yards per game. During his tenure, he became the winningest coach in school history, with an overall record of 160–108–8. The Cougars finished the season ranked in the *Associated Press* Top-10 four times and finished eleven times in the *Associated Press* or *United Press International* Top-20.

His teams played inside Sanford Stadium twice, tying Georgia 10-10 in '68, and beating the Bulldogs in '74 by a final score of 31-24. During the '68 game, Houston outplayed Georgia, but only led 10-7 because the hard-hitting Bulldog defense caused so many fumbles. The game ended in a tie after Georgia stopped a Houston drive at the Georgia nine-yard line. Then, Mike Cavan moved Georgia down the field, to the Houston 22-yard line, where Jim McCullough kicked a 38-yard field-goal to tie the game 10-10.

Singularly Greatest Performances

From a statistical perspective, most collegiate football games end without any excitement, coming to a close with a grumble as the winning team assumes the victory formation. However, at times, there are unique games that do end with a bang, as one team pulls out a late stand, a last-minute score, or a miracle. When eleventh-hour upsets do occur, a player's singular effort can either be immortalized, or shattered, by his team's failure to back-up his phenomenal performance. When a loss does happen, despite an individual player's Herculean efforts, it culminates in massive disappointment over what should have been a celebrated event.

Football is a team sport, and each season, as exceptional players take the field, a very select few will deliver the aforementioned Herculean performances. On those rare occasions, when an individual athlete has had the game of a lifetime, it's clear to all watching that an extraordinary event has occurred. When alumni, students, and fans have the privilege of observing a remarkable event, where a distinctive player has had a phenomenal game, the ticket stubs, programs, and any other artifacts of the game, are kept as souvenirs and family heirlooms, to be passed down to future generations to keep those memories of yesteryear alive.

Unfortunately, football, the ultimate team sport, makes it virtually impossible for an individual player to overcome his own team's deficiencies, or the other team's superiority. Thus, whether or not his team wins, or loses, it should not diminish what an individual player has accomplished. Even when the most valiant efforts of one player are insufficient to guarantee victory, his performance still warrants recognition. As such, some singularly great performances identified in this chapter involves players who were on the losing team.

As a gentle disclaimer, there was certainly no feasible way to highlight every great singular performance in the history of Sanford Stadium. For every Herculean effort recognized in this book, there are many left off this list. While plenty of athletes have played great games inside of Sanford Stadium, the following ten players, listed in chronological order, were recognized as having the singularly greatest performances inside the Mecca of the South.

Vernon "Catfish" Smith, Georgia, October 12, 1929

Athens listened to the tune of the Yale's band play the "Boola" song, along with the war cry of the Southern Bulldogs when 30,000 frenzied football fans stormed the gates of the Classic City for the dedication of the new Sanford Stadium before the Yale-Georgia football game.

Georgia had generously let its visitors, Yale, have the shady side of the field on which to sit. Georgia's game plan sprang out of Rockne's cleverly masked cut-in maneuver. The method caught Yale shifting the wrong way several times; however, line pressure from Georgia's undersized team forced the breaks that helped the 'Dogs upset Bulldogs of Yale. Vernon Smith, Georgia's rugged sophomore end, was the biggest factor in the exploitation of Yale.

Every football game must have its heroes, and Smith stole the show. Catfish scored both of Georgia's touchdowns, blocked a Yale punt, intercepted a lateral pass, forced Yale into a safety by means of a punt angled into the extreme corner, made 15 tackles, and had seven deep punts. He untiringly kept a big rod in the pickle for the defending national champion Eli all afternoon.

Oddly, Smith began the game as though he might be the goat. Early during the game his vertical punts, the ball traveling almost straight-up, had Georgia in hot water throughout the first period. The capacity crowd began mumbling unkind words about Smith, but that was before he did his Doctor Jekyll to Mister Hyde transformation and won the game for Georgia. Before it was over, he was the main factor in defeating a very powerful Yale 15-0. It would be a high carnival in Athens on the evening following the amazing upset.

Charlie Trippi, Georgia, November 2, 1946

Led by Charlie Trippi, the Bulldogs all-around All-American, and one of the greatest defensive backs in the history of the South, passed for one score and sprinted 46-yards for another, as Georgia blanked highly ranked Alabama 14-0, on a wet, soggy field.

On the first play after Georgia's Dick McPhee made an interception, Trippi fired a pass to Dan Edwards for a touchdown. The unique part of the play was Trippi passed, while falling backwards, and Edwards caught the ball diving forwards, after Hal Self, trying to be a little too selfish, had batted the ball into the air.

During the 1940s, it became a custom for Trippi to take-off on at least one long run in each game; Alabama was no exception. In the waning minutes of the second quarter, Trippi started the scoring march with a 33-yard aerial to Johnny Rauch, where Rauch got down to the Pachyderm's 46-yard line. Then, after two pass plays failed, Trippi took a shovel pass from Rauch, rounded the right end, plowed through two defenders, applied an extra burst of speed to explode through three other tacklers, who were dangerously near the sidelines, and roared 46-yards to pay-dirt. George Jernigan split the uprights as Alabama bowed its head in defeat.

Georgia went on to an undefeated season and was selected as national champions in several polls. Alabama, the defending national champions, would prove to be the toughest game of the season for the 'Dogs.

Charlie "Choo-Choo" Justice, North Carolina, October 2, 1948

The Indian-Summer kissed the thousands of shirt-sleeved fans that packed scenic Sanford Stadium on the afternoon of October 2, 1948. The fall frenzy of football gripped Athens for one rip-roaring weekend. Long before kickoff, the masses began their twisting pilgrimage towards the scene of the battle, their paths studded with program and soft drink vendors. On-the-spot picnickers, predecessors to the tailgaters, spread their blankets on any available smidgen of grass and made themselves at home.

For all practical purposes, Athens might has well have been moved to Carolina, or vice versus. Those black and yellow North Carolina auto license plates were as thick as fleas on a hound dog.

After the ball game was all over, and the fans, representing at least fifteen states, started their journey back home, there was one complete phrase that fully summed up the result. There was no doubt about it—"Justice reigned supreme! Justice had been served!"

The one-man scoring demonstration by Charlie Justice— three touchdowns in two quarters…put his All-American honors in a box, and tied it with a ribbon. The "Carolina Special" was probably the only train in history that ran its "Choo-Choo" behind boxcar interference. However, a toast was in order for Coach Butts and his Bulldog coaching staff, who had concocted the defensive strategy that almost accomplished the nation's number one upset of the day.

The crowd was dumb-founded when Georgia won the toss and chose to kick-off—something a Butts' team rarely ever did. Georgia's defensive tactics, coupled with its waiting for the breaks, was perfectly planned. Their break was Eli Maricich's 75-yard pass interception, but their downfall was not opening-up soon enough in the second half. Once Georgia opened its bag of aerial tricks in the fourth period, it was too late.

Both teams had gone with a new technique called the "two-team system." It employed two eleven men teams, who specialized on offense or defense. It was one of the first times fans could see a football game with four different teams on the field during the same game. On several occasions, both teams were penalized for excessive time while getting extra men off the field.

Plus, the mystery of how Carolina's kicker, Mike Rubish, was able to kickoff in his stocking feet, and how he got his shoe back, had finally been solved. Rubish, who booted in his stocking feet, hopped downfield on the play, then went to a pre-arranged spot on the sideline, met a trainer, who gave him his shoe. The "re-shoeing" took place between plays, something that had baffled the sports world for some time.

Georgia derailed the Carolina "Choo Choo" for over two quarters. Then Justice switched from coal to electrical energy in the second half and made three "express run" to the Georgia goal. Written on Charlie's caboose was "North Carolina 21 – Georgia 14."

Maricich tacked Georgia's hopes to a high-flying overhead cloud in the first quarter when he intercepted Hosen Rogers' pass at the Georgia 25-yard line, and set sail down the north sidelines for a 75-yard scoring sprint that had all 44,000 fans on their feet. Not a Tarheel touched goal-bound Eli. Georgia converted the extra-point and led 7-0. Then, Justice checked-in at the pay window, in the third stanza, for Carolinas' initial counter.

Justice was the man of the hour. Besides scoring all of North Carolinas' touchdowns, Justice was a thorn in Georgia's side. The Tarheel Titanic attempted 21 passes and completed 14. His total offensive effort was 106 yards.

The nearest thing to Charlie Trippi that Athens fans had seen since he departed, Justice proved his calmness under fire late in the ball game. In the fourth quarter his center made a bad snap, a low one, and the ball got away from "Choo Choo," rolling back several yards. He raced back, picked-up the ball, surveyed the field and then flung a 30-yard pass, complete to Georgia's 12-yard line. It was a Trippi type play, executed perfectly by Justice.

Statistically, it was the greatest game ever for the legendary "Choo-Choo" Justice, at least as a North Carolina Tarheel. Justice handed Georgia, the eventual Southeastern Conference Champions, its only loss of the regular season during this auspicious meeting.

He gained a total of 304 yards in leading Carolina to its victory. The stat sheet showed Justice had a 9-yard touchdown run and a 13-yard touchdown run in the 3rd quarter, then an 84-yard punt return for a touchdown in the 4th quarter.

The crowd had unexpectedly witnessed Georgia take a 7-0 halftime lead over the Tarheels, a 13-point favorite. Despite 222 total yards being gained at halftime, the Tarheels were held scoreless, as Georgia executed two goal line stands, culminating in fumbles. The game's first score was when Georgia's Maricich returned the aforementioned interception nearly 75-yards.

During the two previous games between these two titans, "Choo-Choo" had been limited to less than 70 total yards rushing; however, on this day, he was virtually unstoppable in the second half. In the third quarter, "Choo-Choo" capped a nine-play, 78-yard drive, with his 9-yard scoring run. Later, from a short punt formation, he rushed for a 14-yard touchdown. In the final canto, "Choo Choo" fielded a Bulldogs punt, faked a handoff, and streaked 84-yards down the sideline for his third touchdown. He finished the game with 106-yards rushing, 198-yards passing, 121-yards on punt returns, and 20-yards on a kick-off return.

With less than five minutes remaining in the game, Georgia's John Tillitski stopped another North Carolina drive with an interception. At that point, the Bulldogs had gained only 40 total yards and no first downs. Johnny Rauch led Georgia down the field and finished the drive with a 29-yard touchdown pass to Gene Lorendo. But, the damage had already been inflicted. North Carolina would hold on to win 21-14. The Tarheels would be ranked number two in the nation less than 48-hours later.

After the game, the smell of burnt rubber, from hot brake linings, blanketed the scene surrounding the stadium as the mass of automobiles crept inch-by-inch from the parking areas. Broad Street resembled a log-jammed river, as motorists tried to buck their way into the open highways. The chorus of horns sounded like a "Victory in Japan Day" celebration.

Oddly, probably one of the hardest hit gentlemen was a rotund fellow who lost quite a roll, betting while the game was in progress. The gambler, seated in the North stands, started off at kickoff giving Georgia and 14 points. The first time Carolina was in scoring distance, he laid even bets the Tarheels would score.

Surrounding fans covered $300 worth on the 14-point bet, and numerous $10 betters covered the scoring march. This kept up during the entire game. As the game neared a close the good-natured fellow turned his pockets inside-out, brought forth 4 one-dollar bills, saying, "...that's all I got left folks." He had lost $1,600 in 1948 currency, or the equivalent of $12,700 in 2015 value.

Pat Sullivan, Auburn, November 13, 1971

There might have been one individual who could throw a football better than Pat Sullivan in 1971. However, this particular entity resided upstairs in Heaven.

After Auburn got through shellacking Georgia, Auburn Coach Ralph "Shug" Jordan even questioned the above statement. "There are plenty of great passers, but what makes Sullivan so great is the way he stands in there and throws with people hanging on him," said Jordan.

Sullivan and Terry Beasley, Auburn's amazing touchdown twins, wore the cloak of the hero in much the same manner, as the way they performed on the football field. With writers from across the nation swarming around their dressing cubicles, the leaders of Auburn's undefeated, fifth ranked Tigers answers questioned with poise and sincerity in a postgame interview.

"Right now, this is the greatest thing that has ever happened to me," Sullivan said of Auburn's stunning 35-20 win over Georgia. The other half of the scoring duo, Beasley, praised the Auburn coaches for the Tiger's win. Asked if he thought Sullivan would win the Heisman Trophy, symbolic of the nation's best collegiate player, Beasley replied, "Shoot, he'd better. He's the best!"

It was Beasley who turned the game into a semi-rout midway through the fourth-period. The Auburn receiver snared a Sullivan pass, bounced off two would-be Georgia tacklers and ran 70-yards for the score that put the Tigers in front 28-20.

After the game, the Bulldogs were miserable, to say the least. Maybe the Bulldog's dejection was most graphically expressed by quarterback Andy Johnson when he flatly stated, "I ain't got nothing to say," and kept walking.

Players who did talk after the game were filled with praise for the pair of Tiger miracle workers, who were just about the only thorn in Georgia's side all day—Sullivan and Beasley.

"Sullivan's a great quarterback, just like everybody says, and Beasley's a great receiver," said Buzy Rosenberg.

Sullivan and Beasley connected two times during the ballgame for scores, and Sullivan hit Dick Schmalz for two other touchdowns. Only one Auburn touchdown was made on the ground.

When Coach Dooley was asked if Sullivan was better than Archie Manning, he replied, "yeah," and punctuated it by reiterating, "… is the best I've ever seen."

Sullivan hit 14 of 24 passes against Georgia for 248 yards and four touchdowns—four knockout punches. Auburn gave Georgia a couple of golden opportunities to fold and Dooley's troops showed their caste by turning the Tigers down. Before most of the 62,891 fans had found their seats, Auburn led 14-0.

Much of Sullivan's superness came on third down situations. In reality, Georgia's defense only got to him twice in the first half. The rest of the time he was lobbing screen passes for first downs or more damaging touchdown passes with defenders closing-in. On two of his scoring tosses, it appeared the Bulldogs had him cornered, but he managed to get the football away.

With the score tied 14-14, in the second quarter, Sullivan faced a third down and six situation at the Georgia 15-yard line. It looked like the 'Dogs had him, and he seemed to be throwing the ball away, but Schmalz leaped high, with hardly any room left in the corner of the endzone, to grab a touchdown pass. A breakdown in the Bulldog coverage left Schmalz open and anybody, but Sullivan, probably would have thrown an incomplete pass.

Earlier he had connected with Beasley for Auburn's second score, and on that play it looked like he threw while he was down.

In the first half the honorable No. 7 faced seven third down situations. He got his team a first down five of those times.

Afterwards, when the questions to Dooley, as it did all afternoon, gravitated back to Sullivan, in reference to how Dooley devised a way to stop him, his response was, "Stop him? Yea—graduate him."

Michael Singletary, Baylor, September 16, 1978

At 6-0, 221 pounds, the Houston, Texas native made an astounding 24 tackles, including six unassisted, against Georgia. His dogfight on Saturday, September 16, 1978, was one of the most dominant performances of a defensive player in the history of Sanford Stadium. And, to be performed by an unheralded sophomore was even more incredible.

An article in the *Athens-Banner Herald* related, "Dooley will have to add a new name to the Georgia backfield, Mike Singletary, Baylor's awesome middle linebacker."

He mercilessly pounded Willie McClendon, along with the rest of Georgia's backfield, the entire afternoon. A singularly dominant feat of this magnitude would not be witnessed again inside of Sanford until Herschel Walker arrived in 1980.

Georgia had been aware of how good Singletary was because during his freshman season in Waco, he had 97 tackles, and he definitely wasn't afraid to put his nose on the football. He was the anchor for Baylor's "4-3" defense.

Through no fault of Singletary, Georgia would come from behind to upset highly ranked Baylor 16-14. Afterwards, Coach Dooley commented, "Singletary is one of the best I've ever seen."

Scott Woerner, Georgia, September 20, 1980

Scott Woerner and his family moved to Georgia, from Texas, when he was in the fifth grade. He would become an All-State quarterback at Jonesboro High School. Conceivably, one of Woerner's most distinguishing characteristics was his enthusiasm, regarding team work, despite personal records of his own. Individual statistics never troubled him; at least not when Georgia was 1-3 in 1979.

Woerner usually played defensive secondary for the Bulldogs. But, he took to the offensive against Clemson in 1980. In fact, he provided the 'Dogs with one touchdown and set-up another, enabling Georgia to upset Danny Ford's Clemson Tigers 20-16.

The first time he got his hands on the ball, he returned the punt 67-yards for a touchdown; minutes later, he ran 98-yards with an interception, halting a Clemson drive in the endzone. Woerner's interception helped set-up Georgia's second touchdown.

It was a switch for the senior, who was really playing the role of backup to Greg Bell. "Greg Bell had two better games than I had," said Woerner. "I knew I hadn't been playing well, and I knew I couldn't make it through the first quarter and he couldn't either."

The first score was set-up after a booming punt by Tiger senior David Sims. "I could hear blocks being thrown," said Woerner. "When I looked down, I could see the hole. Chris Welton threw a real good block." After breaking a few tackles along the sidelines, it was a footrace to the goal line, with Woerner out distancing the punter.

Clemson came right back down the field after Woerner's touchdown, but was turned back by none other than Woerner, who grabbed a Homer Jordan pass in the endzone and headed the other way. "I caught the ball out of the endzone, I think. I thought I better bring it out," said Woerner.

The decision was correct as he had a wall of blockers to lead him down the sideline. Once he got past the initial pack he seemed to have clear sailing for another touchdown; however, Clemson tailback Chuck McSwain caught-up with Woerner at about the 10 yard line, and brought him down on the two-yard line, 98-yards from where Woerner had begun his jaunt.

Woerner, who had a better reputation for good hands than speed, admitted he was tired after the two runs. "In this heat, I start with a 4.6 (speed in the 40 yard dash) and end with a 4.8." The heat was a factor in the game. The temperature was in the 80s and the humility was 97 percent.

Woerner felt Georgia had a score to settle after the '79 loss to the Tigers' in Death Valley. "Last year we went up there, and got our butts beat," he said. "We decided that wasn't going to happen down here." But, for awhile in the first half, it appeared Clemson would take the game away from Georgia. The Tigers scored 10 points in the first half, to get within striking distance.

In the second half, it was Georgia who came out fired-up, and when Georgia got the ball, it was Woerner who was on the field, leading cheers, with a raised clenched towel toward the sky.

The Bulldogs did manage to generate enough offense to stave off a Clemson rally that was brought on, oddly, by Woerner. He almost became the goat of the game when he was called for pass interference at the 'Dogs 10-yard line, with less than two minutes to play in the game.

"I saw him (receiver Jerry Gaillard) at the last second," said Woerner. "We were both just going for the ball. Our feet got tangled-up. It was a judgment call." The call was a controversial one, but Safety Jeff Hipp got Woerner off the hook with his interception at the one-yard line.

During his high school days in Jonesboro, Woerner was an all-purpose man, capable of running the offense. The cornerback said it sure felt good to get back on the offensive side again, even though it was only for two plays. Asked after the game if he had ever had a better game at Georgia, Woerner responded, "No, that is probably the best." He would become Georgia's all-time punt returner, and play several years in the National Football League.

Herschel Walker, Georgia, October 31, 1980

There had always been doubts about Georgia's school record for most yards rushing in a single game, but not after Halloween, 1980. On October 31, 1980, Herschel Walker reached his apex, statistically, and cleared-up the matter for all-time when he ran through, over, around and between Vanderbilt tacklers, and would be tacklers, for 283-yards on 23 carries.

He scored three touchdowns on runs of 60, 48 and 53-yards, pacing Georgia to a 41-0 win. The Wrightsville youth, who had an automobile accident that week, just like his head coach, averaged 12.3 yards per carry in bettering Georgia's old record of 239-yards, set by the immortal Charlie Trippi, in 1945, against Florida.

"Anytime you break a record established by Charlie Trippi," said Coach Dooley, "that is quite an accomplishment. Herschel had three great runs. He has that kind of speed."

Walker had been a mere mortal since the first quarter of the Texas Christian University game. He suffered a sprained ankle and exited the game with just 68-yards. The following week, against Ole

Miss, he gained 44-yards on eleven carries, despite an off week to heal. After the game, Walker said he was still not 100 percent.

"I'm getting better," said the sensation in all his humility. "I've still got a little soreness in my ankle. It slowed me down. On two of the touchdown runs, I wasn't going as fast as I can."

If Walker could do that when not 100 percent, what could he accomplish when healthy? "I really don't know how good I can play," he said. "A lot I do surprises me."

It didn't surprise Georgia's fans; however, who had already come to expect great things from this young man. After six games into his college career, he had gained 746-yards, an average of 124.3 yards per game. He would increase that average to 159.9 yards per game before the season was over. Walkers shattered Willie McClendon's single season rushing record, too.

Hemingway would have had trouble describing Walker. Shakespeare would grope for words. Grantland Rice would be stumped. How do you adequately describe the feats perpetuated by the feet of Walker against Vanderbilt? He rushed for 283-yards on 23 carries; 207-yards by halftime, enroute to breaking Trippi's 35-year old one-game rushing record of 239-yards-set in 1945.

To describe Walker's performance just open your dictionary. Let the words flow: Incredible, Magnificent, Tremendous, Virtuoso, Remarkable, Unbelievable, etc.... There were 59,506 unbelieving witnesses who would have sworn he was unbelievable, playing like he belonged on another planet.

The very first time Walker touched the football, he galloped 60-yards for a score. The next time he ran with it, he "only" got 38-yards. That's 98 yards in two carries, or an average of 49-yards per rush. His third attempt was for 12-yards, giving the great freshman 110 yards before the crowd had gotten comfortable in their seats.

By intermission, Walker had gone over 200-yards and there was talk he might challenge Eddie Lee Ivery's NCAA mark of 356-yards. But Walker finished the last half with 76-yards and came out of the game with 9:21 left to play. His 283-yards fell three short of the freshman one game record set in 1977 by North Carolina's Amos Lawrence.

Unquestionably, Walker could have gone over 300-yards for the day, but Vince Dooley let him become a spectator most of the final period. For Walker, it was the greatest afternoon of his short, but brilliant college football career. It was the highest single-game rushing total in college football for 1980. For Dooley, it was an amiable afternoon.

The game started on a bleak note for Vanderbilt. Georgia won the coin toss and elected to receive. Vanderbilt had a terrible kickoff and the 'Dogs took the ball at their own 38-yard line. On the third play of the game Walker gave an indication as to what kind of afternoon it was going to be. He took a handoff from Buck Belue, roared right up the middle, flattened a couple of would-be Vanderbilt tacklers, like a runaway locomotive, and sprinted 60-yards for a touchdown. Rex Robinson came-in and nailed his eighty-second straight extra-point and the 'Dogs were up 7-0, with only 1:14 seconds of time being used up.

Coach Dooley, his wife Barbara, and son Derek, were in a car accident two had days before the game. Dooley suffered a broken nose and eleven stitches in his lip. He looked like he had been in the ring with Larry Holmes for 15 rounds. The Georgia team gave Dooley the ball, to present to Mrs. Dooley after the 'Dogs one-sided walker past the winless Commodores. Georgia, 3-0 in the Southeastern Conference, and 6-0 overall, were assured its number six ranking wouldn't be tarnished.

Kevin Butler, Georgia, September 22, 1984

In their seven previous games against each other, Georgia and Clemson had won three each, and tied one. In 1984, Clemson was ranked number two in the nation and was expected to play for the mythical national title. Georgia was ranked twentieth in the nation, and was an underdog by three-and-a-half-points. It would be the first time Georgia was an underdog inside Sanford Stadium since 1979, when the Bulldogs defeated Louisiana State University.

During the final quarter, Georgia had rallied to take the lead 23-20, after Kevin Butler kicked another field-goal. Clemson immediately roared back down the field to tie the game at 23-23, very late in the contest. Then, Georgia, led by Todd Williams, raced down the field until it was faced with a fourth down at Clemson's 44-yard line, with 17 seconds remaining in the game.

Butler had missed a 26-yard field-goal earlier in the game. It was his first miss of a field-goal under 30-yards since his freshman season in 1981; however, Coach Dooley wanted Butler to attempt a 60-yard field-goal. As he jogged onto the field, to attempt the game winning try, the only person who said anything to him was his holder, Jimmy Harrell, who simply said, "... keep your head down, and kick it hard." It would be the longest and potentially most celebrated field-goal, in Southeastern Conference history.

The ball was set-down between the fifty yard line and Georgia's 49 yard line. Butler took his accustomed three steps back, and two steps to the side, from the kicking tee. His holder, Harrell, took the snap, and Butler boomed a perfect 60-yard kick through the uprights as Sanford Stadium became undeniably desensitized.

Afterwards, with eleven seconds left to play, Clemson's Ray Williams would catch Butler's kickoff on his own 20-yard line and run 10 yards. There he stopped, and threw the ball across the field to his teammate, Terrance Roulhac, who would go to the Georgia 35-yard line before being run out of bounds. The clock had expired, and Georgia upset Danny Ford's second ranked Clemson Tigers.

Robert Edwards, Georgia, September 19, 1995

When Herschel Walker played at Georgia, Coach Dooley referred to him as "Ol' Man River" because, no matter how much he got hit, he just kept rolling along. Coach Goff discovered another great tributary among his ranks, and that one was named Robert Edwards, who came to Georgia as a cornerback. Then, before the 1995 season started, he was converted to tailback.

On September 19, 1995, before a sell-out crowd of 86,117, and a regional television audience, Edwards did something that neither Walker, nor any other Georgia player had ever achieved inside of Sanford Stadium. He scored a record five touchdowns. In the process, he led Georgia to a stunning 42-23 season-opening win over South Carolina. Had he not fumbled a toss sweep into the Gamecocks' endzone, late in the first half, he would have had six touchdowns. On the afternoon, he carried the ball thirty times for 169-yards, 123-yards came in the momentum-turning second half.

South Carolina had provided the stage for Robert Edwards' coming-out party. In the first half of his first start, Edwards had only amassed 46 yards and Georgia trailed 14-7. However, after the Gamecocks opened the second half with a field-goal, to extend the lead to 17-7, Edwards broke the game wide open. Within a seven minute span, Edwards would haul in a 45-yard touchdown, along with two more scores.

Robert Edwards, 1995

The game turned on Edwards' self-discovery. He gained 11 yards in the first quarter, 35 in the second, 55 in the third, and 68 in the fourth. Four of his carries ended in touchdowns. He showed a gift as a receiver, too, pulling away on a 45-yard pass play.

D.J. Shockley, Georgia, September 5, 2005

He sat around four years waiting to become Georgia's starting quarterback, which gave him an abundance of time to visualize greatness. Even so, he never foresaw his first start being so nice. Shockley threw five touchdown passes and ran for another score, leading the thirteenth ranked Bulldogs to a stunningly easy 48-13 victory over the eighteenth ranked Broncos of Boise State.

"It really hasn't hit me yet," Shockley said, surrounded by reporters and cameras in the locker room afterward. "There's no way I ever could have imagined something like this in my head. It's too big."

Jared Zabransky and the high-scoring Broncos were completely besieged by Georgia's refurbished defense, which didn't appear to have any difficulty supplanting David Pollack, Thomas Davis and Odell Thurman, three defensive stars who moved on to the National Football League, or defensive coordinator Brian Van Gorder, who moved on the National Football League, too.

For Boise State, ranked in the preseason for the first time, the icebreaker was a harsh tutorial in big-time football. "We got spanked," Coach Dan Hawkins said. "Georgia is a very good football team. That had a lot to do with it."

Shockley took over as the starting quarterback after redshirting his first year and backing-up David Greene for three seasons. The senior had big shoes to fill—Green, after all, had been the winningest quarterback in Division I-A history.

Georgia fell right into place with Shockley at the helm. In truth, he tied Greene's school record for touchdown passes during a single game—in only three quarters—and demonstrated an ability to run, are area Greene had been profoundly deficient.

In all, Shockley completed 16 of 24 passes for 289-yards—statistics that would have been even better without four dropped passes. He rushed five times for a team-leading 85-yards; however, one 23-yard run had been brought back because of an illegal block.

Zabransky had four interceptions, two fumbles before he was finally put on the bench minutes before intermission. In less than 30 minutes, any hope he had for possible Heisman consideration ended on a hot, muggy afternoon inside of Sanford Stadium. He failed to return for the second half, and was unable to talk with the media because he was hooked up to IVs.

Shockley had been anxious over his first start; however, he swiftly put the jitters behind him. He tossed a 40-yard touchdown to Kenneth Harris, then a 20-yard pass to Danny Ware and, finally, a 56-yard bomb to Martrez Milner. Next, he tossed two touchdowns to Sean Bailey on two straight scores. The first one was for 31-yards, and the last one was for five yards. Additionally, he had scored Georgia's first touchdown on a 14-yard run—proving he was a decent prognosticator, too.

Georgia's domination continued in the second half when the 'Dogs took the second-half kickoff and scored in less than two minutes, making the score 31-0. Shockley tossed another pass to Milner, who caught it on the fifty yard line, broke a couple of tackles, and went the rest of the way, unimpeded. Milner had three catches for a staggering 111-yards. The score was 38-0 before Boise State got on the scoreboard. "It was well worth the wait," stated Shockley.

The mantra of the crowd on the south-side of Sanford Stadium was, "D.J.! D.J.! D.J.!" While those on the north-side shouted, "O-ver-rated!" as the Broncos trudged off the field.

D. J. Shockley, 2005

Twenty-Five Significant Opposing Players

The ancient Greeks said it best when they reproved "a healthy mind within a healthy body." By its nature, the game of football is extremely intellectual, necessitating near genius strategists, paralleling a chess game. In actual fact, it underscores the highest permutation of scholarly and brute proficiency.

Moreover, during the early days of college football, some faculty believed student enthusiasm for the violence of football would enable the institutions to improve the all-encompassing belligerent conduct of its undergraduates. In truth, most would not disagree football constitutes one of the most interesting and entertaining spectator events in the history of our modern civilization. It is the quintessential equalizer of blood-thirst for society's prevailing athletics.

Though an inherently violent sport, football teaches the consequences of time management, the value of teamwork and the necessity to cultivate the mind and body. It has the ability to unite a diverse population, while aiding with instilling civic pride. In some convoluted way, it can even provide an insight into the often brutal nature of our world.

In fact, changes in college football emulate those events of our society. In truth, one of the most significant chronicles in the annals of twentieth century colligate football would to be the way college football nullified draconian customs and introduced black athletes to the vices and virtues of college football in the South. In 1969, forty years after its dedication game, a running back for the Tennessee Volunteers, Lester McClain, would become the first black player to play a varsity game inside Sanford Stadium. This book briefly glimpses at the dilemma of the sluggish entry of black athletes into football at major southern institutions. For this reason, McClain was included amongst the twenty-five most significant opposing athletes.

Now, in addition to the Heisman Trophy winners who have played inside of Sanford Stadium, the following twenty-five players hold the distinction of being the most important opposing competitors who helped add to the sanctity of Sanford Stadium.

Odell Cornelius Beckham Jr., Louisiana State, Sept 28, 2013

He was born in Baton Rouge, Louisiana on November 5, 1992. Later, he attended Isidore Newman School, in New Orleans, where he lettered in football, basketball and track. Beckham played quarterback, receiver, tailback and cornerback. During his junior season, he caught 45 passes for 743-yards and ten touchdowns. As a senior, he caught 50 passes, for 1,010 yards and 19 touchdowns. He signed a scholarship with Louisiana State in February 2011.

During his freshman season, Beckham started nine of 14 games, recording 41 receptions for 475-yards and two touchdowns. In 2012, his sophomore season, he started 12 of 13 games and had 43 receptions, for 713-yards. In 2013, his final season, he was selected as the winner of the Paul Hornung Award, presented annually to the most versatile player in major college football. He finished the season with 57 receptions for 1,117 yards and eight touchdowns.

In 2013, against Georgia, he had six receptions for 118-yards, and 175 yards on kickoff returns. Despite his remarkable numbers, Georgia would ultimately win the high scoring event 44-41.

Cornelius O'Landa "Biscuit" Bennett, Alabama, Sept. 2, 1985

Bennett was born on August 25, 1965, in Ensley, Alabama. He was nicknamed "Biscuit" because of his strong appetite for his mama's biscuits. While at Ensley High School in Birmingham, he played several positions, including halfback. In addition to football, he was an excellent basketball and baseball player. In football, he was an All-State performer during his senior season, gaining over 1000 yards, on 101 carries.

In the spring of 1983, he signed with Alabama. He played for the Pachyderms from 1983-1986, earning four letters. One of the University of Alabama's all-time defensive greats, Bennett would become a three time All-American.

In 1985, his Alabama team defeated Georgia 20-16. He recorded 14 tackles, while anchoring the line of scrimmage for the Crimson Tide. His play helped guarantee Alabama its first victory inside of Sanford Stadium since 1972.

In 1986, during his senior season, he earned the Lombardi Award, Southeastern Conference Player of the Year award, and finished seventh in balloting for the Heisman Trophy. He had 287 tackles, 21 ½ sacks, and three fumble recoveries.

James Eric Berry, Tennessee, October 11, 2008

Berry was born on December 29, 1988, in Fairburn, Georgia, where he attended Creekside High School. He emerged into a standout at quarterback and receiver and led Creekside to an overall record of 37-5 as a starter. Additionally, he ran track and set the state long jump record at 22'-8' and the 200-meter dash at 21.76 seconds. Berry was member of the 4 x 400 state title relay squad, and a constituent of the National Honor Society with 3.75 grade-point average.

He signed a scholarship with Tennessee in 2007. Known as "The Fifth Dimension," he was a three-year starter—and a three-year celebrity for the Volunteers. He picked off 14 passes in his career and had 494 interception-return yards, including three returns for touchdowns.

He won the 2009 Jim Thorpe Award, as the nation's top defensive back and finished his career with 245 tackles, 17 pass breakups, two forced fumbles and four fumble recoveries. In 2008 and 2009, Berry was a consensus All-American and was selected as the Southeastern Conference Player of the Year in 2008.

When the Volunteers played Georgia in 2008, he proved to be the quintessential defensive back Tennessee was known to torment Georgia with during the 1990s. He picked-up a 46-yard fumble and returned it for a touchdown, plus he had two pass deflections, five tackles, and an interception returned 54-yards. Miraculously, the 'Dogs still managed to win the game 26-14.

Fred Biletnikoff, Florida State University, October 17, 1964

Born and raised in Erie, Pennsylvania, Biletnikoff was the son of Russian emigrants who arrived in America during the Russian Civil War. In Erie, he attended what was then known as Technical Memorial High School, later identified as Central Tech, whose athletic field now bears his name. In 1961, after turning down other notable offers, Biletnikoff chose Florida State University, in Tallahassee, where he was a member of the Lambda Chi Alpha fraternity.

In 1962, Biletnikoff missed several games during his first varsity season because of a broken foot. In 1963, he returned and played on both sides of the ball, leading the team in receptions and interceptions. In a game against Miami, he returned one interception 99-yards for a touchdown.

On October 17, 1964, Georgia ventured into the world of "Top-10" football. It was Coach Dooley's first year as head coach. It would be Biletnikoff's first and only game inside of Sanford Stadium. He would guide Florida State to a 17-14 triumph.

It was a heart-breaking loss for the Bulldogs, who rallied from a 10-0 deficit to take a 14-10 lead with 6:21 remaining. Everybody in Sanford Stadium was convinced an upset was in the making. Everyone, that is, except Seminole quarterback Steve Tensi and halfback Biletnikoff. Tensi filled the air with passes and Biletnikoff pulled them in. The last one went for 26-yards and the winning touchdown. Biletnikoff had eight receptions for 114-yards.

Brett Lorenzo Favre, Southern Mississippi, September 15, 1990

He was born on October 10, 1969, in Gulfport, Mississippi. Favre attended Hancock North Central High School, where he was an All-State baseball and football player. In truth, he played quarterback, punter, placekicker, and lineman during his senior season. In 1987, he received only one scholarship offer, from Southern Mississippi, and he accepted it.

During his freshman season with Southern Miss, he was buried deep on the depth charts as the seventh-string quarterback. In a power struggle, he insisted on playing quarterback, but Southern Miss wanted him as a defensive back. As if by divine intervention, he would take over the starting position in the second half of the third game of the year, against the Tulane Green Waves. He would never surrender his starting quarterback position for the remainder of his time at Southern Miss.

On July 14, 1990, before the start of Favre's senior year, he was involved in a near-fatal car accident. When going around a corner, less than a mile from his parents' house, Favre lost control of his car, which flipped three times and came to rest against a tree. Six weeks after this incident, he led Southern Miss to a comeback victory over Alabama. The following week, he led Southern Mississippi into Sanford Stadium.

Georgia had watched film on Favre all week, and knew he would be the most elusive quarterback they'd face all season. In fact, he would only be brought down once, late in the first period, on a third-and-six play, for a loss of 13-yards.

After six minutes into the second half, and his team ahead 10-6, Favre eluded the grasp of defensive tackle Mike Steele and found his 6-foot-4 wide receiver, Michael Jackson, wide open on the left sideline for a 62-yard scoring strike. "We had the quarterback sacked and the next thing you know, the ball is in the air," said All-American outside linebacker Mo Lewis. "One minute he's in your hand, the next minute the ball is in the air."

Coach Curley Hallman was philosophical about his team, who had beaten Alabama the previous week. "It was a tough loss, Hallman said, "They're all tough when you lose them, just like they're all big when you win'em."

The gutsy Favre, who underwent abdominal surgery on August 8, 1990, after the automobile accident, never missed a game. Against Georgia, he completed 11 of 20 passes for 136 yards, and two touchdowns, with no interceptions. His 62-yard touchdown pass to Jackson almost broke the 'Dogs' back; however, Georgia would hold on for an 18-17 win.

He was impressed with the Bulldogs' defensive linemen by committee. "There's no doubt they were good," said Favre of the Bulldogs defense. "They were weak in spots, but they played us tough. We put in some new packages this week, but it seemed like every time we went to the line, they knew what we were going to do. They were the better team today."

He would have 15 games during his college career where he compiled more than 200 passing yards. Of those 15 games, five were for over 300-yards. He ended his career with 7,695 passing yards, 52 touchdowns, and 34 interceptions.

John Allen "Hawg" Hannah, Alabama, October 7, 1972

He was born on April 4, 1951, in Canton, Georgia and raised in Albertville, Alabama. He went to Baylor School, in Chattanooga, Tennessee, where he wrestled, played football and ran track. In 1967, he won an individual national championship, in wrestling, at the National Prep Championship. In 1969, he went back to Albertville and played his senior season of football there.

He signed a scholarship with Alabama, where he played tackle and guard from 1970 through 1972. He earned consensus All-American honors twice, in 1971 and 1972. Additionally, he was on the Alabama wrestling and track teams.

His only appearance inside of Sanford Stadium came in 1972. The big question, prior to the game, was whether Georgia's defense could slow down the Alabama wishbone, fronted by the most dominant offensive line in the nation.

The Alabama wishbone turned-out to be as good as advertised when they defeated Georgia 25-7. The majority of the yardage gained by the Crimson Tide was behind All-American Hannah, where they gained 263-yards against Georgia's stingy defense. The Tide controlled the ball for over thirty-seven minutes.

Afterwards Hannah, a 270 pound hulk of a man, and generally considered the nation's top professional prospect, stated, "We're not the team we were last year, yet, but we're not as far off from it as we were a week ago. I would like to say I was impressed with Georgia. They hit hard, were very dedicated and never quit."

Chet Hanulak, University of Maryland, October 13, 1951, and October 11, 1952

Hanulak was born on March 28, 1933, in Hackensack, New Jersey. He played at Hackensack High School and is considered its greatest athlete of all-time. In 1950, he signed a scholarship with the University of Maryland where he starred in both football and baseball. He sat out his first season because freshman weren't allowed to play on the Varsity. Later, it was no shock to anybody, who had observed him perform, as to why his moniker happened to be "Chet the Jet." He had an extraordinary amount of speed.

In 1951, Hanulak would emerge into one of the Terrapin's stars, and was a vital piece of Maryland's 1951 and 1953 National Championship football teams.

Most experts consider Hanulak the most powerful runner of his epoch. In 1950, the year prior to his arrival on Maryland's varsity, Georgia soundly defeated an unprepared and unconditioned Maryland team in the season-opener. In 1951, the Bulldogs were thought to be the Terrapins' toughest game. Maryland, considered by many to be greatest opposing team to ever play inside Sanford Stadium, soundly defeated Georgia 43-7, as Hanulak rushed for 115-yards, and scored two touchdowns. He went on to lead Maryland to a 10-0 record and its first National Championship.

In 1952, Hanulak rushed for 107-yards and two touchdowns as the Terrapins beat Georgia 37-0. His punishing style of running eventually devastated an overmatched Georgia defense. At the end of the third quarter, Coach Jim Tatum took Hanulak out of the game.

As a senior, Hanulak sprinted through defenses, and helped Coach Tatum's team defeat Georgia 40-13, in College Park, Maryland. He finished the '53 season with an average of 9.78 yards per carry, establishing an Atlantic Coast Conference (ACC) benchmark for highest per-carry rushing average during the league's first season of existence. Hanulak was a pivotal part of the '53 Maryland machine that went 10-1, and won the national title.

Additionally, Hanulak led the ACC in rushing in 1953 with 753 yards in his only season in the conference. His overall career rushing average was 8.13 per carry and his career rushing total was 1,544 yards. A three-time letterman for Maryland (1951-52-53), he earned All-American and first-team All-ACC honors in 1953. He played on three Maryland varsity teams that had a combined record of 27-3, and won two national titles.

Lionel James, Auburn, Nov. 14, 1981 and Nov. 12, 1983

James was born on May 25, 1962, in Albany, Georgia. Despite his diminutive stature, James became a successful running back and receiver at Dougherty High School, in Albany. He played under Luther Welch, whom James called "the toughest coach in the world." After leading his team to the state playoffs, James would sign a scholarship with Coach Pat Dye's Auburn Tigers in 1980.

After getting the lion's share of carries in 1981 and 1982, he would split the backfield with Bo Jackson in 1983. Still, James remained a pivotal part of Auburn's 1983 Southeastern Conference (SEC) championship team, and Sugar Bowl champions. Nicknamed "Little Train," because of his size, his namesake in the Lionel electric train company, and his determination to succeed as an athlete, he would forever go down in Auburn folklore for his play in the '83 game against Georgia.

In 1983, the wishbone was hitting on all cylinders against fourth-ranked Georgia, in Athens. James accounted for 47 of the Tigers' 286-yards against the nation's top rated rushing defense. "We went into that game really poised," James says. "A lot of people said we didn't have a chance to win, but we knew our team was good. Coach Dye would say things before the game like, 'What are you going to do if we have a seven-point lead in the fourth quarter? What are you going to do if we're 14 points behind? You need to have a plan.' We hadn't really thought like that before."

As destiny would have it, Auburn would have to go into Athens and take the SEC crown away from three-time defending champion Georgia. With Herschel Walker gone to the pros, the Tigers trusted its defense to win the championship. The winner would be declared the SEC Champions.

Auburn scored its only touchdown of the game in the first quarter. After creating a fumble, and getting some hard runs out of Jackson, Auburn was suddenly sitting on the Bulldog's three-yard line. Then, Jackson made a vital block, devastating a defensive player on the corner, and sprung the "Little Train" into the endzone, untouched. Two Del Greco field-goals were eventually tacked-on, and the defense held off a wild Georgia comeback attempt. The final score was 13 - 7.

The War Eagles, a member of the nation's strongest conference, had gone from the cellar of the league in 1980, to winning it four seasons later, the duration of James' Auburn career. James, who was only 5'- 6" and 170 pounds, emerged into one of Auburn's all-time great running backs. During his four years, he accounted for over 3,300 total yards at Auburn.

Calvin Johnson, Jr., Georgia Tech, November 27, 2004 and November 25, 2006

He was born on September 29, 1985, in Newnan, Georgia. He was 6'- 4" at Sandy Creek High School, in Tyrone, Georgia. His size and athletic skills set him on the path to greatness.

In 2003, he signed a scholarship with the Georgia Institute of Technology. His enormous size, 6'-5", and 240 pounds, coupled with his incredible, 4.35 speed, caused Johnson to create a disproportionate amount of attentiveness from opposing defenses while in college.

During his freshman and sophomore seasons he had relatively modest receiving numbers; however, as a junior, he erupted for 1,202 receiving yards and 15 touchdowns. In 2006, he was selected as Biletnikoff Award winner, as college football's top receiver. Additionally, he finished tenth in voting for the Heisman Trophy. For his career at Tech, he had 178 receptions, 2,927 yards and 28 touchdowns.

In 2004, his first game inside of Sanford Stadium, he had five catches for 44-yards and no touchdowns. In 2006, during his final visit into Sanford Stadium, the superior play of Georgia's Paul Oliver held Johnson to two catches for 13-yards, and no touchdowns. Georgia Tech would lose both games against Georgia.

Quintorris Lopez "Julio" Jones, Alabama, September 27, 2008

He attended Foley High School in Foley, Alabama, where he played for the Foley Lions High School football team from 2004–2007. During his junior season of high school, Jones quickly emerged into one of the nation's top high school prospects. He caught 75 passes for 1,306 yards and had 16 touchdowns. In 2007, he participated in the High School Under Armour All-American game. Later, he ran a 4.45-second 40-yard dash at the Baton Rouge Nike camp, and he recorded an event-best 38.6-inch (980 mm) vertical jump.

Listed as the number one receiver in the nation out of high school, he signed with the University of Alabama on February 6, 2008. Jones quickly became an impact player and fan favorite with the Crimson Tide. During his three years with Pachyderms, he accumulated 179 receptions, 2,653 yards, and fifteen touchdowns. He had eight career 100 yard receiving games and was a unanimous 1st Team All-Southeastern Conference selection in 2010.

Jones made his only visit into Sanford Stadium on September 27, 2008. He had his breakout performance as he caught five passes for 94 yards, including a 22–yard touchdown reception from John Parker Wilson.

It was christened the "Blackout Game," when Georgia wore its black jerseys and its fans wore black; however, the game turned into an embarrassment. The biggest cheers came from the white-clad Alabamians, sprinkled throughout the massive stadium. Eighth ranked Alabama looked imposing by whipping third ranked Georgia 41-30. The game was not as close as the final score indicated. The Tide jumped out to a 31-0 lead in the first half before the 'Dogs managed some cosmetic scores in the waning minutes of the game.

Lee Roy Jordan, Alabama, September 23, 1961

Born on April 27, 1941, he was the fourth of five sons born to Walter and Cleo Jordan. Jordan grew-up picking cotton, and tending cattle on the family farm. He attended Excel High School in Excel, Alabama, where he was a standout fullback. During these critical years of growing-up, he developed a strong work ethic upon which he later relied to succeed on the gridiron. Auburn would initially offer Jordan a scholarship; however, for some unknown reason, the Tigers later withdrew its offer. In 1959, he signed a scholarship with the University of Alabama and Coach Paul Bryant.

Jordan arrived on the Alabama campus in 1959. Because freshmen were not eligible to play on the varsity team, Jordan did not begin playing for the Crimson Tide until 1960. From 1960 through 1962, he became one of the greatest players in Alabama football history. During his sophomore season he helped the Crimson Tide finish with an 8–1-2 record. He would be selected as 1960 Bluebonnet Bowl Most-Valuable Player against Texas.

Alabama's Lee Roy Jordan, 1961

During the three years that Jordan played, Alabama posted a record of 29-2-2. In 1961 and '62, he led a defense that allowed 25 and 39 points, respectively. In 1961, his junior season, he was an integral part of the Alabama team that finished with an 11–0 record, won the Southeastern Conference, and the national championship. The season included six shutouts, including a 34–0 win over Auburn. The Crimson Tide won the Sugar Bowl 10-3 over the Razorbacks of Arkansas. He earned All-American honors and won the Lineman of the Year award.

In 1962, Jordan's senior season, Alabama finished 10-1, and ranked fifth in the country. His greatest performance as a collegian would come in his final game in the 1963 Orange Bowl. Playing in front of a crowd that included President John F. Kennedy, Jordan earned Most Valuable Player honors by making 30 tackles and leading the Tide to a 17-0 victory over the University of Oklahoma.

During his career for Alabama, Jordan received high praise from Coach Bryant, who stated, "He was the finest football player the world has ever seen. If runners stayed between the sidelines, he tackled them. He never had a bad day; he was 100 percent every day in practice and in the games."

His only time inside of Sanford Stadium occurred in 1961, when the Alabama defense held Georgia to only one first down. The Bulldogs experienced trouble with an amateurish offensive unit throughout the first part of the game. Alabama's short, yet consistent ground game enabled the Tide to move the ball at will.

The All-American Jordan led his Alabama forces with punishing tackles and kept Georgia from penetrating Tide territory, except minutes before the half, when the 'Dogs made it all the way to the Alabama 45-yard line. Early in the fourth quarter, after Alabama's first string had been removed, the 'Dogs made it to the Pachyderm's 41-yard line before being stopped.

Defensively, Jordan logged twenty-one tackles. He spearheaded a charge that held Georgia scoreless until the final play of the game. Dale Williams, Georgia's back-up quarterback, came off the bench and tossed a touchdown as time expired. The try for two points failed, and it was all over. The final score was 32-6.

Charles Ronald "Choo-Choo" Justice, N. Carolina, Oct 2, 1948

He was born on May 18, 1924, in Ashville, North Carolina. Justice would become a high school football legend in the Smokey Mountains. America was involved in the World War II when he graduated high school, and as a result, he joined the Navy.

While in the military, he played for the Bainbridge Naval Base football team on the coast of Maryland. While playing football on the base, he earned his nickname "Choo Choo." An officer, who was observing the game, commented to a reporter, "Look at that guy run. He looks like a runaway train. We ought to call him Choo Choo."

After Justice was discharged from the military at the conclusion of World War II, he was heavily recruited by Duke, North Carolina, and South Carolina. He was quoted as saying he believed an athlete should play in the state he was going to make his career, so he selected the University of North Carolina.

Being a war veteran, he knew he had no need of an athletic scholarship. Justice sent a proposal to the universities asking each to allow him to attend on his G. I. tuition money and grant the scholarship to his wife. Only the University of North Carolina accepted his proposal. Thus, Justice played collegiate football at North Carolina, under Carl Snavely.

Justice played tailback from 1946 through 1949, and emerged into a national phenomenon while playing several positions, including tailback, safety, quarterback, and punter. During his four year career, he ran or threw for 64 touchdowns, while rushing for 3,774 yards and passing for 2,362 yards. Additionally, the Tarheel football team experienced some of its greatest success during the post-World War II years. The team appeared twice in the Sugar Bowl and once in the Cotton Bowl—the first three post-season bowls ever for the Tarheels.

Justice was named an All-American in 1948 and '49, and finished second in the Heisman Trophy voting both years. He would later be named the Most Valuable Player of the 1950 College All-Star game, when he led the college team to a 17-7 win over the Philadelphia Eagles. He rushed for 133-yards, 48-yards more than the entire Eagles team. He had runs of 33 and 45 yards and caught a pass for 40-yards.

Justice was a breakaway runner with a career average of seven yards per rush. He accomplished half a dozen touchdown runs of 65-yards or more, including a 74-yard touchdown scamper against General Neyland's powerful Tennessee defense. Besides a great runner, he was an excellent kicker. Coach Snavely said, "Justice is the most dependable kicker I've ever coached."

Because he was not too big in stature, the Tarheels provided some extra-large offensive linemen, who balanced Justice's lack of size. His two biggest linemen were Ted Hazelwood, who was a 224 pound tackle, and Chan Highsmith, who a 215 pound center.

Regrettably, from a statistical perspective, Justice would have his finest game as a North Carolina Tarheel against Georgia. In 1948, he gained a total of 304-yards in leading Carolina to a 21 to 14 win on that fateful day in Sanford Stadium as he scored all three touchdowns for Carolina. He made two runs from scrimmage of nine and thirteen yards, then, in the fourth quarter, he scored his last touchdown on an 84-yard punt return.

Dwight Douglas "D. D." Lewis, Miss. State, September 23, 1967

Lewis was born on October 16, 1945, in Knoxville, Tennessee. In 1963, he was a high school All-American who shunned the Volunteers to sign a scholarship with Mississippi State. After sitting out his freshman season, he would later become an All-American center and linebacker in 1966 and '67. As a matter of fact, Lewis was one of the last two-way players in Division-I football as he led Mississippi State in tackles during his three years on the varsity. He was selected as team captain his senior season.

Despite being on teams that went 7-23, Lewis was selected All-Southeastern Conference (SEC) twice, and was first team All-American his senior year. He was repeatedly anointed as the top linebacker in the SEC. Actually, Lewis made a very distinct impression on all rival coaches. Coach Paul Bryant once called Lewis, "… the best linebacker in the country."

Lewis won several awards to include: SEC All-Sophomore Team (1965), All-SEC (1966–67), SEC Defensive Player of the Year in 1967, and *United Press International* All-American 1967. He was selected to play in the Senior Bowl, the Coaches All-American Game, and the Blue-Gray game.

His only time inside of Sanford Stadium was on September 23, 1967, when Georgia defeated Mississippi State 30-0. The 215 pound senior, and captain of Mississippi State, dominated on defense and offense. On one play, he hit Georgia quarterback Kirby Moore so hard, as Moore attempted to run a sweep pattern around the right side, Moore was not able to return to the game. Despite the score of the game, Lewis was in on thirteen tackles and completely controlled his section of the field.

Lester McClain, Tennessee, November 1, 1969

The University of Tennessee football program excluded blacks from 1891 to 1967. While the Southeastern Conference (SEC) was considered the "final citadel of segregation" in college football, when integration finally arrived, it moved swiftly from each corner of the conference. A key explanation occurred near the end of the 1960s, when the US Department of Health, Education and Welfare commenced to threatening to pull federal funding from schools not in compliance with the Civil Rights Act of 1964.

On April 14, 1967, Albert Davis of Alcoa, Tennessee, accepted a football scholarship offer from the University of Tennessee. His signing officially ended more than seventy years of racial exclusion in Volunteer athletics. When an entrance score controversy kept Davis from attending the university, actual desegregation on the playing field fell to Lester McClain.

McClain, born on September 17, 1949, attended Antioch High School, in Nashville, Tennessee. In 1967, he signed a scholarship to attend Tennessee. He was a three-year starter as a receiver, catching 70 passes for 1,003 yards and ten touchdowns. Additionally, he rushed for 123-yards on 30 carries, and scored two touchdowns. He returned eight kickoffs for 168-yards.

In 1968, he earned a varsity football letter, and would become the first African-American to do so in the Southeastern Conference. The desegregation of football proceeded reasonably smooth at Tennessee, although resentment expressed by McClain, near the end of his college years, created a commotion.

On November 1, 1969, McClain became the first black athlete to play inside Sanford Stadium. Tennessee was ranked third in the nation when they went into Sanford Stadium and pounded Georgia 17-3. The loss effectively eliminated the defending SEC champions of another conference championship. McClain, who was primarily used as a receiver, played sparsely in the game, catching one pass for 23-yards. When McClain caught that one pass, he wasn't black or white, he was a football player.

Ironically, the previous season, his first varsity game was against Georgia. McClain had the best game of his career that day in Neyland Stadium against the 'Dogs. His 34-yard reception gave Tennessee a first down, at the Volunteer's 48-yard line. His catch kept a critical drive alive, and put Tennessee in position to tie the eventual SEC Champions 17-17.

Darren McFadden, Arkansas, October 22, 2005

McFadden was born on August 27, 1987, in Little Rock, Arkansas. He attended Oak Grove High School in North Little Rock, where all the recruiting networks rated him as one of the top-five high school athletes in the country. In addition to being selected Player of the Year for the state of Arkansas, by the *Arkansas Democrat-Gazette*, he was a *Parade* magazine All-American.

In 2005, after receiving over 70 scholarship offers, he signed an athletic scholarship with the University of Arkansas and Coach Houston Nutt. During his three year college career, he would go down as the second greatest tailback in Southeastern Conference (SEC) history, second only to Herschel Walker.

On October 22, 2005, during his freshman season, he would make his only appearance inside of Sanford Stadium. Georgia jumped-out to an early lead; however, after the 'Dogs' D. J. Shockley went down to an injury, the Razorbacks were able to keep the game close. McFadden had 31 carries for 190-rushing yards, and two touchdowns. The first score was a stunning 70-yard run. Later, he scored on a one yard plunge with 4:53 remaining in the game. The late score pulled the Razorbacks to within a field-goal, but the Bulldogs, the eventual SEC champions, were able to hold on to win.

McFadden would finish his freshman campaign with 1,113 yards rushing and eleven touchdowns. In '06, he rushed for 1,647 yards, scored fourteen touchdowns, and would become the first sophomore to win the Doak Walker Award, as the nation's top collegiate running back. Then, in 2007, he went for 1,829 yards rushing, while scoring sixteen touchdowns. He won Doak Walker

Award for the second time, too. Moreover, he won the 2007 Walter Camp Award as the nation's best player. Besides being a two-time consensus All-American, he finished runner-up in the Heisman Trophy balloting during his sophomore and junior seasons. In three years, he had a total of 4,589 yards rushing, and scored 41 touchdowns. In the "Wild Hawg" formation he completed 14 of 22 pass attempts for two touchdowns. Utilized on special teams, he had 926 yards on kickoff returns, and scored one touchdown.

Elisha Archibald "Archie" Manning III, Ole Miss, October 12, 1968 and October 10, 1970

Archie Manning was born on May 19, 1949, in Drew, Mississippi. He was a legendary quarterback at Drew High School, in addition to being an outstanding baseball player, who was drafted by several major league organizations. He received scholarship offers from Tulane, Mississippi State and Ole Miss; however, in December 1966, he signed a grant-in-aid with the University of Mississippi, in Oxford.

In 1967, after arriving in Oxford, Manning played on the freshman squad because freshman couldn't play on the varsity. His exploits, while quarterbacking Mississippi's undefeated freshman team, quickly garnered him notoriety across the nation. In 1968, he was quickly named starting quarterback by Coach Johnny Vaught. Manning would remain the starting quarterback for all three seasons.

In October 1968, during Manning's first visit into Sanford Stadium, Coach Erk Russell's defense didn't stand by idly while Georgia's lethargic offense waited to get going. To the satisfaction of the 56,111 fans, the 'Dogs limited the versatile offense of Ole Miss to only two first downs in the second half.

Both teams displayed stingy defenses during the first quarter. However, early in the second quarter, the undefeated Rebels relied solely on the passing of Manning. He moved the ball 51-yards in four plays, scoring the only touchdown of the first half. The drive started on the Rebels' own 49-yard line, as Manning completed passes of 11, 29, and 10 yards, the last of which was good for a touchdown. Jack Simcsak, of Ole Miss, kicked the extra-point to put the Rebels up 7-0.

Early in the third quarter Georgia intercepted a Manning aerial on the Rebels' 21-yard line. The 'Dogs were unable to move the ball, and sent Jim McCullough to boot the first of two field-goals. Georgia, the eventual '68 Southeastern Conference champions, handed Ole Miss its first loss of the season in front of a nationally televised audience. Manning ended the day with three interceptions, and one fumble.

Two years later, on October 12, 1970, Manning, the embodiment of the sprint-out, made his second trip to Sanford Stadium. The outcome would be much different. Coach Dooley knew if Georgia had any chance to win, they'd have to stop Manning from sprinting out, where he liked to reverse his field. Coach Russell's defense made special precautions to trail back, so Manning wouldn't attempt to go the other way.

For three quarters on that ill-fated day, Georgia proved Manning, the most celebrated collegiate player in the country, was a mere mortal. However, after a good jolt, Manning led the Ole Miss Rebels to a 31-21 conquest of the 'Dogs. Afterwards, he stated, "We got a big scare today. Whether anybody had thought about it before or not, today we saw there was a good chance we could get our tails beat. This was a big hill for us to get over. It marks the best start we've had since I have been playing here."

Coincidently, Manning had been slowed by a groin injury he suffered the previous week against Kentucky. However, he managed to toss enough bombs to knockoff Georgia. In fact, he had his hands on every score. The groin impairment slowed him down enough to limit him to completing only 16 of 30 pass attempts for 244-yards. He gained 32 rushing yards, despite being caught from behind the line of scrimmage twice.

He did, however, throw three interceptions, two to Buzy Rosenberg, and one to Bill Darby. Still, for three quarters, Coach Russell's planning for the defense and its ensuing execution had stopped Manning as best as he could be stopped. Manning, for all his ingenuity, could only dent the Bulldog roadblock for three touchdowns during that span. Two of those were homeruns that damaged Georgia. It seemed as though when Manning had to get something done, he simply got it done.

After the game, Coach Dooley declined to direct any public denigration at any particular turnover throughout the game. "We were beaten by a better football team," he said, and then he amended the statement. "Really, we were beaten by one football player. Manning, who was the difference in the game."

As far as the Ole Miss Rebels, Manning was optimistic. "Well, we do have four of our next five games at home and I definitely would rather play in Oxford than here," he laughed, motioning to Sanford Stadium.

Manning never came close to winning the Heisman Trophy because in reality, the Heisman is not won on the field, but instead it is an outgrowth of the Saturday work of the most unlikely people, sports writers. Most experts faulted the lack of Southern tack by Mississippi as the main reason Manning never won a Heisman Trophy. In fact, the Rebels made Manning off-limits when addressing the press. Mississippi's exclusion policy most definitely cost Manning the Heisman Trophy.

From an historical perspective, he ended his career at Ole Miss with 5,576 yards of total offense, and 56 touchdowns. In addition to his jersey, No. 18, being retired, the posted speed limit on campus at Oxford was changed permanently to 18 M.P.H. In 1969, during the first national prime time broadcast of a college football game, he threw for 436-yards and three touchdowns, and rushed for 104 yards, in a 33-32 loss to Alabama. He earned All-America and All-SEC honors in 1969 and 1970, while finishing fourth in balloting for the Heisman Trophy in 1969, and third for the award in 1970. In 1972, he was selected number two overall, by New Orleans, in the National Football League Draft.

Peyton Manning, Tennessee, Sept 10, 1994 and Oct 12, 1996

Born on March 24, 1976, he played high school football at a private school in New Orleans, Louisiana. Rated the top quarterback prospect in the nation, he stunned most people after he decided to join the University of Tennessee, and Coach Phillip Fulmer, instead of signing a scholarship with his daddy's alma mater, the University of Mississippi.

In 1994, as a freshman, Manning started the season as the third-string quarterback, but injuries to Todd Helton, and Jerry Colquitt afforded him an opportunity to take the reigns during the Mississippi State game, a 24–21 loss.

When Tennessee rolled into Sanford Stadium, the Vols were ranked twelfth in the nation. Its massive offensive line subsequently manhandled Georgia's smaller defense, allowing Tennessee running backs to combine for 325-yards, and average 6.6 yards per carry. The Vols made no secret about their game plan. With Manning starting his first game, the Volunteers ran the ball 71 times, while limiting Manning to 13 pass attempts.

Manning and the Vols defeated Georgia 41-23, and left the Bulldogs shaking their heads as they left Sanford Stadium. Manning was selected as Southeastern Conference (SEC) Player of the Week, and would go on to become the 1994 SEC Freshman of the Year.

Two years later, on October 12, 1996, he demonstrated why he was a Heisman Trophy front-runner when he turned Sanford Stadium into "Peyton's Place," during Tennessee's 29-17 thriller. He flung the ball with pinpoint exactness, connecting on 31 of 41 passes for 371-yards and two touchdowns. But it wasn't merely the utter degree of numbers, it was the way they came that made Manning's performance unforgettable.

In the first half, Manning played faultlessly, completing 18 of 24 passes for 181-yards, but he failed to lead the Vols to a single touchdown. "As an offense, we've played better," Manning said. "We made things too hard on ourselves in the first half."

Manning busted out of his slump in the second half by opening-up the half with three straight touchdown drives. The touchdowns gave the Volunteers a 29-10 lead. During the Vols third possession of the half, Manning had two unconceivable plays. The first came with under two minutes remaining in the third quarter, with the Vols on the Bulldogs' 30-yard line. Manning tripped on the exchange from center, and while falling, he did something every coach would tell a quarterback not to do. He launched a throw near the sidelines, as he was falling rearward. Jermaine Copeland, who was heavily covered, managed to catch the ball for a 16-yard gain and a first down.

Later in the drive, Manning accomplished an even more bizarre act. Tennessee had a third-and-three, from the Bulldog's 5-yard line, and he aimed to slip the ball over for the first down. Manning was obstructed by a wall of tacklers; however, he refused to hit the dirt. He spun to his right and located Marcus Nash for a 5-yard score.

During Manning's four year college career, he passed for 11,201 yards, and scored 89 touchdowns, while winning 39 of 45 games as a starter. He would earn several prestigious awards during his senior season, including consensus first-team All-American, the Maxwell Award, the Davey O'Brien Award, and the Johnny Unitas Award, among others; however, he did not win the Heisman Trophy, finishing runner-up to Charles Woodson.

Richard Blair Modzelewski, Maryland, September 23, 1950, October 13, 1951 and October 11, 1952

He was born on February 16, 1931, in West Natrona, Allegheny County, Pennsylvania. Modzelewski played football, baseball and basketball at Har-Brack High School. He was highly recruited by colleges in the northeast, but in 1950, after an incredible high school career, he signed a scholarship with Coach Tatum's Maryland Terrapins. He sat out his freshman season, but moved into the starting lineup his sophomore year, after an injury sidelined the Terrapins' starting tailback, Ray Krouse.

In 1951, while playing Georgia, his second quarter fumble recovery and huge defensive plays afforded the Terrapins the momentum essential to rout the Bulldogs 43-7. Coach Tatum's Maryland team would go on to win its first mythical national title.

Modzelewski remained the starter for the next two seasons, earning All-American honors as a junior and senior. On October 11, 1952, his officious performance guaranteed Maryland's sixteenth straight victory as it overpowered Georgia 37-0. He anchored the defensive line, making twenty-one tackles, nine solo, and kept Georgia out of the endzone. He went on to win the Outland Trophy, as the nation's best lineman. In 1953, with Modzelewski getting the lion's share of the rushing yards, Maryland would win its second national title in three seasons.

Joe Namath, Alabama, September 21, 1963

Namath was born on September 21, 1944, in Beaver Falls, Pennsylvania. His family, of Hungarian descent, came to America to work in the eastern Pennsylvania coal mines. As such, he grew-up in the Lower End Neighbourhood of Beaver Falls. Namath attended Beaver Falls High School where he emerged into an outstanding football, baseball and basketball player.

In 1960, Namath's high school team won the Western Pennsylvania Class AA championship with a 10–0 record. After he graduated, he received several offers from Major League Baseball franchises; however, he elected to sign a scholarship with Coach Bryant's Alabama Crimson Tide in 1961. After leading the Alabama freshman team to an undefeated season, he received significant playing time on the varsity in 1962, where his offensive coordinator was Howard Schnellenberger.

In 1963, Namath was selected to be the successor of Pat Trammell, who had quarterbacked Alabama to the national title in '62. Alas, Namath would have his best game against Georgia. In 1963, the Pachyderms were a 17-point favorite against the 'Dogs, but most experts thought it would be much more unbalanced. The 19-year old phenomena completed ten of fourteen passes for 170-yards and three touchdowns, guiding Alabama to a 32-7 triumph.

It had been a warm, muggy day in late September when Namath played his only game inside of Sanford Stadium. A crowd of 34,980 fans watched as Georgia won the coin toss, and elected to kickoff to start the game. Initially, it looked like Coach Griffith's strategy would pay off. On the Tide's second play from scrimmage, Georgia's sophomore defensive end, Ken Davis, tackled the big bomber quarterback, and forced a fumble on the 26-yard line.

The fumble gave Georgia the early momentum and a first down deep in Alabama territory. Then, Georgia instantly scored a stunning touchdown. It marked the first time Georgia had scored a touchdown against Alabama in two years. The lead would not last long as Alabama stormed down the field on its next series.

Still, Namath and the Tide had to scramble for its 32 points. All but the first touchdown—a 47-yard pass from Namath to Charles Stephens, that was part of a 70-yard Alabama retaliatory drive—was the culmination of Bulldog generosity, in the form of either fumbles or pathetic offensive blocking.

In addition to Namath's 170-yard passing performance, he gained 36-yards rushing on ten snaps from center. The next season, in Tuscaloosa, Namath spearheaded a 35-0 rout of Georgia, enroute to the 1964 National Title.

During his career at Alabama, he completed 203 out of 374 pass attempts for 2,713 yards, twenty-five touchdowns, and nineteen interceptions. He rushed for 655 yards on 190 rushing attempts. Alabama went 29-4 with him as the starter.

Sterling Sharpe, South Carolina, 1983, 1985 and 1987

Sharpe was born on April 6, 1965, in Chicago, Illinois. He grew-up in Glennville, Georgia, and attended Glennville High School, where he played quarterback, tailback and linebacker. In '83, he signed a scholarship with South Carolina and Joe Morrison.

When the Gamecocks played Georgia in '85, the one play that stuck out the most to Georgia's defensive coordinator Bill Lewis was when Carolina quarterback Mike Hold threw in the flats from the Georgia 33-yard line. Sharpe caught the ball, then eluded Michael Willis, Tony Flack and Gary Moss, who had come over to assist. Moss attempted to push Sharpe out of bounds; however, Sharpe slipped away and raced down the sidelines for a touchdown, leaving a host of Bulldogs in a fruitless chase. The score put the Gamecocks within six points, at 20-14, but Georgia eventually pulled away to win 35-21.

Then, in 1987, the combination of quarterback Todd Ellis and Sharpe, amassed some extreme statistics as Sharpe burned the 'Dogs' secondary with eleven catches for 144-yards, however, none of those receptions were within the ten-yard line. The 'Dogs would win the hard fought contest 13-7. Though Sharpe's statistics inside of Sanford Stadium were phenomenal, he went 0-3 in Athens.

During his career, he caught at least one reception in a record 34 consecutive games, and notched 10 games of 100-plus yards receiving. He led his team in receiving for three seasons, and helped the Gamecocks to a berth in the 1987 Gator Bowl. A team captain his senior season, he received the Enright Award for leadership, and played in the East-West Shrine Game and the Senior Bowl. He would end his Gamecocks' career with an astounding 169 career receptions for 2,497 receiving yards and 17 career touchdowns. Sharpe was a first-team All-America selection in his senior season.

Michael "Mike" Singletary, Baylor, September 16, 1978

Singletary was born on October 9, 1958, in Houston, Texas. He attended high school at Evan E. Worthing High School. In the ninth grade, he was an All-State guard and linebacker. Despite early concerns about poor grades affecting his eligibility to play football, his grades miraculously improved. After a star career at Worthing, he was awarded a scholarship to Baylor University, and would meet an important mentor in his life, Coach Grant Teaff.

He stood 6'-2" and weighed 221 pounds while at Baylor. He played middle linebacker and continuously unleashed his power on opposing teams. In 1978, his sophomore season, he had an All-American performance against Georgia. On one specific play, Singletary knocked over two pulling linemen, before flattening the ball carrier. He knocked Georgia's Matt Simon out of the game. It was a shocking collision, made even more extraordinary by the fact Singletary, the Southwest Conference (SWC) Defensive Player of the Year in 1978, '79 and '80, had lost his helmet during the play.

An article in the *Athens Banner Herald* stated, "Coach Dooley had to add a new name to the Georgia backfield in 1978. Mike Singletary, Baylor's awesome middle linebacker." In fact, Singletary did spend most of the afternoon in the Georgia backfield. He made an unbelievable 24 tackles, six solo, and 18 assists. Singletary, who played havoc with the Georgia backs all afternoon, stopping them time and time again for losses and no gains, wasn't overly impressed with Dooley's offensive unit.

"They (Georgia) have a pretty good offense. However, I think we have a better defense, we just didn't prove it today," he stated. Singletary did have praise for the Bulldog running backs he met, usually greeting them head-on. "All the backs I hit were darn good running backs," he sighed.

Singletary was not afraid to put his nose on the football. Although not sought after in high school, because of his supposed lack of speed, Singletary emerged as the anchor of the Bears 4-3 defense. In 1977, his freshman season, he recorded 97 tackles.

"Mike is one of the most intense young men I have ever been around. He has a chance to become one of the finest linebackers we're ever had at Baylor," Coach Teaff stated.

When asked to comment on Singletary's performance, including his 24 tackles, Teaff only replied, "I just wish he had gotten 27 or 30."

He earned All-American honors in his junior and senior seasons, where he averaged 15 tackles per game. In 1978, he established a team record with 232 tackles, including 35 in a game against the University of Houston. In 1980, during Singletary's senior season, Baylor won ten games, marking the first time in school history that had been accomplished.

Additionally, Singletary was the only college junior to ever be selected to the All-SWC team during the 1970s. He was a two-time recipient of the Davey O'Brien Memorial Trophy. At the time, the Davey O'Brien Trophy was awarded to the most outstanding player in the southwestern part of the United States, and had yet to become the quarterback-centric award it would later emerge into. He lettered four years and had a total of 662 tackles. In 1978, he reached his apex with thirty-six tackles against Arkansas, and thirty-one against the Ohio State Buckeyes.

Kenneth Michael "Ken" Stabler, September 18, 1965

In 1945, Stabler was born on Christmas Day, in Foley, Alabama. He attended Foley High School and led Foley to a 29-1 record during his career. He earned the nickname "The Snake," from his high school coach following a long, winding touchdown run. In 1964, he signed a scholarship with Alabama.

In 1964, because of NCAA regulations, freshmen were ineligible to play varsity, and Stabler played for the freshman team. In 1965, Stabler was used sparingly to starter Steve Sloan as Alabama opened the season inside of Sanford Stadium. Stabler, went 3 for 11 in passing for 26-yards. Georgia would upset the Tide 18-17, after the "Flea Flicker" beat Alabama as time expired. The Pachyderms would go on to win its second consecutive National Championship, finishing the season with a record of 9-1-1. Alabama defeated the Nebraska Cornhuskers in the Orange Bowl 39-28.

In 1966, as a junior, he took over the quarterback position full-time. He led the team to an undefeated, 11–0 season which ended in a 34–7 rout of Nebraska in the Sugar Bowl. However, in 1967, during his senior season, the offense struggled, and the performance of the defense slipped. The Tide finished with an 8–2–1 record. Though the season was lackluster, Stabler would provide a memorable moment in the Iron Bowl. Trailing 3–0 in a game drenched by rain, Stabler scampered through the mud for a 53–yard, game-winning touchdown. The Tide won 7–3 at Legion Field.

While at Alabama, Stabler completed 180 of 303 pass attempts, for 2,196 yards, and 18 touchdowns and 18 interceptions. He had 265 rushing attempts for 838 yards and nine touchdowns. Alabama went 28-3-2 during his era.

Bryan Bartlett "Bart" Starr, Alabama, October 31, 1953, and October 29, 1955

Starr was born on January 9, 1934, in Montgomery, Alabama and was the son of an Air Force non-commissioned officer. He played for Lanier High School, in Montgomery, Alabama. After being selected as an All-American, he received scholarship offers from schools across America, and he strongly considered going to play for Kentucky and Coach Bear Bryant.

In 1952, he elected to sign a scholarship to attend Alabama. That year the Southeastern Conference made an exception to authorize freshmen to play on the varsity because of the Korean War. Though Starr didn't start his freshman season, he earned significant playing time. In fact, during the Orange Bowl, he completed eight of 12 passes, accounting for one touchdown, as Alabama destroyed Syracuse 61-6.

In 1953, Starr entered his sophomore year as Alabama's starting quarterback, safety and punter. He averaged 41 yards per punt, ranking him second in the nation, behind Georgia's Zeke Bratkowski. Regrettably, he was injured while practicing punts, and consequently, his playing time was regulated to "clean-up" duty.

On October 31, 1953, 29,000 fans inside Sanford Stadium watched as Starr's Alabama team defeated Georgia 33-12, ending a two game winless streak on Homecoming in Athens. The first Tide touchdown was set-up after Thomas Tharp returned a punt for 86-yards, down to the Bulldogs' two-yard line. On the next play, Starr tossed a quick touchdown pass to Joe Cummings, to give the Tide a 7-0 lead. After Georgia tied the game, Starr came back and completed a 31-yard strike to Bobby Luna to put Alabama up for good. The Tide won the Halloween contest as Starr passed for three touchdowns. The Pachyderms would finish with a 4-5-2, and its coach, Red Drew, was fired at the end of the season. He was replaced with Coach J. B. Whitworth.

In 1954, Coach Whitworth conducted a youth movement at Alabama. In fact, only two seniors started for the team as Alabama struggled to back-to-back 4-5-2 seasons. In 1955, Starr's senior season, he rarely played while healing from a back injury he sustained at practice. In front of over 29,500 Homecoming fans inside Sanford Stadium, his Tide would lose to Georgia by a score of 35-14. Starr completed seven of nine passes, for 130-yards.

At the conclusion of the season he played briefly in the Blue–Grey Bowl of 1955. During his career, he completed 155 of 285 pass attempts, for 1,901 yards, ten touchdowns and twenty interceptions. His statistics at Alabama were good enough to get drafted by the Green Bay Packers. He quarterbacked the Packers to several World Championships during his Hall-of-Fame career. In addition, he had a 1-1 record inside of Sanford Stadium.

Reginald Howard "Reggie" White, Tennessee, Sept. 5, 1981

White was born on December 19, 1961, in Chattanooga, Tennessee. He played football at Howard High School. In his senior season, he had 140 tackles, ten sacks, and was a *Parade* magazine high school All-American.

In 1980, he would eventually work his way into the starting line-up at Tennessee. The following season he played his only game inside of Sanford Stadium. Known as "The Minister of Defense," he dominated the line of scrimmage as the Vols' left defensive end. He tormented Georgia's right tackle with his original bump and club moves. From a three-point stance, he would anticipate the snap count, blast up-field, shrug his shoulders before tossing aside yet another lineman and move inside to take a shot at Buck Belue.

Georgia won the game 44-0, but White's performance was admirable. He registered seven tackles. For the season, he ended-up with 112 tackles, in only eight games. He was named to the All-American team by *The Football News*. In 1982, he was named All-American, but was consistently bothered by an ankle injury, and his production dropped-off. He registered 47 tackles, thirty-six solo, and led the team with seven sacks. Then, in 1983, he exploded by registering 100 tackles, seventy-two solo, fifteen sacks, nine tackles-for-loss, and had one interception. He earned consensus All-American honors, was selected Southeastern Conference Player of the Year, and became a Lombardi Award finalist.

Against the running game, White was a force who enjoyed both the power to shed blockers at the point of attack, and the speed to chase down ball carriers from the weak side. This skill set earned him All-American honors. During his career with Tennessee, he had 293 tackles (201 solo), 32 sacks, 19 tackles-for-loss, four fumble recoveries, and seven batted-down passes.

Jon Steven Young, Brigham Young University, Sept. 11, 1982
Young was born on October 11, 1961, in Salt Lake City, Utah. He attended Greenwich High School, in Greenwich, Connecticut. In 1978 and '79, he earned All-State First Team honors as the starting quarterback for the Cardinals, under head coach Mike Ornato. In two seasons, he rushed the football 267 times for 1,928 yards. Greenwich ran the option offense, where the pass was always the second option, so subsequently he only completed forty-one percent of his passes, for a mediocre 1,220 yards.

After losing the state title game, Young was heavily recruited by the University of North Carolina, who wanted him to play quarterback in the option offense. However, he ultimately decided to attend Brigham Young University (BYU), in Utah. During his freshman season, after struggling with throwing the ball, the coaching staff considered switching him to defensive back simply because of his pure athleticism. He worked diligently to improve his passing skills and eventually succeeded Jim McMahon, the Cougars record-setting quarterback.

On September 11, 1982, he played in his only game inside of Sanford Stadium. Young passed the majority of the game, amassing 285-yards in the air, but he tossed six interceptions. Georgia's defense was able to hold in crucial situations, and miraculously held the most prolific passing team in the annals of Sanford Stadium to only 14 points. Georgia won 17-14.

In 1982, Young was named All-American and won the Davey O'Brien Trophy. He finished second in voting for the Heisman Trophy behind Nebraska running back Mike Rozier. He finished his college career with 592 pass completions, for 7,733 yards and 56 touchdowns, along with 1,048 rushing yards and 18 touchdowns on the ground.

Notable Georgia Players of Sanford Stadium Era

College football is the essence of all things Americana. It is our most popular sport because of its tenacity, violence, and speed. It is the quintessential chess match, where players shift positions, react, dominate smaller battles, and apply their craft for the good of the team. To win as a unit, each individual must know his assignment and sacrifice himself for the benefit of the whole.

It can often appear rude–even illogical–to recognize an individual player ahead of his team. In truth, every game equals nothing more than an accumulation of players waging individual battles. In fact, each season there are many football games decided by improbable events, and won or lost by the performance of distinctive players engaged in the aforesaid individual battles.

Over the past eight decades, Georgia has been the home of some of college football's most gifted athletes. A few of them were rare athletes who could have excelled during any era of college football; however, of all these stars, which special ones are worthy of even greater singular tribute? Who are the élite of the élite? Who is worthy of recognition as one of the most notable to have played inside of Sanford Stadium?

As strenuous as it is for scholar athletes to perform at an optimum level for long periods of time, on occasion, there are particular players who unmistakably standout over their teammates. Certainly, some positions are naturally more high prolife, and undeniably afford some players better opportunities to have monumental plays that will garner media attention. Of these players, some have formed the building-blocks of great Georgia teams; however, occasionally, there is an elite athlete who completes the team—who elevates the 'Dogs to their pinnacle.

When it comes to deciding the most notable Georgia players of the Sanford Stadium era, there are always caveats because players are products of their era. Listing the zenith of its players sounds straightforward enough, but with more than eighty years of history to scrutinize, encompassing over six thousand players, the undertaking immediately develops into a monumentally divisive assignment. Especially since the majority of Georgia players never made any All-Southeastern Conference or All-American teams, yet, all contributed to the inherent legacy of making Sanford Stadium one of the greatest stadiums in the annals of American sports history.

Without any extra ado, the following Georgia players, listed in alphabetical order, directly contributed to making Sanford Stadium one of the most storied stadiums in America. The stars aligned for them.

Champ Bailey, Cornerback, 1996-1998

Bailey, born on June 22, 1978, in Folkston, Georgia, was regarded as one of college football's greatest multiple threat players of all-time. He played in 33 games at Georgia, and recorded 147 tackles, had two fumble recoveries, one forced fumble, eight interceptions and 27 passes defended. He was All-Southeastern Conference (SEC) first-team as a sophomore and junior.

In 1996, as a freshman, the 6'-0" 184 pound Bailey was clocked at a league-best 4.29 seconds in the 40-yard dash, an element that later became a leading talent indicator in recruiting. As a member of the Georgia track team, he set a school indoor long jump record with a leap of 7.89 meters at the SEC Indoor Track and Field Championships. He set a school indoor long jump record in 1998 of 25-10 3/4 feet to finish third at the SEC Indoor Track and Field Championships.

In 1998, he had 52 tackles, and three interceptions. On offense, he registered 47 receptions, for 744 yards and five touchdowns. Additionally, he had 84 yards rushing on 16 carries; 12 kickoff returns for 261-yards and four punt returns for 49 yards. In fact, after the first three games, he was Georgia's leading receiver, while maintaining his starting defensive back position.

On offense and defense, the two-way All-American provided Georgia with the big plays it needed to overcome four fumbles to defeat Wyoming 16-9. He caught three consecutive passes, including a 51-yard touchdown, on a four-play series, and accounted for all of Georgia's 85-yards on the drive. In fact, during the game, he was in on 18 offensive plays and 38 defensive plays. He finished the game with a one-handed interception, six receptions for 100-yards, while scoring one touchdown. Similar to Charlie Trippi during the '46 Tech game, Bailey succumbed to leg cramps that kept him on the bench for most of the second half.

In 1998, Bailey averaged 103.5 all-purpose yards per game, and logged 957 plays (547 defense, 301 offense and 109 special teams) on the way to earning consensus All-American and first-team All-SEC honors, while claiming the Bronko Nagurski Trophy, as the nation's top defensive player. Against Virginia, in that season's Peach Bowl, he caught three passes for 73-yards, including a 14-yard touchdown. He rushed three times for nine yards, returned five kickoffs for 104-yards, and had a punt return for 12-yards. On defense, Bailey had two tackles and a pass deflection. During his three year career, Georgia went 12-6 inside of Sanford Stadium.

Benjamin Franklin "Buck" Belue, Quarterback, 1978-81

Belue, who started all four years for the Valdosta Wildcats, verbally committed to Georgia after his team's 16-14 loss in the '77 state championship game against Clarke Central. During his four year career, he led Valdosta to a 34-14 record.

In 1978, his freshman season at Georgia, he was an understudy to the Bulldogs' starting quarterback, Jeff Pyburn. In the season opener against Baylor, he tossed an interception on his first pass attempt; however, later that season, he would redeem himself in the Georgia Tech game.

It was a freezing day on December 2, 1978, when Belue entered the game, late in the second quarter. Georgia was down 20-0. The ultimate field general, his determined leadership would help breathe life back into the Bulldogs, while directing the 'Dogs on a 55-yard scoring drive against its most hated rival.

Later, with 5:52 seconds left in the game, and Georgia down 28-21, Belue led the 'Dogs' on an 84-yard touchdown drive. Faced with a fourth down and three, he rolled to his right, and hit Anthony Arnold on a 43-yard touchdown play to make the score 28-27. Coach Dooley elected to go for the two-point conversion, instead of settling for a tie. Belue faked a handoff to fullback Matt Simon, then, pitched to Arnold, who sprinted into the endzone for an unbelievable 29-28 come-from-behind win.

On November 7, 1980, Belue played his most unforgettable game at the World's Largest Outdoor Cocktail Party. Earlier, on that fateful day, Georgia Tech had tied number one ranked Notre Dame 3-3, opening the door for the Bulldogs to move-up to number one for the first time since 1942. However, with 1:35 seconds remaining in its game against Charlie Pell's Gators, Georgia fell behind 21-20.

The 'Dogs were on their own eight-yard line, with a third down and 10-yards to go. Belue rolled out to his right and passed to Lindsay Scott, who was all alone in the middle of the field after a Florida defensive back fell down. Scott hauled in the football and outran everybody 93-yards for the season saving touchdown.

On January 1, 1981, in the Sugar Bowl against Notre Dame, Belue guided Georgia to a 17-10 victory over the Fighting Irish. Amazingly, he only completed one pass; however, his leadership was indispensible. Georgia won its first national title since 1942.

In 1981, as team captain, Belue led Georgia to its second straight Southeastern Conference title. He would play a crucial role in numerous Georgia victories during his four year career. He never lost to Georgia Tech or Florida during his career and from 1978 through 1981, Georgia went 21-4 inside of Sanford Stadium.

John Phillip Brantley, Jr., Linebacker, 1984-1987

Brantley was born October 23, 1965, in Wildwood, Florida. After an All-State high school career at Wildwood High School, he signed with Georgia in 1983. He'd become a four year letterman, and a standout linebacker from 1984-87. He recorded two of the top four single-season tackle totals in Georgia history with 160 in 1986 and 154 in 1987. His 415 career tackles stills stands as one of the best totals for any Bulldog.

In 1986 and 1987 he was named All-Southeastern Conference and Georgia's Most Outstanding Defensive Player. In 1987, he was captain of the defense, and was named the Defensive Most Valuable Player of the Liberty Bowl when Georgia defeated Arkansas 20-17.

Brantley played some of his best football when the Bulldogs returned to his home state. Most notably, while wearing "Nasty" on his arm tape, he recorded a team-high seven tackles and notched both a tackle-for-loss and a sack when the Bulldogs upset the top-ranked Gators 24-3 in 1985. In 1987, he would help Georgia to a 23-10 win in Jacksonville as a senior.

Brantley was selected by the Houston Oilers in the 1988 National Football League draft. After playing with the Oilers, he played with the Washington Redskins and the Cincinnati Bengals during a four-year professional career. After retiring from football, he returned to the Athens area. He remained an active supporter of the program and helped spearhead the Bulldogs' initial involvement to build a home through Habitat for Humanity in 2002.

Georgia went 18-6 inside of Sanford Stadium during his four year career.

Edmund Raymond "Zeke" Bratkowski, Quarterback, 1951-1953

Born on October 20, 1931, he played for Georgia from 1951-53. His passing statistics appear appalling with 68 career interceptions—an NCAA three-year record which possibly will never be broken. However, he was an excellent example of a good quarterback on bad teams, as Georgia went 15-17 from 1951 through 1953. Still, his passing skills were definitely feared by all opposing defenses. In addition to his superior passing ability, Bratkowski was an excellent punter, averaging 40 yards per punt.

He was twice the Southeastern Conference (SEC) passing leader under Coach Wallace Butts. During his three-year career with the Bulldogs, he completed 360 passes for 4,863 yards. He was considered college football's greatest quarterback in his day, and was the NCAA's all-time leading passer until 1961. He led the NCAA in punting his senior year with a 42.6 yard average.

Between 1951 and 1953, he broke the SEC total offensive record, previously held by the University of Kentucky's Vito (Babe) Parilli. His mark stood for 27 years until broken by Herschel Walker (1980-82) with 5,259 yards. Additionally, Bratkowski had a posse of receivers in Harry Babcock, John Carson and Zippy Morocco.

Bratkowski passed Georgia into the winning column in 1952. The Bulldog fans were entertained by seven wins and his tosses to Carson, Babcock, Arthur DeCarlo, Bobby Dellinger, Jackie Roberts, Dexter Poss. and Lauren Hargrove. Babcock, with 32 receptions, led the SEC and earned All-America honors. Bratkowski completed 131 of 262 pass attempts, for 1,824 yards.

In 1953, Georgia only managed three wins as the 'Dogs went 3-8; however, Bratkowski and Carson formed an All-America combination that season. Moreover, those eight losses were the most by any Coach Butts' Georgia team.

Bratkowski would be drafted by Chicago where he played five seasons for the Bears. Later, he played three years for the Los Angeles Rams before being signed by Vince Lombardi for the $100 waiver fee. He would become the "super sub" to Bart Starr.

In Green Bay, he was nicknamed "Uncle Zekie." He became an ideal backup and spot starter during the Lombardi championship era. In a 15-year National Football League career, Bratkowski passed for 10,345 yards and 65 touchdowns. Furthermore, Georgia went 5-7 inside of Sanford Stadium during Bratkowski's era.

Kevin Butler, Kicker, 1981-1984

Butler was born in Savannah, Georgia on July 24, 1962. He played high school football in Stone Mountain, Georgia, where he attended Redan High School. In 1979, during the state championship game against Marist High School, he kicked a 44-yard field-goal that won the state title game.

After the game, Coach Dooley spoke with Butler outside the locker room, and reminded him Georgia's kicker, Rex Robinson, would be graduating the following season. In 1980, Butler had been greatly recruited; however, he sustained an injury in the first game of his senior year. Torn knee ligaments ended his season and the scholarship offers he had received from college programs all over the country suddenly vanished. Only one coach, who had been so interested in him the year before, stood by Butler as he went through surgery to repair the damage to his leg.

In 1981, Butler began his career as the Bulldog's kicker. He kicked 19 field-goals to tie an NCAA freshman record. The 94 points he accounted for that year were the most ever by a kicker from the Southeastern Conference (SEC). He would become a two-time All-American, and a four-time All-SEC selection. At the end of the 1984 season, he was Georgia's all-time scoring leader with 353 points. He kicked 77 field-goals and 122 extra-points. The Bulldogs won two SEC titles during his career.

In 1982, his 59-yard field-goal against Ole Miss set a school record. In 1983, he made a number of decisive kicks as a junior, including a crucial extra-point in 10-9 win over Florida, and a 10-9 win over Texas in the Cotton Bowl.

His accuracy on field-goal attempts of 50 yards or longer was 52.4 percent. In total, he had field-goals of 59, 53, and 52 yards. His longest field-goal was a 60 yard game winner against Clemson in 1984. He was 122 for 125 on extra-points and 77 for 98 on field-goals. From 1981 through 1984, Georgia had a 38-8-2 record, with two losses in the Sugar Bowl against Pitt and Penn State, respectively, while beating Texas in the Cotton Bowl and tying Florida State in the Citrus Bowl. Georgia went 22-2 at home during his career.

While in the National Football League, he went on to become the all-time leading scorer, among kickers, for the Chicago Bears. He would become the first placekicker ever inducted into the College Football Hall of Fame.

Spurgeon Ferdinand "Spud" Chandler, Quarterback, 1929-1931

He was born on September 12, 1907, in Commerce, Georgia. He attended Franklin County High School where he was a standout quarterback and defensive safety. In 1929, he signed a scholarship to attend the University of Georgia. He turned out to have an exceptional athletic career in football and baseball. He was a genuine triple threat left halfback, in the Notre Dame Box formation, and a first-stringer for three years with the Bulldog from 1929-1931.

He was one of the "Flaming Sophomores of '29," who blanked Yale 15-0, in the dedicatory game of Sanford Stadium. In fact, he tossed a touchdown pass to Vernon Smith to help defeat Yale. Chandler was a good punter, and a very good defensive back.

Additionally, he ran track, pitched for Georgia's baseball team and almost led the Diamond 'Dogs to the 1931 conference title. After graduating with a degree in agriculture, he spent five seasons in the New York Yankees.

He was a great athlete, but an even greater competitor; a very conscientious player, who blamed himself, never others, whenever he did not do as well as he wanted. Coach Mehre recalled how Chandler had almost failed a course in plowing at Georgia. His professor discovered Chandler had left almost half an acre unplowed because he had cut corners. Chandler corrected the mishap and graduated on-time. The Bulldogs went 8-3 inside Sanford Stadium during his era.

John "The Rome Rocket" Cook, Quarterback, 1943 and 1946

World War II prevented eight Southeastern Conference (SEC) teams from playing football in 1943. Coach Wallace Butts contemplated dropping football, only one day before Georgia's season opener. He elected to go ahead and play the season, in spite of the team being made up of primarily 17-year-old freshmen, who were too young to be drafted into World War II, or players who were medically disqualified (F-4s) from military service.

During the 1943 season opener, Georgia's unexpected 25-7 upset victory over Presbyterian caused Coach Butts to realize his team might be better than originally forecasted. Plus, he found his next star player in the process—Johnny Cook.

John Cook, 1945

Cook, "Rome's Gift to Athens," was a spectacular forward passer, reminiscent of Heisman Trophy-winner Frank Sinkwich. Though smaller in stature than many football players, Cook was very successful when handling the pigskin. In 1943, he scored four first-half touchdowns during a 46-7 thrashing of Virginia Military Institute at a game played in Atlanta. His four scores included a 78-yard rush, and an 80-yard punt return. His touchdown record would not be broken at Georgia until Robert Edwards scored five touchdowns against South Carolina in 1995.

He was the only first-team All-SEC selection for the '43 'Dogs, as he led the nation in passing, completing 73 of 157 passes for 1,007 yards and eight touchdowns. He rushed for 361-yards and nine touchdowns. He tied for fourth in the nation in scoring, tallying 72 points on twelve touchdowns.

After the '43 season ended, Cook followed the same path as most other athletes of his era, and joined the military. He would not return to Georgia until the '46 football season. However, instead of returning to Georgia's lineup as its star tailback, Cook found himself primarily sitting on the bench because there was overwhelming depth in the team's backfield, including the immortal Charlie Trippi. After finishing second in scoring in the SEC, as a 17-year old freshman, he did not score a single point in his second and final year as a Georgia Bulldog.

As of 2015, Cook still remained the only Georgia Bulldog to ever lead the country in passing. Additionally, besides Sinkwich, he was the only Georgia player to finish in the Top-10 in passing and scoring during the same season. Georgia went 10-0 inside Sanford Stadium during his two years of playing for Georgia.

Roy Curtis, Defensive Tackle, 1980-83

He was a three year starter at Southeast High School, and earned three letters in basketball and football. Additionally, he was first team selection All-Tri State squad in 1979. He signed a scholarship with Georgia in 1980, and was member of greatest recruiting class in Georgia football history.

He knifed through the opposing offenses, and often tossed the opponents for consistent losses. He had a certain something that distinguished a great player from just an average player. Some people called it natural ability, fortitude, spirit, or whatever you desire. Whatever it was, Curtis possessed it.

He was an outstanding defensive tackle, and was credited with numerous tackles, and assists. His highest output came in 1981 - '82 seasons. Georgia never lost a game inside of Sanford Stadium during his era.

Raymond Lamar "Racehorse" Davis, Receiver, 1939-1942

He was born on June 15, 1921, in Brunswick, Georgia. He attended Glynn Academy, where he was sought after by several major colleges, but signed a scholarship with Georgia in 1939. As Loran Smith once wrote, "…to achieve greatness, it's almost a prerequisite for you have a fascinating nickname." Babe Ruth was known as the "Sultan of Swat," Red Grange was the "Galloping Ghost," and Charlie Trippi was the "Scintillating Sicilian." Lamar Davis was the "Racehorse."

His nickname, "Racehorse" simply meant one thing, he was fast. Unfortunately, playing in the same backfield with Frank Sinkwich and Trippi meant he didn't get the ball too much; however, when he did get it, he didn't break stride until he arrived in the endzone.

In 1940, against Tulane, he returned a kick-off for 96-yards and a touchdown. In 1941, he had 198-yards receiving in an era when the top quarterbacks only threw for 300-400 yards for an entire season. Additionally, he averaged 28.5 yards per reception, and had 19 receptions for a total of 542-yards. He had approximately 464 punt return yards, including an 85-yard kickoff return for a touchdown against powerful Dartmouth. In 1941, his most memorable play came against the War Eagles. As the final horn sounded, Sinkwich tossed Davis a pass that he caught and ran 65-yards for a touchdown to beat Auburn 7-0.

In 1942, his Georgia Bulldogs finished 11-1, and defeated UCLA in the Rose Bowl to win the national title. His longest touchdown that season was a 90-yard reception against Cincinnati. He would score 145 career points, 24 touchdowns: 17 receiving, three rushing, and four on kickoffs and punt returns.

He was a member of the 1942 "Dream Backfield" with teammates Sinkwich, Trippi, and Dick McPhee. He started three seasons for Georgia, and the 'Dogs went 10-2-2 inside of Sanford Stadium during this era.

Thomas Antonio Davis, Safety, 2002-2005

Davis was born on March 22, 1983. Growing-up in Shellman, Georgia, he was considered the toughest man on the field when he played "kill-the-man-with-the-ball." In fact, when he got the ball, nobody could catch him, much less kill him. On the football team at Randolph-Clay High School, he was so versatile he played eight different positions.

Davis was a sought-after high school prospect who received over thirty scholarship offers. In 2001, he eventually signed an athletic scholarship to attend Georgia. While at Georgia, he shuffled between linebacker and safety. Yet, despite the constant shuffling of positions, he was selected as an All-American during his senior year.

In 2003, following his sophomore season, he earned second-team All-Southeastern Conference (SEC) honors. In '04, he was recognized as a first-team All-SEC selection and a consensus first-team All-American. In thirty-nine career games, he was effective as both a linebacker and a free safety, recording 272 tackles, 18 for a loss, 10.5 sacks, three interceptions, six forced fumbles and nine fumble recoveries.

While in the National Football League, he started a youth organization—the Thomas Davis Defending Dreams Foundation—that emphasized education, leadership development and volunteerism, in an effort to build solid citizens of the future. He admitted he felt uneasy discussing the value of a degree without having completed college himself. He returned to Georgia and graduated with a degree in consumer economics. Georgia went 18-1 inside Sanford Stadium during his time with the 'Dogs.

Robert Edward Dellinger, Tailback, 1951-1952

Born in Columbia, South Carolina, Dellinger graduated from Berkley High School, in Monks Center, South Carolina. He was a highly recruited football player in high school, making a trip to the Orange Bowl, as Clemson's guest, before eventually signing a scholarship to attend Georgia.

"I liked Coach Wallace Butts and Georgia from the beginning," Dellinger related, "and was influenced by Coach Quinton Lumpkin who really was good to all the players in those years. We appreciated Coach Lumpkin. Mainly, I wanted to see if I could play in the Southeastern Conference. Georgia played big time football and I wanted to be a part of that."

Dellinger played varsity football at the University of Georgia in 1952, where he will forever remain in the record books with his

76-yard touchdown run, from scrimmage, against Miami. It was the first touchdown ever scored inside the new Orange Bowl.

In 1952, he led Bulldog rushers, with an average of 5.4 yards per carry. During the first three games of the season he had 124-yards on 23 carries. Other running backs who shared duties with the legendary running back were Charlie Madison, "Foots" Clemens, and Fred Bilyeu. He was Georgia's leading scorer, where he scored four rushing touchdowns, including the aforementioned 76-yard dash against Miami.

After a brilliant sophomore season, his future looked incredibly bright; however, '52 would end-up being his last season of college football. It had to do with a run-in with Dean of Men, William Tate, and a story which wound-up with a fascinating twist. Dean Tate suspended Dellinger for taking part in panty raids the spring following Dellinger's sophomore season. The Dean held no grudge toward the rebellious student, and would later invite him back to join the team.

Among his achievements as a Bulldog running back was the unique scoring circumstance of the 1952 Miami game when he scored on the last Georgia possession of the first quarter and the first Bulldog possession in the second quarter.

"Zeke Bratkowski threw a pass to me, but Gordon Malloy of Miami, who had started his career at Georgia Tech, batted the ball in the air, and I caught the deflected pass and ran for a 32-yard touchdown. After the kickoff, Miami started a long drive which carried over into the second quarter but we took over on downs. I remember the ball was on our 24-yard line. On the next snap, I ran a trap play for a 76-yard touchdown. The newspapers made a big deal out of that and I guess that is the most memorable thing to happen to me while at Georgia."

In 2013, the former "South Carolina Mr. Football" award recipient would be inducted into the Berkley High Sports Hall of Fame. Georgia went 1-2 inside of Sanford Stadium during his one varsity season.

Terrence Edwards, Receiver, 1999-2002

Edwards was born on April 20, 1979, in a county named after General George Washington in 1784, five years before he became the nation's first president. Edwards attended Washington County High School, where he, along with his brothers Robert and Chris, along with Takeo Spikes turned the Golden Hawks of Washington High School into a state powerhouse, winning state titles in 1994, '96 and '97. During his senior season, he made nearly every high school All-American publication in the nation, e.g. *Parade* magazine, *CNN-SI* Top 100 Players in the Nation, Rivals, etc..... In his final season, he passed for over 3,400 yards, tossed 36 touchdown passes, and only had three passes intercepted. In addition to quarterback, he played defensive back, and had nine interceptions, and 88 tackles.

In 1999, he signed a scholarship with Georgia, where he played from 1999 through 2002. In '02, he caught 59 passes for 1,004 yards and eleven touchdowns, while helping guide Georgia to its first Southeastern Conference (SEC) title in twenty years. And, throughout his career, he had ten games where he had at least 100 yards receiving.

He broke all the school's reception records during his four year career. In fact, he caught 204 passes for an astounding 3,093 yards and thirty touchdowns. His yardage total was a SEC record at the time, and his 204 receptions rank second all-time in the conference. As of 2015, he still ranks as the number one receiver in the history of Georgia football.

Georgia went 21-4 inside of Sanford Stadium during his era.

Fred Gibson, Receiver, 2001-2004

Gibson was born on October 26, 1981, in Waycross, Georgia, a city located on the environs of the Okefenokee Swamp. He attended Ware County High School, where, during his final season, he caught 50 passes for 1,000 yards and 12 touchdowns. He was named Region Offensive Player of the Year, first-team All-Region, and *Florida Times Union* Super 24. After being heavily recruited by most schools in the South, especially by Florida's Steve Spurrier, he signed a scholarship with Georgia in 2001.

During his freshman season, he was quickly tossed into action, and started three games. On the season, he had 33 catches for 772 yards and six touchdowns. In 2002, he would start eight games, and finish the season with 43 receptions for 758 yards and four touchdowns. Additionally, he had a total of 460 yards on 19 kickoff returns, and scored one touchdown. In 2003, he tallied 36 catches for 553 yards, and three touchdowns. Finally, in 2004, he made first-team All-Southeastern Conference honors, while catching 49 passes for 801 yards and seven touchdowns

Some of the highlights of the "Waycross Wonder" were when he broke Georgia's single game receiving record with 201-yards against Kentucky in 2001. Another memorable moment was in 2002, when he helped Georgia win its first Southeastern Conference title in twenty years. During the season opener, against Clemson, he ignited Georgia by returning a 91-yard opening second half kickoff return for a touchdown. Georgia won the game 31-28.

Gibson closed out his Georgia career with 161 catches for 2,884 yards and 20 touchdowns. His receiving totals rank second in school history behind 3,093 for Terrence Edwards, and Gibson's 161 catches rank third behind Edwards (204), and Brice Hunter (182). Gibson had five rushes for 23-yards, and thirty-five kickoff returns for 866-yards, and one touchdown. The 'Dogs went 22-3 inside of Sanford Stadium and had an overall record of 42-10 during his era.

Max Jean-Gilles, Offensive Line, 2002-2005

Jean-Gilles was born on November 19, 1983, in Miami, Florida. He was selected first-team All-State and All-County during his junior and senior seasons at North Miami Beach High School. Additionally, he was a Prep All-American, and was rated as the top offensive lineman in the country. He was a three-year team captain and played in the '01 Georgia-Florida All-Star game and the Florida-California game. He was a two-way lineman, registering 197 knockdown blocks during his career and 94 tackles, with eight sacks, five fumble recoveries and seven blocked kicks on defense and special teams.

In 2002, he signed a scholarship with Georgia. He displayed a strong work-ethic, and was used as a reserve offensive tackle as a true freshman. He started the Southeastern Conference (SEC) title game as a third tackle, playing tight end. In 2003, he registered 58 knockdowns as the starting "tight" tackle, earning second-team All-SEC honors. In fact, in a game against Arkansas, he was selected as SEC Lineman of the Week, producing eight knockdowns. He came up with a key block on a 1-yard touchdown run by Brannan

Southerland. Later, he leveled defensive tackle Marcus Harrison as D. J. Shockley connected on an 11-yard scoring pass to split end Bryan McClendon.

Max Jean-Gilles, 2004

In 2005, during his senior season, he was a first-team All-SEC selection and was recognized as a consensus first-team All-American. He was a key member of the Georgia team that defeated the Bayou Bengals of Louisiana State University 34–14, to win the '05 SEC title.

Most experts considered him the most dominant guard of his era. He was a massive drive blocker, with excellent power and surprising quickness for a player of his herculean size. As a pure, physical mauler, he had the strength to create rush lanes and emerged as the model of consistency and durability for the 'Dogs. He never missed any games because of injuries. Georgia went 26-2 inside Sanford Stadium during his era.

Ray Goff, Quarterback, 1973-1976

Goff was born on July 19, 1955, in Moultrie, Georgia. He was a high school All-American quarterback for Coach Bud Willies and the Moultrie High School Packers. After leading the Packers football team to a 28-4 record in three seasons, he had college recruiters from all across the nation pursuing him.

In 1973, he signed a scholarship with Georgia and Coach Vince Dooley. "I really don't know why I came to Georgia," recalls Goff. "Now that I look back, I wouldn't have it any other way. It's been great here."

Like many outstanding athletes, Goff was thankful for those who helped him obtain the point of success he had at Georgia. "My father had a great influence on my life. If not for him, I probably would not have played college football.

In 1974, Goff played second fiddle to Georgia's starting quarterback Matt Robinson. In 1975, Goff would earn the starting job and come within a game of leading Georgia the Southeastern Conference (SEC) title. An upset loss to Ole Miss cost Georgia the championship.

In 1976, Goff would take Georgia to the Promised Land as the 'Dogs won SEC title. He was selected as the 1976 SEC Player-of-the-Year, an honor only four Bulldogs had received since the establishment of the conference in 1932.

Some of his best performances came during his senior season. He had two runs for over seventy-yards against Clemson, in Death Valley. When Georgia played Ole Miss, in Oxford, he connected with Gene Washington on a 75-yard touchdown pass. A week later, during the Vanderbilt game, he had a 63-yard touchdown jaunt. However, he had his best game against Florida. The winner of the "World's Largest Outdoor Cocktail Party" would claim the SEC title. The 'Dogs found themselves down 27-13 at halftime; however, Goff led the Bulldogs back to a 41-27 victory. He would pass for 37 yards, and connect on two touchdowns. Georgia rushed for 184-yards and three touchdowns, while Goff earned national player of the week honors for his performance.

He would finish tenth in the Heisman Trophy voting. Then, three weeks later, Georgia lost 27-3 to Pittsburgh in the Sugar Bowl, as Tony Dorsett rushed for 203-yards, and led the Panthers to the 1976 national title. Georgia would go 19-4 inside of Sanford Stadium during Goff's time with the Bulldogs.

Adriel Jeremiah "A. J." Green, Receiver, 2008-2010

Green was born on July 31, 1988 in Summerville, South Carolina. He attended Summerville High School, where he stared in basketball, track and football, and played wide receiver for the Green Wave of Summerville.

He instantly made the recruiting radar of schools across the country when, as a high school freshman, he tallied fifty-seven receptions for 1,217 yards and eight touchdowns. In 2006, his sophomore season, he was a *USA Today* All-American first team following his seventy-five receptions for 1,422 yards and sixteen touchdowns. As a junior, he had sixty receptions for 1,203 yards and fourteen touchdowns. His 5,373 career receiving yards rank second in the all-time career receiving records of the National Federation of High Schools. In 2008, he was the top rated receiving prospect in the nation, and was ranked as the best player in the country by *Sports Illustrated,* after he caught 72 passes for 1,437 yards and 15 touchdowns.

On February 6, 2008, he signed his letter of intent with the University of Georgia where he would become an immediate impact player for the Bulldogs. In the fourth game of his collegiate career, against the Sun Devils of Arizona State, he had eight catches for 159-yards and one touchdown. He would finish the season with fifty-six catches for 963 yards and eight touchdowns, while leading the Southeastern Conference in receiving yards. In 2009, he had forty-seven receptions for 751 yards and six touchdowns, despite being injured the last three games of the season.

Unfortunately, in 2010, he was suspended for the first four games of the season after a controversy, involving the alleged selling of an autographed bowl game jersey to an unscrupulous person, who marketed amateur athletes. Despite the set-back, Green finished the season with a team high fifty-seven receptions for 848 yards and nine touchdowns. He ended his three seasons at Georgia with 166 receptions for 2,619 yards and 23 touchdowns. During his career at Georgia, the 'Dogs would go 13-5 inside of Sanford Stadium.

David Norman Greene, Quarterback, 2000-2004

He was born on June 22, 1982 in Snellville, Georgia. While attending South Gwinnett High School, in Snellville, Georgia, Greene was a two-sport standout as a quarterback, and as a right fielder in baseball. In football, he led his team, a perennial loser in high school football, to two consecutive playoff appearances. As a senior, he completed 134 passes for 2,102 yards, and nineteen touchdowns. He was a much sought after recruit, who received numerous scholarship offers from schools across the country.

In 2000, he signed a scholarship with Georgia, but would be redshirted by Coach Jim Donnan. In hindsight, Coach Donnan later stated, "... had I known how great a quarterback he was, and that I was going to be fired after an 8-4 season, I would have pulled Greene's redshirt and played him."

In 2001, during Coach Richt's first season as head coach, Greene emerged as the starting quarterback and passed for 2,889 yards and seventeen touchdowns. In 2002, he passed for 2,989 yards and nineteen touchdowns, as he led Georgia to its first Southeastern Conference (SEC) title since 1982. He was unanimously selected as the 2002 Offensive Player of the Year for the SEC. In 2004, Greene made 214 consecutive pass attempts without an interception, and led Georgia to a 10-2 record, including an Outback Bowl win against Wisconsin.

Greene's career was one of the most prolific in Georgia football history, as he passed for an astounding 11,528 yards, seventy-two touchdowns, and recorded forty-two career wins as the 'Dogs starting quarterback. Georgia went 28-4 inside of Sanford Stadium during his time with the 'Dogs.

Todd Gurley II, Tailback, 2012-2014

Gurley was born on August 3, 1994, in Baltimore, Maryland. He attended Tarboro High School in Tarboro, North Carolina, and was a three-sport star in football, track and basketball. During his junior season, he began attracting national attention after gaining a total of 1,472 yards rushing and 26 touchdowns. In 2011, as a senior, he was the North Carolina Player of the Year after totaling 2,600 yards and 38 touchdowns.

In 2012, he signed a scholarship with Georgia. During his freshman season, he rushed for 1,385 yards, on 222 carries, and scored seventeen touchdowns. Unfortunately, his final two seasons were marred by injuries and scandal. In 2013, his sophomore season, he sustained an ankle injury against Louisiana State, during the fourth game of the season, and subsequently lost considerable playing time. He ended the season by scoring a very respectable ten touchdowns, and rushed for 989 yards, on 165 carries.

In 2014, he was the leading candidate to add another prestigious Heisman Trophy to the Butts-Mehre Heritage Hall. In the season opener against Clemson, he had 293 all-purpose yards, while rushing for 198-yards on 15 carries. He scored three touchdowns, as Georgia rolled to a 45-21 victory. After an impressive start to the season, he was everybody's front-runner for the Heisman Trophy. Then, there was that fateful day of Thursday, October 9, 2014.

Gurley would be indefinitely suspended, by the University of Georgia, because of an ongoing investigation over his alleged violation of an NCAA rule involving the selling of his autographs on various pieces of memorabilia, e.g. jerseys, etc.... After rushing for 911 yards, on just 123 carries, he was suspended for four games. When he returned for the Auburn game, his Heisman hopes were gone. Georgia beat the War Eagles; however, Gurley tore his ACL late in the game, ending his career at Georgia.

Todd Gurley, 2012

During his three year career, he rushed for 3,285 yards, averaging 6.4 yards per carry, and scored 36 touchdowns. Georgia went an amazing 18-2 inside of Sanford Stadium during his era.

Rodney Craig Hampton, Tailback, 1987-1989

Hampton was born on April 3, 1969, in Houston, Texas, less than four months before Apollo 11 made its landing on the moon. He played tailback for Kashmere High School, where he was a high school All-American. In 1987, after receiving scholarship offers from major universities across the country, Hampton signed a grant-in-aid to play for the Georgia Bulldogs of Coach Vince Dooley

In 1987, he arrived in Athens as a high school all-everything from Texas. During his freshman season, he cemented himself as what would end-up being the last great tailback of the Vince Dooley era. The majority of Georgia football historians claim Hampton was the second best tailback of the Dooley era, even though his numbers didn't fundamentally add reinforcement to these assertions, when compared to Lars Tate, or even Willie McClendon.

Rodney Hampton, 1989

After rushing for nearly 1,000 yards his freshman year, including 227-yards against Ole Miss, Hampton dropped off the radar in his sophomore campaign because he shared running back duties with the legendary Tim Worley. However, he would bounce back as a junior, when he recorded over 1,000 rushing yards. During his final game as a Bulldog, Hampton scored three touchdowns in the '89 Gator Bowl. He proved to be a workhorse, who was one Georgia's all-time leading rushers.

His overwhelming success as a junior led him to declare early for the National League Football draft before his eligibility at Georgia had been completed. In 1990, Hampton was selected by the New York Giants in the first round, twenty-fourth overall. He would play his entire eight year career with New York. He earned a Pro-Bowl selection in 1992 and '93, won a Super Bowl, and was the Giants' all-time leading rusher at the time of his retirement.

During his three-year career at Georgia, he had 2,668 rushing yards, including the highest single-game all-purpose yardage of 290 yards. He had 3,582 all-purpose career yards. Georgia went 14-4 inside of Sanford Stadium during his three years.

Glynn Harrison, Flanker/Tailback, 1972-1975

Harrison was born in Atlanta, Georgia, on May 25, 1954. When Bulldog legions talk about the best running backs in Georgia history, many might not remember Harrison, who never made any All-American teams. However, he was definitely in the class of great Georgia All-American tailbacks like Charlie Trippi, Herschel Walker, Garrison Hearst, Todd Gurley and Knownson Moreno.

Harrison, who came to Georgia, from Columbia High School in Decatur, Georgia, was an All-State running back. Even though high school games were much cooler, because those games were played at night, Harrison preferred playing college football. "It's more glamorous because of the bigger bands, larger crowds, and the enthusiasm," he related.

Nineteen seventy-two was the last year freshman weren't eligible to play on the varsity, so Harrison played for the "Bullpups." During his sophomore season, Coach Dooley wanted to get Harrison's speed into the Georgia lineup. Georgia utilized him as a specialist in covering kicks and returning punts. Harrison sometimes substituted for Jimmy Poulos and Horace King.

He would make several notable runs for Georgia during his legendary career. His first big run was a punt return in '73, against Tennessee, where he returned it 42-yards. Later that season, against Florida, he had an 87-yard off tackle burst for a touchdown that was nullified because of a penalty. In 1975, against Tech, on Thanksgiving night, he had a renowned 78-yard run for the 'Dogs.

Harrison was the type athlete coaches wanted on their teams. In addition to being one of the best running backs in the

Southeastern Conference, he was modest, and studious. In fact, contrary to what one might have thought of him, he did his best studying during football season. "After practice you're too tired to do anything else, so you might as well sit down and study," he commented.

Although Harrison wasn't superstitious enough wear a rabbit's foot or a lucky charm, he had a certain chair he always sat in for team meetings. "Ever since we've been meeting in that room, I've sat in the middle of the back row," he said. Once, just to make Harrison mad, his roommate sat in the chair and refused to move, "I think I had a bad game that week," Harrison reminisced.

Dan MaGill referred to him as "Gliding Glynn" Harrison, though he was called "Scooter," in the locker room. The legend averaged an astounding 6.37 yards per carry during his career and the 'Dogs went 17-6 inside of Sanford Stadium.

William Coleman "Bill" Hartman, Jr., Fullback, 1934-1937

Born on March 17, 1915, in Thomaston, Georgia, he started his football career in Madison, Georgia. He played high school football in Madison, afterwards, he moved to Milledgeville where he played two seasons of football for Coach Wallace Butts at Georgia Military College.

In addition to Georgia, several other schools were interested in Hartman, particularly Auburn and Tech. In 1934, he signed with the Bulldogs and played fullback and punter for Coach Harry Mehre.

In 1936, at the Polo Grounds, in New York, he gained national attention. Georgia faced an undefeated Fordham team that featured its famed "Seven Blocks of Granite," whom Vince Lombardi was a member. The Bulldogs outplayed the Rams in a 7-7 tie that knocked the New Yorkers out of a Rose Bowl bid and an opportunity to play for the national title. Hartman's performance won him the acclaim of Eastern sportswriters.

The legendary Damon Runyon wrote a front page article about Hartman's "grand feat," and Arthur Daly called him "magnificent."

"His face bore a huge grin throughout the contest," wrote another reporter, "as he kidded the "Seven Blocks of Granite" after each of his smashing tackles."

In 1937, during the Tech game, the first half had ended in a scoreless tie. Afterwards, Tech directed the second half kickoff towards Hartman. It had been well known he'd been hobbled by injuries earlier in the season. Still, injuries and all, Hartman grabbed the football at his seven-yard line, and quickly fumbled it. As Yellow Jacket players swarmed around him, he casually picked-up the football, and proceeded to return it 93-yards for a touchdown. He had trouble decelerating because of his gimpy leg, and ran through a wire fence at the end of the field.

Earlier in the same season, he had an 82-yard punt return against Tulane; however, in 1967, his record setting punt return would be broken when Spike Jones' returned an 87-yarder against Auburn. Hartman, the quintessential Bulldog, suggested an asterisk should be placed by Jones' record because, as he joked, "Mine went out of bounds at the four-yard line on the fly, and Jones had the help of a 30-mile-an-hour wind."

The Tech touchdown was Hartman's most famous touchdown in a career filled with numerous great endeavours. Less than two weeks after the Tech game, he stood in the center of a darkened field at Miami's new Orange Bowl, while President Franklin D. Roosevelt threw a switch, at the White House, that lit up the stadium. After the dedication ceremonies came to a close, Hartman led his team to a 26-0 victory over a powerful Miami team in his last game in a Georgia uniform.

At the end of the season, Hartman was selected as an All-American and unanimous All-South choice. He was chosen as a member of the 1937 "Mythical Eleven," a team selected at the end of each season by a board composed of Coach Howard H. Jones from Southern California; Robert C. Zuppke from Illinois; Frank Thomas at Alabama, Temple's Glenn S. "Pop" Warner, and sports writer Christy Walsh, of the *International News Service*.

In 1941, after Hartman completed two years in the National Football League, he joined the Georgia coaching staff under Coach Butts. As a coach, he always considered the 1942 Orange Bowl the highlight of his coaching career. "We were leading Texas Christian, 33-7, at the end of the first half, and I have never seen such an offensive display of power in my life against a good team!"

After almost 15 years away from the sidelines, Hartman confessed he missed the good things of coaching, but not the headaches. The positive points were, "...the actual time on the field and the excitement of competition the day of the game." What he didn't miss was what practically all coaches throughout history have complained about. "Recruiting can be awfully demanding and frustrating. And, watching those films for hours upon hours were the things that made coaching tough." Georgia went 12-5 inside of Sanford Stadium during his playing career.

Leonard Moore Hauss, Center, 1961-63

Hauss was born on July 11, 1942 in Jesup, Georgia. He attended Jesup High School, where he played fullback. After an injury to his knee, he was told he'd never make the varsity team; however, with lots of hard work and perseverance, he made the team and rushed for 1,500 yards and scored fifteen touchdowns his senior season. He led Jesup to the 1959 Georgia State Class AA football championship and was named to the All-Region, All-State, All-Southern and prep All-America teams.

"If you grew up in Jesup, as I did, you were expected to play football," Hauss stated. "I was playing on a sandlot team when I was six years old. Everybody in the neighborhood had a football. The person who really got me started was a school teacher, and later my Jesup High B-team coach, Mr. Frank Hammond."

If you were in Jesup on Friday nights, during the Hauss years of 1956 through 1959, you would not have found anyone at home during football season. The citizens were all at the football stadium when its Jesup team was home, or in Thomasville, Valdosta, Waycross or Rossville, when the team was away.

He was heavily recruited by Coach Butts, Coach Dodd of Georgia Tech, and Coach Jordan of Auburn. In 1961, he signed a scholarship with Georgia and he became one of the greatest centers in the school's history. He played for head coach Johnny Griffith and strengthened his knee by running up and down the steps of Sanford Stadium. In 1962 and '63, he was selected on the All-Southeastern Conference team.

In 1964, he was drafted by the Washington Redskins, in the ninth round (115th overall) of the National Football League draft. He eventually started his first game, at center, during the fourth game of the '64 season, a job he would not relinquish until retirement. He led the Redskins to Super Bowl VII in '72, where they faced the undefeated Miami Dolphins. He started 192 consecutive games for the Redskins between 1964 and 1977, and was named to the Pro Bowl each year between 1967 and 1972. Georgia went 4-7-2 inside Sanford Stadium during his era.

Gerard Garrison Hearst, Tailback, 1990-1992

Hearst was born on January 4, 1971. He played high school football at Lincoln County and was coached by Larry Campbell, whose 477 football victories rank third all-time nationally. Hearst set numerous high school rushing records while leading the Red Devils to a state title. The high school All-American received numerous scholarship offers from schools across the country.

In 1990, he signed a scholarship with Georgia. His great vision and skilful footwork made him one of the nation's hardest running backs to confront. In 1992, he'd finish third in the Heisman Trophy voting after rushing for 1,547 and scoring nineteen touchdowns. He was selected as a consensus All-American in 1991 and 1992. In '92 he won the Doak Walker Award, and was selected as the Outstanding Collegiate Athlete of the Year, as well as the Southeastern Conference Player of the Year.

During his three year career, he rushed for 3,232 rush yards, averaging 6.0 yards per carry, and scored 33 touchdowns. He had a total of 3,934 all-purpose yards.

Georgia went 15-3 inside of Sanford Stadium during his three years.

Billy Henderson, Tailback, 1946-1949

He was born William Bradford Henderson in Dublin, Ga., on June 2, 1928. His athletic ability was discovered on the dusty sand lots of Macon, Georgia. During his high school days, he was twice named All-American, in both football and baseball. In truth, he had been drafted by the Chicago Cubs after his senior year; however, he signed a scholarship with Georgia.

At Georgia, he played on two Southeastern Conference (SEC) Championship football teams, and led the baseball team in hitting four consecutive seasons, with a .345 batting average. In 1946, he was an All-SEC performer in football and baseball. He is still considered one of the greatest all-around athletes in Georgia sports' history.

Henderson played two years of professional baseball with the Chicago Cubs franchise before joining the coaching ranks at Macon's Willingham High School. He coached at Macon's Mount DeSales High School, the University of South Carolina, Furman, Athens and Jefferson before beginning his twenty-three year reign as head coach at Clarke-Central.

Arguably one of the greatest and most successful coaches in Georgia high school football history, his value system encompassed dedication, courage and achievement, but above all, honesty and decency. Georgia went 16-4 inside of Sanford Stadium during Coach Henderson's four years with the 'Dogs.

Terrell Lee "Terry" Hoage, Safety, 1980-1983

Hoage was born on April 11, 1962, in Ames, Iowa. In 1968, his family moved to Huntsville, Texas. He attended elementary, middle, and high school in Huntsville. In middle school, and high school, he played football, basketball, and ran track. He played quarterback and free safety at Huntsville High School. He was an All-State safety and had been recognized as an All-Trinity Valley and All-District player for three straight seasons.

Hoage was very lightly recruited; however, he initially received several letters from football programs in the now defunct Southwest Conference. Suddenly, schools drew back. It wasn't until later that Hoage and his parents discovered a recruiter, either with Texas or Houston, passed the word he was too slow and "not a winner." Hoage's name had become kryptonite and an outcast.

Interestingly, Georgia did not come to Hoage; instead, he solicited Georgia. If not for a family friend, at Sam Houston State University, where Hoage's father was a biology professor, Hoage never would have stepped foot on the Georgia campus. The family friend had strong ties with Georgia, and, at the Hoage family's request, he sent Georgia film footage of Hoage.

The Georgia coaching staff was impressed with Hoage and immediately offered him a scholarship. He signed a grant-in-aid with Georgia in 1980, where he would hone his skills and become one of the greatest defensive safeties, and rovers, in school history.

During his freshman season, he rarely played; however, during the week before the 1981 Sugar Bowl, he blocked three field-goal attempts in practice and was quickly promoted to the special teams unit. During the biggest game in Georgia football history, against Notre Dame, he blocked a field-goal that set-up Georgia's first score.

During his junior season, he made 101 tackles and his 12 interceptions were the most in the country. In 1983, he sustained an injury against lowly Tulane, causing severe tendinitis to his ankle, and knee. In truth, because of this injury, he only started five games, and missed three games during the season. However, when he did play, he made 60 tackles in those five games, and blocked two field-goals in a game against Clemson to preserve a 16-16 tie. In the Bulldogs' 20-13 victory over Vanderbilt, he intercepted one pass in the endzone and later, in the fourth quarter, he stretched his body out and diverted another one with the tip of his index finger.

He earned Southeastern Conference Defensive Player of the Year honors twice and was named a Heisman finalist in 1982—a rarity for a defensive player in any era of college football. Additionally, he was recognized as a consensus first team All-American during his junior and senior seasons. Coach Dooley called Hoage, "... the best defensive player I've ever coached and maybe the best one I've ever seen." Hoage graduated from Georgia in '85 with a bachelor's degree in genetics, with a 3.85 grade point average.

During his four-year stint with Georgia, the Bulldogs went 43-4-1, captured three conference titles and a national championship. Georgia was 17-1 inside Sanford Stadium during his playing days.

James Hurley, Defensive End, 1967

He was the first black member of the Bulldogs' football and track team. In 1968, he was on the track team and played on the Junior Varsity football team; however, he never played varsity. Hurley, from Atlanta, had walked-on to Georgia's football team earlier that fall, made the junior varsity squad, and started at defensive end. The following season, he was awarded the Bill Mundy Award for having the highest academic average on the team.

Hurley was never given a spot on the Bulldogs' varsity because "the competition was too intense," according to freshman coach John Donaldson in November of 1971. Hurley transferred to Vanderbilt, and was awarded a scholarship and lettered in 1970.

Almost a decade after the University opened its doors for all people, the Georgia football team integrated between the hedges. "The times were changing," coach Dooley related. "They were changing with the integration of the schools. There were too many athletes leaving the South to go North."

Jarvis Jerrell Jones, Linebacker, 2011-2012

Jones was born on October 13, 1989, in Columbus, Georgia. In 2007, he led Carver High School to a state title. As a high school All-American, he was selected to play in the U.S. Army All-American Bowl where he was recognized for his superior play.

Jarvis Jones, 2011

In 2008, Jones signed a scholarship to play for the Southern California Trojans. He played for the Trojans only one season because of a neck injury. The Men of Troy ruled him medically ineligible to play for the Trojans. Jones subsequently transferred to Georgia after he was medically cleared to play by the Georgia medical staff. Jones would be a two year starter at Georgia.

During his two seasons, he posted 13.5 sacks in '11, and had 14.5 in '12. With 28 sacks in two seasons, he was on pace to break Georgia's career mark of 36 sacks; however, he declared for the National Football League instead of returning for his senior season.

Jones, a two-time All-American, was the driving force of the defense, and an undisputed leader. In '12, he was named First Team All-American, SEC Defensive Player of the Year, and was voted, by fans, as the 2012 Premier Player of College Football. Georgia went 11-1 inside Sanford Stadium during his two years with the Bulldogs.

Andy Johnson, Quarterback, 1971-1973

He was born Anderson Sidney Johnson, on October 18, 1952, in Athens, Georgia. Johnson attended Athens High School, now Clarke Central, where he was an All-State quarterback. He was highly sought after by numerous southern institutions after leading his team to the state championship against the Valdosta Wildcats.

In truth, the 1969 Wildcats had outscored their opponents by an astounding total of 402-7, in twelve games before the championship matchup with Athens. The state title game ended in a tie after Johnson threw a touchdown pass, on a tackle-eligible play, to make the score 26-24, with only 25 seconds left. Next, he passed to Gray Sellers for the two-point conversion in order to tie the game. Athens and Valdosta were declared 1969 co-champions.

Andy Johnson, 1973

After Johnson completed his incredible high school career, college recruiters from around the nation attempted to lure one of the most mobile quarterbacks in the country to their school. He signed a scholarship with Vince Dooley's Bulldogs on December 24, 1969.

During his freshman season he played for the "Bullpups." It would be another three years before the NCAA lifted its restrictions on freshman playing on the varsity. In 1971, as a sophomore, he led the 'Dogs to an 11-1 record, while passing for 341-yards and rushed for 870-yards. The 'Dogs only loss was to Pat Sullivan's Auburn. As a team, Georgia rushed for 3,337 yards, while scoring thirty-nine rushing touchdowns, for an average of 303.4 yards per game on the ground.

The success enjoyed in 1971 didn't carry over into the '72 and '73 seasons. In 1972, the Bulldogs finished a lousy 7-4, and lost the Tangerine Bowl 21-10, to Miami of Ohio. Then, in 1973, Georgia went 7-4-1. Johnson passed for 506 yards that season and, in his final game as a Bulldog, led Georgia to a 17-16 win over the Terrapins of Maryland in the Peach Bowl.

His name probably won't be on too many listings of Georgia's all-time greatest quarterbacks, but his record of 23-7-2, as a starter, including that 11-1 season in 1971, can't be ignored. Johnson tossed ten touchdowns and seventeen interceptions during a career where he only attempted 286 passes, for 1,514 yards. Additionally, he rushed for 1,799 yards, including twenty-one rushing touchdown. Georgia went 12-4 at home during Johnson's playing career.

Horace King, Tailback, 1971-1974

He was born Horace Edward King on March 5, 1953. He grew-up in the Rocksprings housing area of Athens. He first excelled at the old Burney Harris High School, where he was the team's most explosive weapon. In 1970, the opening of Clarke Central meant he would have to spend his final year of high school at another school.

During the early '70s, the doors were beginning to open for black athletes in the South. King would help pave the way for future generations. "The legacy in Athens, a lot of people don't know this, especially in the black community, runs real, deep," King said. "People long before us paved that legacy, and we got to live it out and play out their hopes, dreams and aspirations." At Georgia, King received the chance to carry on that legacy to a higher level.

"He came in as a class with the first group of black athletes, and sometimes it is difficult for a local kid to handle all of the problems associated with being the first," Dooley related. "He did it with grace, and by concentrating on getting his degree and playing football. Those two things were his emphasis and he almost shut everything else out."

In 1970, after being recruited by Mike Castronis, King signed a scholarship to attend the University of Georgia. On December 13, 1970, Richard Appleby, Clarence Pope and King, all of Athens, became the second group of black football players to sign a letter of intent with Georgia, joining Chuck Kinnebrew of Rome, and Larry West of Albany, who had signed a week earlier.

On September 16, 1972, Appleby, King, Pope, Kinnebrew and West became the first black football players ever to compete for Georgia's varsity inside of Sanford Stadium. King emerged as the star of the class after electing not to follow in the footsteps of other Southern black athletes who headed elsewhere to play football. "Initially, I was going to move out of the South and go to Michigan State because of race relations," King said, "but when it was all said and done, my mom told me she wouldn't get to see me play."

He would become a three-year starter and an All-Southeastern Conference (SEC) selection as a wingback and tailback. He gained 1,287 yards rushing, including 19 rushing touchdowns. In 1974, his senior season, he finished as the third leading scorer in the SEC with twelve touchdowns, while earning a reputation as an athlete who would get the ball into the endzone.

Of the five Bulldogs who broke the color line on the gridiron in 1971, Kinnebrew and Horace King received their college degrees, Clarence Pope and Larry West became ordained ministers and Richard Appleby runs a multi-million dollar business in Hawaii. Georgia went 16-6 inside of Sanford Stadium during King's three years on the varsity.

Kent Lawrence, Tailback, 1965-1968

Lawrence was born on June 3, 1947, in Anderson, South Carolina; however, he grew-up in Clemson. As a child, he had been afflicted with rheumatic fever, and was told he'd never be able to play any sports. However, he worked his way into condition, and in spite of his small frame, played football at Daniel High School, in Central, South Carolina. In 1965, after high school, he signed a scholarship with Georgia. He would become one of the Bulldogs' all-time great players, and was a three-year varsity letterman.

In 1965, freshman weren't allowed on the varsity, and he played with the "Bullpups." His first varsity game was in 1966, at Jackson, Mississippi, against Mississippi State. The regular starter, Randy Wheeler, was injured after being tackled by D.D. Lewis, thus opening the door for Lawrence to enter the game. Lawrence rushed for 66-yards as he guided Georgia to a 20-17 win.

Lawrence was a member of Coach Dooley's championship teams in 1966 and '68. He finished his college career with a 4.1 yards rushing average, gaining 922 yards with eight touchdowns. As a receiver, he caught 47 passes for 646 yards, and as a kick returner, he had 795 yards, averaging 22-yards per return.

In 1967, against Southern Methodist in the Cotton Bowl, he had a phenomenal game. On the second play of the game, he blew through a huge hole over left tackle, cut towards the east sideline, and using his speed, sailed 74-yards for the 'Dogs first touchdown. He rushed for 149-yards in Georgia's 24-9 win.

Additionally, he was a track star at Georgia, and once defeated O.J. Simpson in the NCAA Indoor 60-yard dash. He tied for first place with Charley Greene, who went on to win the Gold Medal in the 100, held in Mexico City in 1968.

In 1968, he was voted Georgia's Most Valuable Player, Most Outstanding Georgia Back and won the Evans Johnson Memorial Award for leadership, loyalty, dedication and sportsmanship. After graduation, he signed with the Philadelphia Eagles, and later played with the Atlanta Falcons. After a three year career in the pros, he returned to Athens. Georgia went 26-6-2 during his three years on the varsity, and 12-0-1 inside Sanford Stadium.

L. Milton "Red" Leathers Jr., Guard, 1928-1931

Leathers' was born in Gwinnet County, Georgia on December 16, 1908. His family moved to Athens in 1910, where he excelled at Athens High School in—football, basketball, baseball and track. In 1928, he signed a scholarship with Georgia. He attended Georgia where he was part of the '29 "Flaming Sophomores," who defeated Yale during the inaugural game of Sanford Stadium.

During his playing days at Georgia, he had a near-death experience after his appendix burst, just after an away game in New York City, against New York University. "He nearly died. In fact, the report surfaced that he had died," stated Bill Hartman, Georgia's kicking coach and a member of Georgia's 1934-'37 teams.

Leathers' was selected to the All-Southern Conference team in 1930 and the *International News Service* selected him as an All-American in 1931. Additionally, he played for the Philadelphia Eagles in 1933, and later served in World War II. Georgia went 13-2 inside of Sanford Stadium during his era.

Quinton Lumpkin, Center, 1935-1938
Lumpkin went to Lanier High School in Macon, Georgia, where he was an All-State performer in football. In 1935, he signed a scholarship with Georgia, and would become one of its greatest centers of all-time.

In 1938, the Macon husky, weighing 215 pounds, was captain of the team and one of the most versatile linemen to ever play at Georgia. He became the first Bulldog to earn All-American honors since Vernon "Catfish" Smith in 1931. Lumpkin graduated in 1938.

In 1942, he returned to Sanford Stadium, as a member of the U.S. Navy Georgia Pre-Flight Skycrackers. The Skycrackers, consisting of professional players and former college players, came to Athens as the Navy set-up training sites for potential aviators at four universities, including Georgia's campus. Over 20,000 cadets went through training at the Athens Navy Pre-Flight School.

The Navy's football team had scrimmaged against Georgia numerous times, and had been scheduled to play Georgia in 1944; however, the game was canceled because Coach Butts felt the two teams were too familiar with each other. Georgia went 13-4-1 inside of Sanford Stadium during Lumpkin's playing career. His Skycrackers went 4-0 inside of Sanford Stadium.

McCarthy, Chris, Fullback, 1979-1982

He was born on June 12, 1960, in Savannah, Georgia. He went to Benedictine High School, where he earned Coastal Empire Back of the Year, as well as rushing for over 1,000 yards his senior season. In 1979, he signed a scholarship to Georgia.

At Georgia, the 5'-11" 220 pound fullback earned three letters in four seasons. He gained over 700 rushing yards during his career; however, he was most famously remembered for giving-up his number "34," so Hershel Walker could wear it. After McCarthy eventually earned the starting fullback position in 1981 and 1982, he developed a reputation for opening-up massive holes, and throwing incredible blocks for Walker.

As a reward for his efforts, Walker invited McCarthy to attend the Heisman banquet in 1982. "You appreciate a teammate who is being honored, you know he deserves it, and you are grateful you could say you perhaps made a small contribution to his winning the Heisman," McCarthy related. Georgia went 21-4 inside of Sanford Stadium during his era.

Willie Edward McClendon, Tailback, 1975-1978

Born on September 13, 1957, he was the oldest of seven children. He grew-up in Brunswick, the son of Willie Hill McClendon, a truck driver who would congratulate him quietly on good days, but needled him when things didn't go well, the type of encouragement McClendon felt was very valuable.

McClendon was 6'-2" and 202 pounds, with amazing speed out of Glynn County, Georgia. After being heavily recruited by several schools, he signed a scholarship with Georgia in 1975. The Bulldogs quickly moved to the I-formation in order to guarantee McClendon's carries could be over twenty per game.

In 1978, his senior season, he was elected captain of the team. His biggest game came against Kentucky in 1978, when Georgia fell behind 16-0. The Bulldogs would come back to win 17-16 with a Rex Robinson field-goal late in the fourth quarter.

To get into position to win the game, the 'Dogs had to drive from their own 25-yard line to the Kentucky 12-yard line as the clock ticked down to less than one minute to play. He carried the ball six times for 36-yards, running over linebackers and knocking them askew, like a tornado slamming into mobile homes. He carried the ball on every play of the drive, except two, when Jeff Pyburn completed passes of 14 and nine yards. He gained the yards necessary to kill the clock, guaranteeing there was no time for Kentucky. Robinson won the game for Georgia 17-16.

Willie McClendon, 1978

Earlier in the season, McClendon broke Frank Sinkwich's long-standing season record of 1,103 rushing yards in a game against Virginia Military Institute; afterwards, photos were taken of McClendon, Sinkwich and a high school running back named Herschel Walker, who had been invited to watch from the Georgia sideline during his junior year of high school. McClendon had eight 100 yard rushing performances, and 2,228 career rushing yards. He averaged 119.3 yards per game. Georgia went 20-4 inside of Sanford Stadium while he played there.

Kirby Moore, Quarterback, 1965-1967
Moore grew-up in Dothan, Alabama and attended Dothan High School where he was a star pitcher in baseball and the quarterback of the football team. He never lost a game during his

high school career. In 1962, during his senior season, he was an All-State AAA quarterback, gaining 1,213 yards passing and 484-rushing.

After graduation, representatives from Alabama and Auburn approached him, but the two schools would only allow him to play football. Then, the University of Georgia entered the scene and Moore elected to attend Georgia, where it was agreed he would play baseball and football. His appearance at Georgia coincided with the arrival of a new coaching staff—Vince Dooley and his associates. With the exit of the old staff went his college baseball career. It turned out for the best, though. The extra devotion to football helped his play tremendously.

In 1963, he was the 'Dogs number one freshman quarterback. After being held out in '64, he returned in '65 to share the varsity signal-calling duties with Preston Ridlehuber. He completed 53 percent of his passes for 487-yards and was Georgia's punter.

Moore always had his best performances against his home-state teams. He threw the pass to beat Alabama in '65, and later that season, against Auburn, he tossed a 92-yard pass. During the '66 season, he led Southeastern Conference (SEC) T-formation quarterbacks in rushing with 489-yards, scored five touchdowns and passed for four more. He guided Georgia to the '66 SEC title.

A celebrated poem was written in his honor—"To A Great One" by Harold Walker, which included, *When the game is nearing the final gun, and we just can't seem to score, we know who will get the job done, you're a winner—Kirby Moore!*

He was undefeated against *Associated Press* Top-10 teams, going 5-0, while going 5-1 against Auburn and Tech. Georgia went 11-1 inside of Sanford Stadium during Moore's playing days 'tween the hedges.

Anthony "Zippy" Morocco, Receiver, 1949-1951

Morocco was born on March 10, 1930, in Youngstown, Ohio. He was the son of immigrants, who migrated to Youngstown, the same area that All-Americans Frank Sinkwich and George Poschner hailed.

Like Sinkwich and Poschner, he was a high school superstar. During Ohio's All-Star prep football classic, Morocco captivated the

31,000 people in attendance by returning the first punt of the game for a touchdown, after weaving fifty-six yards. He scored twice more, and gained the attention of scouts from across the country.

A standout athlete in football and basketball, Morocco signed a scholarship to play football with Georgia, after being convinced to attend by Charlie Trippi. From 1949 through 1951, he averaged 9.9 yards per carry and his punt return average was 14.2 yards. In 1950, he returned a punt ninety-yards for a touchdown against Furman University. Later that same season, in the Presidential Cup Bowl game, against Texas A&M, at Maryland's Byrd Field in College Park, he returned another punt sixty-five yards for a touchdown. He wore number 23 at Georgia, and most fans of that era simply called Morocco "23." Georgia went 8-8 inside of Sanford Stadium during his four year career.

Knowshon Rockwell Moreno, Tailback, 2006-2008

He was born on July 16, 1987, in New Jersey. He recruited himself to Georgia by sending videos of his high school highlights, and once even took a train to attend one of Georgia's football camps. After reviewing his videos, and observing his performance at the camps, the Georgia coaching staff offered him a scholarship. In 2006, he signed a scholarship to attend Georgia.

In 2006, during what should have been a very special season, with the correct tailback, Moreno subsequently redshirted; however, he returned in 2007, as a redshirt freshman.

After an enormous spring camp, Moreno shared time with Thomas Brown, as the starting running back in the season opener against Oklahoma State. He had a total of 70-yards rushing on 12 carries, with two receptions for 51-yards in the 35-14 Georgia win over the Cowboys. The following week, against South Carolina, Moreno had the lion's share of rushes, with 14 carries for 104-yards; however, he was taken out of the game on the final series. Georgia lost at home 16-12. Later that season, against Vanderbilt, Moreno was elevated to starting tailback when it was announced Thomas Brown would be sidelined with a broken collarbone. Moreno responded with 157-yards rushing in a 20-17 win.

During 2007's World's Largest Outdoor Cocktail Party, twentieth-ranked Georgia defeated ninth-ranked Florida 42-30, as Moreno rushed for 188-yards on 33 carries, scoring three touchdowns. The following week, against Troy State, he rushed for 196-yards, and became only the second player in Georgia history to rush for over a 1,000 yards in his freshman season. He would finish the season with 1,334 yards on 248 carries. He scored 14 touchdowns, and added 253 receiving yards on 20 receptions.

In 2008, he finished the season with 1,792 yards of total offense, rushing for 1,400 yards, while getting 392 receiving yards, and scoring 18 touchdowns. He was named first-team All-Southeastern Conference for the second consecutive year, and was a second-team All-American. He had a career total of 2,734 rushing yards, averaging 5.5 yards per carry, and scored thirty touchdowns. Georgia went 10-3 during his two seasons on the varsity.

Aaron Murray, Quarterback, 2010-2013

Murray was born on November 10, 1990, in Tampa, Florida. He played for Plant High School in Tampa, and verbally committed to Georgia in April of 2008. He broke his leg during his senior season, however, he returned in time to lead his team to the state championship in one of Florida's highest high school classifications.

In 2009, his freshman season, he would redshirt because of an injured shoulder he suffered in practice. Georgia subsequently struggled to an 8-5 record, with Joe Cox as its quarterback. Murray would emerge as the starting quarterback in 2010.

In 2010, a 34-31 overtime loss to Florida might have been Murray's most memorable performance of the season. The Gators went up 21-7 at the half and Murray rallied Georgia. Coach Richt's team exploded in the fourth quarter, scoring three touchdowns, including two touchdown passes and a 1-yard run by Washaun Ealey, tying the score at 31-31. Murray was 18-for-37, for 313-yards, and three touchdowns. He would set a Georgia freshman record with 3,049 passing yards.

At 6'-1", and 211-pounds, Murray helped Georgia reach the Southeastern Conference (SEC) championship game on December 1, 2012. Georgia played Alabama, the number two ranked team in the nation. Murray played an excellent game as Georgia came-up five yards short of winning the championship. His final pass, which was intended for Malcolm Mitchell in the endzone, was instead deflected by Alabama's linebacker C.J. Mosley. The football fell into the hands of a falling Chris Conley, who successfully made the catch, but had lost his balance and was promptly tackled in the field of play on the five-yard line. The remaining seconds ticked off the game clock as the Alabama Crimson Tide held on to win the slugfest 32-28. The Pachyderms went on to defeat Notre Dame 42-14 and won the 2012 Bowl Championship Series national title.

Murray became the first quarterback in the SEC to pass for 3,000 yards during all four years as a starter. He ended his Georgia career with a total of 13,166 passing yards, 396 career rushing yards and 121 touchdowns. From a statistical perspective, he was the greatest Georgia quarterback of all-time. Georgia went 16-2 inside of Sanford Stadium during his four year career.

James Edward Orr, Receiver, 1955-1957

Orr was born on October 4, 1935, in Seneca, South Carolina. After a very successful two year career as his high school quarterback, he signed a scholarship with the Clemson Tigers. However, he later transferred to Wake Forest before finally walking-on at Georgia. While with the Bulldogs, from 1955—1957, he had over 700 yards receiving, and five touchdowns.

He came to Georgia in the fall of 1954, from Seneca, where he had won fame as a basketball player. Orr had played some football, but had not been considered good enough to be given a scholarship to play at the college level. Subsequently, he became a walk-on at Georgia, where he teamed with quarterback Dick Young and twice led the Southeastern Conference (SEC) in receiving (1955) with 24 catches for 443-yards and three touchdowns; then, in '57, he had 16 catches for 237-yards and two touchdowns.

During the 1956 season he lost his bid to successfully defend his SEC receiving title because Georgia had planned to build its offense around a running game, rather than a passing attack. Georgia's backfield coach, Johnny Rauch, wanted the passes to be saved in order to catch the defense off guard, and not to be used as the main offensive instrument.

In 1957, despite Georgia's run oriented offense, Orr still led the conference in receiving. He led the conference in punting, too, averaging 38.1 yards per punt. Unfortunately, he had been unable to break the school record of 42.6 yards per punt, established by Zeke Bratkowski in 1953.

Without question, he and Young formed the top passing combination in the conference. Additionally, Orr made the All-SEC Academic Team and was chosen for the Blue-Gray All Star Classic. Georgia would go 4-6 inside of Sanford Stadium while he was a Bulldog.

Later, Orr would become a legend in the National Football League (NFL), where he teamed up with quarterback Bobby Layne, to win several championships. He had over 400 pass receptions and 8,359 receiving yards, during an era when the NFL didn't pass a lot.

George Edward Patton, Defensive Tackle, 1963-1966

The city of Tuscumbia, Alabama is famous for being the birthplace of two legends–the late author and lecturer Helen Keller, and George Patton, the two-time All-American tackle for the Georgia Bulldogs. In fact, he hailed from a football playing family. His oldest brother, Jim, played on Alabama's 1961 national champion team and another brother, Houston, played at Ole Miss.

Although Patton had established himself as an All-State quarterback, by throwing fourteen touchdown passes his senior year at Deshler High School, it was another Deshler player, Vance Evans, who brought recruiter Spec Towns and Coach Griffith to Tuscumbia. Both players would sign a scholarship to Georgia.

In 1963, Patton was 6'-3" and 210 pounds, and played quarterback for the Georgia "Bullpups," the junior varsity team. Because of his versatility and ability to play any spot—he eventually played multiple positions.

In 1964, when Coach Dooley was hired as head coach, Patton was moved to tackle after Coach Dooley observed the first scrimmage with Patton playing quarterback. Patton would become a legend on the defensive side of the football.

"Coach asked me about the position switch," he said. "I told him it didn't matter to me. I just wanted a job."

On the first play of his varsity career, against Alabama, Patton sacked Joe Namath for an eight-yard loss. It was a precursor of events to come. He spent the next two seasons chasing quarterbacks, fighting off blocks, intercepting passes and receiving passes on tackle eligible plays.

"He kept us fired-up," said Bill Stanfill, his All-American teammate. "He was like a coach on the field. He could diagnose plays. He was at the right place at the right time."

Coach Dooley stated, "He was one of the finest college football players I ever saw."

Like the general for whom he was named, as good as Patton was as a player, he was even better as a leader. He was captain of the 1966 Georgia team, which won the Southeastern Conference (SEC) crown, losing only one game, by one point, on an 11-game schedule. The '66 Bulldogs finished fourth in the *Associated Press*'s final poll of the season.

Patton earned numerous awards. He was a two-time All-American selection, a three time All-SEC selectee, and winner of the Jenkins and Whitworth awards, symbolic of Georgia's finest lineman.

During the 1966 Cotton Bowl game, Coach Dooley put him in as quarterback for one series of plays. He ran the ball only once, but gained fourteen yards to help lead the Bulldogs to a 24-9 victory over Southern Methodist University.

Patton's most memorable moment on the gridiron was in 1965, when he intercepted a pass and returned it 56-yards for a touchdown against defending national champion Alabama. The play led the Bulldogs to a stunning 18-17 victory. During his three seasons on the varsity, Georgia went 11-2 inside of Sanford Stadium.

Jimmy Carl Payne, Defensive End, 1978-1982

Payne was born on February 9, 1960, in Athens, Georgia. He was an All-State performer at Cedar Shoals High School where he was recruited heavily by Tennessee; however, he signed a scholarship with Georgia in the spring of 1978. Between 1978 through 1982, he became the only five-year letterman in modern Georgia football history. During the 1979 season, Payne was injured in the third game of the year and received a medical redshirt.

Payne, one of the greatest defensive players ever at Georgia, was a pivotal member of the 1980 National Championship team. During the 1980 season he had 85 tackles and seven sacks, as a defensive tackle and linebacker. In 1981, Payne logged 12 sacks.

During his time at Georgia, the Bulldogs won three straight Southeastern Conference (SEC) championships in 1980, '81 and '82.

And, easily could have won the SEC in 1978 and '79. In 1981, his hit on Auburn's quarterback, Ken Hobby, caused a fumble in the third quarter, and was a crucial part of Georgia prevailing in that ballgame. With Georgia leading 17-7, he hit Hobby as he dropped back to pass, creating the fumble that Tim Crowe eventually recovered. Georgia took a 24-7 lead, and held on for a 24-13 win.

Buck Belue, Jimmy Payne, Mike Steele, and Herschel Walker

Payne earned All-SEC team accolades for three seasons and was an All-American defensive tackle in 1982. Vince Dooley said, "I believe Jimmy was one of the three best pass rushers to play at Georgia, along with Bill Stanfill and Richard Tardits." Georgia went an amazing 25-0 inside of Sanford Stadium during the five year career of Jimmy Payne.

David Pollack, Defensive End, 2001-2004
He was born on June 19, 1984 and attended Shiloh High School, in Snellville, Georgia. In football, as a senior, he was a Class 5A All-State selection and the Atlanta Touchdown Club named him the Defensive Lineman of the Year.

Pollack signed a scholarship with Georgia in 2001. His remarkable agility, sense of presence, and big-play-thought process enabled him to become the sack-and steal leader for the Bulldogs. In 2002, against South Carolina, when Georgia didn't score an offensive touchdown, Pollack's play was the difference in the game.

Pollack had emerged from relative obscurity to become a three-time All-American and Georgia's most decorated defensive player of all-time. He was selected as a member of the All-Southeastern Conference (SEC) team and to the All-American team in 2002, '03 and '04.

In 2004, he received an incredible amount of awards at the end of his senior season at Georgia. In addition to being recognized as the top college defensive player in the nation, he was a three-time All-American, received the 2004 SEC Player of the Year Award, won the 2004 Chuck Bednarik Award, given annually to the top collegiate defensive player, earned the 2004 Ted Hendricks Award, given annually to the top collegiate defensive end, and won the 2004 Lombardi Award, presented to the top defensive or offensive collegiate lineman who, in addition to outstanding performance and ability, best exemplifies the discipline of Vince Lombardi. Additionally, Pollack received the 2004 Lott Trophy, given to a defensive player exemplifying integrity, maturity, performance, academics, community, and tenacity.

He recorded 36 sacks during his collegiate career and Georgia would go 24-3 inside of Sanford Stadium during his four year reign.

George Poschner, Receiver, 1939-1942

He was born on January 15, 1919. He and Frank Sinkwich both had played football at Chaney High School, in Youngstown, Ohio. At Chaney, he was the leading scorer on his basketball team, and captain during his junior year. He was considered to be too small to play football his first year in high school, but would eventually make the All-City team in 1936-37. Later, when Sinkwich was recruited by Georgia, he accepted the scholarship on the condition Poschner be given a scholarship, too.

Poschner was one of the most high-spirited players who ever played for Georgia. There was no player in America who needed to win more than Poschner. He never gave opponents a minute's rest while he was in the game.

As a freshman, Poschner started out as a 160-pound wingback, and was on the bottom of the depth charts. Consequently, he was moved to receiver before the end of his freshman season. The scrawny third string freshman would surface as a first-string end during his sophomore season.

In 1940, he came through in such a fashion that he beat out Loiver Hawk, Tommy Malone, and Carl Grate. Van Davis was moved to right end to substitute for Jim Skipworth. Fans would long remember Poschner's ferocity and stamina displayed in '40.

In 1941, Poschner weighed 165-pounds, but his play throughout the year was so exceptional the Associate Press selected him as a member of its All-Sophomore team. As a testament to Poschner's stamina, after breaking his arm against Alabama, he was forced to come out of the game to have his broken arm taped-up. Afterwards, he went back into the game and took everything the Pachyderms could throw at him.

In 1942, time after time, Poschner was the sparkplug in stopping teams when they got deep into Georgia territory. In fact, during the Kentucky game, he broke through the Kentucky line, and left no doubt in the minds of the Kentucky team they had five men in the backfield, and one of them was George Poschner.

During the '41 Ole Miss game, Poschner made a play seldom accomplished. He rushed the passer and intercepted the pass on the same play. This play was typical of what opposing quarterbacks faced with Poschner; the danger of having the ball intercepted and, or tackled by the same player.

It was known throughout the South that Poschner played his best when the game was in doubt. He was a money player, playing the type of ball that might be the payoff on any play. The most celebrated event in Poschner's collegiate career came when he caught two fourth-quarter passes, from Sinkwich, in a 21-10 win over previously undefeated Alabama in '42. His performance afforded Georgia an opportunity to win the national title after the 'Dogs went 11-1 and beat UCLA 9-0 in the Rose Bowl.

In 1942, in a game against Cincinnati, Poschner caught five passes, for a total of 83-yards, while playing a stellar defensive game. He would leave no question in the minds of Bulldog supporters he was an All-American. In truth, prior to the game,

Poschner had been thought of as a great defensive end, but a fair receiver, being surpassed only by the nation's leading receiver, "Race Horse" Davis.

During Poschner's tenure with the Bulldogs, he was a member of one of the most successful classes in the history of Georgia football. He participated in the '42 Orange Bowl and the '43 Rose Bowl. He was an All-American who was later selected in the eighth round of the '43 National Football League draft by the Detroit Lions; however, his destiny would be the military.

On January 8, 1945, Poschner found himself at the base of a German machine gun nest in one of the most vicious battles of World War II, the Battle of the Bulge, on a below-zero day. "I got my men together, put my machine gun on my hip and started charging," he recalled. "The next thing I knew, I had been hit in the head and was lying in the snow."

In truth, Poschner would lay in the snow for several days before being discovered. The frost bite took a tremendous toll. His legs were amputated below the knee, and his fingers, on his right hand, were removed. His left arm and hand were left paralyzed.

Our nation's second highest award, the Distinguished Service Cross, along with the Bronze Star and the Purple Heart were bestowed upon him. His citation described how he stormed an enemy machine gun nest and killed over twenty German soldiers.

A *New York Times* report on his injuries observed, "His brilliant pass receiving added much to the reputation of All-American Frank Sinkwich, of Youngstown, as a forward passer." The news report related Poschner's mother advised Coach Butts of her son's case. Poschner was respected as much for his military valor and cheerful sanguinity, as he was for his remarkable accomplishments on the gridiron. Georgia would go 10-2-2 at Sanford Stadium during his four year career.

In 1982, Sinkwich lauded Poschner at a testimonial dinner held at Youngstown's Croatian home. "Knowing George has made me stronger all my life," Sinkwich said.

John "Johnny" Rauch, Quarterback, 1945-1948

He was born on August 20, 1927, and went to Yeadon High School. At the age of 14, he was diagnosed with a heart murmur and had been instructed to give-up all sports. Ignoring these dire warnings, Rauch became a three-sport high school star, before he put together an outstanding career at Georgia.

In 1945, Georgia was switching to the "T" formation, where the quarterback would serve as the offense's primary passer. As a result of the switch, during a recruiting trip, Coach Butts talked Rauch out of signing with Tennessee. With the 'Dogs, Rauch was switched from tailback to quarterback, and promised he'd start under center for the Bulldogs as a true freshman.

As promised, Rauch did start at Georgia as a true freshman. In fact, during his first game, he led the Bulldogs to a 49-0 victory over Murray State. The legend would start 45 consecutive games at quarterback, from 1945 through '48, where he led the 'Dogs to an overall record of 36-8-1. Included in those conquests were four straight bowl game appearances, and the undefeated season of 1946.

On an individual level, Rauch was selected as first-team All-American during his senior season, and left the school as college football's all-time passing leader with 4,044 yards. The record stood for thirty years. He rushed for thirteen touchdowns during his career, caught three touchdown passes, returned a fumble for a touchdown, and had thirteen interceptions. The 'Dogs would go 14-3 in games played inside Sanford Stadium during his career.

Rex Robinson, Kicker, 1977-1980

Robinson was born on March 17, 1959, in Marietta, Georgia. He grew-up watching the National Football League's latest curiosities, soccer style kickers, such as Jan Stenerud, Garo Yepremian, and Pete and Charlie Gogalak, on television each Sunday. Later, he tried to imitate what he saw them doing. By the time he reached high school, he was receiving a great deal of attention. In fact, while on Marietta's junior varsity team, he kicked a 51-yard field-goal and a local Atlanta area news station, Fox Channel 5, sent a crew out to verify the feat.

In 1976, during his senior season in high school, he received several scholarship offers, but selected Georgia, where he would replace Allan Leavitt. Robinson played as a freshman, and was the team's leading scorer. Moreover, he made the '77 All-Southeastern Conference (SEC) freshman team.

Robinson missed his first ever attempt at an extra-point, but would not miss another one the rest of his career at Georgia, making 101 straight. He made the first team All-SEC in 1978, '79 and '80, and the *Playboy* magazine's All-American team in '79 and '80.

In 1980, he made the Walter Camp, Football News, Football Writer's, and *United Press International* All-American teams. The highlight of his career was defeating the Irish of Notre Dame 17-10, in the 1981 Sugar Bowl, in New Orleans, Louisiana. The Georgia Bulldogs were selected as the 1980 National champions.

He was one of Georgia's greatest placekickers of all-time, and entered into the fabled SEC record books via points scored by kicking. He was a classic example of letting his action on the field speaks for itself. He let his foot do the talking. To see him on campus, in his casual attire, it was hard to envision the pudgy, short-haired Marietta, Georgia product as one of the best kickers in collegiate football.

"Kicking is more of an individual game," Robinson said. "Aside from helping the team in a winning effort, I have to derive my personal satisfaction to making goals that help my team. It may be consecutive extra-points, kickoffs going into the endzone, or career field-goals. I've worked to reach the goal to be one of the better kickers at Georgia, and if that's accomplished, then I've helped my team."

He finished his career with a field-goal percentage of 88.2%, 269 points, 56 field-goals, and 101 consecutive extra-points. He had six field-goals of over 50-yards, with two 57 yarders in '80. He would be drafted by the Cincinnati Bengals during the sixth round in '81. And, he played for the New England Patriots during a strike shortened season in '82. Georgia would go 18-8 inside of Sanford Stadium during his monumental career with the 'Dogs.

Frank P. Ross, Linebacker, 1977-1980

Born in Barcelona, Spain, on March 1, 1959, he went to high school at Eastside, in Greenville, South Carolina, where he lettered all four years. He signed with Georgia in the spring of 1977.

The 6'-1" and 215-pound linebacker was the kind of athlete coaches admired and respected. "He's a fierce competitor and has a great willingness to work hard," linebacker coach Chip Wisdom said. "He's a self-made football player. He made himself into a good linebacker with hard work." In fact, Ross would be voted Georgia's Best Conditioned Athlete three years in a row.

He suffered a series of injuries in 1979, and worked to remain in shape in the off-season. According to Wisdom, his efforts did not go unnoticed. "Frank's injuries handicapped his playing time," said Wisdom. "The injuries happened at crucial times, and he had to miss some games, so he never could quite establish himself as a front line specialist." However, Ross could not be stopped by torn ligaments in his knee, a broken toe, a broken thumb, a dislocated shoulder or a small fracture in his ankle. He never lost sight of his goals. Where someone else might have given-up, Ross continued to work himself hard.

Ross captained the 1980 team, and against Clemson, he racked-up an impressive 17 tackles. In an extraordinary move, he managed to block the Clemson pass that resulted in Jeff Hipp's game-saving interception.

Looking back at his years in Athens, Ross never had any second thoughts about coming to Georgia. "I'm glad I picked Georgia," he said. "It has the prettiest campus, and lots of great people. I don't regret choosing it as my school." In the summer of 1980, he remained optimistic about the 1980 season. His personal goals were for the entire team to do well. "When you shoot for number one, you don't just go for number one in the Southeastern Conference," he said. "I'd like to see Georgia tops in the nation."

Georgia had an overall record of 32-13-1 from 1977-1980., and went 18-8 inside of Sanford Stadium during his career.

Theron Coleman Sapp, Receiver, 1956-1958

Sapp was born on June 15, 1935 in Dublin, Georgia. The youngest of ten children, he attended Lanier High School, in Macon. He played both ways, and helped lead Lanier to the State Class AA championship. Though recruited heavily by both Auburn and South Carolina, he signed a grant-in-aid with Georgia in 1955.

During the North-South High School All-Star game, he suffered a serious injury to his vertebrae and was told by the attending surgeon not to play football again because the slightest of hits could be lethal. Coach Butts and Quinton Lumpkin came to the hospital and told Sapp he had his scholarship no matter what. He spent his entire freshman year at Georgia in a head-pelvis body cast.

Coach Butts told him he should not play football again, however, Sapp convinced his coach otherwise. He spent his sophomore year with the Bullpups, and his junior and senior years on the varsity, where he bullied his way up the middle 258 times.

His greatest day came on November 30, 1957. It was freezing, but an enchanting afternoon for Bulldog fans at Grant Field. A wind blew out of the northeast while over 40,000 fans came to see if Tech could make it nine consecutive victories over Georgia. The Bulldogs were suffering their third consecutive losing season, and had not scored a touchdown against Tech in four years.

Some say, with a single touchdown, Theron Sapp did as much for Georgia honor as anyone in Bulldog history. After a scoreless first half, Sapp recovered a fumble at midfield. On third and 12, at the Tech 39-yard line, quarterback Charlie Britt hit Jimmy Orr with a 13-yard pass for a first down at the Tech 26-yard line. From that point forward, it was all 100 percent, unadulterated Sapp.

Sapp crashed into Tech's front-wall on six consecutive plays, getting down to the Tech 1-yard line. On fourth down, Britt handed off to Sapp, who powered his way into the right side of the Tech line and scored the Dogs' first touchdown against Tech since '53. It would be the only touchdown of the game. Ken Cooper made the extra-point, giving Georgia a 7-0 victory.

Sapp only scored six touchdowns during his Georgia career, but he did as much for Georgia pride with that one touchdown as anyone in Bulldog annals, including Frank Sinkwich, Charlie Trippi or Herschel Walker.

Furman Bisher, described the bedlam on the field: "Men kissed men. Women kissed women. Sapp's teammates swarmed over their now immortal hero, whose ninety-one yards on twenty-three carries led the team to the oh so saccharine conquest." Sapp gave credit to Orr and Cooper for the blocks which allowed him to score the game winning touchdown.

Legendary Georgia Tech Coach Bobby Dodd said of Sapp, "Walker won the national championship for Georgia and was awarded the Heisman trophy, but to older Bulldogs, who suffered through the 1950s, Sapp's breaking the drought was greater. He silenced eight years of bragging from Tech fans, students and alumni. Breaking the drought was a remarkable achievement."

> *You can rave about your Sinkwich*
> *And Trippi's praises sing,*
> *While talk about the "Bowl Days"*
> *Still makes the welkin ring.*
> *But to all Bulldog supporters*
> *In every precinct in the South,*
> *I propose a hearty toast*
> *To the man who broke the drouth!*
> *Rise up you loyal Georgians*
> *From Tybee Light to Rabun Gap,*
> *Here's to the Macon Mauler,*
> *The mighty Theron Sapp.*
> *I have seen some lovely paintings*
> *In galleries of art,*
> *Gorgeous sunsets on the water*
> *Which stirred the inner heart.*
> *But of all the wondrous visions*
> *Ever seen by eyes of mine,*
> *I'll take old number forty*
> *Crashing through that Jacket line.*
> *And so down through the ages*
> *Whenever Bulldogs meet,*
> *Whether in the peaceful countryside*
> *Or on a crowded street,*
> *The word will still be carried*
> *By every loyal mouth -*
> *Let's stand and drink another toast*
> *To the man who broke the drouth!*
>   - Harold M. Walker, 1958

Sapp's jersey number 40 was retired two months after the '58 Tech game. His jersey, along with Sinkwich's, Trippi's and Walker's, hangs in the lobby of the Butts-Mehre Building at the University of Georgia. Sinkwich gained 2,271 yards and scored 30 touchdowns, Trippi 1,669 yards and 32 touchdowns and Walker

5,259 yards and 52 touchdowns. Sapp rushed for just 1,269 yards, but he ripped the Jackets' line to shreds in breaking the drought. Georgia went 4-6 inside Sanford Stadium during his career.

Jacob E. Scott, III, Safety, 1967-1968

He was born on July 20, 1945, in Greenwood, South Carolina. His family moved to Athens, Georgia, when he was four years old. His mother, Mary Scott, believes one person who had the greatest influence on Jake's life was Cobern Kelly, the director of the Athens YMCA.

When Scott was 12, he was a member of Athens' YMCA boy's football team, which won the national championship. Scott then attended Athens High School for two years before his family moved to Virginia, where he attended Washington and Lee High School, in Arlington. Scott, who played fullback and outside linebacker, later attended Bullis Prep School, in Silver Springs, Maryland. In 1964, while at Bullis, he played flanker and tailback and was named the outstanding prep player of Washington, D.C.

It wasn't until Scott arrived at Georgia that he made a name for himself. He wanted to play wide receiver, but the Bulldogs had depth there, and needed help in the secondary. Coach Dooley moved Scott to defensive back. In truth, he was the number one safety on the freshman team in 1966, but he missed a quarter of school that year because he was academically ineligible.

Scott played on the varsity at Georgia in 1967 and '68, where he led Georgia in interceptions each season, with six and ten, respectively. In 1967, Scott was named first-team All-Southeastern Conference (SEC) defensive back by the *Associated Press*. Then, in 1968, he was selected as the *Associated Press* and *United Press International* All-American teams.

There might not have been a more prolific two-year player at Georgia than Scott. He led the SEC in interceptions during both of his seasons at Georgia. During an era controlled by the run-heavy offenses, no defensive back made more plays while the ball was in the air. His career highlights included two interception returns for touchdowns against Kentucky, and a punt return for a touchdown during a win over Tennessee.

Coach Dooley suspended him prior to the 1968 season; however, at the urging of teammates, Dooley let Scott back on the team and the Bulldogs won the SEC Championship that season and Scott was named the conference's Most Valuable Player. Georgia went 9-0-1 inside of Sanford Stadium during his reign in Athens.

Jake Scott, 1968

Incredibly, Scott's National Football League career was possibly more remarkable than his college days. After leaving Georgia a year early, to pursue a one-year stint in the Canadian Football League, Scott was signed by the Miami Dolphins in 1970. He played in five consecutive Pro Bowls, to go along with three Super Bowl appearances. In 1972, his Miami Dolphins went undefeated, won the Super Bowl and he was selected as the Super Bowl VII Most-Valuable Player.

Richard Vershaun Seymour, Defensive End, 1997-2000

He was born on October 6, 1979, in Gadsden, South Carolina. He attended Lower Richland High School, in Hopkins, South Carolina, where he was selected as first team All-Region. He earned first team All-Area honors, and as a senior, was voted the team's best defensive lineman. Additionally he was team captain, won an All-Area Player of the Week award, and led his team to four "All-Area Team of the Week" honors. In 1997, he signed a scholarship to attend Georgia.

At Georgia, the housing and economics major was a four-year letterman. He played in a total of 41 games where he finished his career with 223 tackles, 9.5 sacks, 25.5 tackles for loss, and 35 quarterback pressures. He was a first-team All-Southeastern Conference (SEC) selection in his junior and senior seasons.

In 1999, Seymour started all eleven games at right defensive tackle. He led the team with 74 tackles, including 38 solo tackles, along with four sacks. One of his biggest games of the season came against his home state team of South Carolina. He had a momentum changing interception, and two sacks to help Georgia defeat Lou Hotlz and his Gamecocks 24-6. During his career at Georgia, the 'Dogs would go 19-5 inside of Sanford Stadium.

Additionally, Seymour was selected in the first round of the 2000 National Football League draft, where he went on to star in seven Pro Bowls, and was a member of three Super Bowl-winning New England Patriots teams. Most considered him to be one of the greatest defensive lineman to ever play the game.

Donald Eugene "D. J." Shockley, Quarterback, 2001-2005

He was born on March 23, 1983, in College Park, Georgia. He played football at North Clayton High School and, as a senior, the high school All-American threw for 1,861 yards, and 11 touchdowns, while rushing for 864-yards and eight touchdowns.

In 2001, Shockley was Richt's first official recruit at Georgia; however, Richt would select redshirt freshman David Greene, as his starting quarterback in '01, while Shockley was redshirted. During Greene's four-year record-setting career, Shockley saw limited playing time in a modified dual-quarterback system.

In 2002, he was a member of the first Georgia team to win the Southeastern Conference (SEC) title in 20 seasons. Shockley completed 32-of-52 passes for 415-yards with five touchdowns, including a 37-yard touchdown pass in the Sugar Bowl win against Florida State. He rushed for 111 yards and two more touchdowns.

In 2003, during an injury riddled season, Shockley finished with 9-of-21 pass attempts for 88-yards and one touchdown. In six games he had 101 rushing yards, and one rushing touchdown.

In 2004, he completed 26-of-60 passes for 464-yards, along with four touchdowns and one interception. In ten games he had 24 rushes for 113-yards. Additionally, he was on the SEC Academic Honor-Roll.

In 2005, he finally became the starting quarterback for Georgia. After the Bulldogs' opening win against Boise State, he was named Cingular All-American Player of the Week for his 374-yard, six touchdown effort against the Broncos. Additionally, he was one of 11 Division I-A football players named to the National Good Works Team, which recognized "players who have devoted themselves to exemplary community service."

He played in eleven of Georgia's thirteen games, completing 173-of-310 passes, for 2,588 yards and 24 touchdowns, with only five interceptions. He gained 322-yards rushing in 78 attempts, and scored four touchdowns. His longest run was 40-yards and his longest pass play was a 56-yard touchdown pass to tight end Martrez Milner—both occurred on September 3, 2005 against Boise State.

During the first half of Georgia's seventh game of the season, against the Arkansas Razorbacks, Shockley sustained a sprained medial collateral ligament in his left knee. Because of his injury, he had to sit out of undefeated Georgia's eighth game of the season, the World's Largest Outdoor Cocktail Party game against Florida. Georgia's back-up quarterback, Joe Tereskinski III, would start in his stead, and the 'Dogs consequently lost its first game of the year 14–10, to the Gators and first year head coach Urban Myers.

Georgia won its conference's Eastern Division and played Louisiana State University in the SEC Championship game. Shockley threw for two touchdowns and ran for another as the Bulldogs won the game impressively 34–14. Shockley was selected as the Most Valuable Player of game.

He led Georgia to a 10–3 record and the number ten ranking. For his career at Georgia, he completed 240 of 443 pass attempts, for 3,555 yards, 34 touchdowns, against only nine interceptions. He rushed for 643-yards. The 'Dogs would go 23-2 inside Sanford Stadium during Shockley's four years on the varsity.

Andre "Pulpwood" Smith, Fullback, 1983 -1984

Smith, whose nickname was "Pulpwood," was given the moniker by Walter Huckabee, a leisure services coach in Coffee County, Georgia. When Mr. Huckabee questioned Smith about how he was able to hit towering homeruns at only 12 years of age, Smith answered with only one word—Pulpwood.

Smith, who played high school football for the Coffee County Trojans, was the 1982 Class AAAA Back of the Year for the state of Georgia. He was drafted by the California Angels while still in high school, but elected to sign a football scholarship with Texas A&M. However, a major recruiting scandal, involving former Coffee County teammate, George Smith, swayed him to sign with Georgia instead.

In 1983, as a freshman, he played in just one game, rushing for 25 yards on four carries against the Kentucky Wildcats. That offseason, he worked his way up Georgia's depth chart. Eventually, by the start of the 1984 season, he was the starting fullback.

When Georgia opened the season against the Eagles of Southern Mississippi, everybody was focused on Lars Tate—the number one running back in the nation coming out of high school. However, Smith was the running back who stunned the Sanford Stadium crowd. In the third quarter, with Georgia holding onto a 16-13 lead, he scored on a 50-yard run, guiding Georgia to a 26-19 win.

In the fourth game of the season, against the Crimson Tide of Alabama, in Birmingham, Smith rushed for 118-yards. On the fourth play of the game he busted a 44-yard touchdown run. Then, on Georgia's next possession, he scored another touchdown on a 34-yard run directly up the middle of Alabama's powerful defensive line. On October 20, 1984, against Vanderbilt, he scored on a 47-yard touchdown run to help Georgia win 62-30. His long scoring runs were eerily familiar of Herschel Walker's tenure at Georgia.

Smith finished the '84 season as the team's leading rusher with 665 rushing yards and four touchdowns. Smith's memorable football career came to an unforeseen end following the '84 Georgia versus Florida State Citrus Bowl game, because of Georgia's drug policy. In the spring of '85, Smith was declared academically ineligible and was subsequently dismissed from school.

His varsity career at Georgia was comprised of thirteen games. His sophomore season of '84 was one of the best single seasons by a fullback at the University of Georgia. The 'Dogs would go 10-2 inside Sanford Stadium during his time at Georgia.

Vernon "Catfish" Smith, Receiver, 1928-1931

Smith was born on January 14, 1908, in Macon, Georgia. His nickname of "Catfish" was attributed to a story about him biting the head off of one as a 25-cent bet while a student at Lanier High School, in Macon. After a brilliant high school career, where he played football and baseball, he was offered a scholarship by then Georgia coach George Cecil Woodruff. In 1928, Smith would sign a scholarship with Georgia's new head coach Harry Mehre.

At Georgia, he quickly emerged into a three-sport athlete. He earned All-Southern Conference honors, as a receiver, for three straight seasons. Later, in 1931, he was named All-American, after leading the 'Dogs to within one game of playing for the national title and a Rose Bowl berth.

Vernon "Catfish" Smith, 1929

On October 12, 1929, he scored all 15 points for Georgia in an upset of Yale—during the dedication game of Sanford Stadium. Smith scored Georgia's first touchdown on a short pass from Spurgeon Chandler, then kicked the extra-point. Later, he tackled Yale's All-American scat-back, Albie Booth, for a safety. To close out the scoring, he recovered a blocked Yale punt in the endzone for his final touchdown.

Smith was the leader of the "Flaming Sophomores of '29." He wore number 9 and in 1935, he was selected to Georgia's "All-Time Georgia Bulldogs football team. Georgia went 9-1 inside of Sanford Stadium during Smith's era, dating back to October 12, 1929.

Matt Stafford, Quarterback, 2006-2008
He was born John Matthew Stafford on February 7, 1988, in the coastal city of Tampa, Florida. His family temporary lived in Dunwoody, Georgia, while his daddy attended graduate school at the University of Georgia. Later, they moved to Dallas, Texas, and Stafford attended Highland Park High School, where he was coached by Randy Allen. In 2005, Stafford was rated the top high school quarterback in the nation by most recruiting sources. In fact, sports analyst Mel Kiper, Jr., boldly projected, ".... when Matt Stafford decides to go into the National Football League, he will be the overall first pick of that draft."

In 2006, after graduating early from high school, he enrolled at Georgia. The 2006 G-Day spring game was a harbinger of things to come after Stafford completed a 60-yard touchdown pass on his first throw of the game. He eventually earned the starting quarterback job that season, and completed 135 out of 236 attempts, for 1,749 yards, seven touchdowns and thirteen interceptions.

In 2007, his most memorable game was against Florida, when he completed 11 of 18 passes for 217-yards and three touchdowns. The game was highlighted after Georgia's entire team rushed the field to celebrate its first touchdown of the game. The victory launched the 'Dogs into the national spotlight. Stafford finished the season by completing 194 of 348 passes, for 2,523 yards, and 19 touchdowns. Georgia finished the season ranked number two in the nation.

In 2008, the team entered the season with the longest active winning streak in the nation, having won its last seven games of the 2007 season. However, that streak ended during the "Blackout" game against Alabama. Stafford finished the season with 3,459 passing yards, 25 touchdowns and ten interceptions.

During his three year career at Georgia, he completed 564 out of 986 attempts, for 7,731 yards, 51 touchdowns, and 33 interceptions. Prone to tossing interceptions, he had come very close to breaking Georgia's all-time single season record for most interceptions of 15, held by his quarterback coach Michael Bobo; however, he only tossed 13 for the year. Stafford finished his career with a 6–3 record in rivalry games, as he went 1–2 against Florida, 3–0 against Auburn, and 2–1 against Tech. Georgia was 14-5 during games played inside of Sanford Stadium during his three year career.

William Thomas Stanfill, Defensive Line, 1965-1968

Stanfill was born January 13, 1947, in Cairo, Georgia. He attended Cairo High School where he played football, basketball and ran track. He was an All-State defensive lineman, and took his team to three semi-final playoff games. He was a state champion in the discus and shot put and was heavily recruited, but eventually settled on signing with Vince Dooley's Georgia Bulldogs.

Besides Herschel Walker and David Pollack, Stanfill was the most decorated Bulldog of all-time. He played defensive tackle for Georgia and earned All-American honors in 1967 and '68. During his senior season he was awarded the Outland Trophy as the nation's best linemen. Additionally, he was selected to the All-Southeastern Conference (SEC) team 1966, '67 and '68, and was the SEC Lineman of The Year in 1968.

Coach Dooley said, "He was everything you'd want in a defensive tackle. He combined speed, size, range, quickness and competitiveness to make him one of the greatest linemen to ever play the game."

In addition to rushing the quarterback, and swatting the football out of the sky at the line of scrimmage, Stanfill specialized in bowling down ball carriers. Often he would pile a would-be blocker into an opposing ball carrier for big losses. He was one of the few football players to go "bowling on the gridiron."

In 1966, Stanfill became a household name after mauling future Heisman Trophy recipient Steve Spurrier during Georgia's 27-10 upset victory over the unbeaten Florida Gators. Though he was only a sophomore, Stanfill led the Bulldogs' all-out rush on Spurrier, sacking him twice and pounding him repetitively, often after Spurrier no longer had the football.

Spurrier won the Heisman Trophy, but the memory of Georgia denying the Gators their first SEC title, coupled with overcoming a 10-3 halftime deficit, still resonated as one of Stanfill's greatest memories. "If I wasn't sacking Spurrier, I was knocking him down," Stanfill said. "He just didn't have time to throw."

On November 5, 1966, it was a cool afternoon, as a sea breeze flowed through the medal girders of the Gator Bowl. Ray Graves' Florida Gators dreamed of winning its first SEC title since the inception of the conference in 1932. The Gators, undefeated and ranked seventh in the nation, were led by Spurrier, the eventual Heisman Trophy winner. Based on its highly potent offense, Florida was heavily favored to defeat the unranked Georgia Bulldogs.

At first, Florida appeared to be the better team. Spurrier led Florida on an 80-yard opening drive that culminated in a touchdown. Later, in the first half, Florida added a field-goal to push their lead to 10-3 at halftime.

Bill Stanfill, 1966

During the second half, Georgia's defense stopped the Florida offense as it kept the pressure on Spurrier. Stanfill, and the other defenders, teed-off on Spurrier time after time, even after Spurrier had already passed the football.

Early in the fourth quarter, on a blitz, Spurrier attempted to dump the ball to his tight end, but Georgia defenders had the play covered. Spurrier's pass was intercepted and returned for a Georgia touchdown, giving Georgia a 17-10 lead they never relinquished.

Dooley felt a close win against Florida wouldn't be enough, so Georgia tacked on a fourth quarter field-goal for a ten point lead. Late in the game, Georgia got the ball back, and instead of courteously taking a knee as time expired, Dooley allowed his offense to score a final touchdown with six seconds left in the game. In what had been a close game, appeared to be a rout of 27-10.

Stanfill added, "Even if he released the ball, his butt was going on the ground." Then he added, "And he didn't like it either. We pounded him. Not only me, but the whole team."

In 1968, during a 51-0 thumping of the Florida Gators, Coach Dooley allowed Stanfill to finish the game at quarterback. The game was in a driving rainstorm, and caused some hard feelings on the part of the Florida fans. At the end of the season, the Litkenhous poll selected the 8-1-2 Bulldogs as its 1968 national champions.

Georgia went 26-6-2, and won two Southeastern Conference titles, 1966 and '68, during Stanfill's days as a Bulldog. The 'Dogs would go 15-1-1 inside of Sanford Stadium during Stanfill's career.

Richard "Le Sack" Tardits, Linebacker, 1985-1988

Tardits was born on July 30, 1965, in Biarritz, France. He grew-up playing junior rugby in France. In 1984, he arrived in Augusta, Georgia as an exchange student. After meeting Mixon Robinson, who captained Georgia's 1971 team, he decided to walk-on to Georgia's football team.

In the spring of 1985, the 6'-2" and 219-pound Tardits had never seen an American football game; however, he walked-on at Georgia, and would eventually become the Bulldogs' career sack leader with twenty-nine. He wanted an American education, and was flabbergasted at the chance to play a game, while getting a free education in return.

Coach Dooley was impressed with Tardits' robustness and athleticism, and gave him an opportunity. Later, Tardits showed Coach Dooley the outline of his intentions and petitioned for any scholarship aid; however, he was informed it would be awkward for him to obtain any scholarship support unless he could help the football team.

During his freshman season, Tardits made the traveling squad and played in nine games. After being briefed he could play special teams, Tardits questioned whether or not that counted as football. He was moved from the tight end position, to defensive end, and after the starter sprained an ankle, Tardits' situation met opportunity. With his upper body strength, quickness, and speed, he had pass-rushing skills that helped him move-up the depth chart. In the spring of 1986, he emerged as the number two defensive end and earned a scholarship.

Richard Tardits, 1988

In 1988, his last game as a Georgia Bulldog would be in the Gator Bowl, which was Coach Dooley's last game as Georgia's coach. Even though he started his career at Georgia as a walk-on, he became the recipient of a scholarship, and at one time held the school career sack record of twenty-nine. In 2004 his sack record was broken by David Pollack.

When his four years of eligibility were up at Georgia, he had earned an MBA degree. He was reluctant to boast, but rarely has any college had an athlete who exemplified the student athlete replica like Tardits. He received an NCAA post graduate scholarship, an amazing achievement for someone who learned to speak English, as a high school exchange student, just a few years earlier. Georgia went 18-5 inside of Sanford Stadium during his four year career.

Fran Tarkenton, Quarterback, 1957-1960

He was born Francis Asbury Tarkenton on February 3, 1940, in Richmond, Virginia. His family lived in the Washington D.C. area until moving to Athens, where his daddy was a Methodist preacher. Tarkenton played for Athens High School, where he led his team to the state title in 1956. In 1957, after being heavily recruited, he elected to sign a scholarship with Coach Wallace Butts and the University of Georgia.

He was a quick success. During an era when schools still had freshman teams, he helped his freshman squad go undefeated. The following season, in 1958, his legend would be born. In the season opener against the University of Texas Longhorns, Georgia was down 7-0 in the 4th quarter. After taking over on their own 5-yard line, Fran Tarkenton, listed as Georgia's third-string quarterback, noticed starter Charlie Britt, the starting quarterback, was still sitting on the sidelines as the offense ran onto the field. Tarkenton rushed onto the field and marched the Bulldogs 95-yards in 21 plays, stunning his coaches.

After scoring, the Georgia coaching staff sent on its kicking team for the extra-point; however, Tarkenton waived them off, electing to go for the two-point conversion, a new rule just instituted that season. He hit a 5-yard pass and converted one of the first 2-point conversions ever attempted. Unfortunately, Texas responded with a drive of its own, and won the game. Still, Tarkenton's fabled folk tale was born.

In 1958, he was an All-Southeastern Conference (SEC) sophomore team selection and an integral player in the Georgia Bulldogs' SEC championship season of 1959. He led a powerful offensive team that was sometimes called "Tarkenton's Raiders," and "Tarkenton's Music Makers."

In 1959, he led the SEC in pass completions and set a conference record for completion percentage, earning him All-SEC quarterback honors. In 1960, he played in the Orange Bowl where Georgia defeated Missouri, on New Year's Day, by a score of 14-0.

In 1960, his senior season, he led the conference in passing with 1,189 yards, and earned the honor of being an All-American. In addition to being a remarkable player, he was an Academic All-American. During his three year varsity career, he completed 186 out of 317 attempts, for 2,100 yards, 18 touchdowns, and 20 interceptions. The 'Dogs would go 12-3 inside of Sanford Stadium during his varsity career.

Charles "Charlie" Trippi, Tailback, 1941-1942 and 1945-1946

Born on December 14, 1920, in Pittston, Pennsylvania, his athletic abilities as a teenager attracted the attention of a former Georgia Bulldog, Harold Ketron, who operated Coca-Cola bottling plants in the area. Ketron offered Trippi a scholarship to Georgia, which he accepted.

In 1941, Trippi signed a scholarship with Coach Wallace Butts' Georgia Bulldogs. Freshman weren't eligible to play on the varsity in '41, so Trippi, playing halfback, led the Bullpups to an undefeated season.

In 1942, midway through his sophomore season with the varsity, Coach Butts swapped All-American halfback Frank Sinkwich to fullback and incorporated Trippi at halfback. Sinkwich would win the Heisman Trophy, but Trippi, his understudy, gained 1,239 total yards and the Bulldogs won the Southeastern Conference (SEC) championship, and were selected as national champions in the majority of polls released during that era of colligate football.

After beating an undefeated Georgia Tech, Georgia was invited to the Rose Bowl, where Trippi rushed for 130-yards en route to a 9-0 victory over the University of California at Los Angeles. Trippi received the Rose Bowl Most Valuable Player honors.

Trippi missed the next two and a half seasons while serving in the Army-Air Force during World War II; however, he returned for the last six games of 1945. In 1946, his senior season, he captained the Bulldogs an undefeated SEC championship season and a Sugar Bowl victory over North Carolina.

In 1946, Trippi won the Maxwell Award, as the college football Player of the Year. However, he was cheated out of the Heisman Trophy when the New York Downtown Athletic Club awarded it to Glynn Davis, of Army, who had a mediocre season. Davis rushed for 712-yards, scored 13 touchdowns, while passing for 396 yards. In contrast, Trippi, who was an excellent defense player, led the SEC in scoring with 84 points, rushed for 744-yards on 115 carries, and passed for 622-yards. Additionally, Trippi was a unanimous All-American selection.

His career offensive statistics at Georgia were very remarkable. He had 1,669 yards rushing, on 260 attempts, and scored 32 touchdowns. He completed 87-of-179 passes for 1,566 yards and 15 touchdowns.

In 1947, after leaving Georgia, Trippi played professionally as a running back with the Chicago Cardinals for nine seasons. In 1947, his Cardinals won the world championship. He played professional baseball with the Atlanta Crackers in 1947, too. In 1948, he coached Georgia's baseball team, and later, in 1951, returned to Georgia and earned his college degree.

Jim Thorpe, the world's all-time greatest athlete, described Trippi as the "best football player" he had ever seen. Bill Hartman christened Trippi as the "greatest defender to ever play for Georgia." Georgia went 13-1 inside of Sanford Stadium during Trippi's career with the 'Dogs.

Hines Edward Ward, Jr., Receiver/Quarterback, 1994-1997

Ward was born on March 8, 1976, in Seoul, South Korea. Later, his family moved to East Point, Georgia, while his daddy, who was in the Army, went to Germany to serve a tour of duty. Ward attended Forest Park High School where he was coached by Mike Parris. Ward showcased his athletic skills as a quarterback, and was two-time Clayton County Offensive Player of the Year. Additionally, Ward was an All-State quarterback his senior season.

In 1994, he signed a scholarship with Georgia. He played quarterback his sophomore season, and set Georgia bowl records for pass attempts, pass completions, and passing yards during the 1995 Peach Bowl, where he completed 31 of 59 passes for 413-yards.

In 1996, as a receiver, Ward had 52 receptions for 900 yards, and he had 26 rushing attempts for 170-yards. In 1997, he hauled in 55 passes for 715-yards, while scoring six touchdowns. He rushed the football thirty times for 223-yards. He had 149 career receptions for 1,965 yards. As a quarterback, receiver and punt returner, he amassed a total of 3,870 all-purpose yards.

Hines Ward, 1996

Incredibly, when Ward entered the National Football League, it was discovered he was missing an anterior cruciate ligament in his left knee, which he lost during a bicycle accident as a child. Ward would go on to win the Super Bowl MVP for Pittsburgh. Georgia went 15-9 inside of Sanford Stadium during Ward's four year career.

Gene Washington, Receiver, 1973-1976
He was born Eugene Washington, on June 6, 1953, in Gadsden, South Carolina. He attended Lower Richland High School, where he ran a 9.2 in the 100 yard dash. In 1973, after being recruited by numerous schools, he signed a scholarship with Coach Dooley and the University of Georgia.

In 1973, his freshman season, he was named to the All-Southeastern Conference freshman first team after compiling 384 all-purpose yards, while only playing in four games before an injury, sustained against Alabama, sidelined him for the season. Astoundingly, he led the conference in kick-off return average during the same injury shortened season.

In 1975, one of the biggest plays of his career came against Florida, when he caught an 80-yard touchdown pass from Richard Appleby, to beat the Gators 10-7. During his four years at Georgia, he had 2,791 total yards. The 'Dogs went 19-4 inside Sanford Stadium during his reign as one of Georgia's all-time great receivers.

William Mike "Moonpie" Wilson, Offensive Line, 1973-1976

He was born on May 28, 1955, in Norfolk, Virginia. His family moved to Gainesville, Georgia, where he played at Johnson High School. In 1973, he was unheralded when he signed a scholarship with Georgia. In 1974, as a sophomore, he started on defense; however, he was later moved to offense, but still played on the goal-line defense.

It's hard to quantify the play of offensive linemen. Yet, Wilson, a mammoth lineman, who opened-up large holes for Georgia's backfield, would earn consensus All-American honors his senior season. As a right tackle, he anchored the offensive line during Georgia's march to the 1976 Southeastern Conference title.

He was chosen in the fourth round of the 1977 National Football League (NFL) Draft. However, he signed with the Canadian Football League's (CFL) Argonauts for the 1977 season. He had an outstanding season, and was named runner-up for the CFL Outstanding Lineman Award. He was named to the All-Canadian All-Star team, too.

His first NFL season was with the Bengals in '78, and he made an immediate impact, starting eight of the nine games he played on his way to becoming a perennial starter. For each of his next seven seasons with the Bengals, he did not miss a game, starting all but one. Additionally, Georgia went 19-4 inside Sanford Stadium during Wilson's time with the 'Dogs.

William "Will" Cordell Witherspoon, Linebacker, 1998-2001

He was born on August 19, 1980, in San Antonio, Texas. Witherspoon's father served in the United States Air Force, and, consequently, Witherspoon's family often moved while he was growing-up. However, his family never lived on the military bases, instead deciding to live within the communities, so the children could experience the culture. In addition to speaking English, he knew how to speak German, and learned to speak Arabic and Swedish.

He attended Good Shepherd Lutheran School in middle school. Later, he played running back for Rutherford High School in Panama City, Florida, but switched to linebacker before his senior year. He was chosen as the *USA Today* "Florida Player of the Year" for his efforts as a senior, where he posted 112 tackles, three sacks, and three interceptions.

He shocked all the recruiting circuits when he signed a scholarship with Georgia, instead of Florida or Florida State. While playing for the 'Dogs, Witherspoon was a starter during most of the Bulldogs' games from 1998 through 2001, including playing in every game as a freshman. He switched between the middle, strong-side, and weak-side linebacker positions. He finished his career with 211 tackles, 3.5 sacks, one forced fumble, and one fumble recovery. He graduated as a landscape architecture. Georgia went 18-6 inside Sanford Stadium during Witherspoon's four years in Athens.

Scott Allison Woerner, Cornerback, 1977-1980

He was born on December 18, 1958, in Baytown, Texas. Later, his family moved to Jonesboro, Georgia. In 1976, as a quarterback, he was a top prospect, coming out of Jonesboro High School. On an official visit to Austin, he was ready to commit to Texas; however, after the Texas versus Texas A&M game, Coach Darrell Royal announced his retirement. A stunned Woerner didn't commit, but instead signed a scholarship with Coach Vince Dooley's Georgia Bulldogs.

"Woerner the Returner" became his byname. He was, without question, one of the more electrifying players to wear the red and black. In 1977, during his freshman season, he sat the single game record for most kickoff return yards, with 190 yards, against the Kentucky Wildcats.

In 1980, when Georgia played Clemson, both teams were very evenly matched. When those situations come about, the only difference in the two teams, you might suggest, would be the home-field advantage. As it turned out, the difference was the play of one player, Scott Woerner.

Early in the game he scored on a 67-yard punt return, then, a few minutes later, Woerner returned an interception 98-yards, to the

Clemson 2-yard line. Buck Belue would sneak the ball into the endzone two plays later. All the offense the Bulldogs could produce thereafter was two field-goals by Rex Robinson. The defense saved the day by rising to the occasion all afternoon.

In 1980, he recorded 488 punt return yards. Overall, he had thirteen career interceptions, 839-yards on kick returns, and 1,077 yards on punt returns. He was a two-time All-American cornerback and his two interceptions against Notre Dame, in Sugar Bowl, helped guarantee a Georgia victory and a national title. Georgia would go 18-8 inside of Sanford Stadium during his impressive career with the 'Dogs. He would be drafted in the third round of the National Football League draft by the Atlanta Falcons.

Scott Woerner, 1980

Timothy Worley, Tailback, 1985-1988

Worley was born September 24, 1966, in Lumberton, North Carolina. He attended Lumberton High School, where he played football and ran track as a sprinter. As a senior, he won the state titles in both the 100 meters and 200 meters dash. His personal best in the 100 meters was 10.44. He came to Georgia as a *Parade Magazine* All-American and the number one rated running back in the nation. He would become an all-star running back at Georgia.

He began his collegiate career in 1985, rushing for 627-yards, while leading the team with ten touchdowns. That same season, during the World's Largest Outdoor Cocktail Party, he scored an 89-yard touchdown run against number one ranked Florida's top rated defense. He finished with 125-yards rushing to spearhead Georgia's 24-3 dismantling of the Gators.

Unfortunately, Worley's sophomore season ended prematurely because of a torn anterior cruciate ligament. The injury was so severe he needed almost two years for rehabilitation, forcing him to sit out all of the 1986 and '87 seasons. He became academically ineligible during that time, and worked hard at a junior college to restore his grade point average, and his eligibility.

Timothy Worley, 1985

In 1988, Worley re-emerged with his focus balanced on both the books and the football field. He led Georgia in rushing with 1,216 yards. He was selected as first-team All-American by Kodak, the Walter Camp Football Foundation, and the Football Writers Association of America. The *United Press International* named him its Southeastern Conference Offensive Player of the Year. He finished his career at Georgia with 2,038 rushing yards, 27 touchdowns, averaging 5.8 yards per carry. Georgia went 18-5 inside of Sanford Stadium during his four year career.

Benjamin Ray Zambiasi, Linebacker, 1974-1977

The legend was born on August 19, 1956, in Valdosta, Georgia. His high school career was spent at Mount DeSales, in Macon, and in Germany. He spent his junior year in Germany, while his father was stationed there with the military. With his seemingly natural football instinct, most observers would argue Zambiasi was always destined to play the sport. But such wasn't necessarily the case with the Mount De Sales High School star.

"I actually had very little desire to play college ball my freshmen and sophomore years in high school," stated Zambiasi. "However, the more experience I got, the more I started enjoying playing and I realized the game wasn't as tough as I thought."

Because of his size, only a few major colleges showed any recruiting interest in Zambiasi. He did, however, by-pass Georgia Tech in signing with Georgia. "I came to Georgia because I felt they had the best facilities in the South," he added.

He was a 200-pound linebacker and lettered as a freshman. He played in four freshmen games for the Bullpups, but it did not take Georgia coaches too long to realize his varsity potential.

Being a firm believer in the defense, Zambiasi pointed to the difference in defensive squads from 1975 to 1976. "We know we're small, but we make up for it with a lot of hustle," he said.

He carried his freshmen talents and abilities into Georgia's opening game against Pittsburgh and came within one tackle of tying the school record for most tackles in a single game. His 12 unassisted tackles and 11 assists were just short of the record held by his linebacker coach, Chip Wisdom. He was complemented by Pittsburgh's Heisman Trophy winner Tony Dorsett when he stated, "The Georgia defense was pretty good, and that left side (Zambiasi) were really hitting hard!"

He ended his career at Georgia with 467 career tackles tackling, 173 of those tackles coming in 1977. Georgia went 18-6 between the hedges during Zambiasi's four year career.

Eric Royce Zeier, Quarterback, 1991-1994

Zeier was born on September 6, 1972, in Pensacola, Florida. He was a military brat who started his football career at Heidelberg American High School in Germany. In the fall of 1988, he led the team to a championship. Later, in 1990, his family moved to Marietta, Georgia. There, he played football for Marietta High School. He emerged into an All-State performer, who garnered several scholarship offers from institutions around the southeast.

In 1991, he signed a scholarship with Georgia, and made his debut against Clemson on October 5, 1991. The Bulldogs won the game 27-12. Zeier went on to start the final seven games of his freshman season and started every game during his final three years with Georgia.

He was one of most prolific quarterbacks in Georgia football history. After quarterbacking Georgia to a combined 19-5 record in 1991 and '92, Zeier's numbers soared as a junior and senior; however, Georgia's one dimensional offenses culminated in terrible seasons. While passing for a combined 48 touchdowns and nearly 7,000 yards in '93 and '94, the Bulldogs went 11-10-1. Yet, Zeier finished in the top-10 of the Heisman Trophy balloting, twice.

He set 67 school records and 18 Southeastern Conference (SEC) records. In 1994, he became the most productive passer in the history of the SEC, and only the third quarterback in NCAA Division I history to throw for more than 11,000 yards in his career. He earned All-Academic honors in 1992 and 1993 and was selected as Georgia's team captain in 1993 and 1994. And more importantly, he had a 4-0 record against Georgia Tech. His record as a starter was 26-14-1, and 18-6 inside Sanford Stadium.

Faceless Five, Georgia, 1980
The front five offensive linemen from the 1980 national title team, Jeff Harper, Tim Morrison, Jim Blakewood, Wayne Radloff, and Nat Hudson, were responsible for getting off the ball and opening cracks for its backfield. These warriors, who Coach Dooley once said, "If I ever had to go to war, those are who I'd want to be in a foxhole with," led the way. They were known as the "Faceless Five," because they hustled namelessly, generating running room for their running backs, including Herschel Walker, whose 1,616 rushing yards broke the NCAA freshman record of 1,586, set by Tony Dorsett in 1973.

Jim Blakewood was an offensive tackle who stood 6'-3" and weighed 235 pounds. He was a top recruit out of Benedictine High School, in Savannah. Coincidentally, Benedictine High School had the most representatives, six, on both Georgia and Notre Dame's teams during the January 1, 1981 Sugar Bowl. He was a regular starter for Georgia and one of the greatest linemen in Bulldog history.

Wayne Radloff 6'-5" and 260 pounds, spent the first ten years of his life in England, where his father was stationed in the United States Air Force. After his daddy retired, they moved to Winter Park, Florida. Besides playing football, Radloff had been a decathlete on the track team at Winter Park High School.

After signing a scholarship with Georgia, he arrived in Athens in the late summer of 1979. He was a behemoth 6-foot-5, 210-pound lineman, yet, he was quick enough to line-up as a fullback. Georgia's weight training program helped add more than 60 pounds, without sacrificing any speed. He had been timed at 4.75 seconds for the 40-yard dash.

Jeff Harper was born on October 27, 1957, in Macon, Georgia. He attended Monroe Academy, and was a three year starter, and an All-State selection. In 1976, he started out playing for the University of Alabama, but transferred to Georgia in 1977. He was an All-Southeastern Conference selection and helped anchor the Georgia offensive line. Harper was immortalized in statue form as one of the two players who carried Coach Dooley off the field after winning the 1980 national championship.

Nathaniel Lamar Hudson was born on October 11, 1957, in Rome, Georgia. The 6'-3", 265 pound Rome native was a preseason All-Southeastern Conference pick by several football magazines. He would open-up gaping holes during the season, and threw a critical block that allowed Buck Belue to toss the 93-yard game winning touchdown pass to Lindsay Scott to beat Florida. He would be selected 139th overall, by the New Orleans Saints, in the 1981 National Football League (NFL) draft.

Tim Morrison was born on December 10, 1958, in Boaz, Alabama. He was a four year letterman at Suwannee High School in Georgia. During his freshman season, he started several games. In 1980, he was voted, by the Bulldog coaching staff, as the "Meanest Mother in the Trenches." He was a mainstay on the offensive line during Georgia's march to the national title.

The 1996 Centennial Olympiad Games

Sanford Stadium played host to the medal competition of men's and women's soccer during the 1996 Summer Olympics. Unfortunately, the required measurements of a soccer field are wider than those of an American football field, and as a result, the hedges surrounding the field were removed. And, to add insult to injury, two international soccer groups complained the field's one-inch-tall rain-draining crown was against Olympic soccer rules.

The Broad of Regents approved a three million dollar contract that allowed the Atlanta Committee for the Olympic Games (ACOG) to hold Olympic soccer inside of Sanford Stadium. The contract stipulated the ACOG would pay the University approximately $1.2 million to level Sanford Stadium's playing field, and to later make the field suitable for football after the Olympic games were completed.

In planning for this necessity, involving the removal of the hedges, cuttings were taken from the original hedges, three years prior to the Olympics, and cultivated at a secret, off-campus site. It was later learned this "secret site" was seventy miles away, at R.A. Dudley Nurseries in Thomson, Georgia.

Sanford Stadium underwent an extraordinary conversion from home of American college football to the host for "world" football. The site and setting were touted as one of the greatest hosts for soccer anywhere in the world as Sanford Stadium greeted teams, and fans, from every continent.

Many Georgia fans believed it sacrilegious for any other sport, besides college football, to be played inside of Sanford Stadium. And, there were indisputably those who believed removing the sacred hedges surrounding the field was blasphemy. However, regardless of a person's opinion, the Centennial Olympic Games of 1996 added an historic chapter to the chronicles of Sanford Stadium.

During these 1996 Atlanta Olympics, women's soccer made its first appearance. And, despite it being the arrival of women's soccer into the Games, the U.S. Olympic Team battled in front of record-breaking crowds.

The six days of games, in hedge-less Sanford Stadium, featured a sold-out men's gold medal game as Nigeria upset

Argentina, 3-2, before a sellout crowd of 86,117. The United States team won the first Olympic women's soccer gold medal with a sensational 2-1 triumph over China, before the largest crowd ever to see a women's soccer game—76,481.

On August 1, 1996, at the gold-medal game, over 76,000 supporters gathered inside of Sanford Stadium to watch the United States and China go head to head. It was the largest crowd in the world to ever attend a female sporting event. At the end of regulation, Shannon MacMillan and Tiffany Milbrett, of the US Olympic soccer team, scored the two goals to defeat China 2-1.

The trek to Olympic gold began with a total of eight teams. In the primary round, each team participated in three games. Afterward, two games were played in contention for a medal. Ties were possible only in the primary round games; however, penalty-kick shootouts decided games in the subsequent rounds.

Each team consisted of sixteen players who took part in the competition, and the 1996 USA Team was comprised of Michelle Akers, Brandi Chastain, Joy Fawcett, Julie Foudy, Carin Gabarra, Mia Hamm, Mary Harvey, Kristine Lilly, MacMillan, Milbrett, Carla Overbeck, Cindy Parlow, Tiffany Roberts, Briana Scurry, Tisha Venturini and Staci Wilson.

Even though there were tens of thousands of fans present during all of their games, and being on the track towards winning Olympic gold, the USA's women's soccer team was never afforded any live coverage during the entirety of the 1996 Games. Team members were upset by this insult, and felt their star-spangled performances were being disregarded and undermined.

The 1996 U.S. Olympic Team had been together throughout the '90s, and the bonds developed helped the sixteen team members to play flawlessly with one another. The players secured their places in history by joining together to accomplish an miraculous moment: being the first team to win a gold medal in the women's soccer event.

However, after the Americans played to a 0-0 draw against China, a team the USA had beaten 2-0 during the third-place match at the World Cup, meant the U.S. finished second in their group, because of goal differences, and had to face a very powerful Norway in the semi-finals.

Inside of Sanford Stadium, the Americans met Norway in a match of incredibly high tension. After eighteen minutes into the game, Team USA fell behind; however, after an Akers' penalty, they eventually fought to tie it up with less than fourteen minutes before the end of regulation.

The match ended in a 1-1 tie, and went into sudden death overtime. After only ten minutes into overtime, MacMillan scored the decisive goal to secure a return to Sanford Stadium three days later. Her goal put Team USA into the gold medal match against China, one of the most dominant women soccer teams of the era.

During the decisive gold medal match, in front of nearly 77,000 fans, MacMillan would again emerge as the heroine. Nineteen minutes into the match a Hamm shot rebounded off the post, and MacMillan seized the loose ball, and opened the scoring. Next, after thirty-two minutes into the match, the Chinese tied-up the game, and continued to keep an enormous amount of pressure on Team USA. Finally, Milbrett put the U.S. ahead, again, with twenty-two minutes remaining in the match.

Foudy, the unsung hero, shepherded her team successfully through some very anxious moments. When the match finally climaxed, Team USA had won Olympic gold with a 2-1 victory over mighty China. A global television audience saw at least portions of the nonstop action.

With approximately twenty-two minutes remaining in the match, the crucial play occurred. Hamm, a graduate of Lake Braddock High School, in Burke, Virginia, passed down the right side to Fawcett, who eluded defender Xie Huilin and glided a flawless centering pass to Milbrett, who had barely beaten the defender, Liping Wang, to the front of the net. China's goalkeeper, Gao Hong, had no opportunity, diving unsuccessfully to her right with Milbrett's shot already well past her and into the net. The bellow that went up reverberated throughout Sanford Stadium.

The U.S. players closed out the most historic women's soccer game ever played by carrying and waving American flags as they circumnavigated the picture-perfect grass field. It was an historic victory commemoration they would by no means ever forget. The uppermost Olympic and international soccer officials paid homage to the smiling Americans during the medal ceremonies that completed the hard-played, dynamic struggle.

The first goal was an incredible shot. MacMillan, who had scored the winning goal against Norway, gave the Team USA an early lead, after she followed-up a shot made by Hamm that hit the post. Kristine Lilly—who played for the Washington Warthogs, a men's professional indoor team—had kicked a crossing pass from the left side. Then, Hamm fired hard; however, the ball recoiled off of Gao's hands, before walloping the right post and bouncing in front to an unguarded MacMillan.

A charged-up MacMillan had been blocked-in close during the twentieth minute, as the U.S. team dominated for the first 23 minutes. But Team USA appeared to tire after that, and the mighty Chinese took control for the remainder of the first half. Liu Ying broke through in the 24th minute, but was shut-off at the last moment by three American defenders. That was a hint that China's offense had been roused.

Milbrett slowed the Chinese, momentarily, by dribbling half the length of the field in the twenty-ninth minute, passing precisely to Hamm, who continued dribbling through traffic before the Chinese recaptured control. Three minutes later, China tied the score. And in an unforgettable example of the hodgepodge of Olympic action, the Chinese had scored just as Michael Johnson was setting his 200-meter world record at Atlanta's Olympic Stadium.

A resounding shout of approval resonated amongst the overwhelming majority of American fans inside of Sanford Stadium, who had been watching Johnson's race on the Jumbotron. The cheering had created the peculiarity of an optimistic response from American fans as the Chinese were attacking with vengeance. The goal came as Sun Wen gently lifted the ball over the head of goalkeeper Scurry, who was coming out to meet her. Chastain tried to catch-up with the slow-rolling ball, but was unable to knock the ball off course.

So, the applause for Johnson rapidly turned into a groan for the U.S. soccer team. China kept up its pressure in the second half. Fifteen minutes into the second half, Scurry had to come out headlong in order to stop a shot by the Chinese's Sun Qingmei, who had busted loose down the middle. But the Americans salvaged their early-game stride, with Hamm's push in the 62nd minute, after she dribbled around Gao, only to be denied by Xie.

But, Team USA had brilliantly, and decisively, kept the action in front of Gao with three more strong forays that China's defenders were hard-pressed to contain. Finally, China's fortress failed as the U.S. soccer team traversed the winning cascade of kicks from Hamm to Fawcett to Milbrett.

In the final moments, Hamm, who had been hampered the week prior to the game with a sore left ankle, was carried from the field on a stretcher. Her hard work was rewarded moments later as another incredibly huge cheer erupted. The game had ended. Hamm made it slowly on to the field, with a few teammates surrounding her, as the others charged past to celebrate an Olympic gold medal victory in 1996.

Once the Olympics were finalized, the newly developed hedges were relocated from Dudley Nursery, back to their home inside of Sanford Stadium. The University made no money from the Olympics because it was not a profit-making adventure for the University. However, the University of Georgia told the United States Soccer Federation it would not be interested in holding a possible World Cup match if the Team USA got the nod.

1996 Olympiads, Sanford Stadium

Thirteen Who Made Supreme Sacrifice

They shall grow not old, as we that are left grow old:
Age shall not weary them, nor the years condemn.
At the going down of the sun and in the morning
We will remember them.
                    Laurence Binyon, September 27, 1914

There are a host of American heroes to whom our country owes a great responsibility and gratitude, to which we won't ever be able to repay. They are, as Sir Winston Churchill so precisely titled them, *"our honored dead."*

During all of America's conflicts, the University of Georgia has had former students, and faculty members, who have made the supreme sacrifice for our country. The flowing thirteen Georgia Bulldogs, who helped sanctify the grounds of Sanford Stadium during their playing careers, paid the ultimate price for America.

Will Burt, 1940-1941

Originally from Macon, Georgia, Burt was a highly sought after high school recruit from Macon High School. He signed a scholarship with Georgia in 1938. Through hard work and diligence, he emerged into one of the finest lineman of his era.

In 1938, he was awarded his letterman jacket by Coach Hollis. He played guard for Georgia and his dominating play opened-up gaping holes for Frank Sinkwich as the 'Dogs won the 1942 Orange Bowl against Texas Christian University. In addition to be an outstanding lineman for the football team, he was a powerful pitcher for Georgia's baseball team, where he won six games for the Diamond 'Dogs.

Shortly after Pearl Harbor, Burt joined the military. While performing flight duties, as an Army bombardier, his aircraft was shot down by German aircraft over the skies of Italy.

Jackson Elliot "Jack" Cox, 1959-1961

Cox, born on August 15, 1941, was from Waynesboro, Georgia. He was an All-State quarterback for Waynesboro High School, and signed a scholarship with Georgia in 1958. While at

Georgia, he played quarterback and was a Rhodes Scholar. He earned two gridiron letters for the Georgia Bulldogs, and was a member of the 1959 Southeastern Conference Champions.

After graduating college, he joined the Marine Corps. In 1967, he was shipped off to Vietnam after his unit from the Marine Corps Reserves were activated. Those who fought beside Cox noted the high degree of bravery and valor he demonstrated while engaged in direct combat action. Cox was killed by an explosion on March 25, 1967, on the hostile terrain of Quan Tri.

Sergeant Dale Spellman, who served with Cox in Delta Company, 1st Battalion, 4th Marine regiment, offered the subsequent homage on Cox's commemorative page: "Lieutenant Cox was a friend and a good platoon commander during my time with him. We shared the same fighting hole in the ambush of September 16 through September 19, 1966. I rotated back to the states in October 1966, so I was not with him the day he was called to the Lord. Lieutenant Cox was a fine man who loved Georgia football."

Samuel P. Eskew, 1968-1971
Eskew was a high school standout from Greenville, South Carolina, who signed a scholarship with the University of Georgia in 1967. Later, he played on Coach Dooley's 1968 Southeastern Conference Championship team. He lettered during the 1969 and '70 seasons, and graduated from Georgia in 1972.

After college he joined the United States Air Force, as a C-130 cargo pilot. On November 30, 1978, he and his crewmen were aboard the four-engine turboprop when they were all killed in a mishap. A bolt of lightning sent the Air Force C-130 Hercules cargo plane hurtling towards the earth during a very violent thunderstorm. They were 25 miles northwest of Charleston, South Carolina.

A spokesman for Charleston Air Force Base related the pilot, Captain Eskew, "reported a lightning strike, and an in-flight emergency was declared, then the aircraft disappeared from radar screens." The aircraft was on a routine training flight to Charleston from Pope Air Force Base, outside of Fayetteville, North Carolina. Part of a torn parachute was found in a tree near the remains of the plane. Officials at Pope identified those aboard the C-130 as: Captain Samuel P. Eskew, the pilot from Greenville, South Carolina; Co-Pilot Captain Mark D. Greer, of Kewadin, Michigan; Navigator

First Lieutenant Daniel K. Morris, of El Monte, California; and Staff Sergeant Bernie C. Finch, a flight engineer from Kingsville, Texas.

The crew had recently been involved in the movement of troops and equipment to and from Jonestown, Guyana, where the Peoples Temple cult members committed mass suicide November 18, 1978.

Winfred S. Goodman, 1939-1941

Goodman, who hailed from Atlanta, was a three sport athlete in baseball, football, and track. He signed a scholarship with Georgia in 1938, and would letter on three Bulldog football squads, beginning in 1939 and culminating with the Orange Bowl team of 1941. He started two seasons on the offensive line and his teammates included Howard Johnson, James Skipworth and Walter Ruark. Like the aforesaid, Goodman went on to serve with distinction in World War II.

On January 24, 1944, he had been reported missing in action after leading his Fourth Emergency Air/Sea Rescue Squadron during the re-capture of the Philippines.

Winston Hodgson, 1937-1940

Hodgson was an outstanding high school athlete who signed a scholarship with Georgia in 1937. At Georgia, he was a superior lineman for Georgia's Bullpups, where he distinguished himself for his courage on the field. In 1938, he was a first-string guard on Georgia's varsity football team. He graduated from Georgia in 1941 and joined the United States Marine Corps shortly after the United States entered into World War II.

In 1942, he was scheduled to attend a farewell ceremony at Sanford Stadium, during Georgia's clash with South Carolina; however, he suffered a fluke shooting accident and couldn't attend.

During one of the final battles of World War II, on May 30, 1945, he led his platoon into battle while on Okinawa. His squad was positioned at the foot of a mountain, as it prepared to attack the Japanese soldiers. His last words were, "I'm going up to the cave to toss a grenade into it, and I don't want any of you following me until I give you the 'all clear' signal."

Unbeknownst to Hodgson, the cavern contained the largest supply of ammunition on the island. Hodgson's grenade caused a tremendous explosion that sheared the tip of the mountain, and the concussion instantly killed him and the enemy troops inside.

Howard "Smiley" Johnson, 1937-1939

Johnson was born in Clarkesville, Tennessee. In high school, he was a superior athlete, who exceled in basketball, baseball, boxing and football. In 1937, he was 5-foot-10 and weighed 160 pounds upon signing a scholarship with Georgia. He was a guard during Coach Harry Mehre's final season.

In 1938, he played for Coach Joel Hunt, during Hunt's only season as head coach at Georgia. Then, in 1939, Coach Butts took over as head coach. Despite the instability within the coaching ranks, Johnson would letter for three seasons at Georgia. He graduated in '39, while serving as an alternate captain.

Johnson wasn't a quintessential hackneyed type football player. He played fullback and guard and was a force to be reckoned with on the field. He had a subterranean southern drawl and didn't drink, smoke, chew or swear. In fact, he was a very polite gentleman who read his Bible every night.

After graduation, he spent two seasons playing for the Green Bay Packers; however, he readily joined the Marine Corps in December 1941, soon after the attack on Pearl Harbor. Johnson was an exemplary Marine during training and was recognized for his leadership and can-do mindset.

He would eventually experience combat in the South Pacific, where he was awarded the Silver Star for bravery while engaged in fierce hand-to-hand combat with the Japanese during the Saipan Operation. Later, his weary unit would be deployed to Iwo Jima.

On February 19, 1945, while engaged in combat operations on Iwo Jima, with the 4th Marine Division, he was killed by shell fragments. Four days later, the Marines raised the U.S. flag atop Mt. Suribachi. Johnson would be posthumously awarded the Gold Star.

The 4th Marine Division suffered 9,098 casualties during the six week operation of taking Iwo Jima. Approximately 1,462 were killed-in-action, and nearly 350 died of injuries sustained during the heavy fighting. Johnson was buried in the division's cemetery, and awarded his second Silver Star, consisting of a gold star "cluster."

In 1949, Johnson's skeleton, along with other Iwo Jima Marines, were removed from the division's cemetery and re-interred in the National Memorial Cemetery of the Pacific close to Honolulu. When his division returned to Maui, they named the new baseball and football field, "Smiley Johnson Field," in his honor. In 1968, George Crumbly, executive director of the Peach Bowl, announced the "Smiley Johnson Award" would go to the game's most valuable defensive player.

Howard "Smiley" Johnson, 1945

Johnson set no records on the football field; however, his name appears on the War Memorial at the University of Georgia campus. Additionally, Johnson's name is in the Packers Hall of Fame at Lambeau Field. In fact, Johnson remains the only player in the history of the Packers who was killed in combat.

Marcus "Lee" Lenderman, 1969-1972

Lenderman was born in Chattanooga, Tennessee. He attended Chattanooga High School where he was an outstanding multi-sport athlete. He set numerous school records, receiving many awards for superior athletic performance, and was recognized for his leadership.

In December 1968, after being recruited by several Southeastern Conference schools, he elected to sign a scholarship with Coach Vince Dooley and the University of Georgia. In 1975, he graduated with honors from Georgia's Terry College of Business. Afterwards, he joined the United States Marine Corps.

Lenderman was a highly decorated and very well respected Marine helicopter pilot, who rose to the rank of Lieutenant Colonel, and earned numerous commendation and service medals for his service before self. In 1993, while on a night time live ammunition training flight, he was killed when his helicopter crashed in the California desert.

Homer Passmore, 1939-1940

Passmore was born in Valdosta, Georgia. At 6'-0" and 170 pounds, he was an excellent high school football and baseball player for Coach Bobby Hooks at Valdosta High School. He signed a grant-in-aid to attend Georgia in December 1938. He was primarily used as a blocking back for the Bulldogs, and was one of the forty-three members of the 1939 "Point-a-Minute" Bullpups football team. He would earn a letter in 1939 and '40.

Passmore had once been recognized in the student newspaper, *Red and Black,* for an ingenious contrivance he built inside of his dorm room. He innovatively fixed his alarm clock so it could be set to turn-on the lights and radio in the morning, while turning-off the lights at night.

He joined the Army-Air Crops shortly after the start of America's involvement in World War II. He was a decorated pilot, who participated in Operation Overlord, a.k.a. the invasion of Normandy. In October 1944, several weeks after the Normandy offensive, he was killed after being shot down over France, while piloting his B-17 Flying Fortress.

Henry Walter Ruark, 1940-1942

Ruark was born in Bostwick, Georgia. In high school he was an outstanding athlete in both football and baseball. In 1939, he signed a scholarship to attend Georgia, during Coach Wallace Butts first season as head coach. After playing one season with the Bullpups, he made the varsity and would letter three years. He was a two-time All-Southeastern Conference guard on the football team.

In 1941, he lettered in baseball, and in 1942, his career culminated with the 'Dogs winning the national championship.

He was an underrated player, who never took a play off. Ruark established himself a superior athlete, and had a decent chance of playing professional football. Four professional football teams, and one baseball team, wanted to sign him. In truth, Ruark had already signed a deal to play for the Cleveland Rams football team at the end of World War II. He graduated from Georgia on June 11, 1943, with a degree in Education.

In August of 1944, Ruark, who was an alternate captain on the 1942 Rose Bowl team, was selected to play in the All-Star game in Chicago, along with fellow teammates Kenneth Keuper, Van Davis, and Charlie Trippi. Throughout the game he was a mainstay for the line and constantly demonstrated commendable ability, regularly batting down passes, and tackling quarterbacks.

Later that year, on November 22, 1944, while serving with the Army's 47th Infantry Regiment, U.S. Ninth Infantry Division, Sergeant Ruark led a five-man patrol up the Roer River, in Belgium, to destroy a German sniper position in a stone house. He was shot in the chest and would be posthumously awarded his second Purple Heart, and the Silver Star. He was laid to rest at the Henri-Chappelle American Cemetery in Belgium.

Robert G. Salisbury, 1937-1939

Salisbury, from Ocoee, Florida, had one of the most comprehensive athletic resumes in the University of Georgia sports' history, where he lettered in boxing, baseball, football and track. In 1937, Salisbury earned his first letter, lining-up in the same backfield as Bill Hartman. He earned a letter in baseball the following season, while earning a boxing letter as part of the same stable of fighters that included Mangle Burg. After earning a final letter in football in the fall of '39, Salisbury added a track award in the spring of 1940, where he won the Southeastern Conference javelin title.

Salisbury served in the Army Air Corp, rising to the rank of Major. In 1952, after serving with distinction during the entire duration of World War II, he became the only Georgia letterman to be killed in action during the Korea conflict.

James Turner Skipworth, Jr., 1939-1940

Skipworth was born in Columbus, Georgia, where he was a star athlete in football, baseball and basketball. In 1938, he signed a scholarship with Joel Hunt's University of Georgia. He would emerge as the captain of Georgia's 1940 football team, and became an all-star player for the football, basketball and baseball teams.

Skipworth played end for the Bulldogs in 1939-40, spending one season as a teammate to Howard Johnson. After a stellar season, he received an offer to play professional football for the New York Giants. After two years in the pros, he joined the United States Army.

In October 1944, his unit participated in the fierce ten month Philippines campaign under Allied Commander Douglas MacArthur. In January 1945, after several months of sea battles, fighting off kamikaze attacks, and heavy artillery assaults, his regiment finally reached Manila and the main island of Luzon. Skipworth was killed while directing firing orders for members of the 6th Division, 1st Infantry Regiment, at Luzon. After his death, he was posthumously awarded the Silver Star for gallantry.

Louis Sutera, Jr., 1964-1965

He was one of eight children who were adopted by Louis Sutera, Sr., a milkman from Miami Beach, Florida, and his wife Ruby Sutera. The kids were from five sets of parents, and all were of different nationalities.

Sutera attended Palmetto High School, in Miami. At 6'-2" and 230 pounds, he was an All-City fullback, who was highly recruited during his senior season with the Panthers of Palmetto High School. In 1963, he eventually signed a scholarship with the University of Georgia. He played tackle, not one of the glory positions like fullback; however, Sutera toiled vigorously in the trenches, while others reaped the praise.

He lettered on Coach Dooley's first two Georgia teams of 1964 and 1965. In 1966, after a stellar career with the Bulldogs, Sutera enlisted in the United States Army before the draft had an opportunity to call him. He was one of only a few Georgia alumni who served in the enlisted ranks. He earned the rank of sergeant while serving as a forward observer doing reconnaissance work.

In February 1967, he deployed to Vietnam with the famed Hawaiian-based 25th Infantry Division, a.k.a. "Tropic Lightning." In 1967, on the day before New Year's Eve, Sutera sustained injuries from sniper fire, near Hua Nghia, and was killed. His name is listed on Panel 33E, Line 5 of the Vietnam Wall.

Tommy Witt, 1938-1940

Witt was born in Louisville, Kentucky. In high school he played for Coach Wallace Butts at Male High School, in Louisville, Kentucky. In 1938, he was highly recruited before finally signing a scholarship with Coach Joel Hunt of the University of Georgia. While with the Bulldogs, he played two seasons at center.

In 1938, at only 180 pounds, Witt was captain of the Bullpups, and one of the best all-around long snappers to ever play for Georgia. Against Florida that season, he played the entire game as the Bullpups triumphed 13-0. He was awarded his letterman's jacket by Coach Hollis at the end of the season.

In 1941, he joined the Army-Air-Corps. After training, he was assigned to the Ninth Air Force. On October 24, 1942, during the North African invasion, he was killed in action after his B-25 was shot down on a bombing mission. He died from wounds received after he attempted to land his aircraft. He received the Distinguished Flying Cross and the Purple Heart. His wife, Mary Frances Witt, received the medals at a ceremony at Fort McClellan.

The citation awarding him the Distinguished Flying Cross, said: "While participating on a combat mission, the aircraft of which he was pilot was badly damaged by enemy fire. Upon his return to the base, he discovered that the hydraulic system had been damaged and it was impossible to lower the landing gear.

"Rather than abandon his aircraft, Lieutenant Witt brought it into the field with a normal landing approach. As he neared the ground, he deliberately drove the wheels against the earth, jarring the gear into the fully-extended and locked position. He made a successful landing."

Three hours after this feat, Witt, a medium bomber, was killed on another mission. The October 31, 1942 Georgia versus Alabama game, played in Atlanta on Halloween, was in his memory.

Sanford Stadium Bulldog Coronation

Contrary to popular belief, the English bulldog was not the original mascot of the University of Georgia, nor was Uga the original bulldog for the school. The original mascot was a goat; however, there has been some misconception about exactly how many goats there were.

One legend says the first goat belonged to Chief Connolly, who auctioned off the goat after Georgia lost to Auburn in 1892. The goat was purchased by West Calhoun, and from there, its whereabouts are unknown; however, there is one other story claiming the first mascot for the University of Georgia, a goat, belonged to Bob Gantt, who was a student at Georgia.

An *Athens Banner* newspaper article, circa 1902, related Gantt dressed his goat in red and black, and brought him to the first game played on January 30, 1892, against Mercer. The article concluded by stating in 1893, after 10 long years of college, Gantt would graduate and take his goat with him.

Afterwards, chaos ensured as Georgia would have several different mascots appearing on its sidelines over the next two decades. Regrettably, at one time, Georgia had occasionally been referred to as "wildcats;" however, there are no records of any cats ever appearing on its sidelines.

In 1894, the first dog would appear on Georgia's sidelines. Charles Black, of Atlanta, would bring his white bull terrier, Trilby, to most of the home games. In fact, for several years Trilby had been kept at the Chi Phi fraternity, off Milledge Avenue.

However, on November 28, 1901, the first mention of "bulldogs," in association with Georgia athletics, occurred almost seven years after Trilby made his first appearance on the sidelines. Per a newspaper article from the *Atlanta Journal Constitution*, there were an abundance of Georgia fans who attended the Georgia versus Auburn game, played in Atlanta, who wore badges saying "Eat'em Georgia" with a picture of a bulldog tearing a piece of cloth. However, it was not until 1920, in a game against Virginia, the nickname "bulldog" was used to describe the athletic teams at the University of Georgia.

Traditionally, the choice of a bulldog, as the Georgia mascot, was attributed to the alma mater of its founder and first president,

Abraham Baldwin, who graduated from Yale University in 1772. Prior to that time, Georgia teams were known as the "Red and Black."

F. J. Ball, an Athens photographer, was the originator of the proposal to use the bulldog as a mascot, as nearly as could be learned, and gave 1904 as the date in which the adoption took place. However, the date of the adoption of bulldog was estimated to be as early as 1890 by some, but as late as 1920 by others.

On November 3, 1920, Morgan Blake, of the *Atlanta Journal Constitution*, wrote a story about school nicknames and proposed using the moniker "bulldogs" for Georgia. He justified it by stating there was a certain dignity about a bulldog, as well as ferocity.

Per legend, on November 6, 1920, while the football team was enroute to a game in Charlottesville, Virginia, for a game with the University of Virginia, the "bulldog" was officially approved as the school's mascot. The players were in a Pullman-car, and a caucus of athletes, along with the Athletic Director Doctor S. V. Sanford, decided on the "bulldog."

The game with Virginia ended in a 0-0 tie, and an article in the *Atlanta Journal Constitution*, written by Cliff Wheatley, on November 7, 1920, sub-headed, "They're Bulldogs Now!" The moniker "bulldogs" was used five times in his story. And, the name has been used ever since.

On November 20, 1920, after Georgia defeated Alabama, the players voted their final approval for the bulldog as their mascot. "Crimson Tide has ebbed into the West, and the Georgia Bulldogs struts unconquered among his native hills," Blake wrote of the 21-14 conquest.

Yet, it wasn't until November 27, 1938, that Georgia would, for the first time in its history, have an official mascot when the football team took the field for Homecoming against Georgia Tech. Research by a *Red and Black* reporter, in 1937, revealed the "bulldog," used as a mascot by the University teams for many years, had been officially approved, but had never been officially crowned.

Administration and athletic officials voiced their wholehearted approval and support of the plan to hold the coronation for a live bulldog, while the band strutted between halves. Professor W. O. Payne, director of athletic, Coach H.J. Stegeman, L. L.

Henderson, dean of administration, and William Tate, dean of freshmen, were especially enthusiastic over these plans of adopting the bulldog to parade in front of the band before all games.

An official coronation ceremony, where the bulldog was crowned as the sanctioned mascot of the University, was held in Sanford Stadium, just prior to kick-off. Wilson Still, of Monroe, campus leader, and Claude Davidson, of LaGrange, editor of *The Red and Black*, were in charge of arrangements for the crowning. The crowd at Sanford Stadium watched the festivities just prior to Georgia's last home football game of the season, as the "bulldog" was officially crowned mascot of the University's ferocious eleven.

A decorated float, draped in red and black, was escorted through town and brought upon the field before kickoff of the Tech game on November 27, 1938. A scroll was presented to President Harmon W. Caldwell, petitioning the canine's official recognition "on this, the start of the eighteenth year since the Georgia football team approved the bulldog as their mascot."

Then, while standing in the middle of the field, Dean Tate stated, "I was a freshman when they first decided to adopt the Bulldog. Most of the present generation doesn't know that our mascot hasn't been the Bulldog since time immemorial....." After Dean Tate's speech, which only lasted five minutes, the crowd enthusiastically applauded and the ceremony was concluded.

The bulldog crowned on that fateful day was the same bulldog which had been on the field at previous Georgia games during the 1938 season. He belonged to Buck Elton, of Atlanta. He would serve for several years before being replaced.

The renowned Quinton Lumpkin, captain of that 1938 football team, said, "...the presence of the live animal improved the fighting spirit of my team, and the caged beast is an attraction for visitors to our campus." Lumpkin further related Georgia's football team had an unrecognized mascot in 1936, which was paraded at some of the games. "The boys thought so much of it that they let the bulldog eat in the Beanery, so we were not allowed to keep him," Lumpkin laughed

In 1942, another bulldog, Bozo, took over the mascot duties. "Battling Bozo," the Bulldog canine mascot registered in pedigreed circles as "Marvin Spido Prosperity," resided in Athens, where his owner, "Red" Barnet, U.S.N., was stationed. Bozo had been to

Howard University, in Birmingham and to the University of Alabama, so he wasn't a freshman at Georgia. In fact, he was an extremely well-educated dog.

The initial thought most had on seeing Bozo for the first time was to cut and run for their lives. Just as they would gather their legs for a flying start, Bozo would lie down and snore. Having reached the ripe old age of four, Bozo didn't caper about, but instead followed the line of least resistance. In his day; however, Bozo could have scared five lives out of the slickest cat in the Classic City.

The Battler was mascot for Howard University's Bulldogs and once issued an open challenge to the Mississippi State hound for mortal combat. Needless to say, the offer was declined.

Every now and then, life had pushed Bozo too close and he went out on a bender. He could naturally lap-up booze. His nastiest characteristic, however, was that of keeping the entire house awake with his loud, almost human-like snore. Probably the noise could be traced to his conspicuous shortage of nose. Bozo was the exact replica of the dog pictured on the school's sticker. He stayed at the Pi Kappa Phi sorority house, whose members had volunteered to keep Bozo.

In the mid-1940s, Bozo the Battler was eventually replaced by two bulldogs, Tuffy and Butch, who served with distinction for many very important football seasons. During this era, several other bulldogs would appear on the sidelines, including Mr. Angel, a white English bulldog, who was owned by Warren Coleman, of Eastman, Georgia. But, Tuffy and Butch were the most recognized mascots.

Sadly, on October 14, 1948, something went out of the lives of all true Georgians when one of the most fee-ro-shus of all bulldogs in captivity climbed those golden stairs. Tuffy, who had faithfully remained beside her bosom comrade through the thick and thin of numerous gridiron battles, pulled in her fangs, and lay still, leaving her side-kick, Butch, as the only remaining Bulldog mascot. In 1948, after a very intense game against Coach Bryant's Kentucky Wildcats, she passed away from a heart-attack.

It had certainly been quit a career for the little bulldog, ever since she and her brother first charged out on the field, having broken away from her owner, Mabry Smith, of Warner Robins, during the Georgia Tech game in 1946. She and Butch proceeded to chase Tech's notorious mascot, Sideways, off the field. After that altercation with Sideways, Georgia fans knew Tuffy and Butch were their new mascots, and mascotin' they did like mascotin' had never been done. First on the field, they were first to engage in combat—one with the other until one of the cheerleaders would separate them, and woe to the good brother who carelessly got a hand or foot too close while doing it.

Butch, 1947

They demanded and got top billing wherever they went. They were officially registered in the state as the Duke and Duchess of Georgia, and were right on hand when Georgia went to the Sugar Bowl, New Year's Day, 1947.

Her epitaph read, "Her life was never gentle, and the elements so mixed in her, that nature might stand up and say, "This was a Bulldog!"

Butch would eventually be relieved of duties by Mike. In 1953, equipment manager "Pap" Eberhardt assumed the duties of managing Mike. The duo of Pap and Mike were conceivably two of the staunchest supporters of the Georgia Bulldogs.

Fifteen years earlier, Pap came from Elberton to take over as the "keeper of the equipment." Besides being responsible for the equipment and seeing the team had the proper gear at all times, he would assume duties of caring for Mike.

Mike had been given to Coach Butts by a friend from Tennessee. Mike, who was three years old in 1955, lived at the field house. He had his own mattress, but liked the beds belonging to the five players who lived upstairs much better. Pap mentioned Mike liked dog food, and the T-bone steak bones from the training table of the players.

At each home game, Mike rode the bus to the stadium with the players and made his "debut" on the field before the referee would blow his whistle for action.

In 1954, one of the strangest things occurred to Pap at the Georgia-Clemson game in Sanford Stadium. There were only a few seconds remaining in the fourth quarter, so Pap decided to start walking with Mike along the sidelines to the bus. Before he knew it, he was hit by a Georgia and Clemson player, who were both falling out of bounds on a tackle. They weren't shaken up too bad, but Pap suffered a broken shoulder.

In 1955, when Mike died, Coach Butts asked the University of Georgia's Sports Information Director, Dan Magill, to keep an eye out for Mike's replacement for the upcoming season.

In November of 1955, Sonny Seiler married Cecelia Gunn. Later, they would receive a belated wedding present from Frank Heard. It was a solid white English bulldog, with bloodlines to Battling Bozo, who attended the January 1, 1943 Rose Bowl game.

They would name the bulldog Uga, after the name was recommended by family friend, Billy Young. In 1956, after dressing Uga in a red sweater with a "G" on the side, and taking him into the stands of the home opener against Florida State, Uga's photos made it to Magill, who briefed Coach Butts.

Uga, and his descendants, have attended every Georgia game since that auspicious day on September 29, 1956, when Georgia defeated a Lee Corso led Florida State team by a score of 3-0.

Uga I would later retire on October 22, 1966, just before kickoff against Kentucky. He handed over the reign to his son. Uga I would die and go to Bulldog Heaven on November 9, 1967. Athletic Director Joel Eaves made arrangements through Georgia's faculty adviser for athletics, Boyd McWhorter, to have Uga buried inside Sanford Stadium. Uga I was buried next to the Georgia dressing room, with a marble marker placed over his grave.

As of 2015, there have been a total of six Uga representatives, and five have been eulogized with the greatest of respect and sympathy. In fact, ministers have made remarks and the University presidents have all paid their tribute to Uga, as they would to any distinguished alumnus.

In 1981, the east endzone was closed-in and the graves of Uga I and II were moved to the west end of the stadium. Later, after the 1996 Olympics, an impressive wall of Georgia red marble housed the vaults of the deceased mascots. An epitaph is engraved on a bronze memorial plaque adorning each tomb. In 1992, a sculptor by Wyndell Taylor, of a bronze, life size statue, representing all of the mascots, was placed at the entrance to stand guard. The mausoleum is accessible to everyone.

In addition to the goats, bull terriers, and bulldogs, Georgia has a human mascot, too. On September 5, 1981, Hairy Dawg, the human mascot, was introduced when Georgia played Tennessee. He was the invention of Tom Sapp, a graphics design major, who designed the Dawg. He had been created in time to witness Georgia beat Notre Dame 17-10 in the Sugar Bowl, on January 1, 1981, but had to wait to be officially introduced to the fans. Hairy Dawg would become such an intricate part of the Bulldog Nation that rights were purchased by the University.

Additionally, in 1940, Sanford Stadium saw its first women cheerleaders, who took their place beside men cheerleaders, for the first time in its history, during the Ole Miss game. The decision of administrative authorities, to permit coeds to act as cheerleaders, came at the climax of a two-year campaign by *The Red and Black*.

Originally, the privilege of women cheerleaders had been officially granted only for the year 1940-41. In the spring quarter, a re-study of the question was made and continuance of the practice was granted. The one year "trial" was to show whether women cheerleaders could operate in a manner that would elicit the support of students, alumni, faculty and friends of the University.

The three original cheerleaders were selected by Dottie Bowen, Charlotte Adams, Florence Lee Callahan, Frank Gunn, Mrs. R.L. McWhorter Mary Ella Soule and Mr. Kenneth R. Williams.

The Stadium, Today and Tomorrow

In good weather or bad, on autumn Saturdays, millions of Americans all over the country swarm into stadiums to enjoy the fun and excitement of college football. Sanford Stadium is no exception, since most of its games have been sold out since the late 1990s. However, who knows how many people have attended or participated in football games, or other events, inside of Sanford Stadium over a span of almost nine decades? Counting every elementary, high school and college football game, the 1996 Olympics, frequent college graduation ceremonies, and a musical concert, 40 million might be a conservative estimate. And each person has their very own unique story to tell about their experience.

One thing is for sure, Sanford Stadium will be around for at least another century. An aged heirloom from some angles, and a shimmering gemstone from others, the stadium rests deep in the Tanyard basin, ready to serve the University of Georgia well into the 21st Century. In fact, for reasons of finances, campus space, and custom, Sanford Stadium will remain the epicenter of Bulldog athletics for the predictable future.

There will be no rhetoric of "build a new stadium" emanating from the offices of Butts-Mehre Heritage Hall. The stadium seems likely to reach its 100th birthday in 2029, because the Georgia Athletic Department, in agreement with the university's administration, is dedicated to preserving and positively enlarging it.

Considered an old stadium, it shouldn't be of any great surprise to learn it has a few cracks and crevices, and necessitates more attention than when it was newly constructed. Similar things could be said about essentially any other archaic collegiate athletic facility, like California's Memorial Stadium, built in 1920, Tennessee's Neyland Stadium, built in 1921, or Louisiana State University's Tiger Stadium, built in 1924.

All stadiums need continual maintenance, and, on occasion, modifications are necessary to meet changing requirements. Once a stadium descends too far behind, attempting to bring it up to date is challenging and extremely difficult—and very costly. Several institutions, Kentucky, Vanderbilt, and West Virginia, to name a few, built new stadiums during the 1970s and '80s. None of those stadiums cost over twenty-two million dollars. In fact the three stadiums were low-budget, considering professional stadiums such as the Cowboy's stadium in Dallas, or the Atlanta Falcon's stadium, cost over one billion dollars each. It definitely benefits any institution with a timeworn, but solid stadium, to supply the obligatory maintenance and alterations.

When a capacity crowd congregates inside of Sanford Stadium for a Georgia football game, not many people mull over its appearance or condition. However, the Georgia Athletic Department has occasionally heard expressions of concern, particularly after several small areas of concrete had been reported cracked.

In 1928, the draftsmen, engineers and laborers on Sanford Stadium did a truly superior job, considering its current condition is incredibly well maintained. In addition to superior craftsmanship, there are many other factors that can be attributed to its robust condition, specifically the temperate climate of north Georgia that has helped the stadium last longer than many other arenas constructed during the 1920s.

During the decade immediately after its construction, the majority of Sanford Stadium's upkeep was day-to-day work, or makeshift procedures not addressing its long-term needs. When Coach Butts became Georgia's head coach in 1939, he expressed his concern about the need to develop better maintenance for the stadium. The preventive maintenance implemented during his reign as head coach helped guarantee the structural integrity well into the twenty-first century.

A lot of events and numerous modifications have taken place in Sanford Stadium since The Page Wire Fence Company, the successful bidder of placing the fence around the stadium, with a figure of $5,044.00, built the fence in 1929. The fence, considered the first modification of the stadium, had been specially built as a link structure of seven feet high, with three strands of barbed wire on top. The contract, calling for the fence to be up by October 1, 1929, was honored. Since then, millions of dollars, involving modifications, have been pumped into the stadium.

In 1940, the first significant modification occurred when field-level lights were added. There were ten wooden light poles, interspersed in the hedges, five on each side of the field. Each pole had twelve lights: three rows of four lights. Georgia subsequently played its first night game against Kentucky on October 25, 1940. In 1941, Georgia played two more night games when the 'Dogs defeated South Carolina 34-6, and tied Ole Miss 14-14. Moreover, between 1943 through 1951, Georgia played nineteen games under the lights.

Then, in 1949, the first enlargement occurred, when approximately two thousand seats were added to the south side, to equal the capacity of the North side (18,000). Over thirty-six thousand spectators could now be seated in Sanford Stadium, which was equipped with an updated radio broadcast booth on the south side, and a glass-enclosed press box directly opposite.

During the early 1950s, over 2,000 concrete seats were added to each side of the press box on the south side. It brought the total capacity to 38,000, including bleacher seats behind the goal posts and above the north stands. That capacity remained enough for many years; however, as the student body continued to expand exponentially, the alumni ranks, along with the population of Athens, got larger, too.

By 1955, the Athletic Association's increasing activities, equipment and facilities, along with its sports program, had outstripped all other sections of the University in total development. New teams taking the field, along with those teams in the historic athletics, had proven beneficial to the institution, and afforded an opportunity for participation to over 400 student-athletes.

In late November of 1962, development director William E. Hudson, announced construction on the proposed $330,000 bridge to span the Stegeman Hall parking lot. He stated the project was planned to be completed and ready for traffic by September 1963. The bridge would connect Field Street, at the GCM Building, with Sanford Drive.

The plans called for the bridge to be thirty-six feet wide, containing three lanes for automobile traffic and approximately ten feet for pedestrian use. William J. Mathias, Director of Traffic, stated, "We expect to take a great deal of traffic off Lumpkin Street. Since it would be a more direct route for the pedestrian, as well as the driver, it would take less time between classes. Additionally, with the widening of Sanford Drive, to four lanes, to coincide with

Baxter Street, more traffic would be allowed to flow off campus in less time."

Unfortunately, the low point of the bridge ended-up very close to the historic flag staffs, just above the entrance into Sanford Stadium. The construction workers had to clip off some of the poles when construction commenced.

Then, in 1963, it was discovered bats were living under the stadium. A rare and endangered species of bat named Grey Bats, called the tunnels below Sanford Stadium its home, and biologist estimate several bat species have been there since the early 1930s. The Grey Bat, which have been reported in only two locations in Georgia, were reported to roost in the large pipes beneath the stadium, which transferred the waters of Tanyard Creek.

Flying into the tunnels to roost, the Grey Bat, among other species, often flew onto the pipes to rest. Since the mid-1960s, Georgia students, getting their degrees in zoology, have gone into the tunnels to study the bats.

These Grey Bats have a typical wingspan of 10 inches, and tip the scales at about 8 grams. It had been aptly named for its dullish-grey color. These bats primarily eat insect, and live in maternity colonies during the spring and leave during the summer. Like all bats, they rest during the day and come out at night to forage and hunt.

These bats roost in these pipes, underneath Sanford Stadium, by clinging to the various cracks, then hang upside down to sleep. In fact, Grey Bats and Pipistrelles, another bat species, are most commonly found beneath the stadium, but several other species have been known to roost in the tunnels. The bats choose those hallow pipes because of the darkness, high humidity and height. The tunnels are higher than most, which means predators can't reach them when sleeping. Yet, despite the bats living underneath the stadium, continual upgrades remained an on-going process up above in the terrestrial world.

During the 1960s, many universities in the South began to significantly expand their stadiums, and Georgia was no different. When Coach Dooley arrived in 1964, he and Athletic Director Joel Eaves commenced to making upgrades to Sanford Stadium. First, the field-level lighting, for years an obstruction for fans in the stands, was removed. Then, almost 8,000 end-zone seats were added, bringing Sanford Stadium's total capacity to 43,621.

In 1967, Architects Heery and Heery, of Atlanta, were hired to plan a major expansion. The expansion planning was very tricky because the stadium was closely enclosed on both north and south sides by academic buildings. The plans went forward, however, and an upper deck of seats were added to each side of the stadium.

Astonishingly, there was no need to demolish or alter any of the surrounding buildings. In addition to the new upper decks, this major addition included a new press box and club seating. In total, 14,972 seats were added to the stadium. The capacity was upgraded to roughly 58,773, at a cost of $3,000,000. The north side had 18,192 seats on the lower level; 1,296 Club level, not including 80 seats in the President's box; 8,760 on the top level, for a total of 28,248 seats.

The south side had 18,289 on the lower level; 930 Club level; 8,760 on the top level; for a total of 27,979 seats. The east stands had 1,146 seats and the west stands had 1,400 seats. It would be the last expansion for thirteen years.

By 1980, the 50 year old stadium's large concrete box culvert had started to crumple. The system was similar to a septic tank. It had ground water, because of low elevation, and the water underground began to collect. Its old, antiquated tile drainage system had lasted a long time; however, it had to be replaced in the summer of 1980.

Then, in June of 1980, the slow erosion of the field prompted a $200,000 development project involving the re-sod of the entire field. The funds were obtained through a private donation. No money from the state was spent on the field. The athletic department elected to raise the money for the project, versus taking funds out of its operating budget. Research revealed the drainage conditions led to compaction, erosion, and settling of the field. As a result of the compaction, a considerable amount of standing water developed, contributing to several sinkholes across the playing field. In fact, in 1979, a four-foot-deep sinkhole developed on field's eastside.

In early June of 1980, Southern Turf Nurseries, Inc., of Tifton, undertook a six-week project to re-sod the field with a tough, fine, all-weather Bermuda grass called "Tifway 19." An underground drainage system, located every twenty feet, was built below two feet of crushed gravel and eighteen inches of sand. The Tifway turf, designed to last from early spring through late fall, would lie down above the sand.

The turf re-sod commenced right after the graduation ceremonies in June, when workers started digging up the old turf. By mid-August, the new, all-weather turf blanketed the field. The sophisticated drainage system, which allowed up to ten inches of water an hour to drain straight through the root system, made for better play in wet weather. Another main feature of the turf included its thicker grass, better growth patterns and a safer playing field. Coach Dooley felt the new turf combined the best features of grass and an artificial playing field and referred to it as "the turf of the future."

Another noticeable change was the new location of the scoreboard. The structure was removed from its perch in the east endzone and placed on poles high above the west endzone, overlooking Gillis Bridge, a.k.a. Sanford Bridge. The iconic Bulldog, holding a board with a nail in it, was removed, and purchased by a local business in Athens, where it is displayed proudly just off of Baxter Street, at 581 South Harris Street.

In addition, a new speaker system was installed on top of the scoreboard, which featured each team's name in lights, versus the old scoreboard which listed the visiting team's name as "Visitors." The back of the scoreboard, looking down at the Stegeman Parking lot, was a huge billboard bearing the stadium's name.

Contrary to popular belief, the project to add 18,000 seats for the season opener against Tennessee, on September 5, 1981, via closing-in the east endzone, had been planned long before Georgia won its national championship in 1980. Some had speculated the revenue garnered from the national championship season prompted this massive construction project.

All those modifications during the 1950s and 1960s were just a prelude to the addition which took place 1981. On September 17, 1980, the University of Georgia's Athletic Department awarded a bid to the Marvin M. Black Company, of Atlanta, for the construction of this proposed colossal Sanford Stadium expansion. The bid of $7,999,000, which won out over bids from three other companies, would cover the construction costs of an 18,000 seat addition to the stadium's east end. "We were very pleased with the bids that came in," Athletic Director for Sports, Coach Vince Dooley announced. "We're excited about moving forward and seeing some physical construction taking place."

The Black company underbid the other three companies by more than $450,000; however, the winning bid was still under the limit set by the Athletic Board for construction costs. Steve Black, the representative of the Black company at the meeting, was satisfied with the outcome. "We feel absolutely fantastic about it," Black stated.

The other companies which placed bids were McDevitt and Street Company with a bid of $8,497,000, Castle Construction Company, Inc., with a bid of $8,739,000 and D. R. Allen & Sons, Inc., with a bid of $8,498,000.

Construction on the expansion commenced right after the insurance bond was drawn up and the Black company signed the construction contract. According to Billy Hudson, Director of Campus Planning, the procedures were "only a matter of form," and construction commenced less than two weeks later.

The expansion was set to be finished by September 5, 1981, for Georgia's home opener against Tennessee. The new construction project gave Sanford Stadium a horseshoe shape and brought the total capacity to more than 76,000. The total cost of the expansion, as approved by the Athletic Board, was approximately $12 million dollars, which included construction, architect and overhead costs. Funding was assumed completely by the Athletic Department, which borrowed the money from several banks in Athens and Atlanta.

To pay back the loans, the Athletic Department used money from its regular operation budget and funds from the Georgia Student Educational Foundation, a separate corporation which handled contributions from Georgia alumni and friends.

The expansion marked progress in Georgia athletics, but unfortunately, it brought to an end the Georgia tradition of watching games from the railroad trestle on the east end of Sanford Stadium. This tradition began during the late 1960s and 1970s, when a multitude of fans began watching Georgia games from the railroad tracks that overlooked the stadium's open east endzone. These "Track People," as they came to be known, were able to watch the game for free, and became a tradition. The enclosure of the east endzone eliminated the view of the field from the railroad tracks and effectively ended the "Track People" tradition.

The "Track People" had taken great pride in sitting out on the tracks, sometimes for days, to claim a spot. To honor the "Track People," for the solemn loyalty and dedication they provided the football program, special t-shirts were developed just for them. On November 27, 1980, when the players arrived at the stadium for the final home game, against hated Georgia Tech, they were all wearing these t-shirts, bearing a picture of the trestle and the inscription "Good-bye Track People." Each player pulled off his t-shirt and threw it into the hordes of well-lubricated fans who were maintaining their free seats for the final time.

In the summer of 1981, following mid-winter delays, construction on the east endzone addition was finally on schedule. The new section, which added approximately 18,000 seats, enlarged the stadium's capacity to 77,0000, making Sanford Stadium the second largest stadium in the South, behind Tennessee's Neyland Stadium, which, at the time, had a capacity of over 90,000 people.

Campus planning director Hudson related they had more daylight and 10-hour work days that enabled the construction crews to catch-up during the month of May. He stated the impending deadline and the importance of having the stadium ready, helped to motivate the crews. By June, seventeen of the addition's nineteen concrete support pylons had been erected. The contractors had completed the five-foot diameter holes designed to hold the other two. "This will be the beginning of the end," Hudson had related in reference to the holes being ready.

With the completion of the supports, contractors commenced with what Hudson called "horizontal work," meaning the installation of the bench seats, club level bathrooms, and concession stands, etc.... The supports, and most of the prefabricated concrete structures, were in place in early July. That was when they had to katie-bar-the-door, because progress quickly moved from that point forward. Additionally, the finishing touches to the storage rooms, located underneath the stands, were completed after the season opening game against Tennessee.

East Campus Road had been closed for over six months, but was finally opened by the end of July of '81. Once the thoroughfare had been reopened, Sanford Drive and Hooper Street, were closed to private vehicles during working hours. Private cars were no longer routed out of the heart of campus, and the orbit bus route was once again headed down East Campus Road, before turning left onto Hooper Street to pick-up students on their way towards the University Health Service and downtown Athens.

The 18,000 season tickets for the seats in the new addition had already been sold. Virginia Whitehead, assistant athletic director for ticket sales, said if the seats had not been ready, the ticket buyers would have received refunds. However, the construction was completed, and the "Track People," who had become synonymous with Sanford Stadium for decades, were done. It would be two years before the next stadium project.

In 1982, lights were installed in the stadium. Unlike the lights mounted in 1940, these lights were not located at field level, but attached to the top of the upper level in order to not obscure the view of the field. The first game under the new lights was on September 6, 1982, when Georgia defeated Clemson 13–7. It would be almost another ten years before the next construction project.

In 1991, a portion of the west endzone was enclosed, creating a "partial bowl" around the lower level of Sanford Stadium. The west stands could not be completely enclosed due to the proximity of Gillis Bridge, a major campus transportation artery to the stadium. The construction project was conducted by the Winter Construction Company, from Atlanta. The expansion cost approximately $3.7 million, and added 4,205 new seats, bringing the total capacity to 85,434. This project commenced immediately after the Georgia Tech game in 1990, and was completed flawlessly and slightly below budget.

Four years later, in 1994, Georgia built thirty luxury suites above the south stands. The expansion cost a total of $18 million, and raised the seating capacity to 86,520. These thirty suites featured two televisions, a fully stocked bar and catered dining, a video recorder, and plush seating and carpeting. Fifty percent of the luxury boxes had been leased to corporations, including Coca-Cola, Miller Brewing Company, Dentsu Advertising and Georgia Crown. The money from that first group of leases covered the costs of skybox construction, and all future profits went to the Georgia Athletic Association during the ensuing seasons.

Initially, there was a five-year commitment required to lease one of these skyboxes, which came in seat sizes of 24, and 16, costing $250,000 and $175,000 respectively. The yearly rent was $50,000 and $35,000. Then, two years later, Sanford Stadium would undergo another unexpected transformation.

In 1996, Sanford Stadium was selected to host the men's and women's gold medal matches for the 1996 Olympiads. Because the width of a soccer field is wider than an American football field, some of the hedges had to be removed. The field would be leveled to soccer field specifications because the field's one-inch-tall rain-draining crown was against Olympic soccer rules.

Over three millions dollars was spent to hold the Olympics at Sanford Stadium. Afterwards, the Atlanta Committee, for the Olympic Games, paid the University approximately $700,000 to ensure the playing field was suitable for football once the '96 Olympics were completed. After this monumental event, it would be another three years before any more work was conducted on Sanford Stadium again.

In August of 1999, a murky, brown liquid was discovered in the south endzone. When the problem initially started, the leak had been dealt with by the Athletic Association, but because they lease the stadium from the University, authority was handed over to the head of the Environmental Safety Division. Afterwards, Legal Affairs took charge, only to have clean-up taken over by the President's office.

The field had been torn-up for several weeks in an attempt to find the source of this underground leak. At one point, the situation was so dire there had been discussions of possibly relocating Georgia's 1999 home games to the Georgia Dome because of the condition of the turf. Luckily, environmental consultants, hired by both the city and the school, discovered the problem involved the drainage system. And, operating in concert with local companies, they completed their field work, and all field repairs were completed ahead of schedule; however, a new sod was planted.

This new type of sod, a type of Bermuda sod called Tifway 419—had approximately three months to grow. The grass needed four weeks of growing before it would be ready to be played on. It would be the first time the grass inside Sanford Stadium had to be re-planted since the 1996 Olympics.

In 2000, the next project involved building more Skyboxes and Club Seats, and it would cost $12 million to complete. The Mitchell Construction Company won the contract, and built twenty new Skyboxes and Club Seats. All of these Skyboxes and Club Seats had already been sold before the project had been completed. The construction increased the total number of suites to fifty.

The largest luxury suite, a 36-person box, rented for $72,000 in 2000, and each suite was leased under a five-year contract. The Athletic Association enjoyed a 100 percent renewal rate on rentals for the existing Sky Suites, and all of the new suites were quickly rented, mainly to alumni.

Additionally, a 400-seat Sky Club was constructed underneath the Sky Suites. The Sky Club provided a lunch buffet and soft drinks in a climate-controlled area. Ticket holders who wished to watch the game from outside were provided seats with red chair backs.

As with all seats inside of Sanford Stadium, the Sky Club tickets were allocated according to the number of priority points earned, based on the amount of money contributed to the Athletic Association. Football season ticket holders were given one point for every dollar they donated to the Athletic Association.

To be eligible for the Sky Club season tickets, season ticket holders had to have contributed $1,000 per ticket. Based on their cumulative point total—the sum of their lifetime contributions to the Athletic Association—top patrons were allowed to purchase Sky Club season tickets. In the year 2000, the last person who earned the privilege of purchasing Sky Club season tickets had accumulated more than 22,000 points. The following year, another project, to enhance Sanford Stadium, had been contracted out.

In 2001, nearly five hundred thousand dollars was spent on widening Sanford Stadium's concourses on the south side of the stadium. The modification was necessary to prevent fans from being crammed into a small area upon entering or departing the stadium. Walls were removed to avoid bottle necks, thus allowing fans to safely spread out. Lights were added to these concourse areas to make it easier for people to enter and leave the stadium.

In 2003, a project had been undertaken to bring the overall seating capacity to 92,746. It involved the addition of another upper deck being added to the north side of the stadium. It added 5,500 new seats, at a cost of $25 million. These upper-deck seats were called the "600 section" of the stadium, and were reserved for the fans of the visiting team. Additionally, all "600 section" tickets returned from opposing teams would be made available for Georgia fans to purchase on a first-come, first-serve basis; however, the face value of tickets for opposing fans are typically higher priced, and the Georgia fans buying these tickets had to pay the full rate. Finally, the next major project for Sanford Stadium would involve its toilets.

During the 2003 season, it was not uncommon to find mud coating the floor tiles inside the restroom at Sanford Stadium. Locks were scarcely found in the restroom stalls, and lines of people would often wrap outside restrooms. And, to the dismay of fans, there often was never any toilet paper or soap available. The restrooms would become so nasty fans avoided them like the black-plague.

To fix the problem, the bathrooms received an overhaul. The stainless steel that had previously divided the stalls and urinals, were replaced by plastic dividers. And, the University hired people to monitor the stalls, and keep toiletries supplied and fresh. Occasionally, attendants were available to keep restroom floors free of dirt and locks were installed to the backs of all Sanford Stadium restroom stalls. The stadium received another facelift in 2004.

In 2004, the stadium reached a seating capacity of 92,746, when twenty-seven Sky Suites were added to the north side of the stadium. The total cost was $8 million. Later, in April of 2005, a brand new $3.9 million scoreboard, approximately forty-nine feet wide, was added. It replaced the 10-year old scoreboard that had sat on posts above the west endzone. In addition to the scoreboard, state-of-the art ribbon boards were added inside the stadium. These boards displayed the score, similar to the old scoreboards, and flashed messages. The cost of the flashing boards was slightly over one million dollars.

In 2011, the scoreboard's screen's size was expanded from 25×46 feet to the full size of the scoreboard which was 52×76 feet. In addition to the upgrade to the scoreboard, the video boards were converted over to full high definition capability. Three years later, another upgrade was conducted on Sanford Stadium.

In 2014, the Reed Plaza area of Sanford Stadium was added. The construction project enhanced much needed amenities and circulation space along the entire north side of the stadium. The zone was converted from a restricted, gloomy alleyway, into an expansive assembly area. An extensive excavation project, along with site utility work, permitted the addition of twenty-four concession points, ninety-six bathroom fixtures, and general landscaping. Reed Plaza significantly upgraded public safety and provided easy access to the central campus locations. Cooper Carry worked with Manning Brothers and Aramark, to design and coordinate concession services. The spaces designed were extremely functional and efficient. More upgrades are pending.

If a plan from university architects gets approved, Sanford Stadium could expand by more than 9,000 seats. The seating expansion would wrap around the east side of the stadium and would bring the stadium's capacity to 101,766. University architects considered filling in the endzone by the Gillis Bridge, but decided it was important to preserve the view of the Miller Learning Center and Tate Student Center.

One alternative considered was to have a raised seating area, connecting the upper deck area with the Sky Box section, while maintaining the view from the bridge. Other proposals were to increase the number of concession stands and restrooms, and to install a Jumbotron outside the east end of the stadium in order to provide fans an opportunity to watch the game from outside.

In addition to these extensive construction and renovation projects constantly engulfing Sanford Stadium, the prospects of holding other events there, while it lays dormant most of the year, have been mulled over. In truth, as early the late '60s, the prospects of having musical concerts there were considered; however, Athletic Director Joel Eaves had steadfastly resisted any type of concerts inside of Sanford Stadium. Some of his justifications were the destruction of the sacred turf, vandalism, and inadequate lighting within the stadium. Thus, the subject lay dormant for over a decade.

In 1985, a local concert promoter, Peter Conlon, approached officials from the University of Georgia, in reference to staging musical events inside Sanford Stadium; however, concerts involving groups like Bruce Springsteen, Jimmy Buffet, Cheap Trick and

R.E.M., were constantly denied, or had very strict limitations. It would take thirty years for technological advances, in proper ways to protect the stadium's playing surface, coupled with new leadership, to rehash the subject of a musical concert inside Sanford Stadium.

James Brown, 1977 Halftime Show

Athletic Director Greg McGarity, who had worked at Florida when Ben Hill Griffin Stadium had been used for concerts involving groups like the Rolling Stones, appreciated the passion fans might show over a concert in their stadium. Hence, an informal exploratory team, involving Associate Athletic Director for Internal Operations, Josh Brooks, and Kevin Purvis, Assistant Equipment Manager, was formed to explore the feasibility of a concert. In turn, they contacted Conlon, who was president of Live Nation Atlanta.

Two years later, after the logistics, finances and contracts were hammered out, the University of Georgia agreed to the terms. The musical group was Jason Aldean, who was from Georgia, and played a musical cross-breed of country, a hyper-modern genre, and hip-hop. There was minimal financial risk to the University because Live Nation paid $250K operational fees to cover security, concession stands, merchandise, police and fire, gate keepers, cleaning crews, and scoreboard operators, amongst others. In turn, Live Nation would keep all the gate revenue; whereas, the

University would control parking for approximately 10K spots around campus, and received ten percent of merchandise sales.

The intense planning for the event was evident to all spectators. There were over 66,000 tickets sold, and the turf was properly protected with a Terraplas-type material, the same material used during commencement ceremonies, and the hedges remained safe. It was an overall good event that ran very smoothly.

Yet, contrary to popular belief, the Aldean concert wasn't the first musical act to perform inside of Sanford Stadium. Other performances typically were regulated to halftime attractions during football games. In fact, the Godfather of Soul, James Brown, performed during several Georgia games in the 1970s and early '80s, usually performing his hit song "Dooley's Junkyard Dogs."

Additionally, other acts incorporated were Andy Griffith performing his infamous monologue "What it Was, Was Football," during halftime of the 1954 G-Day game, and Bill Anderson performed "Rocky Top," with Georgia's Redcoat Band at halftime of a rain soaked Tennessee game in '72. In 1938, President Franklin Delano Roosevelt spoke at the commencement, and Prince Charles attended the Homecoming game against Kentucky in '77.

One thing is for certain, as long as the ticket office has to turn back thousands of ticket requests each season, it will continue to prompt the expansion, along with alternatives uses of Sanford Stadium.

Sanford Stadium Scoreboard, from Gillis Bridge

Evolution of the Hedges

In 1908, five years after Doctor Sanford arrived in Athens, Charles Martin reached the Classic City. Following his time serving during World War I, he would spend the rest of his life living out his dream of working for the University of Georgia. He worked almost every job in the Athletic Department, from ticket and business manager to advertising agent.

There never would have been the slogan "tween the hedges," if Martin had not conjured-up the inspiration of planting rose hedges around the field. His plan was created in 1925, after he received an invitation from Alabama's Business Manager of Athletics, Thomas Joyce, to accompany him to the Rose Bowl. While in Pasadena, California, Martin was mesmerized by the beautiful hedge of roses around the field at the Rose Bowl. The idea had been planted.

In 1929, when Doctor Sanford's vision of having the "best football stadium in the South," was gradually turning into steel and concrete reality, Martin believed rose hedges would not only titivate the new stadium, but differentiate it from the other stadiums being built in the "pre-stock market crash" building expansion taking place on campuses across the country. But there was a problem.

Personnel from Georgia's horticulturists department related roses would not thrive in north Georgia's humid climate. Instead of planting roses, they suggested the privet ligustrum be used. Reluctantly, it was then determined Georgia's new gridiron would instead be bordered by privet Ligustrum, and not a hedge of roses.

Unbeknownst to many, the privet ligustrum is a weed, and an insidious one. It had been brought into the United States in the early 1800s. This semi-evergreen, deciduous shrub, not only is poisonous to horses and mildly toxic to humans, but is capable of overrunning a habitat and eliminating native species.

The decision to plant these shrubs was a last-minute resolution. The hedges were trucked in from Atlanta, and planted just hours before the dedication game against Yale. Under the cover of darkness, the hedges were planted into the red Georgia earth by workers using shovels and flashlights. It was October 12, 1929, a significant juncture on which the most famous plants in football, if not all of sports—the idiosyncratic privet hedges surrounding the field at Georgia's Sanford Stadium—were first planted.

The stadium dedication had been a very stressful occasion for Martin, as he was the game's primary promoter. With over 30,000 fans, along with governors from nine southern states cramming into the stadium, he successfully ensured an orderly egress of all attendees after the game was completed.

The game against Yale would turn out to be one of the greatest sports days in Georgia football history. The game went off without a hitch, and the newly planted hedges added decor and elegance to an epic day. Almost nine decades later, these hedges, and its decedents, have witnessed over 400 Georgia football games, numerous graduation ceremonies, the Olympiads, and a concert.

Yet, in 1993, one of the largest storms in Georgia sport's history erupted. Atlanta had been selected to host the 1996 Summer Olympics, and Sanford Stadium was selected as the location for the soccer matches. Because regulation soccer field measures approximately 115-yards by 74 yards, the hedges, on the east and west endzones, would have to be removed. Coach Dooley, Georgia's Athletic Director, knew Georgia people would be less than enthralled with the idea of removing the hedges.

Unfortunately, it proved to be a controversial measure, because it had not been general public knowledge the hedges would have to be removed to accommodate the Olympic soccer competition. To head-off an international disaster, the school embarked on a project to save the tradition and install replacement hedges, at a cost of $100,000, to the Atlanta Committee for the Olympic Games.

In 1993, the school cultivated thousands of genetically correct potted plants and grew them for three years at a clandestine site. The 4-inch cuttings were grown into shrubs 54 inches high and 24 inches wide, and were replanted where their ancestors reigned.

The original hedges planted by Martin, a Georgia football symbol and tradition, would see their last games against Florida and Auburn in 1995; however, the actual removal of the hedges didn't occur until after the inter-squad spring G-Day game, in April 1996.

As a matter of fact, during the removal process, it was discovered the hedges were diseased—they were deteriorating from an incursion of nematodes, or microscopic worms—necessitating their timely removal. Officials felt the timing was very good because some of the hedges' roots had gotten into the irrigation system. The 60 year old hedges had to be leveled because of the compressed root system that had been created after decades of spreading.

Two sets of hedges were grown—one set in Thompson, Georgia, and another set in an undisclosed location in Florida. Two sets were necessary to insure the school has an ample supply. Georgia football tradition would be maintained as three-year-old sprigs of the hedges were planted as surrogates before the first home football game in the fall of '96. "These are the sons and daughters of the mother and father hedges, they are of the same lineage," said Athletic Director Vince Dooley, circa '96.

From July 28 - August 2, 1996, the men's and women's soccer finals, and semi-finals, were held in Sanford Stadium. Nigeria and the United States would win the men's and women's football gold medals, respectively, at 'the hedge-less stadium.'

Once the Olympics were over, the newly-grown hedges were transported from their off-site location to the stadium. As planned, more than 2,400 plants were transplanted, with those new plants grown from pieces of the old hedges. The vigorous cuttings had been nurtured into mature hedges before its homecoming into Sanford Stadium, where they were transferred in a ceremony linking Dooley and other Georgia dignitaries. The result culminated in what the Georgia family refers to as "Hedges II."

The descendant cuttings quickly rooted in the stadium's hallowed ground. According to Georgia's Director of Sports Turf and Grass, the hedges grow eight months of the year, at a rate of approximately three feet per autumn.

But in spite of their status as campus symbols, the hedges endure a substantial amount of mistreatment each fall. Television camera crews habitually swathe the hedges with cables and signs. And, fans, players, possums, and insects have damaged the hedges.

Despite the abuse the hedges take, they remain a cosmetic touch to the stadium. In addition to being aesthetically pleasing, the fabled hedges have proven to be an effective measure of crowd control. Even though a major traffic path to exit the stadium from both stands runs directly alongside the hedges, fans have only stormed the field and torn down the goalposts once in the majestic history of Sanford Stadium. That disastrous event occurred on

October 7, 2000, when Georgia finally beat the Volunteers of Tennessee for the first time since the late 1980s. It would be a difficult recovery for Hedges II.

In truth, in April of 2001, the historic hedges of Sanford Stadium were still recuperating from the damage sustained on that fateful day. After beating the Volunteers, Georgia fans struggled to get onto the field, while destroying the Chinese Ligustrum hedges.

During the impromptu celebration, some people stood on the hedges, damaging the stems. The plants suffering the most were on the north side and both endzones. Those hedges unable to survive the attack were dug up and replaced with plants grown from a piece of one of the hedges in a nursery.

The replanting was much different than what occurred for the '96 Olympics. The damaged administered by Georgia fans was intensive. The cost was well over $10,000. There were approximately 20-30 hedges used to replace those hedges receiving the most extensive destruction. Still, there have been other events involving the desecration of the hedges.

In 2008, Georgia Tech players, and fans, commemorated their first win over Georgia since 2000 by breaking off pieces of the hedges and putting the stems in their mouths. The loss was the first Coach Richt had ever experienced against the Gnats.

Ironically, there has been some discrepancy about the correct type of hedge planted at Sanford Stadium. There are many who believe the hedge is an English privet hedge. However, the experts, botanists from the University, claim the hedge is composed of Chinese privet, Ligustrum sinense.

Regardless if it is a weed, or an English privet, one thing is for certain, the Sanford Stadium grounds crews spends an average of sixty hours per week maintaining the field, and ensuring the hedges, and field, remains in top shape throughout football season.

In reality, looking after the stadium, and its hedges, necessitates a staff of ten full-time employees, along with 10 to 12 students from the school's turf program. However, only three individuals are honored with the privilege of trimming the hedges.

For decades, grounds keepers tackled the daunting task—the hedges, which line both sidelines and endzones, covering approximately 3,000 square feet—with everything from traditional, arm-powered metal shears to electric clippers. In the 21st Century, approximately seven or eight sets of gas-powered trimmers and weed eaters, with various lengths and sizes of blades, enables the grounds keepers to complete the job in about two hours. But with the added challenge of a level cut, it is two hours of incredibly hard, focused, and intense work.

The end product is the recognizable, box-shaped hedge, 5 feet tall and 5 feet wide, which has not only bordered the Bulldogs' games in an aesthetically pleasant, historic perspective for over eight decades, but served a sensible reason. The hedges, and the metal fence embedded therein, have proved extremely efficient at crowd control. In fact, on November 16, 1935, the hedges aided Georgia fans who had courageously prevented Louisiana State fans from rushing the field after the Bayou Bengals beat the Bulldogs.

Presently, the field, and the hedges, are protected by a state-of-the-art camera surveillance method, and trespassers, be they harmless, inebriated college kids or would-be ruffians, are met with a loud, ear-splitting siren that sends them stampeding for the nearest way out. As a compulsory safeguard against any possible thefts, plant sickness or annihilation, replacement hedges are maintained at an unrevealed locality in case of an emergency.

The hedges were a splendid, iconic and pea green, long before the famous Boston ivy began clambering along the scarlet brick ramparts of Wrigley Field. In fact, the hedges were there long before the radiant, budding multihued of azaleas first arced athwart on Augusta National. For over eight decades, to be exact. They will stay into the next century. The hedges are an exclusive Georgia tradition.

Hedges, Sanford Stadium, circa 2014

Attendance at Georgia Football Games in Sanford Stadium

Every effort has been made to provide a complete and reliable list of attendance figures, although for a handful of games, no attendance data was available. From 1929 through the '60s, we should beware of too many round numbers, which were often little more than a sportswriter's extemporaneous guess.

Additionally, other factors, like quality of opponents, extreme weather, "body-bag games," The Great Depression, World War II, Homecoming, etc..., had a major influence on the crowd size. As an example, on November 25, 1950, in a game against Furman, the temperature was 11 degrees, and subsequently the attendance was less than 1,000 people; however, the average attendance for the other four home games was 28,875. Moreover, since the late '90s, all games at Sanford Stadium have been sold out; but, sometimes the amount of tickets sold far exceeded the number of people who were actually in attendance.

1929
Yale (Oct 12)—33,000
Auburn (Nov 16)—12,976
Georgia Tech (Dec 7)—20,000

1930
Oglethorpe (Sept 27)—25,328
Mercer (Oct 4)—21,321
North Carolina (Oct 18)—26,210

1931
VPI (Oct 3)—27,381
Vanderbilt (Oct 24)—29,231
Tulane (Nov 14)—39,400
Georgia Tech (Nov 18)—10,321

1932
VPI (Oct 1)—9,543
North Carolina (Oct 15)—3,100
Florida (Oct 29)—10,000

1933
North Carolina St (Sept 30)
Tulane (Oct 7)—10,000
NYU (Oct 28)—25,000

1934
Stetson (Sept 29)—2,132
North Carolina (Oct 13)—2,402
North Carolina St (Nov 17)—8,000
Georgia Tech (Dec 1)—22,000

1935
Mercer (Sept 28)—24,500
Furman (Oct 12)—35,000
Alabama (Oct 26)—25,000
LSU (November 16)—30,000

1936
Mercer (Sept 26)
Rice (Oct 17)—9,500
Tennessee (Oct 31)—12,000
Georgia Tech (Nov 28)—25,000

1937
Oglethorpe (Sept 25)—4,500
Clemson (Oct 9)—8,000
Mercer (Oct 23)—5,000
Tulane (Nov 13)—12,000

1939
Citadel (Sept 30)—7,000
Holy Cross (Oct 14)—15,000
Mercer (Nov 4)—6,000
South Carolina (Nov 18)—29,742

1941
South Carolina (Oct 4)—21,000
Ole Miss (Oct 10)—25,000
Dartmouth (Nov 22)—18,000

1943
Presbyterian (Sept 17)—6,005
Tennessee Tech (Oct 1)—8,000
Wake Forest (Oct 8)—14,899
Howard (Oct 29)
Presbyterian (Nov 5)

1942 (Georgia Pre-Flight)
N. Carolina Pre-Flight (Oct 10)—18,400
Jacksonville NAS (Oct 30)—15,800

1945
Murray State (Sept 22)
Clemson (Sept 29)—27,650
LSU (Oct 20)—30,000

1947
Furman (Sept 19)
LSU (Oct 4)—44,500
Alabama (Oct 25)—48,000
Clemson (Oct 31)--46,300

1938
Citadel (Sept 24)—16,553
Furman (Oct 9)—17,900
Mercer (Oct 15)
Georgia Tech (Nov 27)—28,000

1940
Ole Miss (Oct 12)—36,000
Kentucky (Oct 25)—17,000
Ga. Tech (Nov 30)—28,000

1942
Furman (Oct 3)
Tulane (Oct 17)—20,000
Georgia Tech (Nov 28)-45,000

1944
Wake Forest (Sept 29)—9,000
Presbyterian (Oct 6)—13,000
Kentucky (Oct 13)—21,000
Daniel Field (Oct 20)—15,000
Clemson (Nov 24)—19,500
Georgia Tech (Dec 2)—26,000

1943 (Georgia Pre-Flight)
Daniel Field (Oct 2)—5,225
Newbery (Oct 17)—3,500
1944 (Athens-Pre-Flight)
Morris Field (Oct 15)—13,000

1946
Clemson (Sept 27)—35,000
Kentucky (Oct 11)—49,800
Oklahoma A&M (Oct 19)—45,000
Alabama (Nov 2)—52,000
Georgia Tech (Nov 30)—55,000

1948
Chattanooga (Sept 25)—30,000
North Carolina (Oct 2)—44,400
Kentucky (Oct 9)—23,000
Furman (Nov 20)—17,000
Georgia Tech (Nov 27)—52,000

1949
Furman (Sept 16)—15,000
Chattanooga (Sep 23)
LSU (Oct 14)—38,000
Alabama (Oct 29)—35,000
Duquesne (Nov 12)

1951
George Washington (Sep 22)—20,000
Maryland (Oct 13)—32,000
LSU (Oct 20)—35,600
Boston Col. (Oct 27)—42,400
Alabama (Nov 3)—44,000

1953
Tulane (Sep 26)—15,000
LSU (Oct 17)—23,000
North Carolina (Oct 24)—26,000
Alabama (Oct 31)—29,000

1955
Vanderbilt (Sep 24)
North Carolina (Oct 8)
Tulane (Oct 22)—27,000
Alabama (Oct 29)—29,500

1957
Vanderbilt (Sep 28)
Alabama (Nov 2)—30,000

1959
Alabama (Sep 19)—40,000
Vanderbilt (Sep 26)—30,000
Hardin Simmons (Oct 10)—22,550
Florida State (Oct 31)—30,000
Auburn (Nov 14)—54,000

1961
Alabama (Sep 23)—44,000
Vanderbilt (Sep 30)—22,000
South Carolina (Oct 7)
Kentucky (Oct 28)—32,000
Auburn (Nov 18)—39,000

1950
Maryland (Sept 23)—35,000
North Carolina (Oct 7)—37,000
Miss State (Oct 14)—25,000
Furman (Nov 25)—1,000
Ga. Tech (Dec 2)—50,000

1952
North Carolina State (Oct 4)—22,000
Maryland (Oct 11)—35,000
Georgia. Tech (Nov 29)—50,000

1954
Clemson (Sep 25)—26,500
Texas A&M (Oct 2)—22,000
Vanderbilt (Oct 16)
Georgia. Tech (Nov 27)—50,000

1956
Florida State (Sep 29)—25,000
Miss State (Oct 6)—25,000
Kentucky (Oct 27)—28,000
Georgia Tech (Dec 1)—50,000

1958
South Carolina (Oct 4)—29,770
Kentucky (Oct 25)—31,000
Citadel (Nov 22)—26,000
Georgia Tech (Nov 29)—41,600

1960
South Carolina (Oct 1)—30,000
Miss State (Oct 15)—36,150
Tulsa (October 29)
Georgia Tech (Nov 26)—55,000

1962
Florida State (Oct 30)—31-300
Kentucky (Oct 27)—29,385
North Carolina St (Nov 3)—35,000
Georgia Tech (Dec 1)—55,000

1963
Alabama (Sep 21)—34,980
Vanderbilt (Sep 28)—22,000
South Carolina (Oct 5)—26,500
Auburn (Nov 16)—35,248

1965
Alabama (Sep 18)—42,500
Vanderbilt (Sep 25)—37,880
Clemson (Oct 9)—45,500
Auburn (Nov 13)—46,812

1967
Miss State (Sep 230—54,512
South Carolina (Oct 7)—58,182
VMI (Oct 21)—50,307
Auburn (Nov 18)—59,060

1969
Tulane (Sep 20)—55,285
South Carolina (Oct 4)—51,781
Kentucky (Oct 25)—55,781
Tennessee (Nov 1)—59,781
Auburn (Nov 15)—59,306

1971
Oregon State (Sep 11)—50,709
Tulane (Sep 18)—54,667
Miss State (Oct 2)—53,003
Kentucky (Oct 23)—57,852
Auburn (Nov 13)—62,891

1973
Pittsburgh (Sep 15)—52,005
Clemson (Sep 22)—48,280
N Carolina St (Sep 29)—52,700
Ole Miss (Oct 13)—57,800
Kentucky (Oct 27)—54,500
Auburn (Nov 17)—59,700

1964
Clemson (Oct 10)—43,621
Florida State (Oct 17)—31,000
Kentucky (Oct 24)—39,000
North Carolina (Oct 31)—40,000
Georgia Tech (Nov 28)—52,500

1966
Ole Miss (Oct 8)—45,200
Kentucky (Oct 220—45,000
North Carolina (Oct 29)—45,321
Georgia Tech (Nov 26)—48,782

1968
Clemson (Sep 28)—59,008
Ole Miss (Oct 12)—56,111
Vanderbilt (Oct 19)—54,342
Houston (Nov 2)—59,381
Georgia Tech (Nov 30)—59,537

1970
Clemson (Sep 26)—55,682
Ole Miss (Oct 10)—54,768
Vanderbilt (Oct 17)—52,344
South Carolina (Oct 31)—57,391
Georgia Tech (Nov 28)—59,803

1972
Baylor (Sep 16)—53,201
North Carolina St (Sep 30)—56,613
Alabama (Oct 7)—60,013
Vanderbilt (Oct 21)—58,141
Tennessee (Nov 4)—60,086
Georgia Tech (Dec 2)—58,374

1974
Oregon St (Sep 14)—49,788
South Carolina (Sep 28)—50,000
Ole Miss (Oct 12)—54,900
Vanderbilt (Oct 19)—51,230
Houston (Nov 2)—52,788
Georgia Tech (Nov 30)—47,555

1975
Pittsburgh (Sep 6)—38,500
Miss State (Sep 30)—43,500
Clemson (Oct 4)—57,800
Kentucky (Oct 25)—50,100
Auburn (Nov 15)—57,750

1977
Oregon (Sep 10)—45,000
Clemson (Sep 17)—55,100
Ole Miss (Oct 8)—56,200
Kentucky (Oct 22)—59,100
Richmond (Oct 29)—48,500
Auburn (Nov 12)—57,500

1979
Wake Forest (Sep 15)—56,000
South Carolina (Sep 29)—60,500
LSU (Oct 13)—61,000
Kentucky (Oct 27)—60,100
Virginia (Nov 3)—59-100
Auburn (Nov 17)—63,000

1981
Tennessee (Sep 5)—82,122
California (Sep 12)—79,400
South Carolina (Sep 26)—82,100
Kentucky (Oct 24)—80,780
Temple (Oct 31)—80,117
Auburn (Nov 14)—82,165

1983
UCLA (Sep 3)—82,122
South Carolina (Sep 24)—82,122
Miss State (Oct 1)—82,122
Kentucky (Oct 22)—82,122
Temple (Oct 29)—81,822
Auburn (Nov 12)—82,122

1976
California (Sep 11)—47,000
South Carolina (Sep 25)—59,935
Alabama (Oct 2)—70,145
Vanderbilt (Oct 16)—59,100
Cincinnati (Oct 30)—49,500
Georgia Tech (Nov 27)—60,500

1978
Baylor (Sep 16)—43,000
Clemson (Sep 23)—60,000
Ole Miss (Oct 7)—58,800
Vanderbilt (Oct 21)—53,800
VMI (Nov 4)—50,200
Georgia Tech (Dec 2)—59,700

1980
Texas A&M (Sep 13)—60,150
Clemson (Sep 27)—61,800
TCU (Sep 27)—59,200
Ole Miss (Oct 11)—60,300
Vanderbilt (Oct 18)—59,300
South Carolina (Nov 1)—62,200
Georgia Tech (Nov 29)—62,800

1982
Clemson (Sep 6)—82,122
Brigham Young (Sep 11)—80,209
Ole Miss (Oct 9)—82,122
Vanderbilt (Oct 16)—82,122
Memphis State (Oct 30)—82,122
Georgia Tech (Nov 27)—82,122

1984
Southern Miss (Sep 8)—81,427
Clemson (Sep 22)—82,122
Ole Miss (Oct 13)—82,122
Vanderbilt (Oct 20)—82,122
Memphis State (Nov 3)—82,122
Georgia Tech (Dec 1)—82,122

1985
Alabama (Sep 2)—81,277
Baylor (Sep 14)—77,190
South Carolina (Sep 28)—82,122
Kentucky (Oct 26)—81,407
Tulane (Nov 2)—81,327
Auburn (Nov 16)—82,122

1987
Virginia (Sep 5)—75,125
Oregon State (Sep 12)—73,211
South Carolina (Sep 26)—82,122
LSU (Oct 10)—82,122
Kentucky (Oct 24)81,911
Auburn (Nov 14)—82,122

1989
Baylor (Sep 16)—82,007
Miss State (Sep 23)—82,122
South Carolina (Sep 30)—80,961
Kentucky (Oct 28)—81,987
Temple (Nov 4)—80,012
Auburn (Nov 18)—82,122

1991
Western Carolina (Aug 31)—85,434
LSU (Sep 7)—85,434
Cal St Fullerton (Sep 28)—85,434
Clemson (Oct 5)—85,434
Kentucky (Oct 26)—85,434
Auburn (Nov 16)—85,434

1993
S Carolina (Sep 4)—84,912
Texas Tech (Sep 18)—74,511
Arkansas (Oct 2)—73,825
Southern Miss (Oct 9)—63,458
Kentucky (Oct 23)—81,307
Auburn (Nov 13)—85,434

1986
Duke (Sep 13)—80,420
Clemson (Sep 20)—81,377
Ole Miss (Oct 4)—80,227
Vanderbilt (Oct 18)—78,642
Richmond (Nov 1)—74,785
Georgia Tech (Nov 29)—82,122

1988
Tennessee (Sep 3)—82,122
TCU (Sep 10)—72,680
Ole Miss (Oct 1)—82,077
Vanderbilt (Oct 8)—81,804
William & Mary (Oct 29)—80,712
Georgia Tech (Nov 26)—82,000

1990
So Mississippi (Sep 15)—79,812
Alabama (Sep 22)—82,122
East Carolina (Sep 29)
Ole Miss (Oct 13)—82,812
Vanderbilt (Oct 20)
Georgia Tech (Dec 1)—82,112

1992
Tennessee (Sep 12)—85,434
Cal St Fullerton (Sep 19)—75,515
Ole Miss (Sep 26)—84,278
Georgia Southern (Oct 10)—85,434
Vanderbilt (Oct 17)—83,067
Georgia Tech (Nov 28)—85,434

1994
Tennessee (Sep 10)—86,117
NE Louisiana (Sep 17)—70,611
Ole Miss (Sep 24)—82,734
Clemson (Oct 8)—86,117
Vanderbilt (Oct 15)—78,741
Georgia Tech (Nov 25)—84,113

1995
South Carolina (Sep 2)—86,117
New Mexico State (Sep 16)—78,911
Alabama (Sep 30)—86,117
Kentucky (Oct 21)—85,412
Florida (Oct 28)—86,000
Auburn (Nov 11)—86,117

1997
Arkansas State (Aug 30)—79,145
South Carolina (Sep 13)—86,117
Northeast La. (Sep 20)—74,113
Miss State (Oct 4)—83,211
Kentucky (Oct 25)—85,672
Auburn (Nov 15)—86,117

1999
Utah State (Sep 4)—86,117
South Carolina (Sep 11)--86,117
Central Florida (Sep 23)—86,117
LSU   (Oct 2)—86,117
Kentucky (Oct 23)—86,117
Auburn (Nov 13)—86,117

2001
Arkansas St (Sep 1)—86,520
South Carolina (Sep 8)—86,520
Arkansas (Sep 29)—86,520
Kentucky (Oct 20)—86,520
Auburn (Nov 10)—86,520
Houston (Dec 1)—86,520

2003
Mid. Tenn. (Sep 6)—92,058
South Carolina (Sep 13)—92,058
Alabama (Oct 4)—92,058
UAB (Oct 25)—92,058
Auburn (Nov 15)—92,058
Kentucky (Nov 22)—92,058

1996
Southern Miss (Aug 31)—81,067
Texas Tech (Sep 21)—73,116
Tennessee (Oct 12)—86,117
Vanderbilt (Oct 19)—80,757
Ole Miss (Nov 23)—76,511
Georgia Tech (Nov 30)—78,065

1998
Kent State (Sep 5)—86,003
Wyoming (Sep 19)—86,117
Tennessee (Oct 10)—86,117
Vanderbilt (Oct 17)—83,911
Ole Miss (Nov 21)—85,445
Georgia Tech (Nov 28)—86,117

2000
Ga. Southern (Sep 2)—86,520
New Mexico St (Sep 23)—85,202
Tennessee (Oct 7)—86,520
Vanderbilt (Oct 14)
Ole Miss (Nov 18)—76,248
Georgia Tech (Nov 25)

2002
Clemson (Aug 31)—86,520
Northwestern St (Sep 21)—86,520
New Mexico St (Sep 28)—86,520
Tennessee (Oct 12)—86,520
Vanderbilt (Oct 19)—86,520
Ole Miss (Nov 9)—86,520
Georgia Tech (Nov 30)—86,520

2004
Georgia Southern (Sep 4)—92,746
Marshall (Sep 18)—92,746
LSU (Oct 2)—92,746
Tennessee (Oct 9)—92,746
Vanderbilt (Oct 16)—92,746
Ga. Tech (Nov 27)—92,746

2005
Boise State (Sep 3)—92,500
South Carolina (Sep 10)—92,746
Louisiana Monroe (Sep 17)-92,746
Arkansas (Oct 22)—92,746
Auburn (Nov 12)—92,746
Kentucky (Nov 19)—92,746

2006
Western Kentucky (Sep 2)—92,746
Ala. Birmingham (Sep 16)—92,500
Colorado (Sep 23)—92,746
Tennessee (Oct 7)—92,746
Vanderbilt (Oct 14)—92,100
Miss. State (Oct 21)—92,746
Georgia Tech (Nov 25)—92,746

2007
Oklahoma State (Sep 1)—92,746
South Carolina (Sep 8)—92,746
Western Carolina (Sep 15)—92,746
Ole Miss (Sep 29)—92,746
Troy State (Nov 3)—92,746
Auburn (Nov 10)—92,746
Kentucky (Nov 17)—92,746

2008
Ga. Southern (Aug 30)—92,746
Central Michigan (Sep 6)—92,746
Alabama (Sep 27)—92,746
Tennessee (Oct 11)—92,746
Vanderbilt (Oct 18)—92,746
Georgia Tech (Nov 29)—92,746

2009
S Carolina (Sep 12)—92,746
Arizona St (Sep 26)—92,746
LSU   (Oct 3)—92,746
Tenn. Tech (Nov 7)—92,746
Auburn (Nov 14)—92,746
Kentucky (Nov 21)—92,746

2010
Louisiana Lafayette (Sep 4)—92,746
Arkansas (Sep 18)—92,746
Tennessee (Oct 16)—92,746
Vanderbilt (Oct 16)—92,746
Idaho State (Nov 6)—92,746
Georgia Tech (Nov 27)—92,746

2011
S Carolina (Sep 10)—92,746
Coastal Carolina (Sep 17)—92,746
Miss St (Oct 1)—92,746
New Mex St (Nov 5)—92,746
Auburn (Nov 12)—92,746
Kentucky (Nov 19)—92,746

2012
Buffalo (Sep 1)—91,238
Florida Atlantic (Sep 15)—92,746
Vanderbilt (Sep 22)—92,746
Tennessee (Sep 29)—92,746
Ole Miss (Nov 3)—92,746
Georgia Southern (Nov 17)—92,746
Georgia Tech (Nov 24)—92,746

2013
South Carolina (Sep 7)—92,746
North Texas (Sep 21)—92,746
LSU (Sep 28)—92,746
Missouri (Oct 12)--92,746
Appalachian St (Nov 9)—92,746
Kentucky (Nov 23)—92,746

2014
Clemson (Aug 30)—92,746
Troy (Sep 20)—92,746
Tennessee (Sep 27)—92,746
Vanderbilt (Oct 4)—92,746
Auburn (Nov 15)—92,746
Charleston S. (Nov 22)—92,746
Georgia Tech (Nov 29)—92,746

Georgia's Series Record at Sanford Stadium, as of 2014

Alabama: 7-12	George Washington: 1-0	Oregon: 1-0
Arkansas: 2-2	Georgia Southern: 3-0	Oregon St: 3-0
Arkansas St: 2-0	Georgia Tech: 27-13-1	Pittsburgh: 0-1-1
Arizona St: 1-0	Hardin-Simmons: 1-0	Presbyterian: 3-0
Appalachian St: 1-0	Holy Cross: 0-1	Rice: 1-0
Auburn: 12-17	Houston: 1-1-1	Richmond: 3-0
Baylor: 4-0	Howard: 1-0	S. Carolina: 22-7
Boise St.: 1-0	Idaho State: 1-0	Southern Miss: 3-1
Boston College: 1-0	Kent State: 1-0	Stetson: 1-0
Brigham Young: 1-0	Kentucky: 28-3-2	Temple: 3-0
Buffalo: 1-0	Louisiana St: 6-7	Tennessee: 7-9
California: 2-0	Marshall: 1-0	Tenn. Tech: 2-0
Central Florida: 1-0	Maryland: 1-2	Texas A&M: 1-1
Centre: 1-0-1	Memphis St: 2-0	TCU: 2-0
Chattanooga: 3-0	Mercer: 18-0	Texas Tech: 2-0
Central Florida: 1-0	Middle Tenn: 1-0	Troy State: 1-0
Central Michigan: 1-0	Ole Miss: 17-4-1	Tulane: 7-2
Cincinnati: 1-0	Miss. State: 9-2	Tulsa: 1-0
Clemson: 20-2	Missouri: 0-1	U.A.B.: 1-0
Coastal Carolina: 1-0	Murray State: 1-0	U.C.L.A.: 1-0
Daniel Field: 1-0	New Mexico St.: 3-0	Utah St: 1-0
Dartmouth: 1-0	NYU: 1-0	Vanderbilt: 27-4
Duke: 1-0	N. Carolina: 5-2-2	Virginia: 4-3-2
East Carolina: 1-0	N.C. St.: 5-0-1	Western Carolina: 2-0
Florida: 1-1	Northeast La: 2-0	Western Kentucky: 1-0
Florida Atlantic: 1-0	Northwestern St: 2-0	Wyoming: 1-0
Florida State: 2-2	Oglethorpe: 2-1	Yale: 1-0
Furman: 9-0	Oklahoma St: 2-0	

Conclusion

Sanford Stadium was built of an interminable concrete, disregarding time, fire and the climatological changes of Mother Nature. It will remain impregnable and sturdy when this generation's great grandchildren occupy their space inside of it, bringing home victories for ole Georgia.

Even before its first game, Georgia's football coach, Harry Mehre, spoke kindheartedly of these "there imposing, gray ramparts." In 1928, the fans, students, and alumni who worked and contributed their hard earned money for its creation knew the importance of what they had accomplished.

If they had merely endowed a huge stadia for Georgia football, their complete satisfaction would have been warranted. However, what they provided the university, and the people of Georgia, had been so much more. The building of Sanford Stadium, and its use in those early years, gave the university a new, refined image of itself. Over the decades, since its construction, Georgia's campus has changed dramatically, and the stadium has remained the primary catalyst for continuing improvements to the campuses hallow grounds.

Typically, people have a propensity to take things for granted, and after eventually growing accustomed to the large stadium, many failed to properly appreciate Sanford Stadium. By the 1960s, the stadium seemed in decay, but its needs were identified and addressed. It remains all encompassing on university grounds, as if conscious of its own place in the history of the institution.

Sanford Stadium has been the setting of many exciting football games, and some are lured to call it "sacred ground." If you go take a seat inside this Mecca of the South on a pleasant day, and have some innate imagination, you can see Charlie Trippi running for touchdowns, Coach Butts' team steamrolling to a 1942 national title, or Champ Bailey making an incredible interception. You can visualize D. J. Shockley annihilating Boise State, and leading Georgia to the 2005 Southeastern Conference title.

Except Sanford Stadium is more than simply a site for hosting college football games. Virtually an entire range of human activity has occurred there at one time or another. There have been people who have died there, graduation ceremonies have occurred, and pregnant women have gone into labor, even though there are no official records of anyone giving birth inside Sanford Stadium. Business transactions have been completed, as well as marriage proposals, and a few informal weddings have occurred between its hedges. And, the origins of many divorces have even been born within these hallow confines. Surrounded by its walls, undergraduates have laughed, blubbered uncontrollably, heard a country music concert, got into fistfights, have had the luxury to sunbathe, imbibe bootleg corn whiskey and studied for exams.

Courageous illustration of a determined future in 1929, Sanford Stadium today echoes the persona and character of Georgia as a premier educational institution. Even the oldest Georgia fans and alumni still recognize it, in spite of recurring construction and alterations. Because of its unifying power throughout the decades, Sanford Stadium remains, unquestionably, the most historic structure on the University of Georgia campus.

Sanford Stadium

INDEX

Abbot, Phillip, 33
Adams, B Pratt, 33
Adams, Charlotte, 355
Adams, Michael F., 184
Akers, Michelle, 336
Aldean, Jason, 369
Alexander, Bill, 82, 209
Allen, David, 136
Allen, Donnie, 110
Allen, Heyward, 64
Alworth, Lance, 204
Anderson, Bill, 370
Anderson, W, 33
Anderson, W. D., 33
Archer, David, 123
Archie, Herman, 143
Arenowitch, T., 33
Ariri, Obed, 131
Arkwright, P.S., 33
Armstrong, A. H., 29
Arnold, Anthony, 123, 128, 265
Arnold, L., 33
Arnold, R.O., 33
Arrington, Rick, 101
Atkinson, D.S., 33
Atwell, Harry, 33
Atwood, T. C., 25
August, Johnny, 83
Bachman, Charles, 54
Backman, S.G., 33
Bailey, Boss, 157
Bailey, Sean, 164, 165, 234
Baines, Luci, 95
Baldwin, Abraham, 29, 31, 34, 35, 36, 350

Ball, F. J., 350
Ball, Reggie, 161
Barber, Fred, 96
Barnet, Red, 351
Barnett, J. W., 14, 23, 33
Barrow, Chancellor, 10
Barrow, Craig, 33
Baskin, Weems, 63, 178
Basler, Norm, 82
Batchelor, Graham, 48, 55
Beasley, Terry, 108, 189, 225
Beaver, Sandy, 33
Bell, Greg, 228
Belue, Buck, 123, 124, 127, 130, 132, 135, 139, 205, 231, 304, 330
Bennett, Billy, 154, 156
Bennett, Joe, 40
Bennett, Joseph, 49
Bennett, Michael, 173, 174
Berryman, Robert, 73
Bessillieu, Don, 115, 125
Beussee, Chief, 38
Bible, Dana, 178
Bierman, Bernie, 51
Biletnikoff, Fred, 95, 238
Billyeu, Fred, 89
Black, C.H., 33
Black, Jr., C.H., 33
Black, Jr., E.R., 33
Black, Steve, 362
Blaik, Earl, 219
Blake, Morgan, 350
Blakewood, Jim, 205, 333
Blandi, Ernie, 66
Bledsoe, Robert, 121

Bloch, C.J., 33
Block, H.G., 33
Bobo, Mike, 165
Bobo, Tim, 140
Boland, F.K., 33
Boland, Joe, 44
Boley, Sidney, 33
Bond, Claude, 33
Boneli, John, 77
Booth, Albie, 31, 39, 318
Booth, G.A., 33
Boston, J.E., 33
Bowden, Tommy, 155
Bowen, Dinky, 80
Bowen, Dottie, 355
Bowen, James, 86, 88
Boykin, S.F., 33
Bradberry, George, 81
Bradley, W.C., 33
Braswell, Kim, 109
Bratkowski, Zeke, 267
Bridges, D.W., 33
Britt, Charlie, 92
Broadway, Jim, 128, 131
Brock, Pope F., 33
Brooke, Jim, 43
Brooks, Josh, 369
Brown, Al, 40
Brown, C.M., 33
Brown, Fred, 93
Brown, James, 119, 369, 370
Brown, Norris, 128
Brown, Thomas, 158, 164, 299
Browne, J.R., 33
Browning, Tyson, 157

Brownson, Nathan, 35, 36
Broyles, Frank, 79, 87, 210
Broyles, N. A., 33
Brumbelow, Mike, 65
Brunson, Lewis, 90
Bryan, W., 54
Bryant, Decory, 155
Bryant, Joe, 119
Bryant, Paul "Bear", 67, 111
Bryant, Vernon "Fats", 43, 44
Bryant, W.M., 33
Buffet, Jimmy, 368
Burrus, E.P., 33
Burson, Joe, 96
Burt, Will, 340
Burton, Charles A., 75
Bush, Jack, 84
Butler, Kevin, 138, 145, 231, 268
Butts, Samuel, 178
Butts, Wallace, 82, 177, 178, 180, 284, 343, 348
Cabaniss, W.H., 33
Caldwell, Harmon, 351
Calhoun, F.P., 33
Calhoun, West, 349
Calloway, Selma, 150
Campbell, Earl, 127
Caraniss, C.D., 33
Carlisle, W.T., 33
Carmichael, Tommy, 103
Carter, Quincy, 152
Carver, Dale, 133, 138, 194
Carver, John, 82
Castleberry, Clint, 70
Castronis, Mike, 293

Cavan, Mike, 106, 219
Cescutti, Brad, 114
Chadwick, Leon, 136
Chandler, Gene, 87
Chandler, Spud, 40
Chapas, Shaun, 171
Chapman, Buck, 55
Chappell, B. H., 33
Charles, Prince, 118
Chase, H. W., 29
Chastain, Brandi, 336
Chris Broom, Chris, 148
Chubb, Nick, 174
Clark, Dickey, 115
Clark, Harman, 65
Clarke, Arthur, 33
Clason, M.B., 33
Clausen, Casey, 152
Clay, R.G., 33
Cody, W.B., 33
Cofley, A. T., 38
Coleman, Warren, 352
Colley, A.T., 33
Collie, Scott, 140
Collins, Pat, 122
Columbus, Christopher, 38
Compton, Charlie, 84
Conley, Chris, 173, 301
Conlon, Peter, 368
Connolly, Chief, 349
Cook, John, 270
Cook, Ted, 77
Cooley, Jimmy, 100
Cooper, Ken, 311
Cooper, William, 49
Corso, Lee, 354
Costa, Anthony, 33
Costa, Lee, 64

Cothran, W.F., 33
Courts, Malon, 25
Courts,, R. W., 33
Coutu, Brandon, 164
Cox, Jack, 340
Cox, Joe, 171, 300
Craft, Lawrence, 117
Crawford, Stan, 103
Creekmore, R.A., 33
Crowley, Jim, 66
Crumley, Jonathan, 198
Culliver, Cal, 114
Cunningham, Alex, 4
Cunningham, W. A., 10
Curran, Rennie, 172
Curri, Fran, 118
Curry, Airese, 155
Curtis, Roy, 271
Dalrymple, Jerry, 51, 52
Daniel, T.H., 33
Daniels, P. J., 157
Dargan, Jr., M., 33
Davenport, U.H., 33
Davidsmeyer, Craig, 74
Davidson, C. J., 175
Davidson, Claude, 351
Davidson, Fred C., 118
Davidson, John, 40
Davis, Ed, 92
Davis, John K., 33
Davis, Lamar, 64
Davis, Louis S., 33
Davis, Sam, 54
Davis, Steve, 112
Davis, Thomas, 153, 234, 273
Davis, Van, 64, 70, 306, 346

Deaton, Mike, 119

DeCarlo, Art, 90

Deleski, Jerry, 84

Dellinger, Bobby, 267, 273

Denmark, R.L., 33

Dennis, J. T., 33

Dennis, John T., 33

Dent, Akeem, 168

Devereaux, Grace, 3

Devers, Clayton, 84

Dick, J. P., 33

Dickens, Marion, 40, 48

Dickens, Phil, 57

Dickerson, R.G., 33

Dismukes, R.E., 33

DiTomo, Anthony, 73

Dobbs, B. S., 33

Dobbs, O. R., 33

Dobbs, S. C., 33

Dodd, Bobby, 57, 80, 82, 102, 204, 209, 218, 311

Doering, Chris, 150

Dolan, Joe, 92

Donaldson, Johnny, 83, 86, 290

Dooley, Vince, 98, 112, 118, 122, 123, 127, 134, 184, 195, 218, 230, 282, 298, 304, 334, 362, 373

Dooley, William Vincent, 181

Dorsett, Luke, 54

Dorsett, Tony, 115, 127, 134, 212, 332, 333

Dorsey, Jr., E.H., 33

Dorsey, Roy, 33

Doss, Noble, 68

Downes, Austin, 47

Dowtin, Marcus, 172

Doyal, Paul H., 33

Doyal, R. L. "Shorty", 181

Draper, J.H., 33

Dudley, A. G., 14, 33

Duke, John, 89

Dulaney, L.C., 33

Dunlap, Edgar B., 33

Dye, Pat, 93, 142

Ealey, Washaun, 171

Eaves, Joel, 137, 181, 354, 359, 368

Eberhardt, Pap, 353

Edwards, Danny, 81, 83, 85, 221

Edwards, LaVell, 141, 209

Edwards, Robert, 232, 233, 271

Edwards, Terrence, 152, 154, 157, 274, 276

Ehrhardt, Clyde, 72

Ella Soule, Mary Ella, 355

Ellis, Jack T., 33

Elton, Buck, 351

English, Gordon, 68

Enright, Rex, 61, 73

Erwin, .C., 33

Erwin, Howell C., 33

Erwin, W. L., 33

Eshmoat, Len, 66

Eskew, Samuel, 341

Etter, Bobby, 98

Eubanks, Johnny, 63

Evans, Bill, 77

Evins, S.N., 33

Faircloth, Mack, 97

Farkas, L., 33

Faust, George, 68

Favre, Bret, 146

Fawcett, Joy, 336

Field, Patrick, 90

Fields, Nollie, 51

Flack, Tony, 138, 140, 198, 257

Fleming, F.L., 33

Flichock, Frankie, 66

Flournoy, W.R., 33

Floyd, Don, 96

Floyd, J. S., 33

Foley, C. B., 33

Ford, Danny, 138, 145, 228, 232

Fortson, Blanton, 33

Fortune, Will, 48

Foudy, Julie, 336

Fox, Sheldon, 125

Foxx, Bobby, 65, 66, 68

Franks, Floyd, 106

Fraser, Y.H., 33

Freeman, Davis, 33

Fulmer, Phillip, 152, 209

Fusia, Vic, 67

Gabarra, Carin, 336

Gaillard, Jerry, 131, 229

Gant, Ray, 161

Gantt, Bob, 349

Gantt, Bryant, 149

Gary, Damien, 153, 154

Gasque, Mike, 130

Gaston, Martin, 54

Gerhart, Tony, 200

Gibson, Fred, 153, 157, 275

Gilbert, Paul, 106

Gilmer, Harry, 83

Gilmore, Lloyd, 48

Gipp, George "The Gipper", 217

Glenn, T.K., 33

Glover, Harry, 51

Goff, Ray, 113, 115, 149, 182, 277, 278
Golden, Fred, 67
Goldstein, J.W., 33
Goodman, Winfred, 342
Goodrum, J.J., 33
Gordon, High, 10
Gordon, Jr., H.H., 33
Governali, Paul, 72
Grady, Henry, 4
Grange, Red, 127, 272
Grant, Cy, 55
Grant, J. W., 33
Grant, Joseph, 55
Grant, Jr., J. W., 33
Grate, Carl, 306
Graves, Ray, 321
Gray, Jr., J. R., 33
Greco, Al Del, 142
Green, A. J., 168, 279
Green, J. J., 173
Green, T.F., 33
Greene, David, 154, 156, 234, 279, 315
Greene, Nathaniel, 35
Greentree, Carl, 33
Grizzard, Lewis, 144
Gunn, Cecelia, 354
Gunn, Frank, 355
Gunn, R. G., 33
Gunter, Kurt, 140
Gurley, Todd, 173, 280, 281, 283
Gurr, Charles Stephen, 14
Haas, H.J., 33
Hackman, Norman, 57
Haffner, George, 132, 148
Hall, George, 30
Hall, J. C., 56

Hall, Lyman, 34, 35, 36
Hall, Roger, 74
Hamilton, Derrick, 155
Hamm, Mia, 336
Hampton, Rodney, 282
Hamrick, Jim, 49
Hanna, Clay, 33
Hapes, Norman, 63
Happ, Pinkus, 33
Hardaway, B.H., 33
Hardeman, R.N., 33
Hardwick, T.W., 33
Hareman, Jr., R.N., 33
Hargett, David, 149
Hargrove, Lauren, 90, 267
Harmon, Norwood, 73
Harold, C.C., 33
Harp, Red, 57, 58, 59
Harper, H. B., 33
Harper, Jeff, 333, 334
Harper, Jimmy, 207
Harris, Kenneth, 234
Harris, Kevin, 141
Harris, Ronnie, 140
Harris, Roy V., 33
Harrison, Glynn, 116, 193, 283
Hartman, Bill, 56, 187, 188, 295, 326, 346
Harvard, Bryant, 93
Harvey, Mary, 336
Hatcher, Dale, 138
Hatcher, J. M., 33
Hatcher, S.B., 33
Hauss, Len, 286
Hawk, Loiver, 306
Hawkins, Dan, 234
Hawthorne, Greg, 121

Haynes, Lamar, 51
Hearst, Garrison, 147, 156, 283, 287
Heath, W. P., 33
Heeler, Randy, 101
Heisman, John, 186, 209
Helms, Art, 70
Helser, D.C., 33
Henderson, Billy, 287
Henderson, Jack, 54
Henderson, L. L., 351
Henderson, Steve, 137
Henley, Terry, 109
Henry, Bunky, 104, 136
Henry, Travis, 151
Herron, Bill, 91
Hester, Marvious, 157
Hickey, R., 33
Hightower, Don, 68
Hill, Drew, 116, 124
Hill, L.D., 33
Hill, T.W., 33
Hilliard,, Ike, 150
Hipp, Jeff, 130, 229, 310
Hirsch, Harold, 14, 19, 33
Hirsch, M. L., 33
Hirsch, M. R., 33
Hoage, Terry, 140, 288
Hobson, George, 73
Hodge, Mark, 125
Hodges, Billy, 80
Hodges, K.B., 33
Hodges, Robert, 33
Hodgson, Morton, Sr, 100
Hodgson, Pat, 95, 99
Hodgson, Winston, 342
Hoequist, Frank, 74
Hofmayer, I.J., 33

Hollingsworth, Gary, 149
Holmes, Eric, 74
Holmes, Mark, 100
Holmes, W. R., 33
Holmoe, Tom, 140
Holtz, Lou, 210
Honeycutt, Robert, 109
Hooper, W.D., 33
Hopkins, I.S., 33
Horton, O.R., 33
Hosch, H. C., 33
Hosch, H. H., 33
Hosch, J. H., 33
Houston, Tom, 33
Hovious, Junie, 63
Howard, Marcus, 163
Howard, Scott, 37
Howell, Clark, 26
Howell, Jr., C., 33
Hudson, Billy, 362
Hughes, Jimmie, 54
Hughes, Lynn, 100, 105
Hughes, Phil, 96
Huhrheinrich, Von, 48
Huilin, Xie, 337
Hunt, Aaron, 155
Hunt, Bobby, 92
Hurley, James, 289
Hurt, S.L., 33
Igwebuike, Donald, 144
Illges, Ike, 33
Ingram, Mark, 167
Inman, E.H., 33
Inman, Hugh, 33
Ivery, Eddie Lee, 116, 124, 230
Jackson, Bo, 142, 242
Jackson, Eddie Ray, 146

Jackson, F.W., 33
Jackson, Jerome, 109
Jackson, Michael, 146, 240
Jackson, Tron, 138, 141, 144
Jacobs, David, 156
James, Lionel, 142, 242
Jaskwhich, Charles, 65
Jean-Gilles, Max, 276, 277
Jefferson, Jordan J., 171
Jenkins, Ronnie, 100, 104
Jernigan, George, 83, 222
Jett, Gardner, 109
Joel, J.B., 33
Johnson, Andy, 108, 226, 291
Johnson, Brad, 104
Johnson, Calvin, 161, 243
Johnson, Henry, 125
Johnson, Howard, 343
Johnson, Kelin, 164
Johnson, P.S., 33
Johnson, Richard Malcolm, 35
Jones, Bobby, 50, 180
Jones, Buck, 77
Jones, C. W., 24
Jones, Chuck, 128
Jones, H., 33
Jones, Howard, 285
Jones, Jarvis, 290
Jones, Preston, 148
Jones, R.P., 33
Jones, Sean, 157
Jones, Sidney, 33
Jones, Tom, 43, 44
Jordan, Homer, 138
Jordan, Lee Roy, 204, 245, 246

Jordan, Shug, 92
Joseph, Jonathan, 158
Joyce, Thomas, 371
Kay, Clarence, 140
Keith, Jeff, 90
Kekhelser, Gene, 67
Kelleher, John, 76
Kelley, Mike, 123, 135
Kelly, Cobern, 313
Kelly, Jeff, 33
Kennedy, Bob, 77
Key, Homer, 52, 55
Key, J. B., 33
Kimsey, Cliff, 64
King, Hardy, 104
King, Horace, 283, 292, 293
King, Kim, 104
King, Tavares, 171
Kirouac, Brett, 154
Kohn, Larry, 104
Kopp, Wynn, 153
Kresser, Eric, 149
Krouse, Ray, 89, 255
Krug, Bill, 115
Lake, Ricky, 106, 109
Lamkin, E.E., 33
Lampe, Elmer, 177
Lancaster, Larry, 93
Lane, Fred, 143
Lane, Tommy, 54
Langdale, Noah, 67
Langley, Dax, 150
Lanier, G.W., 33
Lanier, Gary, 116
Lanier, Hollis, 33
Lastinger, John, 138, 140, 142

Lautenschlaeger, Lester, 207
Law, Bob, 56
Lawrence, A.A., 33
Lawrence, Kent, 103, 293
Lawton, A.R., 33
Leahy, Frank, 179, 213
Lear, Jimmy, 204
Leathers, Milton, 49
Leathers, Red, 40
Leavitt, Allen, 114
Lee, Florence, 355
Lee, Rodney, 125
Leebern, Don, 93
Lenderman, Lee, 344
Lewis, Jacob, 74
Lewis, Jeff, 118
Lilly, Kristine, 336, 338
Lippitt, A.L., 33
Little, John, 198
Lombardi, Vince, 268, 284, 305
Long, Chuck, 198
Long, Leo, 76
Lott, Anthone, 150
Lowe, Ernest A., 33
Lowry, Tommy, 108
Lumpkin, B.C., 33
Lumpkin, Quinton, 56, 65, 178, 273, 295, 310, 351
Lyndon, A.J., 33
Lyndon, Mary D., 11
MacDougald, A., 33
MacDougald, D., 33
Maddox, G.E., 33
Maddox, Ralph, 40, 45
Maddox, Red, 48
Maddox, Robert F., 33
Maffett, Herbert, 43, 44

MaGill, Dan, 284, 354
Mahaney, J. L., 33
Majors, Johnny, 192, 210, 212
Malone, Tommy, 306
Mancha, Vaughn, 84
Manget, Luke, 157
Manne, M.L., 33
Manning, Archie, 106, 218, 226, 251, 252
Manning, Jake, 70
Manning, Peyton, 210, 253
Marinaro, Ed, 108, 188
Martin, Billy, 66
Martin, C.E., 33
Martin, Charles, 7, 8, 371
Mason, Charles, 103
Mason, Hutson, 174
Massaquoi, Mohamed, 160
Mathews, George, 79, 87
Mathias, William, 358
Maxwell, Dick, 55
McAfee, George, 67
McAlpin, Henry, 33
McAshan, Eddie, 135
McBride, Ricky, 121, 126
McCall, H.H., 33
McCall, Kenneth, 81
McCampbell, George, 55
McCarthy, Chris, 296
McCartney, J.D., 33
McClain, Lester, 236, 249
McClatchy, Grace, 3
McClendon, Bryan, 159, 277
McClendon, Willie, 121, 124, 127, 227, 230, 282, 297

McCrary, Bull, 40
McDaniel, Sanders, 33
McDorman, C., 33
McEver, John, 57
McFalls, Doug, 95, 96, 97
McGarity, Greg, 369
McGonigal, F. M., 33
McGugin, Dan, 48
McKenzie, E., 33
McKenzie, Isaiah, 174
McLee, Kevin, 112, 116
McPhee, Dick, 83, 86, 221, 272
McVea, Warren, 219
McWhorter, M.P., 33
McWhorter, R. L., 33, 355
Meadow, W.K., 33
Meekins, Eric, 154
Mehre, Harry, 28, 33, 38, 48, 51, 54, 62, 63, 66, 85, 176, 177, 284, 343
Meigs, Josiah, 36
Meldrim, P.W., 33
Mell, Thomas S., 33
Mettenberger, Zach, 173
Michael, D.B., 33
Michael, Max, 33
Michel, Sony, 174
Middlebrooks, G., 33
Miles, L.A., 33
Miles, Robert, 131
Miller, Prince, 167, 168
Miller, W. Paul, 33
Milner, Martrez, 234, 316
Mitchell, Frank R., 33
Mitchell, Roger, 110
Mitchell, William, 82
Mixon, Billy, 90
Mizell, Warner, 44

Modzelewski, Ed, 89
Moon, E.T., 33
Moore, Bernie, 179, 202
Moore, George, 123
Moore, Kirby, 99, 100, 103, 249, 297, 298
Moore, R. L., 33
Moot, Buster, 52
Moreno, Knowshon, 163, 166
Morgan, Marshall, 174
Morocco, Zippy, 90, 127, 267
Morris, Lee, 33
Morrison, Tim, 333, 334
Morton, J White, 33
Mosely, Reid, 81, 87
Moses, Ronnie, 106
Moss, Gary, 198, 257
Mossmer, Wallace, 74
Mott, Norman, 49, 54
Moye, George, 54
Munson, Larry, 37, 111, 112, 144
Murdock, Charles, 79
Murdock, Les, 95, 96
Muyres, Jeremy, 157
Myers, Denny, 69
Myers, J. S., 33
Myers, Urban, 316
Narramore, Lee, 96
Neill, Cecil, 33
Nelson, L.W., 33
Nettleton, George H., 36
Neuhaus, Steve, 100
Nevin, James B., 33
Newell, Bruce, 101
Newman, H.A., 33
Neyland, Robert, 56, 213

Nicholas, Ira C., 25
Nicholson, Lowry, 33
Nickparson, S.H., 33
Nix, Abit, 33
Nixon, Charlie, 80
Nord, Greg, 119
Norris, Ulysses, 113
Nowak, Steve, 62
Nutt, Houston, 250
Odom, Benton, 33
Oliver, Jr., W.M., 33
Oliver, Paul, 161
Orme, Charles D., 33
Ornato, Mike, 262
Orr, James, 301, 311
Osgood, Simon, 54
Outlar, Jesse, 38
Overbeck, Carla, 336
Owens, Jeff, 172
Page, J.E., 33
Palmer, Shelton, 3
Palmer, W.R., 33
Palmer, W.R.M., 33
Palmisano, G., 33
Parker, R.S., 33
Parks, Tim, 134, 194
Parlow, Cindy, 336
Parris, Mike, 326
Parrish, Joel, 115, 117
Paterno, Joe, 192
Patrick, J.K., 33
Patterson, Billy, 67, 68
Patton, George, 98, 100, 104
Paulk, Jeff, 128
Payne, Billy, 101
Payne, Francis, 52
Payne, H. B., 33

Payne, Jimmy, 121, 304
Payne, W.O., 33
Peabody, George Foster, 4
Peake, Charone, 175
Pennington, Durward, 91
Perkins, Marion, 56
Perl, Al, 80
Perry, Lawrence, 50
Perry, William 'Refrigerator", 138
Peterson, Bill, 98
Philot, Jr., T.M., 33
Piasecky, Alex, 67
Pollack, David, 234, 304, 323
Pollard, Al, 114, 116
Pomeroy, E.E., 33
Pond, Raymond W., 76
Poole, Jim, 68
Porter, J. H., 33
Porter, Jim, 59
Poschner, George, 64, 70, 85, 187, 202, 298, 305
Postero, Frank, 33
Poulos, Jimmy, 109, 283
Pritchett, Ed, 95
Prokop, Eddie, 72
Purvis, Kevin, 369
Pyburn, Jeff, 113, 122, 124, 265, 297
Qingmei, Sun, 338
R.E.M, 369
Raber, Dick, 90
Raber, Richard, 90
Rabon, Matt, 150
Radloff, Wayne, 138, 140, 333, 334
Rafney, "Red", 66
Rakestraw, Larry, 181
Ramsey, Derrick, 119

Randall, Jimmy, 73
Rauch, Johnny, 83, 222, 224, 301
Rawson, Lamar, 93
Ray, David, 99
Ray, James, 106, 109
Redfearn, J.A., 33
Reynolds, D. W., 33
Reynolds, H. I., 33
Reynolds, Homer, 3
Reynolds, Jim Tom, 13
Rice, Grantland, 50, 218, 230
Rice, Sidney, 159
Richard B. Russell, 46, 50
Richards, W. A., 33
Richardson, Al, 125
Richt, Mark, 60, 158, 163, 184
Ridlehuber, Preston, 94, 95, 96, 298
Ritter, Tex, 80
Roberts, Jack, 40, 47
Roberts, Tiffany, 336
Robinson, Matt, 112
Robinson, Mixon, 322
Robinson, Rex, 121, 128, 130, 132, 135, 231, 268, 296, 308, 330
Rockne, Knute, 176, 201, 217
Rogero, A. L., 54
Rogers, George, 132, 194
Rogers, Pepper, 116
Roosevelt, Franklin Delano, 370
Rosenberg, Buzy, 226, 252
Ross, Frank, 309
Rothschild, M.D., 33
Rothstein, Benny, 40, 44

Rourke, Jr., J., 33
Rowe, H. J., 14, 33
Royal, Darrell, 329
Ruark, Walter, 342, 345
Rucker, Adrian, 115
Russell, Erk, 114, 133, 183, 192, 251
Russell, Richard B., Jr., 46
Rutledge, Jeff, 113
Saban, Nick, 165, 199
Saint John, Herb, 84
Salisbury, Robert, 346
Sams, Albert D., 33
Sams, W.A., 33
Sanchez, Jeff, 140
Sanders, "Spec", 66
Sanders, Jeff, 115
Sanford, C.S., 33
Sanford, Lucius, 116
Sanford, Steadman Vincent, 1, 2, 3, 6, 7, 25, 33
Sanks, Jasper, 151
Sapp, Theron, 310
Sapp, Tom, 355
Scarborough, C.G., 33
Schmalz, Dick, 108, 226
Schnellenberger, Howard, 256
Scott, A.W., 33
Scott, Lindsay, 124, 132, 135, 266
Scott-Wesley, Justin, 172
Scruggs, Ted, 76
Scurry, Briana, 336
Seaboard and Southern Construction Company, 23
Seagraves, H.L., 33
Secontitae, Vincent, 73
Seiler, Sonny, 195, 354

Self, Hal, 83, 84, 221
Sellers, Terry, 100, 104
Seltenreich, John, 77
Seritchfield, John, 73
Seymour, Richard, 314
Shank, Jeff, 125
Sherman, Mercer, 33
Shockley, D. J., 153
Showers, Shea, 150
Shugart, Tate, 74
Sibley, John A., 33
Sibley, W. Hart, 33
Simcsak, Jack, 251
Simmons, Willie, 155
Simon, Matt, 124, 258, 265
Simpson, O. J., 127, 294
Sims, Dave, 116
Singletary, Mike, 121, 227, 258
Sinkwich, Frank, 7, 60, 63, 67, 69, 116, 127, 179, 186, 188, 202, 203, 270, 272, 297, 298, 307, 311, 325
Skipworth, James, 347
Slade, Lester C., 33
Slaughter, N.G., 33
Sloan, Steve, 98, 259
Smaha, Jiggy, 98
Smiley, Julian, 106
Smith, C.D., 33
Smith, Dan, 116
Smith, Doug, 142
Smith, George B., 33
Smith, Johnny, 123, 125, 136
Smith, Jonathan, 83
Smith, Loran, 272
Smith, Marby, 352

Smith, Marion, 33
Smith, Musa, 152, 154, 156
Smith, Royce, 110
Smith, Sidney, 33
Smith, Vernon "Catfish", 39, 295
Smith, Victor, 33
Sneed, Bib, 59
Snelling, Charles M., 14, 19, 23, 33, 47
Snow, Lenny, 104
Southerland, Brannan, 164, 276
Spalding, Hughes, 33
Sparks, A.O.B., 33
Spooner, Phil, 96
Springsteen, Bruce, 368
Spurrier, Steve, 102, 104, 149, 157, 183, 198, 216, 320, 321
Stabler, Ken, 204
Stafford, Matthew, 161
Stanczak, Frank, 76
Stanfill, Bill, 100, 105, 182, 215, 303, 304, 320, 321
Stark, Troy, 151
Starr, Bart, 268
Stasica, Stan, 61
Steadman, Charles, 3
Steel, Mike, 240, 304
Steele, Dick, 90
Steele, John, 116
Stegeman, H. J., 33, 350
Stegeman, Herman James, 8, 24
Stephen, Alexander H., 180
Stephens, Travis, 151
Stewart, J.P., 33

Stewart, Ronnie, 122, 125, 135
Still, Art, 118
Still, Wilson, 351
Stolz, Charles, 55
Stout, Cole, 175
Stouter, Nellie Agnes, 181
Stovall, Hefey H., 73
Suggs, A. J., 152, 157
Sullivan, Pat, 108, 188, 225
Sullivan, Phil, 109
Sullivan, Willie, 48
Summerlin, M.T., 33
Sutera, Louis, 347, 348
Swift, C.J., 33
Swift, George P., 33
Swift, H.H., 33
Sylvester, Steadman, 74
Tabor, Jr., T.O., 33
Talley, Greg, 146
Tallmadge, Jr., J.E., 33
Tarkenton, Francis, 91, 179, 324
Tate, Ben, 165
Tate, Steve C., 33
Tate, William, 129, 274, 351
Tatum, Jim, 89
Taylor, Bob, 99
Taylor, Jim, 146
Taylor, Nate, 138
Taylor, Tony, 162
Taylor, Wyndell, 355
Teaff, Grant, 120, 258
Tensi, Steve, 95, 239
Tereskinski, Joe, 83, 86, 115, 316
Terrell, Raymond, 63
Tew, Lowell, 84

Thigpin, Bealand, 74
Thilenius, Ed, 37
Thomas, F.W., 33
Thomas, Frank, 82, 285
Thomason, George M., 23
Thomason, Stumpy, 44
Thomey, Ted, 61
Thornton, Jr., A.E., 33
Thorpe, Jim, 127, 238, 326
Thurman, Odell, 234
Tichenor, W.R., 33
Tift, M.W., 33
Tift, Richard, 33
Tigert, J. J., 30
Tiller, W.G., 33
Timmons, Charlie, 68
Tinsely, Gaynell, 202
Tinsley, Jack, 80
Tompkins, H.B., 33
Torrance, C.C., 33
Towns, Bobby, 93
Towns, Forrest, 178
Towns, Spec, 57, 302
Trippi, Charlie, 7, 70, 75, 82, 84, 85, 116, 127, 179, 187, 203, 205, 221, 223, 229, 272, 283, 299, 311, 346
Trosper, Dave, 119
Troutman, H.S., 33
Troutman, R. B., 33
Trumbull, J. H., 30
Trussell, C.A., 33
Tuberville, Tommy, 164
Tully, Darrell, 68
Turpin, W.C., 33
Tutwiler, M.N., 33
Van Gorder, Brian, 234
Vaught, Johnny, 100, 217

Venable, Oscar, 33

Venturini, Tisha, 336

Vickers, Jimmy, 93

Walden, Bobby, 92

Walker, Grover, 75

Walker, Herschel, 7, 127, 131, 132, 134, 136, 137, 139, 142, 182, 186, 192, 194, 195, 205, 227, 229, 232, 243, 250, 267, 283, 297, 304, 311, 317, 333

Walker, Watson, 33

Wall, J. T., 156

Walsh, Blair, 170

Walsh, Christy, 285

Walston, Robert, 90

Wansley, Tim, 151

Ward, Bobbu, 89

Ward, Hines, 151, 326, 327

Wardla, W.C., 33

Ware, Danny, 158, 234

Ware, Larry, 148

Ware, S.J., 33

Warner, Glenn "Pop", 10

Warren,, Jimmie, 143

Washington, Gene, 112, 116, 278

Watkins, Coot, 44

Watson, Branham "Blue", 31

Watson, Deshaun, 175

Weaver, Mike, 140

Wen, Sun, 338

West, Carl, 133

Westbrook, C., 33

Westbrook, Joe, 44

Wheatley, Cliff, 350

Whelchel, Puss, 13

White, H. C., 35

White, Joseph, 48

White, Jr., J., 33

White, R. P., 33

White, W. P., 24, 33

Whitehead, Virginia, 364

Whitman, G.P., 33

Whittaker, W.C., 33

Whittemore, Charlie, 132

Whittington, W.W., 33

Wilkes, Reggie, 117

Wilkinson, Bud, 99

Williams, Bulldog, 84, 87

Williams, C.F., 33

Williams, Dale, 246

Williams, Elijah, 151

Williams, Freddie, 119

Williams, Kenneth, 355

Williams, Quincy, 142

Williams, Rayfield, 112

Williams, Todd, 143, 231

Wilson, Felix, 119

Wilson, Mike, 117, 328

Wilson, Staci, 336

Wisdom, Chip, 309, 332

Witherspoon, Will, 328

Witt, Tommy, 348

Woerner, Scott, 124, 128, 130, 133, 136, 227, 329, 330

Wolf, Raymond B., 65

Womack, Jimmy, 132

Woodruff, George Cecil "Kid", 14, 18, 19, 25, 33

Woodruff, J.W., 33

Worley, Tim, 330, 331

Wright, Barry, 33

Wright, Max, 33

Wuerffel, Danny, 150

Young, Barry, 140

Young, Bob, 24

Young, Dick, 301

Young, LeRoy, 54

Young, Steve, 139, 209

Youngblood, Kevin, 154

Zabilski, Joe, 66

Zabransky, Jared, 234

Zambiasi, Ben, 115, 332

Zimmerman, Don, 51

Zuppke, Robert C., 285

Zwiezynski, Walter, 66

Made in the USA
Lexington, KY
06 October 2015